THE GOSPEL IN ART

HOFMANN: CHRIST AND THE RICH YOUNG MAN

THE GOSPEL IN ART

ALBERT E. BAILEY

DIRECTOR OF RELIGIOUS EDUCATION
WORCESTER ACADEMY, MASS.
LECTURER IN RELIGIOUS EDUCATION
NEWTON THEOLOGICAL INSTITUTION

Author of

"On Nazareth Hill," "The Wise Man's Story"
"Art Studies in the Life of Christ"

PILGRIM PRESS
BOSTON   CHICAGO

THE PILGRIM PRESS
BOSTON

To
My Daughter
Lois

CONTENTS

Contents

Contents

THE POINT OF VIEW

INTRODUCTION

THE POINT OF VIEW

THIS book is not an art course in the usual sense. Though it is based upon certain masterpieces of art, and discusses some of the matters that are usually treated in art books, with many aspects of art it has nothing whatever to do. It is not concerned, for example, with the historic development of painting; it has little to say about technique; biography plays small part in it. These are all matters worth while, but aside from the purpose of this study.

But the book is an art course in the sense that it studies a number of paintings to discover their spiritual values. It takes the finished product of the studio and asks of it, "What excuse have you for being? What qualities have made you live these decades, these centuries; have caused the eyes of men to turn toward you and their hearts to burn as they think of you?" Or perhaps one should say more accurately that the book sets the reader down before these treasures, one by one, and demands of him, "What do you see, what do you feel? Do you discover clearly what the artist has tried to say? Does your heart respond to its beauty? Does the great theme with which it concerns itself shine down on you from the canvas with a new significance, transfigured by the insight, the skill, the emotional coloring of this creative personality?" If you can give a positive answer to these questions, the painting has significance for

3

you; but if your answer is negative, no matter how much you may know about the history or the technique of art, you have failed to grasp the essential picture, either because the picture has no essential worth or because you have not yet learned how to find it.

The pictures of this book have been selected because in some measure they speak of religion. They hint at some ·connection between this world of fact in which we move and the infinite spiritual world that penetrates it and gives it meaning. Jesus lived so continuously and so fully in both worlds that no artist can depict an incident in his life without reminding us to some extent of both. Both elements are present in varying degrees in the story of his birth, his growth and ripening, of his call to a specific task, of his friendships and his labors, his successes and disappointments, his tragic end.. Take out from these human happenings the spiritual element, the element that speaks of joy and peace, of love and sacrifice, of consciousness of a mission, of pity for suffering, hatred of sin, intolerance of selfishness in high places, devotion to the truth; take out faith and the ever-present consciousness of God in which these elements are rooted, and what have we left? Surely nothing that is worth an artist's time to depict. But if the painter has given us a glimpse of these unseen realities, he has not only illuminated for us the life of Jesus, but he has revealed to us something of eternal truth, which is as much truth for us and for all men as it was for Jesus. He has shown us what Harnack calls " Eternal life in the midst of time, under the eyes and by the strength of God." It is these spiritual values that

4

give significance to a great work of art; indeed, without the presence of such values a work of art can hardly be called great.

It is the purpose of this book to help you discover and appreciate the religious element in art; to study art not for art's sake but for your sake; to strengthen your grasp upon the things that are unseen and eternal.

HOW TO STUDY A PICTURE

A. *Find the Facts.* — Some pictures are so simple that a glance serves to show their contents. No prolonged study is necessary to grasp Murillo's Magdalene (p. 213); it is a portrait of a woman looking upward. Hardly more pains will be required to master Zimmermann's Christ and the Fishermen (p. 145); it consists of four men in earnest conversation, with a glimpse of a lake, a boat and a man beyond. But when one is confronted with such a picture as Hunt's " Finding of Christ in the Temple " (p. 105) the task to master its details is considerable. Here one must adopt a method of procedure in order not to overlook some of the significant details.[1]

First take the building. What strange architecture! It is neither Egyptian nor Assyrian nor Greek nor Roman. The rear wall seems to be a screen of metal or of pierced marble, the pattern a beautiful diaperwork and the frieze a series of circles inscribing arabesques. The ceiling is coffered, each beam bearing intricate ornaments in fayence designed from the elements of pine-cones and grapes and pomegranates.

---

[1] It may be necessary to consult a larger reproduction, perhaps in your public library.

From each panel hangs a chandelier of silver, with egg-shaped lamps of crystal. The pillars are clusters of shafts or stalks bound round with a golden vine and terminated by capitals that are fashioned upon palm and lotus motives. The whole is dainty and airy and fantastic, a flowering of the exuberant imagination of the East, though trained and modulated by the hand of fitness. One valve of the great door stands wide in front of us. It is overlaid with plates of gold and ornamented with a wheel-like pattern of papyrus blossoms interspoked with buds of the same. Above the wheel is an inscription: *"Et statim veniet ad Templum suum Dominator quem vos quaeritis."* There are tear-shaped bosses on the door, and a spiral band set with great crystals. The very threshold is ornamented with pomegranates and papyrus leaves. Surely all this painstaking wealth of detail is here for a purpose!

Turn now to the surroundings. Through the window (in the original) a hill with buildings. On the right, leaning against the doorpost, a blind beggar, and below in the courtyard, workmen hewing a large stone preparatory to placing it in the unfinished colonnade. Beyond are cypress trees and a suburb of white houses on the slopes of Mt. Scopas. The open doors, the screens, the brilliant Syrian sky, the birds flying in and out of the Temple, all speak of Spring.

Now look carefully at the persons. In the background do you see a man holding back a sheep and counting his money? A little procession of four is going somewhere within the temple: the woman fondles a baby, the man beside her carries a lamb on his shoulders, a priest with a censor walks in front of

6

them, and a boy with a harp leads the way. A money-changer at his table is weighing gold. Again, near the center, a boy is throwing up his scarf to scare away the birds. To the left, a servant with a long rod is lighting a lamp. Coming now to the nearer persons, do you see that three of them carry musical instruments — a small harp, a larger harp and a sistrum? A well-dressed servant pours wine into a crystal bowl and will hand it to a rabbi. A little boy slyly kisses the skirts of the silken wrapper of the Holy Book; another small boy with a fly-whisk forgets his task while his thoughts fly out of doors with the birds.

Now the rabbis. They are all richly dressed and brilliantly turbaned. The old blind man to the left hugs a huge roll of the Law. The knobs of it and the pendants are of silver; the precious parchment is covered with crimson velvet embroidered with golden vine-wreaths and the mystic name of Jehovah — the Tetragrammaton, or four triangles, in an endless line. The second rabbi holds a little cubical box, a phylactery, containing the promises of Jehovah to the Jews. The third rabbi, who has evidently been conducting the argument, pauses during the interruption with a roll of the Prophets in his hand. The fourth rabbi wears a phylactery on his forehead to show his piety, and is not modest enough to remove it even in the temple of Jehovah. He holds a reed pen and with it sums up on his fingers the whole argument; while above him bends a Levite over his harp to point a finger of scorn at the boy and his peasant parents. The fifth rabbi pours a libation from his wine-glass. The sixth casts an acrid glance at the young Jesus, and the last slumps in his place like a lump of dough.

Over against these are the Holy Family: Jesus, the strong, clear-faced, barefooted peasant boy; Mary, the anxious mother, whispering her reproach; Joseph, the robust carpenter, his shoes slung over his back, his hand upon the mother's hand upon the boy's shoulder as if to draw the boy homeward.

Go over these details again, perhaps again; shut your eyes and still go over them until at will you can recreate each one. This picture is now to be your permanent possession, hung forever on the walls of your memory. It is different from all others, it is precisely this and nothing else. Holman Hunt painted it, and its name is " Finding of Christ in the Temple."

B. *Note the Arrangement of Facts.* — This is what is technically called Composition. It means that the artist has grouped his figures, his lines, his light and dark spots so that without any effort on your part your eye will be led to the center of the picture's interest. For a great picture is not a mere assemblage of objects; it is an ordered assemblage. The artist has in his mind one, or at most two, dominant ideas, and he is indeed a bungler if he cannot give you a hint where to look for them. All else is subordinated to these, all others point to these, take their value from their relation to these. This subtle leading of the mind may be accomplished in several ways. Contrasts or gradations of color may effect it; placing the important figures in the foreground, making them larger, making them distinct while the others are more or less hazy. But the most effective method is to make the important lines lead to the center of interest, as all rays of light focus in the sun.

Turn again to Hunt's picture. What is the center

of interest? Naturally you say, the Holy Family; they are in the foreground and are larger than the other persons. And of this group of three, which one is the center? The boy; for the thoughts and the looks of the parents are focused on him. This group is distinct from the rest. Now it would have been

CUT SHOWING HOW THE LINES OF COMPOSITION FOCUS ON THE LEADING OBJECT

easy and in a way natural to have grouped the rabbis together on the left of the picture and to have made them eagerly discuss the boy among themselves while the parents were engaged with their son; but this would have split the picture into two parts and divided our interest between the two. Hunt has grouped the rabbis there, but their interest is still the boy. They are looking his way or thinking his way; and if our eye wanders over to them it comes back again on the

9

bridge of their interest. In this way Hunt has kept the picture a unity and has singled out in that unity the dominant personality. Moreover, the lines of the rabbis, their robes and accessories, the Levites behind, the perspectives of the building and landscape, all lead to the center. Start where you will on the edges of the picture and somehow your glance gravitates inward. Let it be the line of robes and toes in the left foreground, or the lines of hands beginning with the fly-driver, or the row of beards or mouths or foreheads, or the curve of the upper left-hand harp, or the feet of Jesus, the heel of Mary, the facial angle of the beggar, or even the birds in the sky, — all these are the beginnings of sequences that lead you, not of course with mathematical precision but yet with sufficient clearness, to the one face that Hunt wishes to burn into your memory. These arrangements are the groundwork of the picture, the skeleton that gives it structure, the logic that gives it form and unity and inevitableness, the psychic gravitation that draws all things to their true center. When you have discovered the composition of this or of any picture, you have not only found a source of æsthetic pleasure but a key to the meaning of the picture as well.

C. *Consider the Meaning of the Facts.* — All that has preceded is preliminary. We have found out what the artist has given us to study, what are its chief and its subordinate themes. The real task is to discover the meaning of the whole, its message, its spiritual value. Some pictures have no message — except to reveal the accomplishments or character of their author. In a certain bar-room in Boston are a couple of marvellous paintings. One represents an old and

10

faded and tattered dollar bill, and does it so perfectly that without the use of a magnifying glass you would take oath that a genuine bill had been passepartouted. The other is the portrait of a rather pretty girl. You raise your hand to brush away a fly that has settled upon her cheek, and you discover to your amazement that the fly is painted on! What is the message of such "art"? The artist is saying to you, "I am so clever that I can deceive even an acute observer like yourself!" or, "I am throwing away great talent and precious time in amusing people"; or, "I see nothing in life worth painting except trifles." This is the message of a large percent of the pictures in our galleries. But when you approach a picture that has been admired for three hundred years, the natural inference is that the artist has said something worth while. All great artists are primarily great men; they have intellectual and spiritual powers above the average, powers of observation, insight, feeling. They see more things, more deeply into the meaning of things, and they feel more strongly about things than we do. When such a man devotes a year, or ten years, of his life, to a certain canvas, it is legitimate to believe that he has tried to express an idea that he was unwilling to let die.

These ideas may be insights or feelings or both. In some pictures the insight predominates, as in the "Temptation" of Cornicelius (p. 134), the "Star of Bethlehem" of Burne-Jones (p. 81), or the picture of Hunt's that we have already considered. In some where the insight predominates it takes the special form of a symbol, as in Bloch's "Come Unto Me" (p. 158), or Rodin's "Prodigal Son" (p. 169). In some

11

pictures the feeling is uppermost, as in Keller's " Raising the Daughter of Jairus " (p. 197), or Rubens' " Jesus in the House of Simon" (p. 212). Perhaps it will be well to examine these types more in detail.

1. *Art as Insight.* — We have already examined the details of Hunt's picture and are now prepared to discover what ideas lie beneath the surface. Hunt has illustrated an incident in the life of Jesus; he has also interpreted it — made its true significance clearer.

Take first, the building. We know that Herod built a magnificent temple for the Jews in order to still their restlessness under his iron rule. Marble was the material, adorned with gold and semi-precious stones. We know a few facts about the general arrangement of the building, but next to nothing about its style. The artists have always represented it as they pleased. Hofmann (p. 104) suggests massive Roman pillars; in another picture he presents an Italian-looking porch (p. 283). Kirchbach (p. 290) paints a noble fortress-like structure, part Roman, part Egyptian. But Hunt has thought more in detail and more deeply. He wanted to suggest size and impressiveness; hence the ample spaces in this loggia or summer house in which the scene is laid, and the colonnades without that speak of still wider areas and other structures. "Seest thou what great stones and what buildings are here?" . . . "Forty and six years was this temple in building," — and not even yet is it completed. These gold-plated and jewelled doors and silver candelabra picture wealth; the arabesque screens, the polychromatic decorations of the ceiling, the motives of the design, are indications that we are in the luxurious East, and that the central shrine of Judaism

12

is calculated to appeal to all the sons of the Dispersion, whether they come from the lotus-dotted Nile,
the pine-clad slopes of the Taurus, or the pomegranate gardens of Persepolis and Babylon. This is no
simple "holy place" where peasants from Galilee may
say prayers to Jehovah. It is a wealthy nation's
temple of which the merchant-princes of Israel in any
land may boast, and in which the pride of Sadducees
like Annas may satisfy itself with pomp and ceremony.
Do you not see that Hunt has symbolized here the
spirit of the proud and selfish and luxury-loving hierarchy of the Jews, that was destined never to find
God in any temple, or in the message of this new
prophet who was greater than the temple?

Again, what does Hunt tell us of these rabbis? Luke
calls them "doctors" (margin, "teachers") and makes
no further comment. But the artist fills the word
full of meaning. Study the faces and the robes; they
show us men of wealth and education, but alas, men
also of cynicism and bigotry. These are the Hypocrites who love to walk in long clothing and to have
the chief seats in the synagogue, that make broad their
phylacteries, that devour widows' houses and for a
pretense make long prayers, that tithe mint, anise
and cummin but leave undone the weightier matters
of the law; whited sepulchres, blind guides that compass sea and land to make one proselyte and then
make him a tenfold child of hell. Is this all here?
Why otherwise should their servant pour wine for
them while they raise not so much as a finger to help
the beggar at the threshold! Why should they bind
on their phylacteries in the house of Jehovah; why in
the very foreground should that blind old imbecile sit

hugging the great law! — And how reverently they regard this sacred book! The little boy with the whisk
is supposed to keep the flies, emblems of Beelzebub,
from defiling it. The boy behind tries to steal its
magic virtue by kissing the hem of its garment; the
mystic name of God on the cover protects it from all
harm. And the cataracts in the eyes of this bibli-
olater are just a symbol of the spiritual blindness of
the leaders of the nation who trust to the letter of
the law and leave undone the weightier matters of the
spirit. This episode of the boy moves half of the
wise ones to mirth and half to anger. Not one, as in
Hofmann's picture, is moved to sympathy with the
lad or has learned a thing from the young prophet's
insight. Hunt may be wrong in his interpretation
of these men, but there is no doubt that he has interpreted.

The figures in the background also add their meaning. Here are a father and mother who have come to
redeem their firstborn as the law prescribes. Those
that sell sheep are there, for not yet has One come
to drive them out. The lamb without spot has been
purchased, and now the worshippers and their priest
move to the sacrifice, as twelve years ago another
father and mother had out of their poverty sacrificed
two turtle-doves. Here in operation is the ceremonial
of the old Covenant, which the writer to the Hebrews
would have us believe to be the fore-type and pattern
of that ampler covenant that God should one day pro-
vide. And has that day arrived of which the prophet
spoke? Has the " priest forever after the order of
Melchizedek " yet arisen, or the " lamb slain from
the foundation of the world " yet been revealed? On

14

the door it is written in Latin and Hebrew, where but for their blindness the rabbis themselves might read, " And the Lord whom ye seek shall suddenly come to his temple " (Mal. 3:1); in the courtyard, the stone which the builders rejected is soon to become the head stone of the corner; and on the threshold, fallen from Mary's dress as she entered, lies a head of wheat in which we recognize the symbol of the Bread of Life.

And now when we come to the Holy Family, what insight has the artist to give? We see an anxious mother, a strong and virtuous father, both relieved to find their lost boy and bent on taking him away at once. This is what we might expect. But the boy is the focus of the picture, and to him we should look for the true significance of the whole scene. He is a strong lad who can saw a plank or walk a hundred miles as well as his elders. His face is truly a lad's face; but the clear eyes show that the soul within has fully awaked; and the only half-yielding body is a warning that his parents must regard him no longer as a child. He has brought no book to bolster up his arguments; he has not been confounding the wise from the chair of authority, as Dürer would have it, or graciously patronizing his would-be helpers, like Hofmann's famous boy Christ. He has reverently and frankly come to learn, and he has found the temple to be in very truth God's house, — not because the doctors of the law have made him wise unto salvation — God forbid! — but because he brought his Father with him. In his soul God has ripened to consciousness, as in our own souls he may ripen today. And though the boy knows it not, on his right is the great tradition he is destined to fulfil and destroy, and

15

on his left is the suffering world he is destined to serve and redeem. In this one canvas, therefore, Hunt has made the past and the future minister to our insight of the present.

This picture represents perhaps an extreme case, for Hunt was an antiquarian and a symbolist who delighted to pack his details full of meaning. But the principle holds for all worthy pictures. The artist does not copy nature merely. He invents, assembles, arranges, emphasizes, in order to speak clearly some message from his soul to ours. It is our business to discover what that message is.

But let us not delude ourselves with the idea that we shall fathom a great picture on first sight. Oftentimes we shall read our own fancies and follies into it; we shall mistake our crude and partial insights for true ones; and as the years go by we shall have to revise if not reverse our earlier judgments. But still the picture glows before us like the Gleam of Merlin, enticing us onward to fresh pursuit of its truth. The picture " grows upon us," we say; which means that we have been growing up to its stature! The greater the picture, the more truly and the more deeply it finds us as our personal development advances; its ever-expanding boundaries englobe more and more of life.

2. *Art as Symbol.* — There is a class of pictures that stands by itself, although in reality it embodies a special form of insight. To it belong those works of art that have a universal significance. In the usual cases where the artist's insight has penetrated beneath the surface and found a meaning, the meaning pertains especially to the particular event or person that he has

16

presented. In the painting we have analyzed, Hunt
has grasped the true nature of the Judaism of Christ's
day, has seen that the boy Jesus stands at the opposite spiritual pole from it, and that the paraphernalia
and pomp of legalism and ritualism will some day
yield to this boy's simple gospel of the indwelling
Father. This is insight into the meaning of a definite
event, of a definite situation, an insight corroborated—
if not, indeed, induced — by the subsequent course of
history. You and I are not very much concerned in
this. To be sure, our heart-beats quicken as the
grand generalization becomes clear to us and we grasp
as from some mountain peak the vast reaches of history that have embodied the Divine plan; but we are
not especially in it. Our lives are in a way external
to it all.

But some pictures are universals. They include not
only their immediate subjects, but you and me. The
artist's insight has been primarily not of a special
event, but of a living and ever-present truth, so that
when the artist has expressed it by means of whatever
persons or events have come to hand, you and I, in
looking at the painting, find ourselves. Such pictures
are symbols. Their function is to embody universal
truth in a special case. Whoever contemplates this
special case with sufficient intensity will suddenly feel
it expand to universal dimensions; and this expansion comes over one with the force of a revelation. A
veil has been lifted, and one sees and feels wonderful
things that it is not lawful for man to utter. What is
a Madonna? Surely not the portrait of an artist's
model and her baby; surely not merely an ideal Mary
and her Christ-child. A Madonna is an incarnation

17

of the mystery of motherhood, of the ineffable meeting of the human and the divine that has occurred not once only in Judea but everywhere since history began, whenever an immortal soul through love has found a body.

In these pictures of the life of Christ there are many symbols. You may detect them by the simple device of trying to find yourself in them. Are you present in Burne-Jones' " Star of Bethlehem "? (p. 81). You may be, if you will dedicate whatever treasure your life contains to the service of Christ, or of his representative — a little child. Are you present in the " Temptation " by Cornicelius? (p. 134). Yes, if you will see that all temptation is spiritual and must be fought out in your own heart. Where are you in Hunt's " Light of the World "? (p. 186). You are behind the door, feeling the mystic summons to open and let the stranger in. You have often stood beside Flandrin's Christ weeping over Jerusalem (p. 276), and seen the crowds stream out from the tenement and the mill and look in vain to the church for the satisfaction of their deepest needs. Even the uniquely personal experiences of the Passion may be universalized if you will reflect that the principle of vicarious suffering and of redemption through sacrifice is fundamental to the spiritual life. This is what Matheson meant when he identified himself with the Sufferer who hung before his imagination:

> " O Cross that liftest up my head,
>   I dare not ask to fly from thee;
>   I lay in dust life's glory dead,
>   And from the ground there blossoms red
>   Life that shall endless be."

18

To a large extent all insights are symbols. It does not take much reflection to think ourselves into any of the world's masterpieces of religious art. Indeed, the endeavor so to do is a spiritual exercise of the highest value.

3. *Art as Feeling.* — Tolstoi has said that art is the language of emotion. By this he means that when an artist has had an experience so deep and rich that he cannot rest till he has made others enjoy it, he puts together on canvas certain devices — lines, colors — which he hopes will arouse in others emotions that are like his own; on precisely the same principle that I now hope, by means of these black marks on white paper, to recreate in your mind ideas that are like mine. With his pigments the artist creates a kind of speech by which his love, his fear, his hate, his sense of beauty, his longing, his aspiration, pass over from his heart to another's. And though the human voice is soon silent and the human heart will one day grow cold, yet because the artist's kind of speech is permanent he can transmit his passions endlessly, as long as there are spectators to pass before his canvas. This is surely a very wonderful performance!

There is no end to the ranges of feeling an artist may utter for us. Sometimes his heart may respond to the sensuous beauty of a rose, or a sun sinking into the sea, or grim clouds darkening the breast of some golden Alp, or the face of a child. Sometimes an act may cause a smile to break, or thrill his soul with a sense of the heroic; or some story will breathe its atmosphere of romance about him and conjure up a world of dreams. Sometimes the mutations of fortune may stamp their dramatic quality upon his imag-

ination, or the unrelieved monotony of poverty fill
him with gloom. Sometimes in moments of deep insight his breast surges with the thrust of tremendous
issues that cross in a trivial event and that drive men
and nations to their destiny. The richer his life, the
wider his experience, the deeper his insight is, the
greater is that store of emotion with which at will he
can flood his canvas. His pictures will be perpetual
reservoirs of life, surcharges of high potential whose
fields of force induce mighty currents in all who come
within their range. No one who has stood before the
Hermes at Olympia, or the Taj at Agra, or the Sistine
at Dresden, or Michael Angelo's great ceiling at Rome,
can doubt for an instant that Art is the language
of emotion.

Perhaps this truth also is worth illustrating from
the pictures we are to study. Take a relatively simple
one, Keller's " Raising the Daughter of Jairus " (p. 197).
The event here recorded has no historical significance,
no special bearing on the life of Christ; there are no
deep meanings to be suggested by symbols or eluci-
dated by the skilful arrangement of details. In other
words, the intellectual element is negligible. But as
soon as your eye meets the picture you feel a pull.
Something grips you. Your attention is fastened now
on the awed and uncertain father and his clinging
wife on the left; now on the strange crowd almost
delirious between fear and joy. You feel the fascination of an act that partly drives you away with an
uncanny terror and partly draws you by its gentleness
and power. Each face has its heart stamped upon it,
and even when hidden, like the woman's at the foot
of the sarcophagus, it sends its shafts just as unerringly

20

to your bosom. What insight is necessary to interpret Christ? His face is peace, his hands are sympathy, his whole body is love. Perhaps you have seen such an one; perhaps he once walked down into the valley of the shadow with one of your dear ones and brought her back from the grave. Then there is no need to tell you what this picture signifies; it is a page out of the book of life.

* * * * *

To understand and appreciate great pictures of any kind it is necessary that one live deeply and significantly. Art has no message for a shallow soul. But those who who have loved and sacrificed, who have known joy and sorrow, who have tasted the bitterness and sweetness of life, and especially those who have reflected upon life to know its true values, will find in great art a perpetual revelation, a perpetual inspiration. Youth is the golden time in which to seek these treasures of experience; for if once our heart is schooled to search for the deep things of life, if it is satisfied early with the beauty of the Lord our God, then like the Psalmist of old, we shall rejoice and be glad all our days.

PICTURES ON THE LIFE OF CHRIST
Arranged in Biographical Sequence

Note on the chronology: It is impossible to construct an accurate biography of Christ from the material in the gospels. While scholars are fairly agreed as to the general drift of events, many of the separate incidents may as well be placed at one

21

point as another. In this book the order given is for the most part that of Stevens and Burton's Harmony of the Gospels in which the various passages that refer to an event are grouped. The numbers in parentheses refer to the sections of this Harmony.

Note on the pictures: The list of pictures here given is not exhaustive, but it includes all the works that one might reasonably wish to consult in studying the subject. Pictures are arranged alphabetically by artists, and their present location is indicated. Letters show what companies have issued reprints in their one-cent-series. (Cosmos pictures are two cents, Medici prints — colored — are twenty-five cents.) There is usually a discount by the hundred.

Black type indicates that the picture is studied in this book. A star indicates pictures recommended also for further study.

Key to letters indicating Publishers:

B =Geo. O. Brown & Co., Beverly, Mass.

Bl =Berlin Photographic Co., 305 Madison Ave., New York.

Br =Braun & Co., 13 W. 46th St. New York. The appended letters indicate size and price of carbon photographs, as follows: F = 8 x 10, $2. R = 11 x 14, $3. I = 14 x 18 to 16 x 20, $5. E = 24 x 30, $18. O = 30 x 40, $25. T = 36 x 54, $65.

C =Cosmos Pictures Co., 119 W. 25th St., New York.

M =Medici series, " Old Masters in Color ": Foster Bros. 4 Park Sq., Boston, Mass.

P =Perry Pictures Co., Malden, Mass.

S =Seemann Three-color prints, $.25, Rudolf Lesch, Agent, 13 W. 42nd St.,New York.

T =Tissot pictures, N. Y. Sunday School Commission, 73 Fifth Ave., N. Y.

TP =Taber-Prang Art Co., Springfield, Mass. The appended numbers indicate size, kind and price, as follows:

Carbon Photographs:	Artotypes:
1 =cabinet, 18 cts.	9 = $3\frac{3}{4}$ x 5", $2\frac{1}{2}$ cts.
2 = 6 x 8", 30 cts.	10 = 11 x 14" paper, 10 cts., colored 25 cts.

Carbon Photographs:

3 = 7 x 9", 50 cts.
4 = 9 x 12", 80 cts.
5 = 13 x 17", $1.50.
6 = 16 x 20", $2.00.
7 = 18 x 22", $2.30.
8 = 20 x 26", $3.50.

Artotypes:

11 = 16 x 20", 40 cts.
12 = 20 x 24", 50 cts.
13 = 20 x 28", 90 cts.
14 = 26 x 32", $1.75,
　　　　colored $3.00.
15 = 28 x 38", $3.00.

16 = U. S. Carbons, 13 x 17", 80 cts., colored, $1.30.
17 = U. S. Carbons, 20 x 26", $1.75, colored, $2.75.
18 = Platinos, 7 x 9", 20 cts., colored 40 cts.
19 = Eureka Carbons, $3\frac{3}{4}$ x $5\frac{1}{4}$", 8 cts.
20 = Color prints, from $2\frac{1}{2}$ to 24 cts.

U = University Prints, Newton, Mass.

W = W. A. Wilde Co., 120 Boylston St., Boston, Mass.

1227 PICTURES

THE ANNUNCIATION TO MARY (§5)
Albertinelli: Florence, Acad. B
Angelico, Fra: Florence, S. Marco corridor, BM
　　Cortona, Ch. of Gesu. M
*Baroccio: Rome, Vatican, B
*Bonfigli: Perugia, Vanucci Gal. U
Botticelli: Florence, Uffizi. PM
Bouguereau: B
Bout: Brunswick Gal. Bl. $1.50
*Bramtot, A: Sparrow: Bible in Art, N. T. p. 17
*Bulleid, G. L.: Sparrow Bible in Art, O. T. Bk. III, p. 28; Bl. $1.25 or $2.00
*Burne-Jones: Eng. Earl of Carlisle C. Bl. $5.00
Christus, P: Madrid, Prado, U
Cima da Conegliano: Petrograd, Hermitage. S. Bl. $1.50
Cossa: Dresden Gal. S
*Credi, Lorenzo di: Florence, Uffizi. US
Crivelli: London, Nat. Gal. UC
David: Vienna Gal. S
Deger: B
Del Sarto, Andrea: Florence, Pitti. BS
Donatello: Florence, S. Croce (relief) U
Dubufe: Bl. $1.25–$6.00
Dürer: Munich, Alt. Pin. S
Ferrari: Berlin, K. F. Mus. U
Francia: Milan, Brera. U
Giotto: Padua, Arena Chapel. U
*Hacker: London, Tate Gal. S
Hofmann: (drawing) B

Holbein: Munich, Pin. U
*Lippi, Fra Filippo: London, Nat. Gal. UM. Bl. $5.00
　　Florence, Acad. U
Martini, Florence, Uffizi. U
Melozzo da Forli: Florence, Uffizi. S
Monaco, L: Florence, Acad. M
Müller, Franz: B. Bl. $1.50–$6.00
Murillo: Paris, Louvre (Immaculate Concep.). BC. Bl. $1.50–$18.00
　　Madrid, Prado (La Purissima). BS. Bl. $5.00–$12.00
　　Petrograd, Hermitage, Bl. $3.50
Ostade: Brunswick Gal. Bl. $1.50
Parsons: Bl. $1.25–$6.00
Reni, Guido: Paris, Louvre, B
Rossetti: London, Tate Gal. BMS
Schaffner: Munich, Pin. S
Seifert: B
Tintoretto: Venice, S. Rocco (detail). UC
Tissot: New York. T
Titian: Treviso, B
Van der Weyden: Berlin, K. F. Mus. U
Van Eyck: Berlin, K. F. Mus. U.
*Veneziano, Lorenzo: Venice, Acad U
Vinci, da: Florence, Uffizi. S, Paris Louvre. U
Viti: Milan, Brera. U

ANGELS AND SHEPHERDS (§10)
Bassano: Rome, Sparrow: N. T. p. 57
Bastien-Lepage: Phila. Widener Col. Sparrow: O. T. Bl. III. p. 38

23

Cabanel: Masterpieces of European
Art
Castiglione: Brunswick Gal. Bl. $1.50
Gaddi: Florence, S. Croce. P
Perrault, H: (Paris Salon, 1896)
Plockhorst: BC
Uhde, von: Die Kunst Unserer Zeit.
Vol. 17

NATIVITY AND ADORATION OF
SHEPHERDS (§§9, 10)
Antwerp, School of: Cassel Gal. S
Bartolommeo: Florence, Uffizi. U
Biscaino: Brunswick Gal. Bl. $1.50
Botticelli: Petrograd, Hermitage, Bl.
$5.00. London, Nat. Gal. M
Bouguereau: Paris, St. Vincent de
Paul. B
Burne-Jones: Torquay Church. Bell:
Sir Edw. B-J. p. 88
Birmingham, church window. Bell
op. cit. p. 78
Correggio: Dresden, Gal. BS. Bl.
$1.25–$12.00
Cosimo: Berlin, U
Craeyer, Gaspard de: Brussels Mus.
U
*Credi, Lorenzo di: Munich Pin. B
David: Vienna Gal. Bl. $5.00
Doré: B
Dürer: Munich. BS
Feuerstein: B
*Firle, W: Bl. $4.50–$15.00
Francesca: London Nat. Gal. Bl.
$2.50
*Ghirlandajo: Florence, Acad. BS
Giotto: Padua, Arena Ch. U
Grass, H: B
Hofmann: B
Honthorst: Florence, Uffizi. U
Vienna, Sparrow, N. T. p. 62.
Lerolle: BC
Lotto, Lorenzo: Brescia, Marti-
nengo Coll. U
Luini: Paris, Louvre. P
Memling: Bruges, Hosp. St. John U
Merson: B
Müller, Carl: B. Bl. $1.25–$18.00
Murillo: Madrid, Prado. B
Perugino: London, Nat. Gal. P.
Vienna, B
*Pierrey, L. M.: Sparrow, N. T. p. 66
Pinturicchio: Siena, Acad. B.
S. M. del Popolo, Rome, P
Rembrandt: London, Nat. Gal. Bl.
$3.50
Ribera: Paris, Louvre. B
Ripert: B
Robbia, Giov. della: Florence, Bar-
gello. U
Roeber: Bl. $1.25–$6.00
Romanino: London, Nat. Gal. U
Rossetti: Sparrow N. T. p. 68
Schaffner: Munich, Alt. Pin. S
Schöngauer: Munich, Alt. Pin. U
Berlin Gal. Bl. $2.50

Sinkel: B. Bl. $1.25–$12.00
*Tintoretto: S. Rocco, Venice, Spar-
row O. T. Bk. III, p. 36
*Uhde, von: Berlin Nat. Gal. S. Bl.
$1.25–$6.00
Van der Goes: Florence, Uffizi. US
Berlin Gal. Bl. $5.00. S
Vecchio, Palma: Berlin: SP
Velasquez: London, Nat. Gal. B
Veronese, Paul: Venice. S. Giusep.
di Castello. U
Vinci, Da: Florence, Uffizi. S
Zurbaran: Sparrow, N. T. p. 69

WISE MEN FROM THE EAST
(§13)
Angelico, Fra: S. Marco, Florence,
PM
Bosch van Aeken: Madrid, Prado, S
*Botticelli: Florence, Uffizi. BMUS
Petrograd, Hermitage, S
Bouguereau: Paris, St. Vincent de
Paul. Sparrow N. T. p. 83
Brueghel, Jan: Vienna, Imp. Gal. U
Burne-Jones: Manchester Gal. U
Byzantine terra-cotta: Bologna, Ch.
of St. Francis. B
Correggio: Milan, Brera. UM
Dürer: (woodcut) Life of the Virgin,
Sparrow N. T. p. 75
*Florence, Uffizi. BMS
*Fiorenzo di Lorenzo: Perugia, Va-
nucci Gal. U
Francia: Dresden Gal. S
Gaddi, Taddeo: Florence, S. Croce.
P
Geertgen: Amsterdam, Rijks Mus.
S
Gentile da Fabriano: Florence Acad.
BSM
Ghirlandajo: Florence, Pitti. B
Florence, Uffizi. B.
Giorgione: Vienna Gal., Bl. $5
Gozzoli: Florence, Riccardi Pal. U
Grien: Munich, Alt. Pin. U
Hofmann: B
Kulmbach: Berlin Gal. US
LaFarge: Boston Mus. F. A., B
Leighton: "Star in the East,"
Temple: Sacred Art, p. 112
*Lippi, Filippino: Florence, Uffizi.
Sparrow, N. T., p. 78
Lochner: Cologne Cath. U
*Luini: Saronno, Pilgrimage Ch. U
Paris, Louvre. B
Massaccio: Berlin Mus. M
Master of Mary's Death: Dresden
Gal. S
Medieval terra-cotta: Bologna, Ch.
of S. Stephano. U
Memling: Bruges, St. John's Hosp.
U
Mostaert: Amsterdam, Rijks Mus,
S.
Madrid, Prado. Bl. $5

Perugino: Trevi, S. M. d. Lacrime. U
Pfannschmidt: B
Piglhein: " Star of Bethlehem." BC
Pinturicchio, School of: Florence,
    Pitti. S
Pisano, N: Siena Cath. U
    Pisa, Baptistery. B
Portaels: " On the way to Bethlehem "
    B
Rossetti: Temple, Sacred Art, p. 115
Rubens: Antwerp Mus. U
    Paris, Louvre (draw.). Sparrow,
    N. T., p. 80
Sarto, del: Florence, Annunziata. U
Signorelli: New Haven, Conn. Yale,
    U
Tintoretto: Venice, San Rocco
*Tissot: Brooklyn Inst. (Approach of
    Wise Men). T
Uhde, von: " Star of Bethlehem." S
Van der Weyden, L.: Antwerp Mus.
    (engr.). U
Van der Weyden, R: Munich, Alt Pin.
    SU
    Berlin Gal.
Van Orley: Antwerp Mus. U
Velasquez: Madrid, Prado. U. Bl. $5
Veronese: Dresden Gal. B
    Vienna Gal. Bl. $5
Vivarini: Berlin Mus. U

FLIGHT INTO EGYPT (§14)

*Angelico, Fra: Florence Acad. M
Bouguereau: B
Brueghel: (slaughter) Vienna Gal.
    Bl. $3.50, $5
*Cazin: Sparrow, N. T., p. 94
Dürer: Little passion series. P
Furst: B
Giotto: Padua, Arena Ch. U
Girardet: Sparrow, N. T., p. 94
Hofmann: BC
Hunt, Holman: Liverpool, Walker
    Gal. C
*Kaulbach: Die Kunst Unserer
    Zeit, 9 : 128
Lingner, O: Bl. $1.25, $2.
Lizen-Meyer: B
Lorrain: Dresden Gal. U
Murillo: Petrograd, Hermitage, Bl.
    $2.50
Plocʹ:horst: B
Portaels: B
Rubens: Cassel Gal. S
Steinhausen: S
Tintoretto: Venice, San Rocco. U
Van Dyck: Munich. B

REPOSE, ON THE FLIGHT OR IN EGYPT (§14)

Altdorfer: Berlin Mus. US. Bl. $3.50
Baroccio: Rome. B
Bassano, J.: Milan, Ambrosiana. U
Benz: B
Bordone: Florence, Pitti. B

Correggio: Florence, Uffizi. B
Cranach: Berlin Gal. US, Bl. $5
Ittenbach: Berlin Gal., Bl. $1.25,
    $4.50
Knaus: New York, Metro. Mus. B
Long, Edwin:
Merson: Hyde Park, Mass., Dr. Geo.
    Kennedy. B
*Morris: " Shadow of the Cross." B
Murillo: Petrograd, Hermitage. Bl.
    $5.
*Pape: " Light in Egypt." Temple,
    Sacred Art, p. 118
Patinir: Brussels Mus. U
Plockhorst: B
Solario, A.: Milan, Poldi Pezzoli. U
Uhde, von: Die Kunst Unserer Zeit,
    vol. 17
Van Dyck: Munich, Alt. Pin. US
    Florence, Pitti. B
Veith: Bl. $2–$6

CHILDHOOD AT NAZARETH (§15)

*Dagnan-Bouveret: " Madonna of the
    Shop " C
Hofmann: (draw.) B
Millais: " Christ in the House of His
    Parents "
Viti: Brescia, Martinengo Col. U

VISIT TO JERUSALEM WHEN TWELVE YEARS OLD (§16)

Angelico, Fra:
Bida: Sparrow, N. T. p. 109
Bramer: Brunswick Gal., Bl. $1.50
Campi: Cremona, S. Margherita
    (fresco). Sparrow, N. T., p. 107
Dobson: B
Duccio: Siena Cath.
Dürer: Rome, Barberini Gal. P
Ferrari: Varallo, S. M. d. Grazie
    (fresco)
*Gebhardt, von: Die Kunst Unserer
    Zeit, 10 : 94
Giordano: Rome, Corsini Gal. S
Hofmann: Dresden Gal. B
Hunt, Holman: Birmingham Gal. B
*Luini: Saronno (fresco)
    London, Nat Gal. Bl. $5.00
    (draw.) Sparrow, O. T., iii : 45
Mazzolino: Berlin Gal.
Mengelberg: " First View of Jeru-
    salem " B
Pinturicchio: Spello, Coll. ch. (fresco)
Ribera: Vienna Gal., Sparrow, N. T.,
    p. 108
Van der Meire: Antwerp Mus. U
Veronese: Madrid. C

EIGHTEEN YEARS IN NAZARETH (§17)

Hunt, Holman: Manchester Gal. B
*La Font: Nazareth, Ch. of the An-
    nunciation. C
Müller, F: C

25

BIRTH AND YOUTH OF JOHN THE BAPTIST (§8)

Angelico, Fra: Florence, Uffizi. P
Baudry: P
Benedetto da Majano: Florence, Bargello. U
Botticelli: Paris, Louvre. C
Boucher: B
Bouguereau: Van Dyck, How to Judge a Picture, p. 71
Dolci: B
Donatello: (relief) Florence, Bargello. U
*Ghirlandajo: Florence, S. M. Novella (fresco). U
Giotto: Florence, Santa Croce
Lippi, Filippo: Prato (fresco)
Luini: Milan, Ambrosiana. M
Murillo: Vienna, B Bl. $3.50 (?) B
Madrid, Prado, B Bl. $5.00
Quercia, J. della: Siena, S. Giovanni. U
Reni: London Nat. Gal. B
*Reynolds: Sir Fred. Cook Col., Sparrow, N. T., p. 104
Rubens: Berlin Gal. C
Vienna Gal. U
Sarto, del: Florence, Uffizi. U
Florence, Pitti, BMS Bl. $5.00
Van der Weyden, R: Berlin
Van Eyck: Berlin Gal. Bl. $5.00
Winterstein: P

MINISTRY OF JOHN THE BAPTIST (§18)

Baudry: B
Bles: Vienna Gal.
Brueghel: Dresden Gal.
Munich Gal.
Cranach: Brunswick Gal. Bl. $1.50
*Donatello: (statue) Florence, Bargello. BU
Doré: B
Geertgen: Berlin Gal. S
Ittenbach: B
Lippi, Filippo: Prato
Memling: Bruges, St. John's Hosp. U
Lübeck Castle. U
*Raphael: Florence, Uffizi. B
Rembrandt: Berlin Gal. Bl. $5.00
Reni: Rome, Corsini Gal. B
Ribera: Madrid, Prado. U
Rodin: Paris, Luxembourg. U
Romano: Rome, Borghese Gal.
Sarto, del: Florence, Scalzo (fresco) Sparrow, N. T., p. 125
Schonbrock: Brunswick Gal. Bl. $1.50
Tissot: Voice in the Desert, Brooklyn Inst. T
*Titian: Venice Acad. BS
Wouvermans: Dresden Gal.
Van Eyck: Ghent, Bl. $5.00
Vinci, da: Paris, Louvre. U

BAPTISM OF JESUS (§19)

Angelico, Fra:
*Bellini, G: Vicenza, S. Corona. U
*Cima da Conegliano: Venice, S. Giov. in Bragora
Caereno di Miranda: Petrograd, Hermitage
David: Bruges Acad. U
Du Mond, F. V.: Harpers Weekly, Mar. 17, 1894
*Francesco, P. della: London Nat. Gal. UM
Francia: Dresden Gal.
Hampden Court
Ghirlandajo: Florence, S. M. Novella
Giotto: Padua, Arena Ch. U
Maratta: Rome, S. M. degli Angeli
Masolino: Castiglione d'Olona
Mosaic: Ravenna. B
Murillo: Siena Cath. U
Patinier: Vienna Gal. S
Perugino: Rouen Mus.
Perugia Gal.
Foligno
London Nat. Gal.
Pinturicchio: Rome, Sistine Ch.
Raphael: Rome, Vatican (fresco)
Sansovino: Florence, Baptistery (sculpt.) U
Stoss: Cracow, S. Florian (sculpt.) U
Tintoretto: Madrid, Prado, Sparrow, N. T., p. 126
Verrocchio: Florence, Acad. UCMS
Veronese: Florence, Pitti, Sparrow, N. T., p. 127

TEMPTATION (§20)

Botticelli: Rome, Sistine Ch.
Cornicelius: B
Ghiberti: Florence, Baptistery (relief)
Hofmann: B
*Morelli: Naples, Casa Maglione, Sparrow, N. T., p. 132
Perugino: Rome, Vatican
Rivière: Temple, Sacred Art, p. 124
Schaeffer: B
*Tintoretto: Venice, S. Rocco, Sparrow, N. T., p. 131
Tissot: T

MIRACLE AT CANA (§25)

Angelico, Fra: Florence Acad.
Burne-Jones: Biarritz (window)
David: Paris, Louvre. U
Doré: B
Gebhardt, von: (fresco) Loccum. Die Kunst Unserer Zeit, 10 : 106
Giotto: Padua, Arena Ch. P
Padovanino: Venice Acad. U
Steen, Jan: Dresden Gal. U
*Tintoretto: Venice, S. M. d. Salute B

*Veronese: Paris, Louvre. U
   Dresden Gal. BS
   Milan, Brera

DISCOURSE WITH NICODEMUS (§28)

Francken, Franz: Vienna Gal.
Gebhardt, von: Bl, $6.00
*La Farge: Boston, Trinity Ch.
Müller: B
Rembrandt: P
Tissot: T
*Uhde, von: Die Kunst Unserer Zeit, vol. 17

DISCOURSE WITH THE SAMARITAN WOMAN (§32)

Biliverti: Vienna Gal.
Burne-Jones: London, S. Peters (window)
Caracci: Vienna Gal., Bl, $3.50
Cranach: Berlin Gal.
Doré: B
Dyce, Wm.: Birmingham Gal., Sparrow, N. T., p. 139
Hofmann: BC
*Lippi, Filippino: Venice, Seminario
Moretto: Milan, Morelli Col.
Reni: Paris, Louvre
Richmond: London, Nat. Gal

PREACHING IN THE SYNAGOGUE (§36)

Bida: B
Doré: P
Tissot: T

CALL OF THE FOUR (§38)

Barocci: Brussels Mus.
Basaiti: Venice Acad. US
Burne-Jones: Cheshire, Ferry Ch. (window)
Craeyer, de: Brussels Mus., Sparrow, N. T., p. 144
Doré: B
Duccio: London, Mr. R. Benson
Ghirlandajo: Rome, Sistine Ch. U
Jouvenet: Paris, Louvre
Mantegna: Padua, Eremitani Ch.
Raphael: London, S. Kensington Mus. B
Rubens: Mechelin
Van Dyck: London, Nat. Gal., Sparrow, N. T., p. 144
Vogel: " Miraculous draught." S
Zimmermann: BC

CALL OF MATTHEW AND FEAST IN THE HOUSE OF LEVI (§42)

Bida: B
Moyaert: Brunswick Gal. Bl. $1.50
Skilbeck: Temple, Sacred Art, p. 131
Van Hemessen: Sparrow, N. T., p. 132
Veronese: Venice Acad. US
   Paris, Louvre. B
Voenius, Otto: Antwerp Mus.

SERMON ON THE MOUNT (§49)

Angelico, Fra: Florence, S. Marco
Bida: B
Bloch: " Come Unto Me." B
*Dietrich: (Is. 32 : 2) Bl, $1.50–$15.00
Doré: B
*Gebhardt, von: Die Kunst Unserer Zeit, 10 : 99
Hofmann: B
Le June: B
Lorrain: London, Grosvenor Col.
Noack: B
Rosselli: Rome, Sistine Ch.
Tissot: T

THE CENTURION'S SERVANT (§50)

Veronese: Vienna. P
   Dresden, Sparrow, N. T., p. 147
   Madrid, Prado. S
   Munich

RAISING THE WIDOW'S SON (§51)

Caracci: Sparrow, N. T., p. 148
Dobson: Temple, Sacred Art, p. 132
Hofmann: B
Palma: Venice Acad. B
Schurer: Sparrow, N. T., p. 149
Tissot: T

ANOINTING IN THE HOUSE OF SIMON (§53)

Bassano, J: Hampden Court
Champeigne: Paris, Louvre
Cranach: Berlin Mus.
Dirk Bouts: Berlin Gal. S
Froment: Florence, Uffizi
Hofmann: B
Jouvenet: Paris, Louvre
Lanzani: Vienna Gal.
Mabuse: Brussels Mus.
Moretto: Venice, S. M. d. Pieta
Rubens: Vienna Gal. W
   Petrograd, Hermitage, Bl, $5.00
Tissot: T
*Veronese: Paris, Louvre. B

MARY MAGDALENE (§53)

Allori: Florence, Uffizi
Batoni: Dresden Gal., C Bl. $1.25–$18.00. S
Bellini, G.: Venice Acad. U
*Byzantine: Florence Acad.
Correggio: Dresden Gal., B Bl. $3.50
Crivelli: Berlin Gal., Bl, $2.50
Dolce: Florence, Uffizi. BC
*Domenichino: Florence, Pitti. B
Edelfelt: S
Giampietrino: Milan, Brera. US
Max: Bl, $1.25, $6.00
Metsys: Antwerp Mus. UM
   Berlin Gal., Bl, $2.50
Murillo: Berlin Gal. B

Rembrandt: Brunswick Gal., Bl, $1.50
Reni: Rome, Capitoline
  Paris, Louvre. B
  Amsterdam, Rijksmus.
Ribera: Dresden Gal.
Robbia, A della: Vald' Ema, Certosa Cloister (relief). U
Scorel: Amsterdam, Rijksmus. S
Titian: Petrograd, Hermitage, Bl, $5.00
  Florence, Pitti. S
Van Orley: London, Nat. Gal. U
Veronese: Turin. Sparrow, N. T. p. 152
Viti: Bologna Gal. U

PARABLES BY THE SEA (§57)

Dietrich: "Sower" Bl, $1.25–$6.00
Hofmann: Preaching from Ship. B
*Joy, G. W.: Pearl of Great Price, Sparrow, N. T., p. 155
Millais: Evil One Sowing Tares.
Millet: The Sower. B
Overbeck: The Sower, Sparrow, N. T., p. 154
Robert: The Sower. B
Tissot: Preaching from Ship. T
*Uhde, von: Die Kunst Unserer Zeit, vol. 17

STILLING THE TEMPEST (§58)

Delacroix: Sparrow, N. T., p. 156
Dietrich: Bl, $1.50–$36.00
Doré: B
Jalabert: Temple, Sacred Art., p. 140

GADARENE DEMONIACS (§59)

*Rivière: Sparrow, N. T., p. 157

RAISING JARIUS' DAUGHTER (§60)

Comb-Hood: Temple, Sacred Art, p. 135
Ecckhout: Berlin Gal., Sparrow, N. T., p. 159
Hofmann: B
Keller: B
*Max: Die Kunst Unserer Zeit 5 : 20, 26
Repin: Petrograd Acad. S
*Richter: Berlin Gal. B Bl. $1.25–$18.00
Tissot: Brooklyn Inst. T
Veronese: Vienna Gal., Bl, $5.00. S

PREACHING TOUR, HEALING SICK, ETC. (§63)

*Aubert: Sparrow, N. T., p. 149
Bida: (Palsy.) B
  (Lepers.) B
  (Blind.) B

Brueghel: (Blind) Paris, Louvre. U
Dietrich: Dresden Gal., Bl, $1.25–$6.00
Doré: (Demoniac). B
Gebhardt, von: (fresco) Loccum. Die Kunst Unserer Zeit, 10 : 102
Goodall: Temple, Sacred Art, p. 129
Hofmann: (Sick.) B
  (Raising dead). P
Plockhorst: (Consoler). B
*Rembrandt: U
Rosselli: (Lepers) Rome, Sistine Ch.
Schaeffer: (Consoler). B
Schönherr: B
Tissot: Brooklyn Inst. T
Uhde, von: Die Kunst Unserer Zeit, vol. 17
Unknown: Ten Lepers. B
Van Dyck: London, Buckingham Pal., Sparrow, N. T., p. 164
Van Leyden: Petrograd, Hermitage. S
Zimmermann: (Consoler). B

DEATH OF JOHN THE BAPTIST (§65)

Civitale, M.: Lucca Cath. U
Donatello: Siena, S. Giovanni (relief). U
Gebhardt, von: "John sends to J." Die Kunst Unserer Zeit, 10 : 94
Ghiberti: Siena, S. Giovanni (relief) U
Giotto: Florence, S. Croce. U
*Lippi, Filippo: Prado Cath. U
Luini: Florence. Sparrow, N. T., p. 142
Masolino: Castiglione d' Olona Baptistery. U
Metsys: Antwerp Mus. U
Moreau: Paris, Luxembourg. U
Puvis de Chavannes: New York, Metro. Mus.
Reni: Rome, Corsini Gal. B
*Rochegrasse: Salome dancing, Temple, Sacred Art, p. 138
Sarto, del: Florence, Scalzo. U
Titian: Venice, S. Giovanni Elymos. U

FEEDING THE FIVE THOUSAND (§66)

Murillo: Seville. B

JESUS WALKING ON THE WATER (§67)

Gaddi: Florence, S. M. Novella. P
Ghiberti: Florence Bapt. (relief)
Giotto: Rome, St. Peters (mosaic) P
*Jalabert: Sparrow, N. T., p. 159
Lanfranco: Sparrow, N. T., p. 160
Plockhorst: BS

THE SYROPHŒNICAN WOMAN (§70)

Vecchio, Palma: Venice Acad., Sparrow, N. T., p. 160

Peter's Confession (§75)
 Perugino: Rome, Sistine Ch. U
 Schwartz, A.: B

THE TRANSFIGURATION(§§77, 78)
 Angelico, Fra: Florence, S. Marco.
  Florence Acad.
 Bellini: Naples Mus., Sparrow, N. T.
  p. 167
 Ghiberti: Florence Bapt. (relief). U
 *Perugino: Perugia, Cambio.
  Perugia Gal.
 Raphael: Rome, Vatican Gal. B
 Savoldo: Florence Uffizi
  Milan, Ambrosiana
 Tintoretto: Brescia, S. Afra
 Titian: Venice, S. Salvatore

WOMAN TAKEN IN ADULTERY
 (§83)
 *Anderson, A.: Sparrow, N. T., p. 171
 Cranach: Munich, Alt Pin. U
  Dresden Gal.
 Francken II: Dresden Gal.
 Gebhardt, von: (fresco) Loccum. Die
  Kunst Unserer Zeit 10 : 106
 Hofmann: Dresden Gal. B
 Lotto: Paris, Louvre
  Loreto
 Marconi: Rome, Corsini Gal.
  Berlin Gal.
 Padovanino: Vienna Gal.
 Palma: Rome, Capitoline
 Poussin: Paris, Louvre
 Rembrandt: London, Nat. Gal., Bl.
  $5
 Rubens: Leigh Court, Eng.
  Munich, Alt Pin. S
 Siemiradski: Paris, Louvre
 Tintoretto: Venice, Acad.
  Dresden Gal.
  Milan, Archduke's Pal.
  Budapest. S
 Tissot: Brooklyn Inst. T
 Titian: London, Duke of West-
  minster Col., Sparrow, N. T.,
  p. 170
  Vienna Gal., Bl. $5.00
 Van der Werff: Munich, Alt Pin.

THE GOOD SAMARITAN (§88)
 Bassano, F: Berlin Gal.
 Bassano, J.: Vienna Gal.
  London, Nat. Gal.
 Dupain, E.: B
 Henner: P
 Penrose: Temple, Sacred Art, p. 141
 Plockhorst: B, Bl. $1.25–$12.00
 Rembrandt: Paris, Louvre
 Veronese: Dresden Gal.

VISIT TO MARY AND MARTHA
 (§89)
 Allori: B
 Burnand: Phila., Bethany Ch., Bl.
  $1.25–$6.00

 Eichstadt: B
 Dietrich: Bl. $1.25–$6.00
 Hofmann: B
 Jouvenet: Paris, Louvre
 Joy, G. W.: (Mary) Sparrow, N. T.,
  p. 171
 Lesueur: Munich
 Siemiradski: B
 Sinkel: Bl., $1.25–$6.00
 Steenwyck: Paris, Louvre
 Velasquez: London, Nat. Gal.

PARABLE OF THE LOST SHEEP
 (§102)
 Dietrich: Bl. $1.25–$18.00
 Dobson: B
 Molitor: B
 Mosaic, fifth cent: Ravenna. U
 Murillo: Madrid, Prado. B
  Madrid, Museum. B
 Plockhorst: B
 Schönherr: B
 Soord: Taber-Prang

PARABLE OF THE LOST MONEY
 (§102)
 Millais: B

PARABLE OF THE PRODIGAL
 SON (§102)
 Batoni: Vienna Gal., Sparrow, N. T.
  p. 183
 *Bechingham, A.: Royal Acad exhib.,
  1893
 Dubufe: New York, Adolf Strauss
  Col. B
 Dürer: (engr.). U
 Francken II: Paris, Louvre
 Gebhardt, von: Die Kunst Unserer
  Zeit, 1908
 Greuze: P
 Guercino: Vienna Gal.
 Holbein: Liverpool, Walker Gal.
 Hunt, W. M.: Boston, Mus. F. A.
 Jordaens: Dresden Gal.
 Kugelgen, von: Dresden Gal.
 Molitor: B
 Murillo: London, Sutherland Col.
  Madrid, Prado
 Puvis de Chavannes:
 Rembrandt: Petrograd, Hermitage
 Rodin: (statue) Paris
 Rosa, Salvator: Petrograd, Hermitage
 Rubens: Dresden Gal.
 *Swan: Temple, Sacred Art, p. 146
 Teniers: Paris, Louvre, Sparrow,
  N. T., p. 182
 Tissot: Brooklyn Inst. T
  (series) Paris, Luxembourg
 Van Hemessen: Brussels Mus.
 Watts, G. E.: Sparrow, N. T., p. 185

PARABLE OF DIVES AND LAZARUS
 (§103)
 Bassano, J.: Vienna Gal.
 Bonifazio: Venice Acad.

Doré: B
Teniers: London, Nat. Gal.
*Veronese: Venice, Acad.

RAISING OF LAZARUS (§105)

Angelico, Fra: Florence Acad. M
*Bassano, L.: Venice Acad.
Bonifazio II: Paris, Louvre
Froment: Florence, Uffizi
Garofalo: Ferrara Gal.
Gebhardt, von: Die Kunst Unserer
Zeit 10 : 110
Ghiberti: Florence Bapt. (relief). U
Giotto: Padua, Arena Ch. U
Guercino: Paris, Louvre
Jouvenet: Paris, Louvre
Mabuse: Busssels Mus.
Outwater: Berlin Gal.
*Piombo, S.: London, Nat. Gal. B
Rembrandt: New York, Yerkes Col.
Rivière: Temple, Sacred Art, p. 148
Rubens: Berlin Gal. BS Bl, $5.00
Tanner, H. O.: Paris, Luxembourg
Tintoretto: Venice, S. Rocco
London, Dorchester House
Vedder: (head of L) Chicago, Stone
Col.
Vischer, P.: Regensburg Cath. U
Voenius: Antwerp Cath.

PARABLE OF THE PHARISEE AND THE PUBLICAN (§109)

*Tissot: Brooklyn Inst. T

CHRIST BLESSING LITTLE CHILDREN (§111)

Ballheim: B
Bourdon: Paris, Louvre
Burne-Jones: Brampton Ch. (window)
Eastlake: Manchester Gal.
Fugel: S
Hofmann: B
Pfannschmidt: Bl, $1.25–$3.50
Plockhorst: B
Rembrandt, School of: London, Nat
Gal. P
*Roederstein: Sparrow, N. T., 123
Uhde, von: Leipsic Mus.
Vorgel: B

THE RICH YOUNG RULER (§112)

Gebhardt, von: Die Kunst Unserer
Zeit, 10 : 94
Hofmann: BC
Tissot: Brooklyn Inst. T
Watts: London, Tate Gal.

BLIND MEN NEAR JERICHO (§115)

Poussin: Paris, Louvre
Van Leyden, L.: Petrograd, Hermitage

TRIUMPHAL ENTRY (§119)

Angelico, Fra: Florence Acad. M
Deger: B Bl. $1.50–$12.00

Doré: BC
Dubufe: Sparrow, N. T., 103
Duccio: Siena Cath. U
Dürer: Little passion series
Eastlake: London, Nat. Gal. B
Flandrin: Br I
Gérôme: Sparrow, N. T., 203
Giotto: Padua, Arena Ch. U
Hofmann:
Hogarth: Passion series

CLEANSING THE TEMPLE (§§27, 121)

Bonifazio: Venice, Ducal Pal.
Dürer: Little passion series
*Gebhardt, von: (fresco) Loccum:
Die Kunst Unserer Zeit, 10 : 102
Ghiberti: Florence, Bapt. (relief)
Giordano: Naples, S. Gerolemini
Giotto: Padua, Arena Chapel
Greco, Il.: London, Nat. Gal. S
Hofmann: B
Kirchbach: B
Rembrandt: (etching)
Tissot: Brooklyn Inst. T
Venusti: London, Nat. Gal. U

PARABLE OF THE VINEYARD (§124)

*Rembrandt: Petrograd, Hermitage.
Bl. $2.50
Melville: B

PARABLE OF THE GREAT SUPPER (§124)

Burnand: Br. F.I.E.

THE TRIBUTE MONEY (§125)

Bida: B
*Massaccio: Florence, Brancacci Ch. U
*Rembrandt: (etching) Sparrow, N. T.
207
Rubens: Paris, Louvre
Titian: Dresden Gal. BC Bl, $15.00. S

THE WIDOW'S MITE (§128)

Bida: B

PARABLE OF THE WISE AND FOOLISH VIRGINS (§131)

Piloty: N. Y., Metro. Mus. BC
*Strudwick: Temple, Sacred Art 154

CORRUPTION OF JUDAS (§132)

Giotto: Padua, Arena Ch. U
Prell: Berlin Gal. P

THE LAST SUPPER (§133)

Angelico, Fra: Florence Acad. M
Bida: B
Bonifazio II: Florence, Uffizi
Venice, S.M. Mater Dom.
Burnand: Bl, $2.00–$36.00
Duccio: Siena Cath.
Dürer: Basel Gal.

Ferrarese: London, Nat. Gal.
Ferrari: Milan, S. M. d. Passione
Gaddi: Florence, S. M. Novella. P
Gebhardt, von: B. Bl, $2.00–$18.00
Ghiberti: Florence Bapt. (relief)
Giotto: Padua, Arena Ch. U
Hofmann: B
Holbein: Basel Gal.
Justus of Ghent: Urbino Gal. U
Raphael: Florence, Sant' Onafrio or Rome, Vatican. P
Riemenschneider: Rothenburg, St. James Ch. (sculp.) U
Rosselli: Rome, Sistine Ch.
Rubens: Milan, Brera. U
Sarto, del: Florence. S. Salvi. UC
Schoenfelein: Berlin Gal.
Unknown: Florence, Egyptian Mus. C
Tiepolo: Paris, Louvre. U
Tintoretto: Venice. S. Rocco. U
  Venice, Giov. Mag., Sparrow, N. T., 215
  Venice, SS. Protasio e Gervasio
  Venice, S. Paulo
  Venice, S. Stephano
Uhde, von: Bl, $6.00
Vicenti: Madrid, Prado. S
Vinci, da: Milan. S. M. d. Grazie. U. Bl, $1.50–$18.00
Zimmermann: B

WASHING THE DISCIPLES' FEET (§133)

Angelico, Fra: Florence Acad.
Bida: B
Brown, F. M.: BS
Cranach: Berlin Gal.
Duccio: Siena Cath.
Dürer: Little passion series
Francken II: Berlin Gal.
Ferrari: Varallo. S. M. d. Grazie
Ghiberti: Florence, Bapt. (relief)
Giotto: Padua, Arena Ch.
Morando: Verona Gal.
Tintoretto: London, Nat. Gal.

THE AGONY IN GETHSEMANE (§136)

Bacon:
Basaiti: Venice Acad.
Bassano: Petrograd, Hermitage
Bellini: London, Nat. Gal.
Berna: S. Gimigniano. M
Bruni: Petrograd, Hermitage
Correggio: London, Nat. Gal., Sparrow, N. T., 233
  London, Apsley House
Cranach: Berlin Gal.
Dolce: Florence, Pitti
Duccio: Siena Cath. U
Dürer: Little passion series
Ferrari: Varallo
Francken II: Berlin Gal.
Giotto: Florence, Uffizi
Greco, Il: Budapest. S

Herbert: Paris, Luxembourg
Hofmann: B. Bl, $1.50–$18.00
Jalabert: B
Liska: B
Mantegna: London, Nat. Gal.
Murillo: Paris, Louvre
Noack: P
Perugino: Florence Acad. U
Schoenfelein: Berlin Gal.
Schongauer:
Spagna, Lo.: London, Nat. Gal.
Tissot: Brooklyn Inst. T
Tintoretto: Venice. S. Rocco
Van Leyden: Passion series

BETRAYAL AND ARREST (§137)

Angelico, Fra: Florence Acad. M
  Florence, S. Marco. Sparrow, N. T., 238
Duccio: Siena Cath.
Dürer: Greater passion series
  Little passion series
Geiger: B
Ghiberti: Florence Bapt. (relief)
Giotto: Padua, Arena Ch. U
Hofmann: Darmstadt Mus., B
Mosaic: Ravenna, S. Apollinare
Van Dyck: Madrid, Prado, U, Bl, $5.00

TRIAL BEFORE THE JEWISH AUTHORITIES (§138)

Angelico, Fra: Florence Acad. M
Duccio: Siena Cath.
Dürer: Little Passion series
Giotto: Padua, Arena Ch.
Holbein: (drawing) Basel Mus.
Unknown: B
Van Leyden: Round passion series

REMORSE OF JUDAS (§138)

Armitage: London, Tate Gal. S
*Meyer: Die Kunst Unserer Zeit 5 : 44
*Dollman: Temple Sacred Art, 165

PETER'S DENIAL (§138)

Angelico, Fra: Florence Acad. M
Dietrich: Bl, $1.25–$6.00
Harrach: B
Ribera: Seville Cath.
Teniers: Paris, Louvre. U
West: Hampton Court, Eng.

TRIAL BEFORE PILATE (§139)

Cagliari: Venice Acad.
Ciseri: Rome, Nat Gal., BC (" Ecce Homo")
Doré: B
Duccio: Siena Cath.
Dürer: Little passion series
Hofmann: P

Holbein: (drawing) Basel Mus.
Multscher: Berlin Gal. S
Munkacsy: Philadelphia, J. Wanamaker, BC
Rembrandt: London, Nat. Gal., Bl, $2.50
Schiavone: Naples Gal.
*Schongauer: Brussels Mus. U
Tintoretto: Venice, S. Rocco. U
Tissot: Brooklyn Inst. T

TRIAL BEFORE HEROD (§139)
Duccio: Siena Cath. Hurll, p. 270
Dürer: Little passion series

SCOURGING, MOCKING, "ECCE HOMO" (§§138, 139)
Angelico, Fra: Florence Acad. M
Antonelli da Messina: Venice Acad. U
Borgognone: Milan, Brera
Botticini: Vienna, Belvedere
Brüggemann: Schleswig Cath. U
Cigoli: Florence, Pitti, Sparrow, O. T., iii : 52
Cima da Conegliano: London, Nat. Gal. U
Correggio: London, Nat. Gal.
Dolce: Rome, Corsini Gal. C
Duccio: (three scenes) Siena Cath.
Dürer: Little passion series
Ferrari: Varallo
Gelder, de: Dresden Gal.
Giotto: Padua, Arena Ch.
Hofmann: B
Holbein: (drawing) Basel Mus.
Lesueur: Paris, Louvre
Luini: Milan, Monast. Maggiore.
Mabuse: Antwerp Mus. U
Mazzolino: Dresden Gal.
Morales: Rome, Corsini Gal. S
Morelli: Berlin, Seeger Gal. S
Murillo: Paris, Louvre
Madrid, Prado, Bl, $1.50
Mignard: B
Piombo: Rome, S. Pietro in Mont.
Pollaiuolo: Florence, Pitti
Rembrandt: Darmstadt Gal. S
Reni: (two pictures) Dresden Gal. BC Bl, $1.25–$5.00 S
Rome: Corsini Gal. B
London: Nat. Gal., Bl, $3.50
Rudinoff: S
Signorelli: Milan, Brera
Sodoma: Siena Acad. U
Solario: Milan, Poldi Pezzoli. US
Tintoretto: Venice, S. Rocco.
Titian: Venice, Imp. Gal. US
Madrid, Prado.
Paris, Louvre. U
Munich, Alt. Pin. S
Van der Werff: Munich Gal.
Van Dyck: Berlin Gal., U. Bl, $5.00

Van Leyden: (two series) round passion
Velasquez: London, Nat. Gal., Bl, $5.00
West: Phila., Acad. Fine Arts.

JOURNEY TO CALVARY
*Aertszen: Berlin Gal.
Angelico, Fra: Florence Acad.
*Beraud: (Paris Salon, 1894) Br
Bouguereau: Sparrow, N. T., 251
Brueghel: Vienna Gal., Bl, $3.50
Cariani: Vienna Belvedere
Crespi: B
Doré: B
Duccio: Siena Cath.
Ghiberti: Florence Bapt. U
Giorgione: Boston, Mrs. J. Gardner U
Giotto: Padua, Arena Ch.
Greco, Il: Munich, Alt. Pin. S
Hofmann: B
Ittenbach: Berlin Gal.
Veronica's Handkerchief, Bl, $1.25–$4.50
Juanes: Madrid, Prado
Kraft: (sculpt.) Stations of the Cross, 1, 2, 6, 7, U
Lesueur: Paris, Louvre. S
Master of Flemalle: "Veronica's Handkerchief," Frankfort Art Inst. S
Max, G.: "Veronica's Handkerchief"
Morando: Verona Gal.
Morales: Paris, Louvre.
Palmezzano: Berlin Gal.
Piombo: Petrograd, Hermitage
Dresden Gal.
Ribera: Vienna Gal., Bl, $5.00
Raphael: Madrid, Prado. C S
Romano, G: "Lo Spasimo" Madrid, Prado, BC, Bl, $5.00–$15.00
Rubens: Brussels Mus.
*Thiersch: B
Tiepolo: Venice, S. Alvise. U
*Tintoretto: Venice, S. Rocco
Titian: Madrid, Prado.
Petrograd, Hermitage
*Unknown, 14th Cent.: Florence, S. M. Novella. U
Van der Meire: Antwerp Mus. U
Van Leyden: Round passion series
Veronese: Paris, Louvre

CRUCIFIXION (§140)
Angelico, Fra: Florence, S. Marco U
Bonat, L.: C
*Bulleid: Bl, $1.25–$2.00
*Burne-Jones: Birmingham, S. Philip's (window), Sparrow, N. T. 260
Cano: Madrid, Prado. U
Carrière: Paris, Luxembourg

Cranach: Weimar, Stadt Kirche. U
David: Berlin Gal., Bl, $3.50
Deger: Bl, $1.25–$3.50
Delacroix: Sparrow, N. T., 261
Delaroche: " Good Friday," Temple
  Sacred Art, 166
  " Night of the Crucifixion," Temple
  Sacred Art, 172
Dürer: Dresden Gal. U
  Greater passion series
  Lesser passion series
Eakins: Phila. Acad. F. A.
Francia: Paris, Louvre
Furst: B
Gaddi: Florence, S. M. Novella
*Gérôme: P
Ghiberti: Florence Bapt. (relief)
Giottino: Florence, S. M. Novella U
Giotto: Padua, Arena, Ch. U
Hofmann: B
Lebrun, C.: Paris, Louvre. U
*Luini: Lugano
*Mantegna: Paris, Louvre, Sparrow,
  N. T., 35
Martini: Florence, S. M. Novella B
Messina: London, Nat. Gal. M
Mosaic: Venice, S. Mark.
Marot: Petrograd. M
Murillo: Petrograd, Hermitage, Bl,
  $2.50
  Madrid, Prado, Bl. $5.00
Munkacsy: Phila., J. Wanamaker. B
Nuremberg Master: Berlin Gal. U
Perugino: Florence, S. M. Mad. dei
  Pozzi. U
  Petrograd. M
Piglhein: " Moritur in Deo "
Pizano, G.: Pisa Mus. (relief) U
Prud'hon: Paris, Louvre. U
Plockhorst: Bl, $1.25–$18.00.
Raphael: London, Mr. Du Mont. M
Reni: Rome, S. Lor. in Lucina. B
Rubens: Antwerp Mus. U
  Paris, Louvre. B
  " Elevation " Ant. Cath.
Schmalz: " Return from Calvary "
Schülein: (sculpt.) Trefenbroun, Abbey
  Ch. U
Squarcione: Pesaro, Ateneo. U
Tintoretto: Venice, S. Rocco. U
  Venice, S. Cassanio, Sparrow, N.
  T., 256
  [Venice, Acad.]
Trubner, Wm.: S.
Unknown, 8th Cent. (fresco): Rome,
  S. M. Antiqua. U
  12th Cent. (fresco): Florence Acad.
  U
Van der Weyden, R.: Madrid
  Prado
  Vienna Gal. S
Van Dyck: Antwerp Mus. U
  Naples Mus. B
  Vienna Gal., M. Bl, $5.00
Velasquez: Madrid, Prado, Bl, $5.00
Wolgemut: Munich, Alt Pin. U

THE DEPOSITION (§141)

Angelico, Fra: Florence Acad. M
Bartolommeo: Florence, Pitti. UM
Correggio: Parma Gal. UC
Dürer: Munich. Alt. Pin. U
Garofalo: Rome, Borghese Gal. U
Giottino: Florence, Uffizi. U
Haarlem, Gerrit von: Vienna Gal.
  Bl, $5.00
Master of Cologne: Paris, Louvre. U
Perugino: Florence, Pitti. U
Rembrandt: London, Nat. Gal. Bl,
  $2.50
  Munich, Alt Pin. US
  Petrograd, Hermitage, Bl, $5.00
Rubens: Antwerp Cath. B
  Petrograd, Hermitage, Bl., $5.00
Tintoretto: Venice Acad. U
Van der Weyden: Madrid, Prado. U
  Bl, $5.00
  Madrid, Escorial
Volterra: Rome: S. Trin. del Monte.
  B

THE ENTOMBMENT (§141)

*Angelico Fra: Florence Acad.
Brown, F. M.: London, Leyland Col.
  Sparrow, N. T.
Caravaggio: Rome, Vatican. U
Ciseri: Locarno. Mad. del. Sasso
Crivelli: Rome, Vatican
Carpi, da: Florence, Pitti
Duccio: Siena Cath.
Dürer: Nuremberg Mus.
  Little passion series
Francia: Bologna. B
  London, Nat. Gal.
Gaddi: Florence Acad.
Hofmann: B
Lippi Filippo: Florence, Uffizi
Marconi: Venice Acad.
Metsys: Antwerp Gal. U
Michelangelo: London, Nat. Gal. U
Morando: Verona Gal.
Pfannschmidt: B
Piglhein:
Pisano, N.: (relief) Lucca.
*Raphael: Rome, Borghese Gal. UMS
Rembrandt: Dresden Gal. U Bl,
  $5.00
Sarto, del: Florence, Pitti. C
*Titian: Paris, Louvre. B
Uhde, von: Die Kunst Unserer Zeit.
  vol. 17
Van der Weyden: London, Nat. Gal.
  Bl, $5.00
  Florence, Uffizi. S

THE PIETÀ (§141)

Bartolommeo: Florence, Pitti. BS
Bellini: Berlin Gal. Bl, $5.00
  Milan, Brera. UM
  Milan, P. Pezzoli. M

Bernini: (sculp.) Rome, St. John Lateran. U
Botticelli: Munich Gal.
Bouguereau: P
Cano: Madrid, Prado. Bl, $4.50
Caracci: Naples Gal.
    Paris, Louvre
Delacroix: Boston, Mus. F. A.
De la Roche: Boston, Mus. F. A.
Francia: London, Nat. Gal. UMS
*Gebhardt, von: Die Kunst Unserer Zeit, 10 : 99
*Giotto: Padua, Arena Ch. U
Holbein: Basel Mus. U
Klinger, M.: Bl. $1.25–$6.00
Mantegna: (engraving) Milan, Brera U
Metsys: Munich, Alt Pin. S
*Michelangelo: (sculpt.) Rome, St. Peters. PC
Morales: Madrid, Academy St. Ferd.
Piombo: Berlin Gal. Bl, $5.00
Poussin: Munich Gal.
Ribot: S
Reni: Bologna Gal.
Santi: Urbino Inst. F. Arts
Sarto, del: Vienna Gal. Bl, $5.00
Tintoretto: Milan, Brera. S
Titian: Venice Acad. U
    Vienna Gal. Bl, $5.00
Van der Goes: Vienna Gal. Bl, $2.50
Van Dyck: Antwerp Mus. (?) U
    Antwerp Mus. M
    Madrid, Prado. Bl, $5.00
    Berlin Gal. Bl, $5.00
Veronese: Petrograd, Hermitage. S

RESURRECTION (§143)

Angelico, Fra: Florence. S. Marco
Bartolommeo: Florence, Pitti. B
Bellini: Berlin Gal. Bl, $5.00. S
Burne-Jones: (window) Hopton, Eng.
Caracci: Paris, Louvre
Correggio: (fresco) Parma Cath. U
Del Garbo: Florence Acad.
Dietrich: Bl, $1.25–$6.00
Duccio: Siena Cath.
Dürer: Greater passion series
    Lesser passion series
Francesca: San Sepolcro Mus. U
Gaddi: Florence Acad.
    Florence. S. M. Novella. B
Ghiberti: Florence, Bapt. (relief)
Ghirlandajo: Berlin Gal.
*Giotto: Padua, Arena Ch.
Hofmann: B
Mantegna: Tours Mus.
    London, Nat. Gal.
Memling: Lübeck
Noack: B
Perugino: Rome, Vatican
Plockhorst: B
Pinturicchio: Rome, Vatican
Robbia, L della: (relief) Florence Cath.

Schönherr: B
Signorelli: Orvieto Cath. U
Thompson: B
Tintoretto: Venice, S. Rocco
Titian: Brescia, SS. Nazero e Celso. U
Uhde, von: P
Vinci, da: Berlin Gal.
Vivarini: Venice, S. Giov. in Bragora

HOLY WOMEN AT THE TOMB (§143)

Angelico, Fra: Florence Acad. S
    Florence, S. Marco
Bouguereau: B
Burne-Jones: P
Caracci: Castle Howard, Eng.
Carlovingian ivory: B
Duccio: Siena Cath. M
Ender: Molde, Norway. B
Goltz: P
Hofmann: B
Lafarge: (fresco) N. Y., Ch. of St. Thomas
Master Lyversberg Pas: Cologne Mus. U
Peschel: U
Pfannschmidt: B
Plockhorst: BC
Schaeffer: B
Spurgenberg: B
Van Eyck, H.: Richmond, Cook Col.

CHRIST APPEARING TO MARY MAGDALENE (§143)

Angelico, Fra: Florence, S. Marco U
    Florence Acad. M
Baroccio: Florence, Uffizi. U
Burne-Jones: England, Mrs. Williams P. Bl, $3.50
Caracci: Petrograd, Hermitage
*Correggio: Madrid, Prado. Bl, $5.00. S
Credi, di: Paris, Louvre. U
    Florence, Uffizi
Duccio: Siena Cath.
*Giotto: Padua, Arena Ch.
Giovanni di Milano: Florence, S. Croce. U
Henner: N. Y. Metrop. Mus. U
Lippi, Filippino: Venice, Seminario
Mantegna: London, Nat. Gal.
Max. G.: Die Kunst Unserer Zeit, 18 : 209
Schongauer: P
Titian: London, Nat. Gal.
Uhde, von: "Easter morning." Bl, $5.00. S

PETER AND JOHN (§143)

Burnand: Paris, Luxembourg. S

DESCENT INTO LIMBO
Angelico Fra: Florence Acad. U
*Skovgaard: Zeitschrift für bildener
  Kunst, 19 : 149

WALK TO EMMAUS, AND SUPPER
(§145)
Angelico, Fra: Florence, S. Marco
Bartolommeo: Florence, S. Marco. U
Bellini: Venice, S. Salvatore. P
Carpaccio: Venice
Craeyer, de: Berlin Gal.
Dagnan-Bouveret: P
Duccio: Siena Cath.
Eichstadt: Bl, $1.25–$6.00
Furst: B
*Girardet: (walk)
  (supper) Sparrow, N. T., 277
Hofmann: B
*L'Hermitte: Boston, Mus. F. A. B
  ("A Friend of the Lowly ") N. Y.
  Metro. Mus. C
Marziale: Venice Acad.
Melchers: Essen, Krupp Gal. S
Melloni: London, Nat. Gal.
Moretto: Brescia, Martinengo Col. U
Müller, C.: B. Bl, $1.50–$12.00
Palma (Vecchio): Florence. Pitti
Plockhorst: B
Rembrandt: Paris, Louvre. P
Romanino: Brescia, Mart. Col. U
Rubens: Madrid, Prado
Sant and Roberts: Temple Sacred
  Art, 177
Titian: Paris, Louvre. B
Uhde, von:
Veronese: Paris, Louvre. P
  Dresden Gal.

APPEARANCE TO THOMAS (§147)
Bacon: "Peace be unto you"
  Temple Sacred Art, 179
Brüggemann: (sculpt.) Schleswig
  Cath. U
Cima da Conegliano: Venice Acad.
  U
  London, Nat. Gal.
Duccio: Siena Cath.
Dürer: Little passion series
Guercino: Rome, Vatican. B
Lippi, Filippino: P
Morando: Verona Gal.
Rembrandt: Petrograd, Hermitage.
  Bl., $3.50
Rubens: Antwerp Gal.
Salviati: Paris, Louvre.
Van Dyck: Petrograd, Hermitage,
  Bl. $5.00
Verrocchio (sculpt.), Florence, Or San
  Michele. U
Zimmermann: Die Kunst Unserer
  Zeit, 4 : 18

CHARGE TO PETER (§148)
Perugino P

Raphael: London, S. Kensington
  Mus. B

ASCENSION (§150)
Biermann: B. Bl. $1.25–$4.50
Brunkal: Bl, $1.25–$6.00
Correggio: Parma, S. Giov. Evang.
Dürer: Little passion series
Giotto: Padua, Arena Ch.
Hofmann: B
*La Farge: (fresco) N. Y. Ch. of As-
  cension
Mantegna: Florence, Uffizi
Pacchiarotto: Siena. B
Perugino: Lyons Mus.
Rembrandt: Munich Gal. Sparrow,
  N. T., p. 283
*Robbia, Luca della: (relief), Florence
  Cath. U
  Verna
Tintoretto: Venice, S. Rocco
Uhde, von: Die Kunst Unserer Zeit,
  17 : 24
Van der Werff: Sparrow, N. T., 282
Wouverman: Brunswick Gal. Bl.
  $1.50

LAST JUDGMENT
Angelico Fra: Florence Acad. U
  Berlin Gal. Bl, $5.00
Bartolommeo Fra: Florence Hosp.
  S. M. Nuova
  (drawing) Florence, Uffizi. U
Leighton: "And the Sea gave up its
  Dead," London, Tate Gal. Bl,
  $6.00 $24.00
Michelangelo: Rome, Sistine Ch.
  BC
Orcagna: Florence, S. M. Novella. U
Rubens: Munich, Alt Pin. US
Signorelli: Orvieto Cath. U
*Unknown: Pisa, Campo Santo. U
  14th cent. (sculpt.): Orvieto Cath.
  U

FACE OF CHRIST
Angelico Fra: Florence, S. Marco
  (Christ as Pilgrim) U
  Florence, S. Marco (with symbols of
  passion) M
  Orvieto Cath. (Christ enthroned)
Baroccio: (" Il Salvatore ") Florence,
  Pitti
Beraud: Bl, $1.25–$6.00
Bida: B
Burnand: detail of " Prayer after
  Last Supper." Bl, $3.50
*Burton: " The World's Ingratitude."
  Temple Sacred Art, 163
Caracci: Dresden Gal.
Correggio: Parma, S. Giov. Evang. U
Heck, R.: P
Hofmann: " Christ and the Rich
  Ruler." C
  " Come unto me." P

35

Massaccio: Florence, Ch. of Car-
mine, "Tribute Money." U
Michelangelo: (sculpt.) Rome, Ch.
of the Minerva. PC
*Mosaic: Venice: St. Mark's. U
Melozzo da Forli: Rome, Ch. of
SS. Apostoli. U
Orcagna Florence, S. M. Novella
(Christ enthroned). U
Raphael: "Transfig." Rome, Vati-
can. U
"Dispute of the Sacrament,"
Rome, Vatican. U
Rubens: Munich, Alt. Pin. "Four
Penitents." U
Sarto, del: Florence, Ch. of Annuni-
ziata
Thorwaldsen: (sculp.) B
Titian: Florence, Pitti
Unknown: (13 cent. sculpt.): Wech-
selburg Castle. U
(14 cent. Ger.): Nuremberg. U
Van Eyck: Ghent. U
Vinci, da: (drawing) Milan, Brera
Viti: Brescia. U

MISCELLANEOUS

Brunkal: "Come unto Me" Bl,
$1.25–$6.00
*Burne-Jones: Mosaic, "Tree of Life"
Rome, American Ch., Sparrow,
O. T., 3 : 54
Dietrich: "Christ's Call to the Sick
and Weary," Bl, $1.50–$6.00
"Behold I stand at the Door,"
Bl, $1.25–$6.00
Dobson: "Peace be to this Home"
P
Hofmann: "Omnipresence of Christ,"
B
"Behold I stand at the Door,"
B
Hunt, Holman: "Light of the
World" BC
Noack: "Christ on Mt. Olivet," B
*Pauwels: "The Prince of Peace"
Bl, $1.50–$6.00
Schonherr: "Behold I stand at the
Door," B
Uhde, von: "Come Lord Jesus be
our Guest." S

CHAPTER I

THE ANNUNCIATION

PICTURES FOR STUDY

Fra Angelico: Annunciation
Crivelli: Annunciation
Rossetti: " Ecce Ancilla Domini "
Murillo: Immaculate Conception

THE story of the miraculous conception of Jesus is found in only two gospels: Mt. 1: 18–25, in which the announcement is made to Joseph, and Lk. 1: 26–38, in which the angel visits Mary. Nowhere else in the New Testament are the incidents in any way referred to. The pictures that follow are based upon the story in Luke.

The narrative is singularly reticent about details. We are told that the place was Nazareth, but we are not told the year, the season, the time of day, how old Mary was, what she was doing, whether she saw the angel or what Gabriel looked like. These deficiencies have been made good by the pious imaginings of later generations. We learn, for example, in the apocryphal Gospel of James that Mary was drawing water from the spring when Gabriel appeared. St. Bernard says that she was reading from the prophet Isaiah, and an early biographer of Mary says that the angel filled the room with a great light. The Protevangelium of James tells us that she had been chosen by lot one of seven to spin the royal purple for a new curtain of the Temple, and the announcement was made while she was at work.

The good monks of Nazareth, both of the Latin and of the Greek rite, have located the scene for us. The Roman Catholics place it in a cave now under the high altar in their church of the Annunciation. A broken ancient pillar marks the spot where Mary stood, and another the position of Gabriel. The Orthodox Greeks, on the other hand, venerate a spot under the altar of their church of St. Gabriel just where the spring that supplies the village issues from the base of the hill. These conflicting traditions and the conflicting beliefs that Christians of all ages have held need not trouble us. They all witness to the central fact that once in this little town the life of God and the soul of man met, and history became different. The ages have not been able to forget that somehow the Incarnation shows at once God's willingness to save and the historic fact that in Christ he has made salvation possible.

The artists have given us scores of Annunciations of all degrees of excellence and insight. In general, the older ones are more theological, the later ones more human. Contrast for example, Bonfigli or Albertinelli or Fra Filippo Lippi, none of them lacking in human quality, with the Rossetti or the sweet waking-dream of Hacker, and the difference will be at once apparent. The pictures are an index of the changed emphasis in our day from dogma to life.

FRA ANGELICO: THE ANNUNCIATION

Fra Angelico (1387–1455)

Original, a fresco in the upper corridor of the monastery of San Marco, Florence, Italy.

Colored reproductions: London, The Arundel Society, No. 61. Chromo-lithograph.

London, The Medici Society, No. lviii. Chromo-lithograph.

O. M. C. 283, Three-color half-tone.

This picture is so plain, so simple, at first sight so lacking in dramatic quality and arresting power, that the novice is likely to pass it by with the thought " One of those old ones! " Nevertheless the world has judged it to be one of the great Annunciations; and not a few of us, when we approach its radiance in the dim corridor of San Marco, yield ourselves perforce to the injunction the Angelic Brother has painted on the border:

" When thou comest before the figure of the spotless Virgin, see to it that the ' Ave ' be not silent through omission."

We are in Italy. Before us is the porch, or loggia, of some simple and dignified building. The ceiling is vaulted. The plain, round arches rest upon plain capitals of modified Corinthian and Ionic design, supported by plain but delicately proportioned columns. The structure bears striking resemblance to the porch of the Church of the Annunziata in Florence which the painter's friend Michelozzo had just designed. Yet this is not a church. The little doorway opening into a tiny room with its tiny grated window suggests not even a home, but rather a monastery. This suggestion is continued by the " mission " style of chair upon which Mary sits, by the uncovered floor of stone, by the absence of any implements of household work and of any trace of comfort. This is a place for meditation. There are no curious people here; the fence limits our eyes and our thoughts to what is taking place within the enclosure. Can it be Mary's home? It is certainly "home" for the monk-painter — the only home he knows. If he must create a home for Mary it shall be of the very kind that is home to him. There too is the little grass plot that he loved within the cloister walls; there are pinks and daisies to tell us it is Spring. And beyond the fence we see only so much of the world as is beautiful and silent — cypress trees and roses. "A garden enclosed is my sister, my spouse." Mary is here alone with her great experience.

Of the two figures in the picture there is no doubt which is the important one. The artist has hinted it in several ways. First he has placed in Mary's vicinity the striking contrasts, so that the eye will be attracted thither: the dark blue of her robe against the pink of her under-garment; the shadow of the cell against the white of the wall and the light of the window. Then he has placed her face in the very center of the right-hand arch, as it were in a frame, and so closely against the corbel of the two rear vaulting-arches that the eye is led to it by them. And if the eye wanders from Mary's face it is brought back involuntarily by other lines that focus upon her: by the curve of Gabriel's wing that projected leads thither, by the line that skirts his robe on the pavement and jumps across to her robe, by the curves of light and shade in the vaulting that spray from each capital above Gabriel's head and converge upon Mary. The artist's intention is perfectly clear: he is telling Mary's story.

40

Yet the angel is not to be neglected. He is a splendid creature. His robe is pink edged with gold and most chastely embroidered; the plumes of his many-colored wings are delicately tinted with rose, violet, green, yellow. Lustrous and pure, he has freshly come from the Divine Presence; without the slightest delay he has spoken his message, " Hail Mary, full of grace! " and now with eager face and reverent posture he is waiting for her response. The painter has no doubt of Gabriel's reality. Gabriel is not a dream nor an apparition; he is of the substance that heavenly creatures are made of — too substantial, in fact, to ever have been borne hither by such wings as he possesses. The good Fra has made him real because to his thinking angels are always real. Has not Dionysius the Areopagite written about them — given the names of the three orders and the three ranks in each, defined their nature and their duties, and even described their armor! In these days we are inclined to minimize the angelic function. Probably the most religious among us prefer to feel that God speaks direct to our hearts, or even dwells within us, and so needs no messenger. Our angels therefore are to all intents poetical symbols of God's presence, — wings for swiftness and strength, for willing service that outstrips the wind; the human face for intelligence and love. But not so in the middle age. Gabriel was objective and real. Mary saw and heard him; she could speak and get responses. And in our picture he stands as we ourselves would have stood had we been the messenger, eager, interested, conscious of a divine errand, and full of reverence and deference to this mortal who of all women has been chosen to be the mother of our Lord.

Turning now to Mary, what interpretation has the artist to offer us? She is a simple peasant girl; hence her inexpensive and modest costume. Her robe is blue in token of her faith in God. She has no devices for increasing her attractiveness, no jewelry or ribbons, no embroidery and lace; her face is not even pretty. There is not a trace of self-consciousness, no feeling of elation or pride or fear. She is simple woman, whose well-ordered mind is reflected in well-ordered surroundings and in the self-contained posture of her body. And note how skilfully the artist has expressed in her figure his ideal. Dr. H. H. Powers has written: "Let the head drop a trifle lower, and instantly it becomes obsequious; hold it a little higher and something of haughty reserve mars the perfect spirit of the scene. Not by the deviation of a hair could this picture be modified without sacrificing something of its spiritual perfectness." Another critic says: "Wonder and inquiry are in her face, but chastened and free from doubt; meekness, yet mingled with a patient majesty; peace, yet sorrowfully sealed, as if the promise of the angel were already underwritten by the prophecy of Simeon."

What, then, has the artist said to us? "Here is simple and pious Mary, chosen of God to be the mother of our Lord; and here is Gabriel who brings her the divine message. Let us revere her for her purity and her lowly acceptance of the Divine will."

> "Virginis intactae dum veneris ante figuram
> Praetereundo cave ne sileatur Ave."

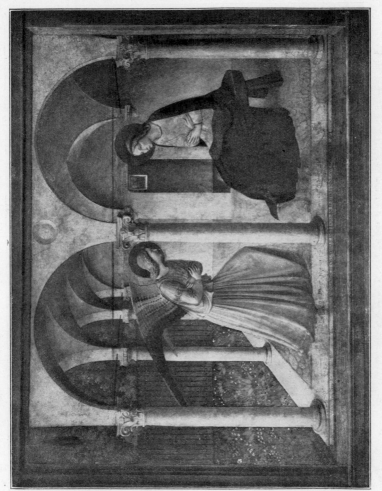

FRA ANGELICO: THE ANNUNCIATION

CRIVELLI: THE ANNUNCIATION

CRIVELLI: THE ANNUNCIATION

Crivelli, Carlo (1440?–1495?)

Original painted for the Church of the Annunziata, Ascoli, Italy,
1486, and given by the citizens as a thank offering for the
liberties conferred on the city by Pope Innocent VIII on the
anniversary of the Annunciation. Removed to the Brera
Gal., Milan, in 1811; sold to private hands in 1815; bought
and presented to the Nat. Gal., London, by Lord Taunton in
1864. Painted on wood, 7 x 5 ft.

Reproduction:

Crivelli takes us into a different world from Fra
Angelico's. Here is no monastic seclusion, no unobtrusive and respectable poverty; rather the full tide of
Renaissance splendor. The Virgin's home is a Venetian palace adorned with sculptured marble, rich in
tapestries, melodious with singing birds and bright
with flowers. The exotic splendor of peacocks and
Oriental rugs vies with the newly-found grace of Greek
art. The scene conjures before our imagination the
great republics of Italy in the fifteenth century, whose
argosies whitened every sea and whose merchant-
princes trafficked in the wealth of Ormus and of Ind.
The painter's own Venice is here — Venice that singlehanded defended Christendom against the Turk, and
took toll of half the world that she might adorn herself as becomes the Bride of the Sea. This is a far cry
from Fra Angelico's simple story, far indeed from the
Nazareth hovel where the scriptural Mary lived.

Nor is this a private experience that is here depicted.
On the steps of the palace at the left a merchant discusses plans with two friars while his little daughter
peeps round the balustrade. A priest pauses at the
corner of the street; a lawyer under the arch medi-

tates his next legal maneuver; overhead on the architectural viaduct another lawyer reads a document to his client. In the distance by the garden wall young people form groups for conversation. The public is very much in evidence — so much so that Mary is overlooked by everybody and half forgotten by us. Even the angel has been waylaid by the enterprising young bishop, and it is a question whether he will get a chance to deliver his message! Could anything be more absurd?

The trouble is with us rather than with the picture. We have failed to get the artist's point of view. The first step in understanding a work of art is to enter sympathetically into the mood of its creator; and in this case such participation is imperative. Crivelli's picture was a thank-offering of the city of Ascoli. Lying on the border of papal and secular dominions, Ascoli was subject to changes in political and economic allegiance that were detrimental to its interests; until at the intercession of their bishop, Prospero Cafferelli, a new charter was obtained from the Pope giving the city autonomy under papal protection. The inscription " Libertas Ecclesiastica " on the frame of the picture is a reminder of this event. Since the charter was received on Annunciation Day it is not strange that the thought of their civic freedom became linked for the people of Ascoli with the Angel's visit to Mary. That is what Annunciation Day meant to them, religion and liberty. In a deeper sense, too, their liberty had sprung out of their religion. Were it not for this blessed annunciation there would have been no Christ, no Christian civilization, no development of free cities wherein wealth might minister to

well-being and art glorify life, no church to hold in
its hand the keys of heaven, no Pope to rule the
faithful in Christ's stead and to confer freedom on
deserving Ascoli! All these blessings have flowed from
the Virgin and her participation in the divine plan.
It is not such a fantastic thought therefore to paint in
one picture the intimate experience of Mary and the
public experience of Ascoli, the mystery of the incarnation and the consequences of redeeming grace, the
Annunciation in its private and personal aspect and
in its cosmic relations. The picture is one grand
symbol: it is what the Annunciation meant to
Ascoli.

Crivelli has filled the canvas with other symbols
also. A ray of light darts from the sky, passes through
a hole in the palace wall which the naïve builder constructed for this purpose, and falls upon Mary. Its
origin is a double " glory " of angels, two rings of
celestial dancers who show forth the joy of heaven
over this event. Along the beam slides the dove,
symbol of the Holy Ghost, — as in King Arthur's
later hall the Grail slid down a beam of light. This
means that God is the prime mover in the event and
that the dove comes from Him. The lilies in the
angel's hand are token of Mary's spotlessness. Emidius, patron saint of Ascoli, holds in his hands a model
of the town. It is his way of saying that the whole
city is here present to participate in the joy of the
event and to offer itself to the Virgin's service. The
fruits of the earth in the foreground, the flowers, the
gorgeous peacock, the parrot, the doves, the rich rug,
the clean street, the beautiful vista and the happy
garden, all speak of joy and prosperity. And the

fact that none of the citizens sees the light or the angel or the bishop is a hint that, after all, this is primarily a spiritual experience of Mary's; these celestial tokens are for her heart alone.

The most attractive part of the picture is the group in the street. It is all animation and good will. The angel is so full of his message that he cannot wait to deliver it to the proper person, but must gossip about it with his friend Emidius; and the saint drinks in the news with a refined eagerness that is tempered with humility, — for in the heavenly hierarchy he is hardly more than a country squire, while the angel is at least a duke. It must have pleased the people of Ascoli to see their familiar saint here. He was their very own. He was the human link that bound them to heaven; the one who carried the city not only in his hands but on his heart, and through whom they dared petition the Virgin and her more august Son; for in those days the common man might not approach the Throne unsponsored! Crivelli has lavished upon these two the principal wealth of color and interest. How aristocratic is the face of Gabriel, his hand how dainty, his costume how supra-mundane! He has robes, to be sure, but growing into feathers at the upper edge. Gorgeous feathers droop like epaulettes from the shoulder, a fantastic head-dress surmounts his wealth of ambrosial hair. His jewelry is of celestial richness; his wings are dyed with the living colors that flashed from the walls of chrysoprase and jasper as he passed through. The saint too is only less splendid: his cope is stiff with thread of gold and his bishop's mitre blazes with precious stones. All this to us is fantastic; but to the simple people of an Italian hill-town it was the very livery of heaven. Anything less gorgeous would have been earthy.

As we turn now to Mary, we feel that the painter has really a spiritual message to express. This gentle and high-minded girl is shown at her devotions: she kneels at her *prie-dieu* and reads from the book of Isaiah — " Behold a virgin shall conceive and bear a son"— at least, St. Bernard in his " Perfect Legend " tells us so. How clean her chamber is! The bed is neatly made, the shelf is duly arranged; she has set her house in order. Indeed she is that perfect woman whom the ancient sage declares to be above rubies in value (Prov. 31: 10–31). But all her thought is now upon the scripture; and as she reads the prophetic words, she feels in her heart that this virgin is she! She crosses her hands upon her bosom — " Behold the handmaid of the Lord; be it unto me according to thy word!" There is no need for Gabriel to speak now, he may return to his celestial choir, for the pious heart of a maiden has outsped his wings in the speed of its desire, and has found God and Heaven in her own soul.

ROSSETTI: " ECCE ANCILLA DOMINI "
(" Behold, the Handmaid of the Lord ")

Rossetti, Dante Gabriel (1828-1882)

Original: 28 x 16 inches, painted in 1849 when Rossetti was but twenty-one years old. Now in the Tate gal., London. The head of the Virgin was painted from the artist's sister Christina.

Colored reproductions: London, The Medici Society, No. xxxii. Chromo-lithograph.

London, The Medici Society, O. M. C. 277, Three-color half-tone.

Why has this simple picture such a hold upon the modern heart? Everybody who sees it loves it, if not at first sight at least ultimately; and those who have come upon its modest pallor among the glories of the Tate will never forget its message to their souls. Its attractiveness cannot lie in richness of color, for it is predominantly white. It cannot be its impressive size that holds us, for one has to hunt to find the little two-foot canvas among its grand companions. It cannot be its novelty of conception, for we have all seen Virgins and lilies and angels before, in not dissimilar attitudes. It is worth while stopping a moment to find an answer.

We have here the work of a boy twenty-one years old. He was a youth who saw visions and dreamed dreams. One of his visions was of Art that spoke to men's hearts not through the inane conventionalities of cows and landscapes and Venuses, but through the sincere presentment of noble experience. One of his dreams was of finding or creating a brotherhood of artists who should make this view of Art their creed. This little picture is his dream and vision realized: it was painted to embody his artistic creed and to fulfil the mutual promise that he and Hunt and Millais had made. And the picture is all Sincerity.

In what way is the picture sincere?

The real Mary was a young girl, — a fact the medieval painters quite forgot. She was not a queen nor the daughter of a merchant-prince; she was a peasant. She did not live in a Venetian palace; she lived in a simple hut with the plainest of furnishings — at least the scripture narrative implies all this. This idea Rossetti paints. The room is poor, but neatly whitewashed; the bed is hardly more than a place to lie, but the linen is white. There is no chair or rug, no scroll

of the prophets or prayer-desk. The only furnishing
is a little hand-loom on which she has been weaving
her ideals — red for love divine, white for the pure in
heart; and the lilies of the pattern, they speak of
spring when the dead heart of earth leaps up to God.
Not a syllable of this need be changed if you trans-
port the painter to the Nazareth of the first century.

There is sincerity also in the portrayal of spiritual
things. Rossetti's angel is not a "show-piece," as
Crivelli's evidently is. He is there merely to remind
us of the heavenly origin of Mary's experience. A
good angel, like a good wine, needs no bush. Fuss
and feathers do not make a seraph. Angels do not fly;
they appear. If one must have warrant that they are
heavenly, let it be through the exceeding whiteness of
plain robes, such that no fuller on earth can whiten
them, and the air bursting into primrose flames under
the feet of the hovering creature — " He maketh . . .
his ministers a flame of fire." If further proof of
supernaturalness is needed, let the face be strong and
sweet and grave, like the face of man — which is the
noblest thing we know. So only can one picture love,
and wisdom that ever wakens, even when they are
divine.

And if you would know what Mary's experience
really was, in part at least, you must study this girl's
face. Do you notice that Mary is not looking at the
angel or at the lily he holds out to her? Do you see
that her eyes are not beholding anything? The painter
means to say that the angel is not there at all. He
must be placed there, it is true, for our sake, and the
dove must be wafted in at the window on the wings
of the white dawn, in order that we dull mortals may

not forget the divineness of this event. But for Mary there is no objective angel: the scripture does not compel us to think so, and Rossetti will not have us think so. The whole transaction is going on behind those eyes of hers — has already gone on, was consummated while she slept; and through the half-unconsciousness of this waking moment Mary is trying to fix the vision lest it fade forever. Gabriel is a transcendent experience in the soul.

What did this experience mean to Mary? It meant a secret that she could not share; it meant misunderstanding and condemnation; it meant participation in a fearful mystery that was charged with significance for all time and for other worlds. If all of this meaning were realized, as in a flash of revelation, by a simple peasant girl, would she look otherwise than this young poet has pictured her? And would the next moment be ecstasy or tears? It was the human side of this experience that appealed to Rossetti; the simple and untutored peasant girl with no dowery but a pure heart and an earnest longing to do God's will, brought face to face with the unescapable and the inscrutable. In his verses to Mary's girlhood he has expressed precisely this moment:

> " So held she through her girlhood, as it were,
> An angel-watered lily, that near God
> Grows and is quiet. Till one dawn at home
> She woke in her white bed, and had no fear
> At all, yet wept till sunshine, and felt awed,
> Because the fullness of the time had come."

It is the utter humanity of this Mary that fascinates us. True to a boyish instinct of what was fit-

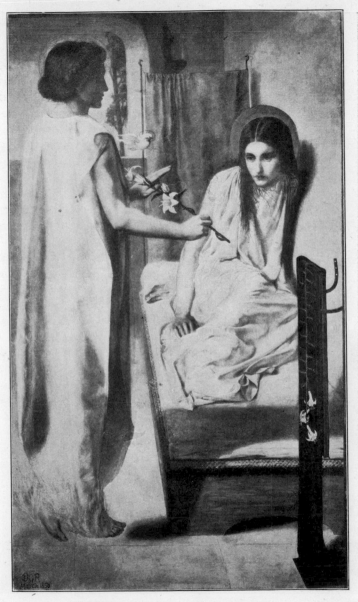

ROSSETTI: "ECCE ANCILLA DOMINI"

MURILLO: THE IMMACULATE CONCEPTION

ting, Rossetti painted in her face the features of his sister Christina. As if he would say to us: "Mary was like this — like my own sister; as pure as she, but not purer; as simple as she; as naturally and as lovingly God's own child as she; longing as earnestly as she for his kingdom of righteousness. And out of his grace God blessed the world through her." Shall we now go a step further? Shall we see in this Mary our own spiritual selves and say, "Be it unto me according to thy word"? Then this picture has accomplished its supreme mission: the unique experience it interprets has become a universal; art has become the handmaid of religion.

MURILLO: IMMACULATE CONCEPTION

Murillo, Bartolomé Estéban (1617–1682)
Original, one of three pictures painted in 1678 for the Hospital de los Venerables in Seville. Taken to France in the Napoleonic wars by Marshal Soult, and when his loot was sold in 1852, bought by the French government for $117,200 and placed in the Louvre, Paris, where it now is. It is reckoned one of the great paintings of the world.
Reproductions: Berlin Photographic Co. No. 119a, various kinds, $1.50 to $18.00.

This picture presents the mystery of the Incarnation. Mary is standing upon the clouds, the crescent moon beneath her feet, the earth nowhere to be seen. Mary is like that person mentioned by Paul who was caught up into the third heaven and saw things it was not lawful for man to utter; only in this case it is not possible for human lips to utter them: they are ineffable.

51

"The Immaculate Conception" is one of those glorious creations that it is granted man to produce only once in a hundred years. The golden light that streams from its heaven brightens half the long corridor of the Louvre where the picture hangs. The blue of Mary's robe is that of our New England skies in May, pure radiance with the emotion of infinite spaces in it. The cherubs that ring the Virgin in a living cloud wit not that their faces shine, but the light of the empyrean still radiates from them. How could a mortal think such heavenly colors!

Yet the glory of this canvas is not its color. It lies in its clear expression of a transcendent mystery and a transcendent emotion.

The first message of the picture is that of the peace of surrender. Mary is not rising or falling; she is not rapt up to heaven in any whirlwind. All the energy of the scene — and it does not lack motion — streams from the palpitating cherubs; she herself is at rest. See how the lights and darks are balanced about the central line of her robe, and note how the eye comes back to her again and again because there is nothing elsewhere to distract it. Mary is in equipoise as if she had found her true center. It cannot be otherwise with her soul: the strain and stress of selfhood have gone and left no trace. She no longer has a personal will; she has surrendered it to His dread keeping. Like Piccarda whom Dante saw in the Heaven of the Moon, she has found in His will her peace.

"E la sua volontate é nostra pace."

The second message is that this experience in its essence is emotional. The composition of the picture clearly indicates this. Begin where you will, the eye is led not only to Mary but to a certain part of Mary's figure. Follow, for example, the line of light that begins with the cherub's foot at the bottom of the picture: it leads you up the leg, the side of his body, his arm, to the upraised arm of the cherub above, to the white edge of Mary's robe, till it disappears beneath her hands. Or starting with the same point and following to the other side of the cherub's body, the eye jumps to the medial line of Mary's robe and thence to the hands. Begin with the faint diagonal cherub in the lower right-hand darkness — you are led past the horn of the crescent to the blue robe and thence to the hands. Begin with the central right-hand cherub, or follow the direction of cherubic legs and arms in any part of the picture, or observe the point on which the eyes of these little creatures are focussed: you are led, not to Mary's face but to her hands. And the hands have sought her breast because the ecstasy of her experience is centered there. Not even does her heavenward look draw our interest — or hers — into the heavens. Her wonderful eyes do not see the glories above; they are no longer organs of vision, but of expression. They are windows through which we may look into a woman's soul at its supreme moment. And this moment is not for her a revelation of divine truth to the intellect; it is a mystical union of the finite and the infinite in her heart. Two supercharged potentials have here found contact and the result is a flash of blinding emotion.

Just what has taken place here? The Word has been made flesh.

* * * *

Is this a unique experience, happening only once in human history? Let the theologians decide that as they will — for doubtless they know the precise limits God has set for himself, the precise boundaries of the human soul. They can tell where dead matter leaves off and life begins; where life ceases to be animal and becomes human; at what point human life becomes divine; and how our bodies can become " temples of the Holy Ghost " without interfering with the chemical, the physical, the sub-human and the human forces that are already tenanted there. But sometimes the poets are wiser than the theologians. Do you remember how King Arthur came, in the Idylls, on the night that Uther died, " moaning and wailing for an heir "? Merlin and his master Bleys

> " Left the still king, and passing forth to breathe,
> . . . .
> Dropt to a cove and watched the great sea fall,
> Wave after wave, each mightier than the last,
> Till last, a ninth one, gathering half the deep
> And full of voices, slowly rose, and plunged
> Roaring, and all the wave was in a flame;
> And down the wave and in the flame was bourne
> A naked babe, and rode to Merlin's feet;
> Who stooped, and caught the babe, and cried 'The King!
> Here is an heir for Uther!' "

When Merlin was questioned later about the birth and nature of King Arthur, he replied in a riddle:

> " From the great deep to the great deep he goes."

You may say that this is just poetry. But if you turn to " De Profundis," written by Tennyson upon the birth of his son, you will find that fancy has given place to conviction:

> " Out of the deep, my child, out of the deep,
> From that great deep before our world begins,
> Whereon the spirit of God moves as He will, —
> Out of the deep, my child, out of the deep,
> From that true world within the world we see,
> Whereof our world is but the bounding shore —
> Out of the deep — thou comest, darling boy!
>
> For in the world which is not ours they said
> 'Let us make man'; and that which should be man
> From that one light no man can look upon
> Drew to this shore."

And when Tennyson draws nigh the verge of life, and he wishes to give the world the Seer's final word on human destiny, one immortal figure alone will suffice:

> " When that which drew from out the boundless deep
> Turns again home."

Conviction has become faith: faith in God as the ultimate source and the ultimate destiny of all human life. Life and death alike are the process of finding

> " Nearer and ever nearer Him, who wrought
> Not matter, nor the finite-infinite,
> But this main miracle, that thou art thou,
> With power on thine own act and on the world.
> . . . .
> Hallowed be thy name — Hallelujah! —
> Infinite Idealty!
> Immeasurable Reality!
> Infinite Personality!
> Hallowed be Thy name — Hallelujah! "

Chapter II

THE NATIVITY

PICTURES FOR STUDY

Merson: Arrival at Bethlehem
Correggio: Holy Night
Van der Goes: Adoration of the Shepherds
Lerolle: Arrival of the Shepherds

LUKE is the only evangelist who gives the story of the birth of Jesus. From his gospel (Lk. 2:1–20) we learn that Joseph and Mary came from their home in Nazareth to Bethlehem to be enrolled in the census, and that while there Jesus was born. On the same night, angels announced to certain shepherds that a Saviour had come, and immediately they went to Bethlehem to worship him. The artists have usually introduced the shepherds into the nativity scene, so that pictures of this event may be called indiscriminately the Nativity or Adoration of the Shepherds.

The scripture says that the birth did not take place in the caravanserai, but it does not say that it took place in a stable. A movable manger could be utilized as a temporary cradle anywhere, and a movable or fixed one is found in every home where animals are owned. Tradition has located the actual spot in a cave adjoining the ancient market-place of Bethlehem. The first to mention this cave was Justin Martyr (d. 165 A.D.). Origen (d. 255 A.D.) confirms the tradition. The empress Helena (c. 325 A.D.) ac-

57

cording to her contemporary Eusebius, transformed the cave into a splendid sanctuary, and her son the emperor Constantine built the imposing basilica that still stands, albeit somewhat restored in the fourth and sixth centuries. Under the high altar is the cave cut in the living rock, set in the marble floor of which is a silver star with the inscription "*Hic de Virginis Maria Jesus Christus natus est.*" A few feet away is the manger — or its modern substitute of marble; for the original (!) wooden one, now plated with silver, has since the twelfth century been preserved in the church of Santa Maria Maggiore in Rome. In most pictures of the Nativity some sort of cave is either painted or symbolized.

The Nativity has naturally attracted the attention of all the major artists. There are at least eighty representations of it extant in the galleries and churches of Europe. From various points of view the story has been repeated over and over, as if it were too precious a heritage ever to be lost sight of, and too universal in its import to be circumscribed by any private interpretation. One might easily fill a book with Nativities alone. The reader is urged to procure if possible some other versions of the story for the purpose of comparison, particularly those starred in the list on p. 24. With all these pictures before you, consider such questions as these: Which of these pictures represents most truly the facts of scripture? the true spirit of the occasion? Just what did this event signify about (a) God's attitude toward man, (b) man's possible relation with God, (c) the interest of man's redemption for all creation, (d) its significance for the whole of history (cf. Brooks' lines, "The hopes and fears of all the years Are met in thee tonight "); (e) the dignity of motherhood. Does any one of the pictures express all of this meaning? Which expresses the most of it?

The reader will not forget to refresh his mind on the hymns that celebrate this event: Luther's " Away in a manger," Brooks' " O little town," Longfellow's " I heard the bells on Christmas day," Lowell's " What means this glory round our feet," Sears' " It came upon the midnight clear," Mohr's " Holy Night," Holland's " There's a song in the air," Wesley's " Come thou long-expected Jesus," Watts' " Joy to the world," and the old English carols like " God rest ye merry gentlemen " and " The first Noel."

MERSON: ARRIVAL AT BETHLEHEM

Merson, Luc Olivier (1846–)

Original, a tiny picture a few inches square, first exhibited in the Paris Salon of 1885. Now privately owned. The *Gazette des Beaux-arts* said of it (Vol. 31 : 492): " It is a charming and delicate little thing. The composition, the color, the feeling, accord so exquisitely with the spirit of the naïve complaint [of the carol]; a little too much insistence on any single trait and the spell is broken, but that word " too much " the artist has not said! "

Reproductions:

This picture was inspired by a naïve Christmas carol in the old style that Merson happened upon. The original and a translation follow:

St. Joseph	St. Joseph
Passons par l'autre rue,	Another street we'll try,
La cour est vis-à-vis.	A courtyard there may be.
Tout devant notre rue	Here before mine eye
J'y vois un grand logis.	Is this grand hostelrie.

59

La Vierge	*The Virgin*
Allez-y seul, de gràce;	Prithee, of your grace,
Je ne puis plus marcher.	No further can I go.
Je me trouve si lasse	Alone seek you a place,
Que je ne puis chercher.	My strength it faileth so.
St. Joseph	*St. Joseph*
Ma bonne et chère dame,	Hostess dear and kind,
Dites, n'auriez-vous point	Pray, of your great pitie,
De quoi loger ma femme	Some little corner find,
Dans quelque petit coin?	To lodge my faint ladie!
L'hotesse	*The Hostess*
Les gens de votre sort	Common folks and poor
Ne logent point céans.	In here we never keep.
Allez à l'autre porte,	Try that other door,
C'est pour les pauvres gens.	'Tis there such people sleep.

The picture and the carol belong to each other, for running through both there is a note of pathos. Here is a human situation that appeals at once to our hearts. This poor girl has travelled all day in order to reach her destination by nightfall. The sun sank as they hurried past the Holy City, the swift Syrian night came down as they reached Rachel's Tomb of sinister omen, and only the moon lighted the rocky stairs that led them up to the khan of Bethlehem. Huddled on its rough hillside lay the little village, checkered silver and ebony against the crisp sky. Not a lamp gleamed from any window; even the dogs were asleep till the footsteps of the strangers aroused them.

" Hurry, Joseph, my hour is come! "

But there is no room at the inn, and the carol tells us why. In vain Joseph's polite request; in vain his expostulations and entreaties. The hard-hearted inn-

keeper's wife thrusts a head and an elbow out of the
window and nonchalantly bids them move on to a less
aristocratic place. Selfishness and the prospect of a
harvest of coin in the morning crowd out the thought
of another's suffering. She does not even offer to sacrifice her own comfort for a night that Mary may have
at least a pallet of straw. " Common folks and poor!"
Was there ever such a pathetic failure of intuition and
sympathy! Surely opportunity knocked at this hostel-
door tonight and will never knock again. Poor Mary
sinks under her burden, and sitting in the street, exhausted, frightened, she wraps her thin garment about
her to keep out the cold. Why does she turn her
head away? Is it a gesture of weariness and pain, or
have the hard face and voice of her sister of the inn
struck her heart with a chill keener than the night
wind? The village dogs scent trouble and come hurrying out of their lairs to add noise and terror to the
scene. Nowhere to go but to the lea of some friendly
wall in a corner of the market-place; and there,
as Joseph keeps the dogs at bay with his staff,
his young wife goes down alone into the Valley of
the Shadow, " While the eternal ages watch and
wait."

Do you not feel that Merson has felt all this? It matters not that his Bethlehem with its unpaved street,
its houses of plaster and thatch, looks more like Brit-
tany than Palestine; the setting is only a background
for a very human story that concerns three people —
helpless and desperate Mary, helpless and exasperated
Joseph and a hard-hearted woman. It is the eternal
conflict of human need and human selfishness that has
been exemplified a thousand times before this night

and a thousand times since, even to this day of grace. It is the sort of situation that Christ's religion is trying to make impossible. "Blessed are the merciful" is one of the persistent and heavenly overtones in the music of the gospel. "Whoso hath this world's goods and beholdeth his brother in need and shutteth up his compassion from him, how doth the love of God abide in him?"

One cannot help feeling also that Merson has here offered us an insight. This is not merely the presentment of a pathetic human situation, it is an episode in history that looks before and after. "The hopes and fears of all the years" are here met, and the light of succeeding centuries shows this hour to be fateful. "He came to his own and his own received him not." They knew not the time of their visitation; darkness covered the earth and gross darkness the people. All the providences of Jehovah from the call of Abraham to the birth of the Forerunner had not availed, so it proved, to prepare the hearts of the chosen people for this new and greatest revelation. And this initial event in the life of our Lord becomes an irony of fate and a prophecy, an allegory of how God's greatest gift to humanity has not been welcome, but how the hard-heartedness of men down through the ages has shut out the heavenly child with his message of good will. More personal still, it is a symbol of our own blind attitude that says, "I am rich and have need of nothing," but knows not that we are wretched and miserable and poor and blind and naked. Merson may not consciously have painted this personal symbolism into his picture; but there is no reason why, if we choose, we may not read it

62

MERSON: THE ARRIVAL AT BETHLEHEM

CORREGGIO: THE HOLY NIGHT

there; nor why we should not use this picture as a comment on Miss Elliott's appealing hymn, " Thou didst leave thy throne," even till we have made our own the prayer of its closing lines:

> " Oh, come to my heart, Lord Jesus,
> There is room in my heart for Thee! "

CORREGGIO: HOLY NIGHT

Luke 2 : 1–20

Correggio, Antonio Allegri da (1494–1534)

Original, 101 x 74 inches, ordered in 1522 by Alberto Pratonero as an altar-piece for his chapel in the church of S. Prospero at Reggio, but not finished till 1530. Duke Francesco of Modena coveted it and *stole* it in 1640, giving the church in its place a copy! His collection of pictures was sold in 1746 to Augustus III, Elector of Saxony, and the Holy Night now divides with the Sistine Madonna the honors of the Zwinger Gallery in Dresden, his capital city.

Reproductions: Taber-Prang, 1, 2, 4.

Braun & Co., R. 1. E. T. Detail I.

Fishel, Adler & Schwartz Co. Artotype, 13 x 18, $.80; colored, $1.50.

In color: Medici Print, Ital., lxiv, chromo lithograph, 15¾ x 11¾, $6. (Mother and child only.)

Seemann Print, three-color half-tone, No. 1008.

Berlin Photographic Co., No. 63a, from $1.25 to $12.00.

Of all the representations of the Nativity, this is the most popular. It is painted in the artist's happy style, and with the full force of dramatic conception and impressive " chiaroscuro." The extraordinary lighting of the picture is a large part of the secret of its power. Notice that the baby is the sole source of the light, and that the intensity diminishes as the light penetrates further and further and loses itself in blackness or in the light of dawn. Correggio may or may not have heard of the tradition that at the time of the birth a bright light shone in the cave (Protevangelium of James); possibly also the thought of Christ as the Light of the World crossed his mind. But more likely he hit upon this device by a happy stroke of genius. At any rate, this particular method of lighting the picture is all his own, this focussing of the white phosphorescence in the child.

It is impossible in a small print to make out the details of the scene, for even in the original they have become obscure through the blackening of age and misuse. It seems certain, however, that the action is set in a decrepit stable built among the ruins of a once stately house or temple. The stone pillar in the center and the masonry on the right are parts of the older building; the rest is wooden beams and thatch, open enough for sun and rain to nourish the growing things that cover the floor. Through the openings on both sides of the pillar one can see a charming landscape — a country house or two, with the sweet light of dawn breaking over hills of blue.

The shepherds have just arrived. The older one, clad in a dull red tunic and carrying a big staff, is a burly, energetic fellow, more like a roistering performer in a medieval miracle-play of this title than a pious shepherd of the artistic tradition. He raises his arm with a gesture of wonder as cyclopean as it is genuine, — or is he taking off his cap in this holy presence? Or perhaps he is telling Mary about his astonishing apparition of angels. If so, Mary is sublimely uninterested! The younger shepherd who holds his big dog in check looks up at the speaker with interest and approval. The good woman by the pillar was on her way to early market, as shown by her basket of goslings, but attracted by the light, she has followed the shepherds into the stable. Her interest, woman-like, is in the baby; the light that radiates from him smites her with an uncanny force from which she instinctively tries to shield herself. In the background the donkey has conceived a notion that there is something besides fodder in his crib; it takes a good bit of Joseph's strength to prevent him from immediately investigating! Beyond the donkey, two men are tying an ox to a post. Correggio may have here conformed to a venerable practice of introducing an ox and an ass as symbols that the Jewish and Gentile worlds are some day to serve the Lord of Glory. But symbolism was foreign to Correggio's nature. It would be nearer the truth to regard the animals as realistic space-fillers.

In the air hovers a group of young angels. When fresh from the painter's hand they aroused the most extravagant enthusiasm by their grace, their joy and their heavenly color. They represent also the accomplishment of a difficult feat of foreshortening in which no doubt the painter took pride. But modern criticism has reduced their worth. It has been pointed out that their heavenly form is combined with an inanity of spirit hard to reconcile with the angelic nature. They are childish creations, innocent because they cannot conceive of sin, but unmoral because they are incapable of any serious purpose. One irreverent critic has even stigmatised the group as a "ragout of frogs' legs!" Perhaps the truth lies between the extremes: the angels are lovely reminders that heaven is in a unique way interested in this event.

Mary and the child hold the center of the picture. The mother, clad in an under-garment of soft blue, a crimson tunic and a dark blue cloak, is kneeling before a crude wooden crib on which is a handful of straw. With her arms she encircles the little one, who is, strange to say, a real baby! Her lovely face is full of joy and tenderness. In fact, it is for the sake of enhancing this little circle of glory that the rest of the picture exists; everything else is vulgar by contrast. The message of the picture, too, is concentrated here, and it differs not at all from the note of all Correggio's art. It is the message of joy: not spiritualized and mystical and theological joy such as bathes the faces of saints in the gardens of Paradise, but pure human joy that springs from perfect inner harmony. Here are a mother and her first child; and the joy of realizing that fundamental relationship is as real and as divine as that of heaven when the morning stars sang together. What need of angels to show us that this is a religious event? No doubt the good Pratonero who ordered the picture and specified that the work should be executed "faithfully and in the best manner," would have objected to an absence of heavenly spectators, and perhaps the artist himself needed them as a further embodiment of the joy he was throbbing to express; but we can dispense with them. The transfigured face of the mother furnishes religion enough for the picture. For when is God ever nearer to a human soul than when he lays a little child in a mother's arms and says, "Inasmuch as thou doest it unto the least of these, thou doest it unto me." No theological conception of the Nativity could stand comparison for an instant, as a working force in the world, with the realization on the part of every mother that God and she are in partnership both in creation and in redemption. Correggio and the middle age would not have interpreted this picture so. But Correggio painted the mother as he saw her; and because he painted truly, he has unwittingly given us the secret of the world's salvation — human love.

VAN DER GOES: ADORATION OF THE SHEPHERDS

Luke 2 : 1–20

Van der Goes, Hugo (c. 1435–1482)

Original: a triptych with figures life size, painted between 1470 and 1475 by order of Tommaso Portinari, agent at Bruges of the Medicis of Florence, the most famous banking and mercantile house of Europe. Portinari gave it as an altarpiece to the chapel of St. Giles connected with the Hospital of S. Maria Nuova at Florence, an institution founded by his ancestor, Falco Portinari, famous as the father of Dante's beloved Beatrice. On the shutters of the triptych are portraits of the donor and his family with their patron saints. The picture stayed in its original position till 1897, when the government bought it for the Uffizi Gallery at a price of 900,000 francs.

Reproductions: In color: Seemann Print, three-color half-tone, No. 1352.

NOTE: It will be advisable to procure a larger photograph for the sake of the detail.

The masterpiece of Van der Goes is included in this study because it furnishes a most instructive contrast to the Lerolle that follows. The two illustrate two different attitudes of mind not only toward the scriptural story but toward religion and life in general, and these two attitudes may be characterized as the medieval and the modern.

The older picture reflects in the first place the religious outlook of the times. It is not a Salon picture but an altar-piece; its subject is not a landscape or a battle but a scene from the Bible. Belief is as yet untouched by doubt: real angels with wings announce the nativity to the shepherds; real angels with heavy robes kneel beside the inhabitants of earth, as substantial creatures as they; the little child has the mature and wise look of a god, and emits light as a token of his divinity, while the hands of all the spectators are folded in prayer and the faces of all are turned toward the incarnate deity. There is no myth or symbol or allegory for Van der Goes in this story; it is all gospel fact, and fact that reveals a segment of a vast and closely reasoned scheme of salvation that was fashioned in heaven and let down to earth. The theology of Anselm and Aquinas is still true. Not yet has the Renaissance made skeptics within the fold.

But the Renaissance is here, the spirit of realism, of delight in nature, of love of the beautiful. Reflections of the growing wealth of the North are here, hints that Bruges and Ghent and Antwerp have monumental buildings of stone, looms for the manufacture of rich stuffs, and mercantile houses that traffic in the jewels of the East; are, in fact, as important stages on the great trade route from York to Delhi as Florence and Venice are. And all of these reflections are so naïvely given! How can

VAN DER GOES: ADORATION OF THE SHEPHERDS

there be a Gothic church and a Romanesque stable in Bethlehem in 4 B.C.? How can angels and shepherds be Flemish, and Joseph good plain Dutch! How can angels perch on rafters or grow wings through a robe of the cloth of gold? How can shepherds hear the angelic song in broad daylight on the hills, and at the same time be worshipping the babe in the stable? These things strike us as incongruous, but the fifteenth century was uncritical: it saw no reason why things should not be painted in this way.

There is something very attractive in this realism. The faces of the chief personages are evidently portraits. Joseph is a substantial slow-witted burgher, who has thought to take off at least one of his wooden shoes before putting his hands together and saying a prayer about something he does not understand! Mary, clad in a robe of deep blue, is fairly intelligent though by no means beautiful; her sad face shows that a mother's intuition has divined a fate of sorrow for her boy. The three chief shepherds are hinds of the field. Look at their hands, their rugged faces, their strange trowel-like crooks, their leathern wallets trimmed with iron. But more particularly, note how their spirit shines through their faces: the third one is unintelligent and timid, but truly interested; the left-hand one is truly devout; the near one is fatherly, and intelligently happy. This is realism of the right sort; the shepherds are the best part of the picture.

The foreground monopolizes most of the delicate beauty of the picture. Notice the wonderful robes — rich brocades and tapestries. The nearest right-hand robe is inscribed with a triple " Sanctus," while the medallions in the border of the robe above Joseph's head are adorned with portraits of Christ. The angelic wings are some of them made of peacock's feathers and some of parrot's. The crowns blaze with great jewels. Between the groups lie the angelic gifts, gorgeous irises, a spray of something like columbine, scattered violets, and a sheaf of grain that symbolizes the Bread of Life. All of these details are lovely, and show that Van der Goes had a feeling for beauty that rivals the greatest of his contemporaries.

This picture, therefore, must have had a great religious value for its generation. It is sincere, it expresses the current view of what actually happened, it presents the heavenly guests in the only guise that would have been intelligible and impressive to the fifteenth century, the delicate beauty of many of its details is most appealing, and its symbolism and the attitudes of its personages are suggestive of worship. But as we now look at things, the eternal verities are most of them conspicuous by their absence.

LEROLLE: ARRIVAL OF THE SHEPHERDS

Luke 2 : 15–20

Lerolle, Henri (1848–   )
Original : painted in 1885. Privately owned (?).
Reproductions: Taber-Prang, 1, 2, 4, 13; Braun & Co., F. I.

When we turn from Van der Goes to Lerolle, we step either forward four hundred years or backward fourteen hundred. The atmosphere of this picture is Palestine, or some primitive land; the underlying conception is as modern as ourselves. We could not ask for more forceful illustrations of the principle that an artist sees his theme through the lens of his world-outlook, than these two paintings afford.

We are standing in a huge and dimly-lighted cave. Great trunks of trees as rafters rest on equally rugged columns and sustain the doubtful roof. Their irregular alignment and untouched naturalness help to produce a feeling that the people of the picture are a simple and untutored folk. Great boulders and the débris of the hill above have all but blocked the mouth of the cave; the shepherds have entered through an opening somewhere behind us. On the left are the supply of fodder and the pitchforks, on the right the feeding-tubs, the animals and some sheaves of grain. This is realism: not the realism that reproduces the environment of the painter, but that earnestly endeavors to paint the scene as it must have been. It is the product of our critical nineteenth century that will not tolerate infidelity to the facts. This critical realism has eliminated the angels — wings, robes, crowns and all; has reduced the shepherds to pretty nearly the elements of humanity, has humanized and socialized Joseph, stripped the baby of his rays of gold and transferred the glory from the child to the mother. Absolutely the only suggestion of the supernatural is this light. We cannot construe it as an attempt to elevate the Virgin above her son, or to glorify the dogma of the " Mother of God "; it may be merely a painter's device to bring into sharp outline the face of Mary. But it may also be taken as a recognition of the profound significance to the world of spiritual motherhood.

The child should have no halo. The light that radiates from the Christ of history was not born with him; it was created by him as his spirit grew from human infancy to divine manhood. Golden mandorlas and aureoles that are out of place in the manger are inevitable at the Transfiguration and the Resurrection. Mary's crown of light, on the other hand, is due now, as a pledge of the glory that is eternally hers as perfect mother. Lerolle has thought this truth out correctly.

The shepherds constitute another piece of critical realism. If you and I had heard the angels' song and had hurried to the spot where the long-expected one lay, would we have crowded curiously to his manger and otherwise made ourselves familiar? I believe that like these shepherds of Lerolle's we would approach with fear and trembling, and with unshod feet gaze at the holy thing from behind the screen of the friendly pillars; we would lift our hand in awe, like the least afraid of them, or raise ourselves on tiptoe in timid wonder like that splendid youth in the rear, or drop upon our knee in the dim sense that we were not worthy to be witnesses of so august and divine an event. These shepherds are just us, in the presence of one of God's mysterious and glorious providences.

For us, then, there is more truth in the strongly human simplicity of Lerolle than in the theologically conceived glories of Van der Goes.

Chapter III

INCIDENTS OF THE CHILDHOOD

PICTURES FOR STUDY

Gentile da Fabriano: Adoration of the Kings
Burne-Jones: Star of Bethlehem
Holman Hunt: Triumph of the Innocents
Merson: Repose in Egypt
Edwin Long: "Anno Domini"

The stories of the Wise Men, the Massacre and the Flight are recorded only in Matthew 2 : 1–23. On the basis of the simple and rather indefinite information there given, pious tradition has built an extraordinary fabric, and Art has adorned it with at least a hundred and fifty paintings. Indeed the Magi seem to have attracted more interest than any other persons in the Bible except Jesus and his mother. A hundred and twelve pictures are devoted to them alone.

The Magi were a class of priestly astrologers and magicians of Persia. In the course of his travels in the East, Marco Polo (14th cent.) came across traditions of them in cities that he visited, Saba and Avah, both about fifty miles southwest of Teheran, and Kashan — " Castle of the Fire-worshippers " — about three days' journey from Avah. (See Jackson: The Magi in Marco Polo, Jour. Amer, Orient. Soc., 26 : 79–83.) Earlier centuries had evolved their nature and nationality from various passages in the Old Testament. The suggestion that they were Arabian came from Ps. 68 : 29 and Is. 60 : 6; that one was

73

Ethiopian is inferred from Ps. 68 : 31. The passages that prove them to be kings are Ps. 68 : 29, 31; 72 : 10; Is. 49 : 7; 60 : 3, 10. The star came from Num. 24 : 17. Other suggestive verses are Ps. 72 : 10–11. According to the Eastern tradition they were twelve in number, but the West has fixed upon three, doubtless because only three gifts are mentioned. In that wonderful relic-discovering fourth century, the bodies of the Three Kings were found in the East and brought by the Empress Helena to Constantinople, whence the Crusaders took them as unlawful spoil to Milan. Frederic Barbarossa presented them to the Archbishop of Cologne, who removed them to that city in 1164. There they now rest in a wonderful golden reliquary in the treasury of the cathedral, and their memory is also preserved in the three crowns on the city's arms. In 1179 their names and ages were definitely assigned as Caspar of Tarsus, aged sixty, Melchior of Arabia and Nubia, aged forty, Balthazar of Saba, aged twenty. All of this romantic tradition lends itself most happily to the fancy of an artist.

Numerous legends of the Flight and Sojourn in Egypt are recorded in the Arabic Gospel of the Infancy and in the Pseudo-gospel of Matthew; but they have only a curious interest and need not be repeated here.

The pious archæologists of the Holy Land have kept pace with the growth of the facts. They show a "Well of the Magi" on the road from Jerusalem to Bethlehem, where the wise men saw the star a second time. In the grotto at Bethlehem is an altar to mark the spot where they worshiped, and where in the

74

fourth century the Epiphany was first celebrated. Leading from the grotto still lower into the rock is a narrow passage and then a chamber where Joseph is said to have had his dream of warning. Descending five steps further we come to the Chapel of the Innocents whither according to a fifth century tradition the mothers fled with their children to escape Herod's fury. In Egypt, too, the scenes of the Flight and Repose have been located. At Heliopolis, seven miles from Cairo, is an old sycamore (planted 1672!), in the hollow trunk of which Mary hid to escape her pursuers, screened from sight by the timely spinnings of a spider. In Old Cairo is the ninth century church of Abu Sergeh in the crypt of which the Holy Family is said to have rested a month; and on the edge of the western desert the Sphinx still refuses to tell whether Mary and the child ever reposed between its paws! It is more than likely that these stories are all pious endeavors to embody in parables the words of scripture, " Gentiles shall come to thy light," and " He shall give his angels charge over thee."

Every one will recall the vivid picture of the Wise Men in Wallace's " Ben Hur," Chap. I. Hopkins' " We Three Kings " is a delightful carol that conforms wholly to tradition. Other suggestive hymns are, Heber: " Brightest and best"; Dix: "As with gladness."

GENTILE DA FABRIANO: ADORATION OF THE KINGS

Matt. 2 : 1–12

Fabriano, Gentile di Niccolo di Giovanni Massi, of (c. 1360 or 1370 — 1428 or 1432)

Original: The painter's masterpiece, a most gorgeous triptych in excellent preservation, painted in 1423 for the sacristy of the church of the Trinità in Florence, whence it was recently brought to the Academy. It is one of the best examples of elaborate altar-pieces of the early fifteenth century, and is still preserved in its fine old original frame.

Reproductions: In color: Seemann print, three-color half-tone, No. 1305. Medici O. M. C., No. 117.

This picture presents four moments of time. In the left lunette the Magi see the star from the top of a mountain. Behind are the sea and ships, below in the valley men busily prepare for the long journey. In the central lunette the procession, with the three kings conspicuous in gold, arrives at Jerusalem to pay its respects to king Herod. The right lunette shows the kings entering the city gate of Bethlehem. The main picture presents a gorgeous procession, the kings and their retinue crowding down to worship at the humble home.

What a brave pageant it is! Not including the Holy Family there are twenty-two men, nine horses, a camel, a grayhound, a lioness, a leopard, two apes, three falcons, a dove, an ox and an ass. This is no religious procession; it is a jolly hunting-party that has stumbled by chance upon this holy group and takes the opportunity to pay its compliments. Look at those beautiful horses with their rich trappings, at the distinguished faces and courtly clothes of the attendants, at the slave kneeling to remove the spurs from the heel of the third king, at the touches of Oriental display in the outlandish animals, at the jessed falcon perched on wrist and the other one in the air that has stooped and trussed its quarry. Look at those gorgeous kings that outshine the princes of fairy-land. This is an illuminated page out of the heart of a medieval romance; or more truly it is a picture of Italy under the spell of Venetian enterprise and splendor, — powerful, luxurious, its heart set on the things of this world even while its eyes are turned toward heaven. Gentile has caught the spirit of it perfectly and has set it forth in a way that has never been surpassed. No other picture of the period can rival this one as a piece of exquisite decoration, or in the care with which the designs and the colors are executed or the low relief in plaster engraved and gilded. The whole thing is a jewel.

Gentile has had in mind the traditions and the appropriate symbolism. The cave and the manger are here; so are the ox and the ass, typical of the Jewish and Gentile worlds. The house to the left is the home of Jesse, father of David, now falling to ruins because the old dispensation it typifies is passing away. The two women who are admiring Caspar's gift are one of them a midwife whom Joseph procured but who arrived too late to be of any assistance, and the other a Mary Salome who came to visit the Virgin at this time. Joseph fulfils the part and age assigned him by tradition. The Pseudo-gospel of Matthew makes him exclaim when selected by the High Priest to be the husband of the fourteen-year-old Mary, "Why do you hand me over to this infant who is younger than my grandsons!" The old carpenter is somewhat awe-struck by all this magnificence. Mary is a very sweet lady who feels herself not altogether unworthy of the honors that are coming to her. She looks with interest and love upon her son, though he needs none of her solicitude or assistance. The baby is quite capable of handling this situation. He looks with benignity upon his worshiper, presents a toe for the ceremonial kiss like his successors the Popes, and lays an apostolic hand upon the bald head. This is not naïveté; this is theology. Remember that the middle age affirmed this baby to be incarnate Deity, who even now has the universe on his mind and sees the end from the beginning.

If there is any religion in this picture it is in the person of the kneeling king. Caspar has humbled himself before the Lord of Glory. His crown is on the ground, his robes of velvet and silk and jewels trail in the dust, and on the face of this wise old monarch is a look of self-abnegation more eloquent than words. So should kings bow before him who has proved himself to be the King of Kings. So have they humbled themselves, from Constantine to Baldwin and St. Louis and the good Victoria; so have the multitudes that no man can number, out of every nation and tribe and people and tongue cast their trophies at his feet and crowned him Lord of All. This pageant of Gentile's is a symbol of the march of the generations past the manger of Bethlehem.

One other little touch is worth noting. Do you see that smooth-faced young man with the turban, standing behind the third king? That is Gentile. It may have been vanity that moved him to paint himself there, but if he were really vain he would have made himself one of the kings. Rather should we think that Gentile wanted by this means to enroll himself among the worshipers of the Child and lay his great art down at his feet; as if he would say to the little babe, " Lord, remember me when thou comest into thy kingdom! "

One is tempted here to contrast Gentile and his greater contemporary Fra Angelico. Both were men of wonderfully sensitive temperament, both were noted for their tenderness and finish. But in spirit their works are as far asunder as the two poles. Gentile is a mirror held up to the glories of this world; Fra Angelico lives and has his being in a transcendental world

> " Where loyal hearts and true
> Stand ever in the light,
> All rapture through and through
> In God's most holy sight."

We would not willingly dispense with either artist. But if we are searching for an interpretation of our own religious life, we can more easily translate Fra Angelico to our needs than Gentile.

BURNE–JONES: STAR OF BETHLEHEM

Matt. 2 : 1–12

Burne-Jones, Sir Edward (1833–1898)

Original: a life-size water-color painted in 1891 and now in the Birmingham (Eng.) gallery. It reproduces with slight modifications a tapestry designed for the chapel of Exeter College, Oxford. The tapestry, woven by Wm. Morris, is a wonder of rich color — dark greens and dull reds. It glows in the soul long after one has seen it, like the memory of some medieval romance. The heart of Pre-Raphaelitism is revealed here: sincerity, feeling, poetic insight, religion.

Reproductions: Photograph by Hollyer, London.

" Do you really think that the story of the Magi is true? " asked a young girl as she watched Burne-Jones paint this glowing canvas.

" It is too beautiful not to be true," was the artist's answer. Perhaps we shall see what Burne-Jones meant.

In the background of the canvas is a forest. It is not the leafy, bird-haunted woodland of summer; the boughs stand naked and comfortless and the pathways beneath are choked with snow. Why did he not create a pleasant setting for his kings? In his beautiful window of the Nativity in St. Philip's church, Birmingham, he again chose a wintry forest. There's a reason; he is challenging our recollection of the great masters of allegory. Do you recall how Spenser's knight in the Faerie Queene once took shelter in a wood and lost his way completely? " This is the wandering wood, and Errour's den," says Spenser. And do you remember how Dante begins his Divine Comedy?

BURNE-JONES: THE STAR OF BETHLEHEM

" Midway upon the journey of our life
I found myself within a forest dark,
For the straightforward pathway had been lost.
Ah me! How hard a thing it is to say
What was this forest savage, rough and stern
Which in the very thought renews the fear.
So bitter is it, death is little more."

To rescue him from his peril God stirred to action two spiritual realms and worked the miracle of Dante's regeneration. The wood stands for Sin, for the demoralization of Dante's own life.

Here, then, is the artist's first message. He has staged the story of the Adoration against the background of lost humanity, that barren waste of error and sin from which, unaided, man can never hope to escape; the antithesis of that garden of trees which God once planted for man but which man lost by his own act

" till one greater Man
Restore us, and regain the blissful seat."

From this forest the kings have been guided by a star. You can see the flame burning between the hands of the angel who hangs in the air motionless before them. Ever since man first pointed a telescope into the sky he has tried to find the Star of Bethlehem. In this picture Burne-Jones shows us why man will never find it: an angel brought it. And what an angel! His wings are huge, many-colored pinions such as may easily bear from the heavenly spaces this "bird of God." His robes are rich beyond dreams; in color and in symbol they bear the blazonry of the courts of heaven. Unseen by either the kings or

81

the Holy Family this iridescent vision waits silently
to shed its light of meaning upon the fateful present.
He is a majestic symbol of God's eternal watchfulness and care; a symbol in human form because no
other could express those attributes of feeling, thought
and will that are not only human but divine. God's
messenger can be none other than the spirit of God.
This star is no mere phenomenon, whether natural or
supernatural, no comet or planetary conjunction;
it is Love, it is Wisdom, it is Act, united in one being
and directed to one end — the salvation of man.

So this is the artist's second symbol: man is rescued
from the forest of his sin only by the guidance of
Divine Grace.

Who are these man thus happily lead to the goal
of their desire? Tradition long ago created them.
Caspar, monarch of Tarsus, is the first; his gift is
gold, symbol of kingship. Melchior king of Arabia
follows with frankincense, symbol of deity. Balthazar
of Saba brings myrrh, symbol of death and burial.
" Kings shall bring presents unto thee, the kings of
Tarshish and the isles shall render tribute; the kings
of Sheba and Seba shall offer gifts. . . . Princes shall
come out of Egypt; Ethiopia shall stretch out her
hands unto God." Burne-Jones' kings are the kings
of tradition, but they are something more; under his
hand they have grown to a fulness of meaning they
never before possessed.

Take old Caspar first. In spite of his crown he is
no king. His robes are quite plain, and were it not
for the sheen upon the folds you would never guess
how rich they are. His delicate hands and features,
the monk-like pose, emphasized by the huge folds of

his garment upon the shoulder, indicate that he is a scholar rather than a monarch. His domain is the realm of thought; his beard is a symbol of the wisdom of experience; his casket studded with jewels is a reminder that "Wisdom is better than rubies, and all the things that may be desired are not to be compared unto it." But Caspar in "following the Gleam" has found one greater than Solomon; and he lays down the crown of his life-achievement at the feet of this little child, while the angel softly whispers to him, "In Him are hid all the treasures of wisdom and knowledge."

Melchior is a warrior. His helmet is of tempered steel. His coat of mail gleams with bosses of polished bronze. His mighty sword, like Excalibur, is forged to carve the casques of men. He too has a crown, not a dainty and fantastic circlet like Caspar's in which is symbolized the brilliancy of intellectual conquest, but such a sign of sovereignty as may survive the shock of battle. Melchior comes in the strength of manhood, type of the great constructive and conquering forces that mold the world to its destiny; type of the kingdoms of this world that shall some day become the kingdoms of our Lord and of his Christ. He waits his turn to surrender his crown and all it signifies, while Uriel chants to his listening heart, "He is the head of all principality and power — to whom be glory and majesty, dominion and power, before all time, and now, and forever more."

Balthazar comes last, child of the opulent East that

> " with richest hand
> Showers on her kings barbaric pearl and gold."

83

His face bears the stamp of luxury. His garments are by far the richest, heavy with jewels and lustrous with the fancies of Oriental looms. Even his sandals blaze and the crown he carries might ransom the kingdom of Golconda. There is no doubt what the artist means here: " The wealth of the nations shall come unto thee; they shall bring gold and frankincense." And as we look across to the little child we seem to hear the seraph speak the words of Paul: " For ye know the grace of our Lord Jesus Christ, that though he was rich yet for your sakes he became poor, that ye through his poverty might become rich."

In this great allegory, then, these three kings stand for man, — man at the summit of his glory and wisdom, in the flood-tide of achievement, in the fulness of power; yet led by divine wisdom and love to lay his treasure, "an offering far too small," at the feet of our Lord. It is a prophecy of what is to be. The kings are the foretypes of that multitude no man can number who shall one day cast down their crowns before the throne and cry: "Worthy the Lamb to receive power and riches and wisdom and might and honor and glory and blessing! "

In contrast to the glory of the kings, Burne-Jones has placed the poverty and simplicity of the Holy Family. Joseph has built a little hut of wattle and thatch for the mother and her child. He has gathered a handful of sticks for the fire, and now returns to find the fire no longer needed and his home invaded by strange guests. Joseph is not used to greatness. He has dropped his axe and stands abashed, perplexed, — good, faithful, unillumined Joseph. Mary too is simple and unschooled. She receives her guests with quiet dignity, though the visit is beyond her interpreting. She will let them leave their gifts and return she knows not whither. The fear that flutters at her heart will die away, and in its place will come the long dumb wonder that will be her treasure through thirty years of waiting. Sweet girl-mother! Little do you know what the years have in store!

And after all the centuries of Christ-childs, Christ-mannikins and theological incarnations, here at last is a baby! Dear timid little creature, he clings to his mother's robe and shrinks from the gaze of these strange men. He offers no playful patronage, as the baby of Gentile's picture does; his two fingers are not raised in papal blessing nor is his toe presented for the kiss of obeisance. The wisdom of the God-head does not radiate from mature features. He is just plain baby. He has not even a halo to differen-tiate him from any peasant's child. And I can almost read a look of disappointment, or at least a question, in the faces of the three great ones, as if they were saying in their hearts, " Is this all?"

Yes, this is all. He is but a pilgrim and a stranger here in this rude hut, the resting-place of a night. He has no court about him but the faithful two. His kingdom, if he has one, is not of this world. His throne is his mother's lap. He is just a little child.

But do you notice that the snow has retreated from this little area where love reigns? That in the wilder-ness have sprung up pools of water? that the waste places are glad like Eden? that the Rose of Sharon flowers in the hedge, and the Lily of the Valley bursts from the ground at Mary's feet? Can it be that love has done this? And can it be that when we also lay our gifts at the feet of a little child in memory of his childhood, God is leading us by his star of duty or of love into the service of his Son? " Whoso shall receive one such little child in my name receiveth me."

HUNT: TRIUMPH OF THE INNOCENTS

Matt. 2 : 13–23

Hunt, William Holman (1827–1910)

Original: Two versions are extant: (1) an original begun in Jerusalem in 1870, continued on poor canvas during his stay of 1873–6, and finished in 1886 after many attempts at repairs; this one, from which our illustration is taken, is now in the Walker Art Gallery, Liverpool — (2) a replica made during 1883–6 for the donor of the first picture. The first one represents two and a half years of solid labor in Palestine, besides the long periods of " incubation " and discouragement.

Reproductions:

Like most of Hunt's work, this picture strikes the average person rather unfavorably at first. Striking it is, even in reproduction, but vastly more so when one stands before the life-sized original in Liverpool and sees how the deep blue of the Syrian night throws a spell over the whole room. Few would call the picture beautiful, some would call it weird; but no one who makes a serious attempt to understand it can deny that it is profoundly interesting and stimulating. It is realism of the most uncompromising kind mingled with a mysticism that is subtle and profound. Ruskin called it the greatest religious picture of our epoch.

Hunt's artistic creed forced him to paint with absolute fidelity to the truth. This is why he went to

Palestine repeatedly, and went with specific themes in mind. In his preparation for this picture he roamed over the Philistine plain till he hit upon a little village, called Shama, that yielded him precisely this background of mountains, this clump of trees and huts and water-wheel, this slight water-course. The flowers of the picture are the very ones that star the Syrian fields in spring; even the dogs that skulk away from the unnatural light are of the ownerless village sort that one meets everywhere in the Holy Land. Hunt found in Jerusalem his donkey, of pure Mecca breed and a descendant of one that Mohammed rode! Mary's under-garment is the wedding dress of Bethlehem, well known to travellers. The little children are Jerusalem babies, selected with infinite trouble and not without opposition from mothers who had strange notions about the influence of paint on death and the judgment. Joseph's bronzed and rugged frame has stepped out of the field or the workshop into this picture, tools, basket, shoes and all. Those who have travelled in Palestine will find here all the atmosphere of the East.

Hunt has followed the tradition of the Eastern church that the flight took place in the month of April when Jesus was sixteen months old. The Holy Family are on the road to Gaza and Egypt, about thirty miles from Bethlehem. They have left the highway and are walking through the fields. Joseph leads the donkey and anxiously looks back at the mountains wreathed in the remnants of a storm that has sprinkled them with snow, and at the watch-fires of Herod's soldiers who are on his trail. Mary, in whose face the traces of anxiety are slowly dissolving before the dawn of hope, is dressing the child with garments she had hastily stored in the saddlebags on setting out.

About the fleeing family dances and floats this triumphal procession of the first martyrs. Mary does not see the children but her son is trying to call her attention to them. Jesus smiles joyously as he recognizes one and another of his little playmates of Bethlehem; he holds out to them a handful of wheat-ears to remind them that he is the Bread of Life. They are in three groups, each distinguished by the particular spiritual state in which its members find themselves at this moment. Leading the procession are the three proto-martyrs, who have reached the full consciousness of their bliss: the first one carries a thurible from which incense is ascending, and his upward prayerful glance shows him to be the priest of the band who offers to heaven the sweet savor of their sacrifice. His two companions in equally joyous mood bear one the palm of victory and one a branch of flowers to strew the way. The second group who have surrounded the laggard foal of the ass and are bringing it to its mother, are decked in chains of flowers like sacrificial victims and carry flowers in their hands. Not yet have they entered fully upon the bliss of their heavenly life; their joy is subconscious. One little fellow is curious about the sword-cut in his garment, under which he can find no traces of the wound that drove him here. The third group come hurrying on behind, fresh from the terror of their taking-off. Pain and sleep are still struggling in their faces. Soon will dawn the heavenly light, sorrow and sighing shall flee away, and God shall wipe away all tears from their eyes. The crown of stars that even now is forming above them will soon break into coronets of joy for each, and the little band that once played about the streets of Bethlehem will be united again in the land of the " remembered dream and the forgotten sorrow."

Hunt has used extraordinary means to show that these children are in a spiritual and not corporeal state. There is first the vague luminosity that rings their bodies round. But, more wonderful, they are borne along on a phosphorescent stream of mystic water, " the river of the water of life that proceedeth out of the throne of God." It is not like the earthly stream, beautiful as that is with its reflection of the stars of hope set twinkling by the plash of Joseph's foot; it is rather like the ghostly billows of pale flame that follow a ship at night in southern seas. And from its surface rise dream-globes that mirror the past and the future in a unity of iridescence that shows life to be glorious and all one when seen under the aspect of eternity. There behind Joseph are Jacob's ladder and the Tree of Life and the Adoration of the Lamb in heaven, fleeting manifestations of the Unchanging One who " sits by the shining fount of life " and pours the eternal flood. Swept into its mighty current are now these little ones, never again to be tossed on the rude sea of time, but rather to move forever in eddies of praise through the meadows of the blessed. This is poetry and mysticism and insight.

The picture is called a " Triumph." It is a triumph of the classic sort, the procession of joy that conducts a conqueror to his throne. A strange " Via Tri-

umphalis " this, that begins with the Massacre of
Innocents and leads to Calvary. But from that
march not only will the Victor return triumphant;
he will lead with him a train of countless children,
as the ages run, saved from pain and disease and
breaking toil by the growing power of his gospel in
men's hearts, given a chance to breathe the sweet
air and live in the sunshine and find God in work and
worship and love, as those who were born before his
coming never could. Not yet is the Age of the
Children fully ushered in, but the night is far spent
and the day is at hand.

MERSON: REPOSE IN EGYPT
Matt. 2 : 14–15

Merson, Luc Olivier (1846–   )
Original: about 4 x 6 feet, painted in 1879 and twice thereafter.
    One at least of the three is owned in the United States, by
    Dr. George Kennedy, of Hyde Park, Mass.
Reproductions: Fishel, Adler & Schwartz Co., New York; Arto-
    type 10 x 18, $.80; colored, $1.50.

This is a very unusual composition. The center of
gravity of the picture seems at first to be on the
extreme left; but if you will observe yourself while
you observe the picture you will find that the moments
of force equalize themselves when your eye rests
somewhere between the sphinx and the fire. On the
one side is the mass of the monument, on the other
the sharply defined though smaller masses of the
streak of river, the donkey and the smoke-stream.
At a point between these your interest hovers, and
while there it becomes infused with the influences of
two powerfully suggestive infinities, the desert and the

HUNT: TRIUMPH OF THE INNOCENTS

MERSON: REPOSE IN EGYPT

sky. The lines of composition, it is true, center in Mary and the child: toward them converge the edges of the sphinx's head-dress, the edges of the sand-drifts, the left paw of the sphinx, Joseph's staff and recumbent form which in turn continue the lines of the saddle and tethering-rope. But the message of the picture is greatly enhanced by the undefinable suggestiveness of the two infinities. It is they that give the emotional undertone to the rest, that add majesty and awe and silence, and conjure forth the powerful fancies that are imprisoned in the magic name of Egypt. The coloring of the original also contributes to the feeling-tone: the night is violet-gray, and the stars are so weirdly created that those of the second and third magnitudes come out only as you gaze long at the sky. And while it is the moon that lights the scene, an orange glow, radiating from the sleeping child, diffuses about the sphinx's heart a warmth as of love in a desolate world.

You are in Egypt at night, and alone except for the sleepers. The wind that by day has piled the sand in drifts now has ceased its play. The smoke from the little fire rises straight as a sword-blade against the background of the darkness. Not a leaf of the scant herbage trembles, not a sound pulses across the waiting air. The desert stretches away illimitably, dead and still. Unruffled the moonlight sleeps upon the narrow mirror of the Nile. The patient donkey, relieved of his saddle, stands by his peg and dreams, too somnolent to bite the spear of grass beneath his nose. Joseph has forgotten his long and anxious tramp across interminable deserts—his bed the sand, his pillow a stone. The baby sleeps in the heaven of his mother's bosom; Mary sleeps in the arms of the sleepless and immemorial sphinx. The whole world is waiting, waiting, waiting.

"Ah, Sphinx of the countless years, tell me your dreams! You front the level moon with a face that baffles me, with eyes that see yet do not reveal, with lips that smile so faintly that while one says 'Lo, there!' the smile becomes a question and the question vanishes. What thoughts dwell in your mind of stone? What hopes or fears flit through the adamantine chambers of your bosom? Are you, too, waiting? and for what?"

"I am the Genius of the Unexplained, the symbol of the Eternal Mystery. I am waiting between the two eternities for him who shall solve my riddle."

"O Sphinx, the world is full of riddles. What is thine?"

"I would know the meaning of Man. Out of the gray dawn of the world he came, and as the centuries fall I have seen his generations file down the long valley, sowing and reaping, dreaming and building, with laughter and tears; till each in his turn reaches the borders of my desert, gazes into my face a moment and vanishes over the horizon of the setting sun. I would know the whence and whither and the all-between — the fountain whence they spring, the river that makes green their footsteps, the ocean whither they flow."

"Thy vigil is ended, Sphinx! In thine own bosom lies the answer. This little child is he who shall teach Man his meaning. Out of the fountain of Immortal Love he came, into the deep of Immortal Love shall he go; and all between — the shadow-valley of the sowing and the reaping, of the dreams and labors, of the laughter and the tears — is watered by the river of Immortal Love! "

LONG: "ANNO DOMINI"

Matt. 2 : 14

Long, Edwin (1829–1891)
Original:
Reproductions:

" The Year of our Lord! " What a momentous turning-point in history, a node where lines of destiny cross! Through millenniums the creative life of God has been unfolding, man has been reaching out and up in rhythmic alternations of growth and arrest, seeking his creator and his Highest Good in fetish and totem, dryad, sun-god, Olympian, through talisman and image and sacrifice and ritual. And now, silently as stars pass to their setting,

"The old order changeth, yielding place to new,"

and God fulfils himself in other and unimagined ways. This silent sweep of history into new courses, this unheralded epiphany of cosmic force in human destiny has caught the imagination of Edwin Long, and he has pictured it here.

The background is old Egypt, the oldest civilization in all the world, whose roots go back not only to the pyramids yonder, peering through the desert haze, but back to the pre-dynastic burials of Abydos and at least fifty thousand years to the pictured rocks

93

of Gerf Hosein. In the year our Lord came, the empire of Egypt had long since set; but the thoughts of Egypt, scattered through the ancient world like spores, were living in a thousand forms and in a thousand cities; and the faiths of Egypt, whether in guise of crudest magic or of loftiest mystery, were flourishing more riotously in the rotten soil of Rome and Ephesus than ever they did at Thebes. Isis, the Mothergoddess of the Delta, whose soul was born when earth and sky first came together, had become for half the Roman world the hope of the lost, the very image of the love and power of Heaven.

In this picture we find ourselves confronting the symbols of this world-old worship. Yonder is the temple shining bright in the sun. Within its hinder area rises the house of the Goddess, solid as the ramparts of Egypt's desert cliffs. Between the Hathorcolumns you can see the cool darkness in which the goddess lives. Round about, the walls protect the sacred enclosure, and in front two monumental pylontowers flank the huge gateway. Every foot of tower and wall is sculptured with mystic characters: the weighing of the soul in the judgment-scales of Osiris; the glories of Isis, her wifely devotion, her magic arts that caused her murdered husband to live again, her faithfulness to their young son Horus, till he avenged his father's death, — these and a hundred other tales in the oldest language of man. And before the pylons sit two giant figures in stone to immortalize some Ramses, Thothmes or Sesostris, who built this temple for his own glory.

Out from between the pylons winds the procession on the feast-day of Isis. You can see the sacred bulls, the priests in white linen or in panther skins, the images, the chariots of state, the nome-symbols on their staffs, the gorgeous fans, and crowned with blue lotus, the ravishing priestesses leading all with dance and tambourine and sistrum. Isis herself is borne in mid-procession, seated on a throne and suckling her infant Horus, the earliest Madonna history knows. She is their Lady of Consolation, their intercessor, the Mother of their god. See how the crowds prostrate themselves before her and hold out suppliant hands. See how the slaves have borne a litter as near the sacred presence as they dare, in the hope that virtue may come forth to heal the sick girl. On our left a despairing mother holds a dying child in her lap, she has tried everything, — images, charms, priests' potions; in vain the little Ethiopian holds before the child a statuette, and the vendor behind brings his trayful fresh from the temple. Only the touch of another Mother can cure this ill; and in the tradition of the Arabic Childhood, Mary does take the sufferer into her arms and heals him. Last of the throng, notice the naked image-seller on the ground, holding up for the Virgin to buy a statuette of Pasht the goddess of purity. Little need has she of its virtue!

This is all the presentment of the magic and the mummery of Egypt, the sensuous glamor of a creed outworn; on the one hand the outward splendor, the wealth, the ritual, the mystery; and on the other, impotence to deal with man's deepest needs of body and soul. This hoary temple of Heliopolis, where Joseph took unto himself to wife the daughter of Potiphera, and where Moses learned all the wisdom of the

Egyptians, is only a mask for degeneracy and ignorance and sin. "Professing themselves wise they became fools, and changed the glory of the incorruptible God into the likeness of an image of corruptible man, and of birds and four-footed beasts and creeping things. Wherefore God gave them up to uncleanness through the lusts of their own hearts."

But God has not forsaken his world. The people that sat in darkness shall now see a great light. It is no fable — though written in the Pseudo-Matthew — that when the Holy Family entered an Egyptian temple the gods prostrated themselves and the lofty pylons shook. Isis and her infant Horus indeed decreased, while the true mother and her Child increased. St. Mark brought the gospel first to Egypt and made it the power of God unto salvation; and his footsteps may still be followed along the valley of the Nile where in temple after temple the zealots of the new faith hammered out the face of the goddess on wall and capital. There today the ruined sculptures stand, mute witnesses of the death-struggle the Son of Mary waged so long ago with the Goddess of the Mysteries. Slowly the lights went out in the abandoned shrines, till in the days of Theodosius by imperial edict Isis became a name without a worshiper.

Thus with the arrival of this little child in Egypt the sin-sick world swings out into a new era — the era of our Lord. It is the era when God and man may meet without the presence of a priestly interloper; when the only pressure God needs in order to save man is to hear the Prodigal's confession, "Father, I have sinned"; when the Kingdom of God, at first

96

within a human soul, works itself out in brotherly love and a regenerate social life. So clear, so simple, but oh, so long in coming! On the dials of time the hand has moved but an inch in two thousand years!

LONG: "ANNO DOMINI"

CHAPTER IV

THE YEARS OF GROWTH

PICTURES FOR STUDY

Millais: Christ in the House of His Parents
Hofmann: Christ and the Doctors
Holman Hunt: Finding of Christ in the Temple
Holman Hunt: Shadow of Death

The scripture is disappointingly silent about the thirty years in Nazareth. We have the statement that this was his home (Mt. 2 : 23); that he " grew and waxed strong, filled with wisdom: and the grace of God was upon him " (Lk. 2 : 40); we have also the wonderfully significant account of his visit to Jerusalem when twelve years old (Lk. 2 : 41–50); and the two verses in Luke (51–52) in which the subsequent eighteen years are summarised. Nevertheless we can reconstruct to a certain extent the setting of these silent years. Edersheim, out of his Jewish lore, tells us of the upbringing of a Jewish child in the home, the school and the community (Life of Christ, Bk. II, Chap. IX and X); George Adam Smith describes for us in wonderfully vivid colors the nature of Galilee and its influence upon history (Historical Geography of the Holy Land, pp. 377–464): other travellers have written their impressions of Nazareth as they have found it (Van Dyke: Out of Doors in the Holy Land, Chap. on Galilee and the Lake), or have transcribed the spiritual meaning of its wondrous panorama (Bailey: On Nazareth Hill). But of direct and authoritative statements of how the boy Jesus grew to manhood there are none.

Fortunately the artists have not tried to fill in this hiatus. They have passed by the foolish traditions of his boyhood, — his wonderful feats of intellect, the miraculous playthings he made, his supernatural works of mercy and egotism, all of which are to be found in the Arabic Gospel of the Childhood and elsewhere. They have confined themselves to the probable and the certain, in which lies all the truth we need for an appreciation of his unfolding personality. Parents, home, work, the fair world without and God within, formed the soil in which this prophet grew to his task.

MILLAIS: CHRIST IN THE HOUSE OF HIS PARENTS

Matt. 2 : 23; Luke 2 : 40, 51–52

Millais, Sir John Everett (1829–1896)
Original: painted in 1849 and exhibited in 1850, his second important Pre-Raphaelite picture. Now privately owned.
Reproductions:

It is strange how prepossessions can alter one's judgment. When this picture was first exhibited in 1850 there were no words in the language strong enough to denounce it: it was called outrageous and blasphemous; and even Dickens, who later became a warm admirer of Millais, called it mean, odious, revolting. The whole trouble lay in the fact that it was an innovation. Hitherto the sacred characters of scripture had been treated in an ideal way, exalted

100

above the common ways of life and separated like holy beings from this work-a-day world. Millais is the first of that school of the last century — men like Von Uhde, Von Gebhardt and Tissot — whose avowed object was to paint the essential idea of sacred subjects in the garb of the present, or at least in the language of sincerity. Today we see no blasphemy in painting Jesus in a carpenter shop; on the contrary, we feel some truths when thus presented that otherwise would escape us. But seventy-five years ago the pious people of England raised hands of holy horror!

When first shown, the picture was inscribed only with a rather inept verse from the Bible, Zech. 13 : 6: "And one shall say unto him, 'What are these wounds in thy hands?' Then shall he answer, 'Those with which I was wounded in the house of my friends.'" The whole scene is conceived in the spirit of perfect sincerity that was the cornerstone of the Pre-Raphaelite creed. This is a real carpenter shop — English, to be sure. Millais painted the one near his home and used the carpenter for his model of Joseph, all but the face which is that of his own father. The small son has been playing around the bench and has torn his hand on a nail. About him the action centers. The father stops his work and leans over with sympathy to advise what to do. Mary in deep solicitude kneels and kisses the little face. Grandmother Anna reaches across the bench to pull out the offending nail with pincers. The carpenter's assistant pauses long enough to look; and little cousin John, with sympathy in his face, carefully brings in a bowl of water. This is all natural, almost naïve, and perhaps a little sentimental. It certainly is interest-

101

ing and for a youth of only twenty-one astonishingly well done.

But the picture illustrates also other dicta of the pre-Raphaelite creed: it is emotional and symbolic, suggestive of thoughts beyond what is given. Do you notice that the wound is in the center of the boy's hand, and that a drop of blood has fallen upon his foot? There is a nail, too, and pincers, that since early times have been symbols of the passion. This accounts for the over-anxiety of Mary — as if her intuition was strong enough to be called prescience, and to foreshadow her greater pangs at Calvary. It is a pretty touch to introduce little John here with his raiment of camel's hair and his bowl. He does not know, but we do, that he will some day use this bowl for the greater purification at Jordan; and his cousin will be there to receive at his hands the final consecration to a world-task. And through the door beyond the wattle-fence we see a flock of sheep, some roaming unshepherded across the wold but most crowding up to the house as if to look for a shepherd. Yes, he is within, the Good Shepherd, but not yet ready to lead the sheep to green pastures and beside the still waters. Some day, when the wounds shall have been made in earnest and death shall have tested his love to the uttermost, the sheep will hear his voice and follow it; and there shall be one fold and one Shepherd.

This is sentiment, poetry; not in itself religion, but suggestive of some of the deep truths of our faith. There is no more satisfactory presentation of the childhood in Nazareth than this of Millais'.

HOFMANN: CHRIST AND THE DOCTORS
Luke 2 : 41–50

Hofmann, Johann Michael Ferdinand Heinrich (1824–1911)
Original: 60 x 80″, painted 1882, now in the Zwinger Gallery, Dresden.
Reproductions: Taber-Prang, 1, 2, 3, 4, 5, 6, 10, 11, 12, 13, 16, 17, 18, 19, 20; Detail of Christ, 1, 2, 4, 5, 6, 7, 10, 11, 12, 13, 16 , 17, 18, 19, 20.
Fishel, Adler & Schwartz, Artotype 13 x 18″, $0.80; colored, $1.50; head of Christ, 14 x 18, and $\frac{3}{4}$ figure, 10 x 18, same prices.

This is one of the most popular pictures ever painted, and deservedly so. It represents the boy Jesus at his most winsome age; it is dignified, reverent, and the original is striking and harmonious in color. There is an earnestness and a spirituality in the face of this lad that marks him at once as an ideal creation. There is no other boy-Christ so beautiful as this. Though the critics have never accorded the picture a high rank, though they have called attention to an air of too conscious superiority about the boy — a suggestion of sentimentality, an over-prettiness — they have never been able to stop with faint praise its triumphal march into schools and homes all over the world.

The swift Bible narrative gives us no details. We are told that the boy was " found in the Temple among the Doctors, both hearing them and asking them questions: and all that heard him were amazed at his understanding and answers." (Lk. 2 : 46–47.) Hofmann has chosen the moment when this discussion is at its height, before the boy's parents have found him. He has given us a hint of the superb architectural character of the temple — the classic pedestals, the pillars of polished marble, the background of heavy draperies that seclude this little company. He had indicated that the Doctors are among the great ones of the Jewish world by giving them all a dignified bearing and costly clothing. It is these accessories that lend such exceptional brilliancy of color to the canvas. But the chief matter of interest and the chief merit of the picture lie in its psychology. Let us consider these men one by one.

Seated on the right is perhaps the chief Rabbi, holding the book of the Law. His chair and the fact of his sitting hint at something that Jesus will say later to his disciples: " The Scribes and Pharisees sit in Moses' seat: all things, therefore, whatsoever they bid you, these do." This figure is the embodiment of self-conscious and strict legalism. Every sentence of the Law is written on his heart and operative in his life — even down to the command in Deuteronomy, " Thou shalt not mar the corners of thy beard." Solomon's seal on the back of the chair is a further hint of wisdom. The rabbi is evidently refuting rather than constructing an argument; his fingers are on chapter and verse, and though he courteously waits for the boy to finish, he will soon open his defensive with guns of all calibers. He represents dignified and intrenched Orthodoxy.

Next to him is one of the most attractive characters in the picture. He has a refined face and an unmistakable kindliness of bearing. His interest is not in the Law, not merely in proving his position, but rather in helping the boy. His pose and his gesture

HOFMANN: CHRIST AND THE DOCTORS

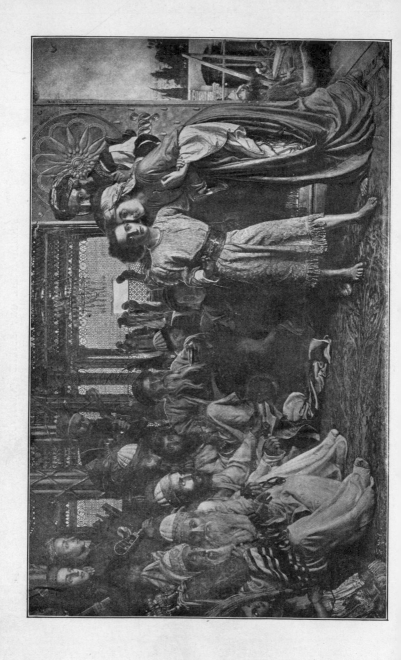

say, " My dear son, what you say is perhaps true, but let us look at it for a moment in this way." And it is significant, is it not, that Jesus is addressing himself to that one of his hearers who is sympathetically trying to understand him. If there is a true teacher in this group it is he.

Between him and the boy is an old man of different type, the oldest and richest and most intense of all. He leans forward on his staff and gives the boy a searching glance not of sympathy but of criticism. This good man is a Bourbon who can learn nothing and forget nothing; he has divided people up into two mutually exclusive classes, the orthodox and the unorthodox, the learned and the unlearned, the saved and the damned. There is a great gulf fixed between these two, so that " none may pass over from thence to us." This boy clearly belongs to the latter class. He is full of heterodoxy, and obstinately refuses to accept the very lucid explanations of the learned brothers on his left. " What is the use of any more arguing with this conceited young upstart? He ought to be sent home with a good caning! "

On our extreme left in the background is the sleek face of one who has little interest in the argument. His mind is not much set upon spiritual things anyway; and he was about to leave when some particularly unorthodox remark caused him to pause and cast a parting look of intolerance at the lad. Jesus may expect no help from him.

One man only in this group — can it be Nicodemus? — has seen new light. He too has been searching the scriptures while the conversation went on, and he has found that the boy's questions open up possibilities of truth of which he had not dreamed. Note the thoughtful gesture, the hand on beard; note the gaze into space and the knitted brow. Some very significant thinking is going on in that judicial mind; a seed has found good soil and will some day ripen into the conviction, " Rabbi, we know that thou art a teacher come from God."

The sweet-faced boy is the center of interest; all faces are turned toward him. But see how skilfully Hofmann transfers our thought from persons to ideas: the boy is pointing to the book, his thought is there. His look of clear-eyed earnestness and his gesture show us that he is full of his Father's business and that he finds his Father's will in the Word he has given. The interpretation he offers is all his own, but the words are the words of the Law and the Prophets. Jesus is still a boy; he is not wise beyond what is written. Moses' seat is still for him the seat of authority, and the most he can hope is to learn from these wise teachers whether the thoughts that have come to his soul as he pondered his lesson at the synagogue or looked down from his eagle's-nest of a home upon the wondrous scenes of his country's history — upon Elijah's place of sacrifice and Deborah's place of victory, on Naboth's vineyard and Gideon's well and the ominous heights of Gilboa — whether these thoughts about God and his kingdom and his Messiah are permissible.

Dear boy, you must understand that they are not. God's word, to be sure, is true, and it is in this book, but not every Rabbi can find it. Go home and think again, and pray and live and learn to know both man and God. Then some day you will return to these blind leaders of the blind and say, "Ye have heard that it was said to them of old time. . . . But *I* say unto you!" Then the breach will be complete; the worn-out garment in which inspiration once clothed itself you will throw away, and you will trust that living and ever-deepening inspiration that comes from direct contact with God.

And they will kill you for it.

HUNT: FINDING OF CHRIST IN THE TEMPLE

Luke 2 : 41–50

Hunt, William Holman (1827–1910)
Original: begun in 1854, finished in 1860 after his second visit to Palestine, and bought by a Mr. Gumbart for 5500 guineas (about $28,000). Now in the Birmingham (Eng.) gallery.
Reproductions:

In painting this picture, Hunt fully showed the heroic qualities that characterized his life. In his two volumes " Pre-Raphaelitism and the Pre-Raphaelite Brotherhood," which is really an autobiography, the artist gives many amusing incidents of his journeys in Palestine, of his embarrassments, sicknesses and dangers, and shows how he was satisfied with nothing short of absolute fidelity to the facts. He tried, for example, to find in the Jerusalem ghetto models for his Rabbis; but they thought he was a propagandist for the London Mission to the Jews, and they would have none of him; those that had agreed to sit they forced to throw up their contracts, and threatened with excommunication all those who persisted. Only after months of persuasion, in Jerusalem,

Bethlehem, Tiberias and elsewhere, did he measurably get what he wanted. He had to leave Palestine before the picture was finished. The model for the boy-Christ he found by visiting all the Jewish schools of London and at last selecting a lad from the school at Red Lion Square, whose frank face and hair of reddish-gold seemed to meet the artist's ideal. In his preparation the painter also studied all the history and all the recorded facts that bore even remotely on the subject, and examined the remains of Jewish, Assyrian and Egyptian architecture to approximate if he could the style of Herod's temple. Little wonder that the picture represents fully three years of solid work.

It will not be necessary to repeat here the analysis of the picture given in the Introduction (pp. 5–16). Suffice it to say that the work combines to a remarkable degree archæological accuracy with symbolism and true spiritual insight. No picture but Hofmann's can stand comparison with it, and Hofmann's is sentimental where this one is strong. The beauty of Hofmann's appeals to every one instantly; but Hunt's is more rewarding to those who will diligently search for its treasures.

HUNT: THE SHADOW OF DEATH

Hunt, William Holman (1827–1910)

Original: begun in 1869 during his third visit to Palestine. Sketched in a carpenter-shop at Bethlehem, the landscape supplied by a visit to Nazareth; finished in Jerusalem in 1872; bought by Sir William Agnew and given by him to the Manchester (Eng.) gallery.

Reproductions:

As far as the writer can discover, no other picture represents Christ as a laboring man. Other artists have painted pretty representations of the boy Jesus helping his father in the shop; but here is the full-grown carpenter, the man of the house, the eldest of many children, earning his bread and theirs by the sweat of his brow. It is said that when this picture was exhibited in the north of England, the hard-working men of Lancashire and Yorkshire saved their weekly pence to purchase two-guinea engravings of it, because it presented to them not the pale Christ of the creeds but a Christ they could understand.

When it was first exhibited in London, Mr. Hunt wrote a pamphlet in explanation of the picture. The following paragraph is condensed from it.

" Mr. Hunt aims to show him as he may have been seen by his brethren while still gaining his bread by the sweat of his face, during his first but longest humiliation. Compelled to realize in his own person the effect of the curse pronounced upon Adam and his posterity (Gen. 3 : 17–19), he has been hard at work all day, and the setting sun tells him that the hour for cessation from toil has arrived, that his day's labor is over. He has just risen from the plank on which he has been working, and is portrayed as throwing up his arms to realize that pleasant sensation of repose and relaxation caused by the inverse action of the tired and stiffened muscles of arm and body; and in perfect harmony with this physical act, so natural and grateful to every one, the Divine Laborer pours forth his soul in fervent gratitude to his Father that the hour of rest his come."

Mr. Hunt then goes on to tell about the details of the picture. The trestle on which the plank has been sawed is of a form peculiar to the East. The saw is designed from early Egyptian representations, which correspond with the modern Oriental form; the teeth are directed upwards so that the cut is made by the pulling stroke. The red fillet with the double tassel at the foot of the trestle is the " aghal " now worn by Syrians, and pictured on the Egyptian monuments. The tools on the rack behind are from a collection of ancient carpenter's implements bought at Bethlehem, and, like the former details, are found in Egyptian paintings long before the time of Christ. The crown in the casket is a combination of the forms of the dynasties of Antiochus and Herod, and of the ancient and modern Persian monarchs. The censer is of cloisonné, used in the East at a much earlier date than that here illustrated. The design upon the ivory surface of the box is almost an exact copy from the ornamentation of capitals still existing in Persepolis. The landscape seen through the window represents the hills of Galilee, with Gebel el-Corwis, the Hill of Precipitation, and further off the plain of Jezreel, and beyond this the mountains of Gilboa and Gilead.

These details, interesting and authentic as they are, are of course the wrappings and the husk; the true message of the picture lies within. It is the thought of the real humanity of Christ. We may perhaps differ from the artist in the view that work is a humiliation or that it is part of man's punishment for Adam's sin. That particular philosophy of toil is rather barren of spiritual helpfulness. Shall we not say rather that toil is God's disguise for the richest blessings he ever gives man, and that through toil Jesus, like all his brethren, came to significant portions of his character. Work gave Jesus his body that stood the terrific strains of the three crowded years; work gave Jesus his knowledge of men, gained in the shop and street and in the character-disclosing episodes of common tasks; work developed his will — the power to undertake, to keep at it, to carry through; and who can doubt that it yielded also the joys of achievement, of the thought made fact, the ideal fulfilled, the service rendered, the burden carried cheerfully, the mother and children provided for. Jesus would be less than the priceless possession he now is to the world if we knew for a fact that he stepped out of heaven straight into his ministry, or that some rich patron befriended his youth, and gave him a soft-snap education at the university. How could such an one say " Come unto me, all ye that labor "? This is the great message of the picture: Jesus won his manhood by toil, and he forever dignified and glorified the humble tasks by which men win their bread. With good right could he preach, for he had worked.

But around these years of toil the artist has let his fancy play. He has bethought him of that visit of the Wise Men and of the gifts they left in token of the child's coming greatness; he has remembered how Mary "pondered all these things in her heart" and contrasted, no doubt, the splendor of the promises and the hopes with the meanness of the actual present. And when she saw her son grow to manhood and settle down into the trade of his father, good and faithful son though she knew him to be, she could but wonder why God had mocked her with such prophecies of greatness. Again and again she would go to the chest where the hoarded treasures were kept, as if to convince herself by the handling of the kings' gifts that those fast-receding experiences were real. It was the only contact she had with the golden hopes of thirty years ago.

Today is one of those days of doubt, those blue days, when the angels' song rings hollow to her memory. And as she fondles the crown and the censer, and now comes to the vase in which the myrrh is kept, — what is that against the wall! Her hand falters, the vase drops, the death-symbol of the myrrh is spilled; a sword pierces her own soul as she sees before her a shadow cast by the failing sun — as of a man upon a cross. Ah, God! can it be a prophecy? Is this the flowering of the seed of pain that was sown so long ago in the Temple, when the spirit descended upon Simeon? And shall her first-born son who was to save his people from their sins become a Savior only by treading the road of death? Upon this day, then, that marks almost the close of Christ's labor as a carpenter and the beginning of his work as redeemer, there falls upon Mary's pathway a shadow of the cross. Henceforth her son goes to a career that she cannot share and cannot understand; ex-

changes the calm and unperplexing tasks of the
workshop, where she could sit and spin her wool in
his blessed presence, for the never-ending strain of a
spiritual ministry and the blame of those he bettered;
leaves behind the little Nazareth home and has nowhere to lay his head till the black hatred of the
world robs her of him forever. This for her boy, and
for her. From this day the shadow of death lies
also upon Mary's heart.

HUNT: THE SHADOW OF DEATH

DEL SARTO: JOHN THE BAPTIST

THE KINDLING OF THE FIRES

When he was about thirty years old, Jesus came under the influence of an extraordinary man whom he later characterized as marking the turning-point in history, from Law to Gospel (Lk. 16 : 16). The stories of this man's birth are given in Luke 1 : 5–25, 57–80. It would seem from this account that John became a desert-dweller when still a child, probably as a member of the brotherhood of the Essenes. Tradition locates his birth at the village of Ain Karim, four and a half miles northwest from Jerusalem, and his "desert" as a solitary spot in the valley of Sorek, an hour's walk further. But when he begins his ministry he appears at the Jordan, eighteen miles east of Jerusalem. In that region we know that the Essenes had their home, living in great austerity as hermits. Such was the magnetic power of John's preaching that it drew crowds from all parts of the land. The best proof that his power over men was extraordinary lies in the fact that it was his touch that waked in Jesus the consciousness of his spiritual mission and destiny. Jesus had a premonition that something might happen if he came into contact with

John. The " Gospel of the Hebrews " — as old as the Synoptic Gospels — tells how the mother and brothers of Jesus urged him to go with them and be baptized; but for a while he resisted the call. His intuition was correct. The greatest possible thing happened, — the awakening of his Messianic consciousness.

A personal description of John and a summary of his message are found in three gospels, Mt. 3 : 1–12; Mk. 1 : 1–8; Lk. 3 : 1–18. These narratives continue with the account of the baptism of Jesus; but the accounts are not clear as to the supernatural elements. Luke does not say who saw the dove or heard the voice; Matthew and Mark say that Jesus saw the dove, but are not clear about who heard the voice. John says that the Baptist saw the dove and had a revelation that this was a Messianic sign. The Temptation that immediately followed is disposed of by Mark in a couple of verses, but the full narrative is given in Matthew and Luke. With the completion of these events, Jesus finds himself in full consciousness of his mission, and he begins almost immediately to preach his gospel.

Art is very rich in representations of John and his ministry, largely because the development of the dogma of baptismal regeneration led to the building and adorning of baptisteries everywhere. John became a favorite patron saint, — as of the city of Florence, for example. Most frequently John is represented as a child with the Holy Family.

ANDREA DEL SARTO: JOHN THE BAPTIST

Luke 1 : 57–80

Sarto, Andrea del (1486–1531)

Original: painted about 1523, probably as a gift to Francis I, whose friendship Andrea wanted to regain; but the picture was finally bought by Ottaviano de' Medici. It is now in the Pitti Gallery, Florence.

Reproductions: Berlin Photographic Co., No. 3862. Photogravure, $20\frac{5}{8}$ x $15\frac{3}{8}$, $5. In color, Seemann Print, three-color half-tone, No. 1049. Medici, O. M. C., No. 280.

This is a very beautiful picture. The young prophet stands at the threshold of manhood, his clear eye fixed on the coming task, his hands holding the symbols of his preparation and his mission. Across his shoulder is the leathern girdle and about his loins is the shaggy pelt of camel's hair. The rich-red robe that falls over his arm is symbolic of his zeal; his left hand carries the parchment on whose message his soul has fed, the scroll of the prophets in whose spirit and power he is to come. In his right hand is the bowl of purification with which some day he will pour the waters of baptism upon the multitudes and upon the Christ. Resting against the stone in front is the slender cross made of the reed-stalks that flourish on Jordan's banks, the sign that in the artistic tradition of the centuries has always marked the Forerunner. The body is wonderfully modelled, — the torso that of a young athlete, the arms formed for action but not distorted with toil, the hands strong and fine and full of character, the face sweet and clear; the unkempt hair blown about his forehead by the desert winds is rich with wild beauty.

> " Large-brained, clear-eyed, of such as he
> Shall Freedom's young apostles be."

Yet one is inclined to recall the criticism offered by Bentley to Pope after reading his translation of the Iliad: " This is a very pretty poem, Mr. Pope, but you must not call it Homer." Lovely though the picture is, if you strip aside the Baptist's symbols you have nothing that will remind you of the Baptist. The gospel says that the child " waxed strong in spirit, and was in the deserts till the day of his showing unto Israel." This boy is altogether too pretty to answer that description. A dozen years of life in the wilds, with meat of " locusts and wild honey," never would have filled out his form with such Athenian grace, or produced a face so unmarred and placid, so cultured and socialized. There is nothing of the ascetic here. There is no uncontrolled fire in the eye, no frenzy of soul ready to burst forth in denunciation, such as marks the young St. John of Raphael; no brooding upon his people's sins until the whole being cries out, " Woe is me if I preach not repentance! " We must remember that in a few short years this youth is to burst like a thunderbolt from the desert; his eccentricities of appearance will draw curious crowds and his violent speeches will set the whole Jewish world on fire. What fore-warnings of this has Del Sarto given us here? Can you imagine these lips saying, " O generation of vipers, who hath warned you to flee from the wrath to come "? or is this the frame of one who came " neither eating or drinking " and who became a by-word among the Pharisees because " he hath a devil "? This is a

very pretty picture but it is not John. Rather it is
Jesus as he might have appeared in the workshop of
Nazareth, or when he walked beside his widowed
mother, her friend and protector, on the yearly pilgrimage to Jerusalem. It is such a lad as every parent
prays may bless his own home. We may love it for
its idealized beauty, but we must look elsewhere for
the Baptist.

RODIN: JOHN THE PRECURSOR

Matt 3 : 1–12; Mark 1 : 1–8; Luke 3 : 1–18
Rodin, Francois Auguste (1840–   )
Original: completed in plaster and exhibited in the Paris Salon of
    1880; exhibited in bronze in 1881; bought by the State for
    the Luxembourg Museum, Paris, in 1884.
Reproductions:

Mr. Frederick Lawton, in his " Life and Works of
A. Rodin," says of this statue: " The model was an
Italian fresh from the mountains of his native country.
He had never posed and was quite unacquainted with
the various noble gestures imposed by academic
stylists. When the man first came to pose, Rodin
ordered him merely to raise his arm and commence
to walk. The model did so. " There, now, stop and
keep that attitude!" The simplicity of the procedure
comes out strikingly in the statue. So spontaneous
is the gesture and so accurately has the posture of the
body between two seconds of movement been marked
and caught that it creates an illusion of motion.
On approaching the figure one gets an equally strong
impression of living mobility in the somewhat gaunt
framework, with its play of muscle and articulation. . . .
But this physical perfection attained by the modeling,

119

though wonderful, is not that which most perfectly entitles the St. John to its high rank. . . . The physical here serves uniquely to suggest the spiritual. The preacher is so entirely unconscious of his corporeity that the spectator transcends it too, and sees at last only a plastic rendering of the Voice crying in the Wilderness."

It is this transcendent quality that makes Rodin's St. John the best representation we have of the great Forerunner. " You feel that a force at once mysterious and formidable sustains and impels him," and that that force has become a part of his character. Put to yourself the questions that were suggested under Del Sarto's picture: Have we here a man who since his childhood has " waxed strong in spirit "? Certainly we have. Walk round the statue and discover how irresistible is the stride, as if the legs were but the automatic means by which an insistent message gets itself carried to its audience; and the arm thrusts itself forward to emphasize the thought even before the thought has risen to consciousness. Has this man been in the deserts, his meat locusts and wild honey? Beyond a doubt. There is not an ounce of fat on this anchorite's body. He has a gait whose barbarian naturalness has never been mitigated by the dancing-master. This is no " afternoon-tea " walk; the strong toes grip the ground like a lion's; the feet are calloused and deformed by the rough stones; the arms and shoulders help out the stride by compensating motion. This preacher never practised before a mirror: Cicero and Wendell Phillips never would have insulted their cultured audiences with such a monstrous pose. John has never thought whether his

audience will like his looks. One idea alone has been
ringing in his ears till it can no longer be suppressed,
" Repent! Repent! " " Nude, mystic, terrible, the
Precursor advances with long strides, announcing the
wrath to come and hastening to his own inevitable
martyrdom."

Could these lips ever have cried to the Pharisees,
" O generation of vipers "? We cannot answer this
question till we enquire in what spirit the words were
said, and till we have asked also whether the lips
could say, " Behold the Lamb of God " and " He must
increase but I must decrease." It is all a matter of
John's character. It is said that Beecher once uttered a sentence of Christ's in three distinct ways in
order to show how the same words can express attitudes of mind and heart that are worlds apart.
The sentence was Christ's denunciation of the Pharisees, — quite similar to John's, — " How shall ye
escape the damnation of Hell! " Beecher's first
rendering expressed anger and hatred, his second
warning, his third melting tenderness and sorrow. We
feel instinctively that Rodin's John is a stranger to
the first of these emotions, but that he might readily
express the other two. For the face is strong but not
bitter, intent on social righteousness but not vindic-
tive, insistent on getting a hearing but modest and
ready to give place to a better preacher. If we read
John's character and this statue aright, Rodin has
expressed clearly these two aspects, its inspired force
and its humility. No other artist has done this.
Donatello's statue emphasizes John's eccentricities of
manner and his dependence upon the prophetic
tradition of the past; Titian's picture gives us the

defiant lion. Rodin gives us the true spirit of the Forerunner, — the divine urge, the responsive will, the fiery, straightforward and untutored presentation, the lack of egotism, the capacity for self-renunciation.

It is possible also that Rodin has hinted something further. Do you observe that he calls the statue not the Baptist but the Precursor? Perhaps, following his philosophic bent, he has generalized this gaunt figure into a type of those countless forerunners that have led the way to civilization and spiritual achievement. Mr. Theodore Child has asked, "Among the socialists, the workingmen, the thirsters after justice in all ages and all countries, do we not still see savage types of affirmation?" Such a "savage type" was John, crying out against the evil but knowing not the pathway to reform; calling, "Repent! Repent!" but lacking the intellectual insight to construct the program that should lead to the new era. There is always need of Jesus who comes eating and drinking and loving and teaching, to supplement John's ascetic gospel of denunciation.

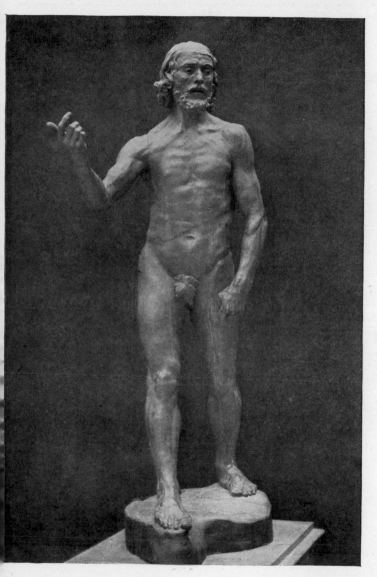

RODIN: JOHN THE PRECURSOR

GIOTTO: BAPTISM OF CHRIST

Matt. 3:13-17; Mark 1:9-11; Luke 3:21-22

Giotto, Angiolo di Bondone, nicknamed Giotto. (1266?–1337)

Original: a fresco in the Chapel of the Arena, Padua. In 1303, Enrico Scrovegni bought the ruins of a Roman amphitheater, erected within the oval a fortified palace for himself and a chapel in honor of the Virgin. This chapel he asked Giotto to decorate in 1306. Here are painted thirty-eight scenes from the lives of the Virgin and Christ, arranged in three tiers under a blue starry vault. The entire inner surface is covered with pictures or other decorations, " pure and radiant in color like the iridescence of a shell "; or, as Quilter expresses it, the spectator stands " in the midst of a gigantic opal." The Baptism (p. 126) and the Triumphal Entry (p. 278) are from this series.

Reproductions:

The reader who is not an art student may perhaps smile at this primitive picture. " This is truly what the baptism did *not* look like," one is apt to say, and there is some truth in the remark. The river Jordan is certainly not a green hump of water, nor do its banks look like shelves on treacherous icebergs; the gospel makes no mention of angels, and the first person of the Trinity did not appear in this event. Yes, but —

In the first place, please notice the date (1306). Recall that for a thousand years before this the only representations of holy persons had been crude carvings on sarcophagi, little symmetrical paintings over altars, and mosaic decorations in which stiff and almost gruesome figures stared at one from a golden wall. Art was decorative — formal, symbolical, conventional. Recall also that Giotto was handicapped by a rule made by the Second Council of Nicæa in 787

A.D., that in all representations of the Baptism, Christ should be in the center, in the Jordan, with John to the left on the shore, angels on the right, and over Christ the glory of God. Giotto was the first to tell a story with pictures, the first to introduce landscape as a background, the first to make his characters do things, the first to suggest by pose and facial expression the thoughts that were going on in the mind. To venture upon these revolutionary changes in artistic tradition belongs to genius. We will forgive, therefore, the shortcomings of perspective and anatomy, and try to enter sympathetically into the story.

Giotto tells us that the baptism occurred in the Jordan near the wilderness of Judea. The desert cliffs rise abruptly on either bank; the green water flows upward to the Savior's waist. This is surely the Savior because his nimbus has a Greek cross on it, and because in the water beside him is a fish. The middle age was quite familiar with the symbol of the fish, the "Ichthus" of the early Christians who saw in its letters the initials of the words, "Jesus Christ the Son of God our Savior"; and they knew the oft-quoted simile of Tertullian that we, as little fishes, are born of water, as was Christ the great fish. Giotto means also to remind us of the conversation that took place before the act; so John looks on with awe while Jesus raises his hands to say, "Suffer it to be so now." John is shown to be a prophet by his bright halo and his garment of camel's hair under his mantle. His disciples are represented by the solemn person with the halo and the curly locks — probably Andrew — soon to become a disciple of Jesus; and the unconverted multitudes are represented by the haloless one. These are all dignified and reverent in the presence of this great event. The painter would not have us forget that Heaven is interested also. How solicitously the angels on our left lean forward and, as tradition requires, hold the garments of Jesus! The Dove issues from the brightness and hovers over the Savior's head; and the Father, made visible for us in the heavens, stretches out his hand to emphasize the words he is speaking, and clasps to his bosom the book of the Word incarnate.

This may not mean so much to us, dazzled as we are by the technic of the Renaissance, but to the unlettered folk of the fourteenth century who could not read the gospel narrative and who we may be sure got little religion from mosaics in an apse, this breath of naturalness, of sincerity, of directness, this gentle seriousness in picturing an act of consecration, must have come like a breath from heaven. This was in very truth the act by which Christ opened the door of salvation to them, by which God " by the baptism of his well-beloved Son in the river Jordan did sanctify the element of water to the mystical washing away of sin." Salvation was thus nigher to them than when they believed.

VERROCCHIO: BAPTISM OF CHRIST

Matt. 3 : 13–17; Mark 1 : 9–11; Luke 3 : 21–22

Verrocchio, Andrea di Michele di Francesco Cioni (1435–1488)

Original (unfinished): 69 x 59″, painted for the monks of Vallombrosa at S. Salvi. On the suppression of the monastery it passed to that of Santa Verdiana, whence it was removed a century ago to the Academy, Florence. It is the earliest existing work of Verrocchio, who was a sculptor rather than a painter, and the only painting of his that has come down to us. Its popularity caused it to become the model for all later representations.

Reproductions: Medici, O. M. C., No. 130.

Seemann's three-color print, No. 1347.

Detail of angels, in color. Medici prints, chromo-lithograph 19 x 10″, Italian lxxx, $7.25.

The stream of the Renaissance has carried us in this painting a century and a half nearer the mastery of technic. Verrocchio has discovered the rules of perspective; the river banks no longer pile themselves up in crude masses, but merge into distant vistas down which in placid reach or in cascade flows the Jordan. He has learned anatomy, for he was a sculptor. This is evidenced by his masterly handling of the wasted figure of John, the athletic form of Christ, and the graceful contours of the two attendant angels. He has learned how to make more varied and explicit the facial revelation of thought. But he has not gained a whit over Giotto in directness or sincerity; both pictures are full of these qualities, and of the religious spirit.

It is worth while to note certain changes in emphasis. In this picture the angels are present as tradition requires, but they have lost their wings, they are reduced in size and they are kneeling; in other words, they have been subordinated. Instead of the fish with its doctrinal symbolism we have pebbles shining through the crystal water. Instead of the burst of glory and the full figure of the Father we have a pair of hands to show whence the dove came. The spectators have vanished. The two chief actors only are here, with no earthly intrusions to distract from the meditative solemnity of this hour.

John steps strongly forward to pour the water. He is the scriptural Baptist, his figure wasted with fasting, his strong jaw and firm mouth indicative of strength of purpose, his eye lighted with inspiration and his head lowered in humility. His cross of reed bears a scroll that interprets for us the thought he now dimly perceives and will later express, " Behold the Lamb of God! " It is by this insight into character that John proves himself to be a prophet. In reverence he performs this ceremony on one the latchet of whose shoes he is not worthy to unloose.

Christ stands in the center of the picture in an attitude of humility, his hands closed in prayer. What may his thoughts be? Is he rejoicing in the fact that he is the well-beloved Son? Does he look forward to the joys of world-conquest and the glorious day when he shall come upon the clouds of heaven? Far otherwise. This is a face of sadness. He has not yet heard the voice that pronounces him to be the Messiah; he has heard only the voice of John calling upon a sinning and a wretched world to repent. The burden of that world is upon his own heart. And just because he wishes to dedicate whatever power he has to the task of saving the world is he here, fulfilling all righteousness by this act of conse-

127

cration; as Isaiah once stood appalled before the sins of the world and cried, " Here am I; send me! " This is an act of self-surrender. And when this Chosen One has reached the point where he can say " Lo, I come to do thy will, O God! " — then the heavens are opened to his spiritual sight, and the assurance, new and overwhelming as a sudden burst of thunder, rolls in upon his soul, " Thou art my well-beloved Son! " Christ came to the baptism sad and perplexed, knowing only the world's need and his desire to help; he went away awe-struck and with the burden of a crushing responsibility on his soul.

Neither he nor John foresaw this outcome, though Jesus had a dim premonition of it. In the Gospel of the Hebrews — as ancient as any of our Gospels — there is an interesting account of how Jesus resisted the invitation to be baptized of John: " Behold, the mother of the Lord and his brethren spake to him saying, ' John the Baptist is baptizing for the forgiveness of sins; we will go to be baptized of him.' But he said unto them, ' What sins have I committed that I should go to be baptized of him? Anything that I have said must have been said in ignorance.' " This reluctance to meet the powerful preacher of righteousness was no doubt a presentiment that the contact would waken to life the powers that were slumbering in him, and would lead to persecution and martyrdom. At all events, a reverent study of the sources leads to the conclusion that on this day and moment, the belief that he was the Messiah of God was first implanted in the consciousness of Jesus. This is therefore one of the greatest turning-points in history.

VERROCCHIO: THE BAPTISM

HOFMANN: THE TEMPTATION

HOFMANN: THE TEMPTATION

Matt. 4 : 1–11; Mark 1 : 12–13; Luke 4 : 1–13

Hofmann, Johann Michael Ferdinand Heinrich (1824–1911)
Original: a drawing.
Reproductions:

Jesus and the devil are here fighting out a quarrel and the devil is getting the worst of it: — that is Hofmann's straightforward interpretation of one of the most mystical passages in the gospels.

We are in the wilderness of Judea. There are stones to suggest one of the three temptations, a city in the distance to suggest another, and a mountain more or less " exceeding high " as a setting for the third. The picture lacks only " all the kingdoms of the world " to be complete. The serpent is there as a symbol of the lost Eden and as a foil to that " greater Man " who shall " regain the blissful seat." An angel in the sky looks on while the uncanny encounter is being fought out; as soon as the place is safe she will come down and comfort the victor.

How does this devil suit you? His toe-nails are claws, there are barbs on his ankles, and his wings are hooked like a bat's. Horns and tail, if he has them, are not visible. He is a right substantial personage weighing a hundred and eighty-five pounds. Where his foot rests the ground smokes. He has bracelets and a crown, very likely of asbestos. He has a hard face, and his gesture and gait show that he is very excited and angry about something. Jesus has been somewhat impressed by these evidences of Infernality, not to say a bit frightened. Still he is in command of himself, though he thinks it prudent to

129

keep an eye on his enemy who is now getting in his rear. "Thou shalt worship the Lord thy God, and Him only shalt thou serve" are the words Jesus has just uttered to show the devil that he is not sufficiently impressive to be mistaken for Deity.

This sort of picture will do for children (sic), but thinking men and women are not so easily satisfied. Was Jesus tempted in this fashion by a devil of this sort? Or, since he was "tempted in all points like as we are," it is fair to ask, Were we ever tempted in this fashion?

It will clarify our minds somewhat if we inquire into the personal history of Satan. He was not present in Eden, as Milton would have us understand, the rôle of tempter there having been played by a snake. His earliest appearance in scripture is in Zech. 3 : 1. In 1 Chron. 21 : 1 (4th cent. B.C.) he stirred up David to take a census; though strangely enough in 2 Sam. 24 : 1 (pre-exilic) we are told that God stirred up David! The Psalms make no mention of him, nor do other books of the Old Testament except the late book of Job, and there we find him to be a hanger-on of Heaven. A little research will show that the Hebrews never heard of the devil till the Exile, when they borrowed him from the Persians. When once borrowed he made rapid strides into popular favor and became part and parcel of the religious imagery of the age; the apocryphal literature of the centuries just before and just after Christ is full of him. Down through the middle ages he terrorized men's souls; but after the Renaissance his power began to wane and his appearances became less frequent. Luther was among the last to see him —

on which occasion he threw his ink-bottle at him. His roaring became fainter in our grandfathers' day, though his name was always uttered with reverence and capitalized when written. Today he is neglected and very much out of style. Microscopes and the alienist and the doctrine of evolution have scared him away to the far-off corners of the world, to China and Tibet. In Kashmir he and his crew infested, till recently, the river Jhelum, and drowned all who entered the water. But even there he had his troubles. An " oldest inhabitant " told the writer that since Dr. Biscoe opened his mission school (he taught all his boys to swim), the devils have left the river!

The devil is an attempted explanation of the sin of the world. For a while the hypothesis worked; but like the Ptolemaic theory, the atomic theory and other postulates of science, philosophy and religion, he was relegated to the scrap-heap when he ceased to explain the facts of life. The facts themselves cannot be so relegated; they are too real and too awful. But if we are going to explain them satisfactorily to our generation we need a finer analysis than Hofmann used in this picture.

CORNICELIUS: CHRIST TEMPTED BY SATAN

Matt. 4 : 1–11; Mark 1 : 12–13; Luke 4 : 1–13

Cornicelius, Georg (1825–1898)
Original: painted in 1888, 31 x 18″, Berlin Nat. Gallery.
Reproductions:

Is it not a marvellous thing that a painter with a few dabs of pigment can produce an emotional effect like this? Here is the whole mystery of the Temptation, not explained but portrayed; and that mystery lies behind those eyes that look not at you, and not through you, but past you to infinite abysses, while the mind within is weighing, pondering, seeking principles, testing conclusions. This great soul is not afraid — he only longs to find his duty; he is not struggling with a divided self, trying to bring the lusts of the flesh and the pride of life under the control of his spirit. He has been for years wholly committed to the performance of duty; but now a great experience has opened a new heaven and a new earth — and a possible new hell. The lines of relationship between the little facts of his former life, the little paths of action that used to run so clearly from duty to duty have been obliterated as by some seismic convulsion; and his naked self stands alone, on the highest pinnacle of earth, with a vast continent of problem and of opportunity stretching below him, the infinite spaces overhead, and God within.

The intensity of the struggle is indicated here in subtle ways: his eyes (in the original) are red with lack of sleep, his hair has been blown into disorder by the wind — for days he has not thought of his personal appearance; his chin rests upon his right hand, as so often happens when one is thinking, but his other hand has gripped the wrist. This muscular tension is a pure reflex from the tensity within.

And the problem? It was whether to trust without further proofs the new revelation that came to him at his baptism. If thou art the Messiah — prove it on these stones. If thou art the Messiah — let all the people see it after the pattern of their expectations.

132

Since thou *art* the Messiah, — rule! It took Jesus forty days to think himself clear of the entanglements involved in these suggestions; but he emerged with his future principles of action settled forever. They are these: I am the Messiah and my work is to establish the Kingdom of God; I will never use my Messianic power for my own gratification; I will never make a spectacle of myself to gain popularity; I will never rule, but only love and help and teach. One has only to think what would have happened to the character of Jesus and to the history of the world had he transgressed one of these principles, to realize that the sublimest issues were involved in this wilderness struggle.

How does Satan come into this experience? Cornicelius has put him into this picture for our benefit, so that we may connect this experience with the scripture account. The tempter's form is a dim background, his face subtly suggestive of evil, and the crown a reminder of the last great struggle of the Master. He is, in fact, the thought of Jesus objectified for us, as if Christ's eyes were lenses through which we could see all the phantasmagoria of evil that is passing before his consciousness. Jesus does not see the devil; he feels him. The devil is an experience.

But the important question remains: did Jesus think of him as an experience, or as an external reality? Probably the latter. In a sense this struggle had an external origin, for the problems of the Messiahship were thrust upon him. In another sense also it was external, though spiritual, for Jesus like ourselves was an ethical dualism; within him was a higher self with which he felt himself completely identified, and a lower self that from childhood he had suppressed so completely that he had lost sight of it. How otherwise could he be in any sense human? To his consciousness, this solicitation of his lower self appeared to come from outside his personality; and explaining his struggle in the imagery of his day he called it Satan. But do not fail to observe that whether we use the mythological language of the first century or the psychological language of the twentieth, the truths are the same: temptation is a reality, and it is inward; yielding to temptation is sin, the choice of the lower alternative; sin works death to our spiritual life, and that "second death" is terrible. Jesus taught these eternal truths with all the intensity of full conviction. "Yea, fear him who hath power to cast both soul and body into Hell."

CORNICELIUS: CHRIST TEMPTED BY SATAN

GHIRLANDAJO: CALLING OF PETER AND ANDREW

CHAPTER VI

THE MINISTRY OF TEACHING

PICTURES FOR STUDY

Ghirlandajo: Calling of Peter and Andrew
Raphael: Miraculous Draught of Fishes
Zimmermann: Christ and the Fishermen
Tissot: Jesus in the Synagogue
Tissot: The Sermon on the Mount
Bloch: " Come unto Me "

Jesus' decision at the Temptation left him no alternative but to work quietly and patiently, explaining his conception of the Kingdom of God to all whom he could reach and winning his followers one by one. He therefore became a teacher. As his fame increased the teaching became preaching, yet his method throughout the ministry was not at all that of the orator who sways men by brilliant rhetoric or emotional appeal but rather that of the interpreter, the explainer, the friend and companion who seizes upon a word in conversation or an object by the roadside and translates it into terms of the spiritual life. Not Preacher but Teacher he was most frequently called by his contemporaries. Jesus had the teaching instinct; he had an enthusiasm for spiritual truth that shows him to be the true successor of the splendid line of prophets who are Israel's glory, and a capacity for pregnant statement that transcends the power of Israel's greatest sages. But he had what is of greater importance for a religious teacher, knowledge of God through personal experience and knowl-

135

edge of the heart of man. It was this knowledge born of insight that gave him such tremendous power in teaching, that enabled him to stand alone against the whole weight of scribal authority, and that forced from his enemies the reluctant confession, " Never man spake like this man! "

Jesus taught first beside the Sea of Galilee. This beautiful lake, some six miles by thirteen, lies in a hollow 680 feet below the Mediterranean. The hills of Galilee run down abruptly to the shore on the north and west, while above its eastern cliffs the level plateau of the Hauran stretches away to the Arabian Desert. Not all of this country was the scene of the gospel ministry, for we never hear that Jesus entered Tiberias, Herod's capital, half way down the western shore, nor any of the numerous cities to the south and east. These were heathen cities like Hippos, Tari-chiæ, Gamala, Bethshan and Gerasa, thoroughly given over to business and pleasure and vice, quite out of sympathy with pious people who were looking for a kingdom of God. Virtually the northern shore and the amphitheater of the plain of Magdala marked the confines of his labor. Here lay the cities of Capernaum, Bethsaida and Chorazin, "wherein most of his mighty works were done," largely Jewish in population and presenting what seemed at first to be promising soil.

It was at Capernaum that Jesus made his home, attracted thither no doubt by his recently formed friendship for the men whom he met while he was with the Baptist. These friends he now invites to become special pupils and co-workers. With these partners in the business of the Kingdom he goes out in wider circles to the villages of Galilee. With each new excursion the crowds increase and the fame of the new teaching flies to the remotest corners of the land. Never again can Jesus be a private citizen. He now belongs to the world. And indeed the great lessons he taught long ago in that obscure corner have reverberated through the centuries and across the seas, till alien peoples and hostile faiths have been compelled to say with Nicodemus, " Rabbi, we know that thou art a teacher come from God."

The artists have given us relatively few pictures of the events from now till the beginning of Passion Week, and these are for the most part poor. The best have been selected for our study, and it is noticeable that of these more than half are by artists of the nineteenth century. This circumstance emphasizes the truth that early art was controlled by the church and was used to glorify the dogmas of the faith. Modern art is free, and it responds to those aspects of religion that lie close to life. Christ a living and serving man means more to our day than Christ an embodied theological formula.

GHIRLANDAJO: CALLING THE DISCIPLES

Matt. 4 : 18–22; Mark 1 : 16–20; Luke 5 : 1–11

Ghirlandajo, Domenico di Tommaso di Currado Bigordi, called (1449–1494)

Original: a fresco in the Sistine Chapel, Vatican, Rome. In 1481 Pope Sextus IV completed a chapel in the Vatican (called henceforth from his name, Sistine) and asked various artists to decorate it, among them Ghirlandajo. This picture is third from the altar on the right wall. The other scenes in the series are from the life of Christ, as the scenes on the opposite wall are from the life of Moses.

Reproductions:

There is no superficial brilliancy in this picture, rather it is grave and solemn and makes its impression only on careful study. In the center of the foreground stands Christ, before whom kneel Andrew and Peter, the first to answer to the call. In the middle distance on the left the scene is repeated: Christ with hand raised calls to Peter and Andrew who are in a boat near the shore. Andrew grasps his net and both prepare to land. Again on the middle right, Jesus stands in a similar attitude, with Peter and Andrew behind him, while Zebedee rows toward the shore a boat in which are his two sons, James and John. The chief actors are all distinguished by halos and their faces are merely conventionalized types. The ordinary spectators have no halos, while each of the fifty-three faces is a distinct portrait, probably members of the Florentine colony then living in Rome. The composition is well balanced without being too formal, the landscape is interesting, the perspective accurate, and the atmospheric effect attractive.

The main question for us is whether this picture

adequately interprets the event. Superficially, yes. The scene is by the sea, the men have been fishing, they heard the call, left all and followed Christ. The multitudes are witnesses of the call, and about the lake are the populous cities and villages in which they straightway began to preach. But the account of this event in Luke 5 : 1–11 shows that an extraordinary happening had preceded it. Having toiled all night and caught nothing, they had let down their nets once more at the command of Jesus and had taken a record catch; whereat all were amazed beyond words, while Peter was beside himself with fear. This miracle gives point to the assurance, " Fear not, from henceforth thou shalt catch men."

Of this astonishment there is not a trace in this picture. Jesus stands in a dignified and not unkindly attitude, bestowing instructions or a blessing on the neophytes, while the newly-called kneel reverently, one listening with crossed arms and the other praying. These saintly and composed men never saw a miracle; nor is there a suggestion of the momentous change this call is destined to work in their lives. They are incapable of vision and enthusiasm. In fact, the disciples are too old to become missionaries anyway! — graybeards both, whose grandchildren are doubtless standing behind them in the crowd. No, this is not an interpretation of spiritual experience. The Pope has ordered Ghirlandajo to paint an appropriate picture and he has painted it, — an excellent piece of work, excellent in all but the perception of inner significance, which it is the function of genius to discover.

The great French sculptor Rodin has said of

artists, " Our eyes plunge beneath the surface to the meaning of things, and when afterwards we reproduce the form we endow it with the spiritual meaning which it covers. . . . In art only that which is gifted with character is beautiful." Ghirlandajo has proved Rodin to be true. Where he did not plunge beneath the surface, in painting Christ and the disciples, the result is merely negative; but where he did so plunge in the case of all the other personages of the picture — those living, energetic Florentines — he caught and painted their spirit *con amore.* Notice that splendid line of eleven heads on the right, every one of them distinctive and forceful, filled with character and therefore beautiful. If Ghirlandajo could have conceived Peter and Andrew and Christ as vividly as he saw his contemporaries, this picture would have been a masterpiece. It is because of the absence of the divine touch in this and similar pictures in the Sistine series that visitors scarcely notice them; rather they fasten their eyes on the wondrous ceiling of Michelangelo where the dead past thrills with passion, an ever-living present.

RAPHAEL: MIRACULOUS DRAUGHT OF FISHES

Luke 5 : 1-11

Raphael, Raffaelo Santi, or Sanzio (1483–1520)

Original: One of the cartoons for a series of tapestries to cover the lower section of the Sistine Chapel below the frescos. This set was ordered by Pope Leo X, and the cartoons were drawn in 1515–6. There are ten subjects illustrating the acts of the Apostles. The drawings were sent to Brussels to the arras-maker and never returned. At the recommendation of Rubens, Charles I of England bought six of them, including this one. After the death of Charles, Cromwell purchased them for the State and they are now in the S. Kensington Museum, London. The tapestries themselves at Leo's death were pawned for 5000 ducats. After the sack of Rome in 1527, they were sold by soldiers and had various adventures; rebought finally in Constantinople and Lyons they were restored to Rome, but when Napoleon took Rome in 1798 they were resold by the soldiers and taken to Paris. Pope Pius VII repurchased them in 1818, since when they have remained in the Vatican.

Reproductions:

How absolutely different from Ghirlandajo's is this work of Raphael. The stately symmetry of the landscape, the dignified multitude, the ecclesiastical looking disciples, the unnatural three-moment presentation have all gone, and in their stead, life, drama, spiritual insight.

The scene presents the unruffled lake of Galilee, with a suggestion of cities and busy people on the distant vanishing shore. Two boats occupy the foreground, or rather two conventionalized objects that stand for boats, — for we must remember that this is a decorative design and not a transcription from life. The miracle recorded in Luke 5 : 1-11 has

141

just been performed; James and John in the further boat are tugging at the breaking nets, while Zebedee with his paddle keeps the boat in place. In the nearer boat Peter and Andrew have succeeded in landing their catch and now are turning in amazement to the author of their good fortune. The cranes in the foreground are screaming their joy, for they will get their share in due time. Conventional and decorative though it is, it is worth a thousand Ghirlandajos.

Consider first these men, and contrast them with the former ones. These are true fishermen, not saints posing. See the knotted arms of James and John, their bent backs, their legs bare above the knee. See the rugged frames, the rough clothes and the unkempt hair of Peter and Andrew, their intensity, their absolute sincerity. There is some use in Jesus' calling men like these; they are good for something! With them he can conquer the world.

But more interesting than the men are their mental states, the way in which they have apprehended this experience. Superficially one might say that there had been no miracle here. Fishermen frequently toil all night and catch nothing; and sometimes they make a lucky strike just as they are pulling home. Zebedee, farthest from the Master, looks at it in this way; he has seen this happen before. James is too busy to think much, but he knows that something strange has happened; he is pulling for dear life. But John has begun to think, and his mind wanders from the fish toward that strange person in the other boat. It is as if the divine radiations from the Master's personality had begun to reach him. They have already reached Andrew, who, nearer the source of power, seems drawn from his place as by a magnetic force (see his hair streaming forward); his look and his gesture show that he is certain this is no mere piece of luck: the Master has caused it and it is a miracle! Peter is fully within the circle of intensity, and the act appeals to him not merely as supernatural but as having a moral quality as well. For the first time in his life he has caught sight of a being of infinite perfection as well as power, in contrast to whom his poor self seems contemptible indeed: "Depart from me, O Lord, for I am a sinful man!" This is always the first effect of a sight of the ideal.

Jesus the psychic center of power is himself calm, almost unconscious of what he has done. Miracle with him is an incident only. His unassuming attitude expresses the ease with which his spirit commands all things, and his hand and eye show that Peter's spiritual state is now the object of his concern. "Fear not, from henceforth thou shalt catch men!" Peter must not remain crushed by his self-abasement, Andrew must not let his astonishment paralyze his activity. There is work to be done! And these splendid follows, all sincerity and enthusiasm and loyalty, are built precisely for this work. So the Master turns the fear and the amazement into high resolve; they leave all and follow him. The miracle of the miraculous draught fades from sight before that greater miracle by which Jesus smites his spirit into the souls of men.

ZIMMERMANN: CHRIST AND THE FISHERMEN

Zimmermann, Ernst Karl Georg (1852–1899)
Original: first shown in the Jubilee Exposition at Berlin in 1886.
Now in the Berlin National Gallery.
Reproductions: Taber-Prang, 1, 2, 3, 4, 13.

Jesus has come upon an old man mending his nets and has sat down on the beach beside him. Two younger men have just landed from their boat, and joining the group are at once caught by the spell of this earnest and kindly teacher. Something of vital importance is under discussion. It is something new as far as the younger men are concerned, for they look into Jesus' eyes with an interest and an intensity akin to astonishment. How quick they are to seize upon the truth and absorb it! "Wonderful! And *true!* Give us more, more!" That is always the response of those who see visions in the days of their youth, before the evil days come with their burdens and their disappointments and their hatreds. We feel instinctively that these young men are disciples already in heart, converts at sight, and that they wait only the word to go forth like "Sons of Thunder" to the great quest. But with the old man it is different. The teaching is hard to take in, limited as he is by moderate capacity for thought, and especially by sixty years of thinking from another angle. To him it sounds fair; he wishes it might be true; but how shall he square it with this and this, that for all these years have formed the warp and woof of his mental fabric? The old brain labors to grasp it all.

And now see the kindliness and the patience of the

144

RAPHAEL: THE MIRACULOUS DRAUGHT

ZIMMERMANN. CHRIST AND THE FISHERMEN

Great Teacher. He does not lightly toss the objections aside, and with a knowing wink to the young men say, "It is all clear to us, of course, but old uncle here is a bit thick." Rather the young men, all eagerness though they are, he ignores for the time, and all his tact and skill are bent to solve the old man's problems. How patiently and at ease Jesus sits on the bank, as if time were no object and the evening would last forever! With what earnestness his head bends forward, and how gently his right hand seeks the other's wrist so that the doubter may never doubt for a moment the teacher's sympathy and comprehension and calm assurance of the outcome. It is a strong face — that profile of Christ's — not the face of a fanatic who will carry his point with the bayonet, nor of the sophist who delights to confuse his opponent with a quibble; it is the face of a friend, who can afford to wait till the light of faith shall dawn and the shadows flee away. What would you and I not give for a look into those quiet eyes, and for a touch of that hand!

And the subject of this conversation? — We may venture to guess that nothing less than the heart of the gospel is being disclosed. Jesus is here showing these simple peasants, who never had time nor wit to master the subtleties of scribal Judasim, that they are God's children and that all He requires are trust in Him, humility, mercy, forgiveness of our debtors; that love of money endangers a man's soul, but that love of one's neighbor is better than whole burnt offerings and sacrifices. This is the simple gospel unmixed with Greek philosophy and Latin theology; the good news that Jesus carried personally into all

145

the villages of Galilee, an evangel so simple that only children can understand it! And that word that he once spoke is as true today as when it was uttered: " Except ye become as little children, ye shall not see the kingdom of God."

TISSOT: JESUS IN THE SYNAGOGUE

Luke 4 : 16–30

Tissot, James (1836–1902)

Original: One of the series on The Life of Christ, painted during the artist's residence in Palestine, 1886–1895. Now owned by the Brooklyn Institute, New York.

Reproductions:

Tissot gives us here, as usual, not an interpretation of a spiritual message, but a picture of the externals of an event, — its backgrounds, its actors. He shows us a real synagogue. It is a fairly commodious building with some pretensions to architecture; at least there seem to be in the background a stone pillar, an arch and a gallery. In the center of this building stands a tribune or raised platform, which is the specially sacred part of the edifice. This and the reading-desk are properly of wood, for they must be movable to accommodate the exigencies of feast-days; but they are not cheap. The pillars of the reading-desk and the ornaments of the pews are carved; so are the sides of the tribune, which also has a prettily patterned balustrade. The lamps that fill the upper space are doubtless the gifts of pious people, who are thus in the person of their gift continuously present in the sanctuary. The lamps are lighted on the greater feast days.

146

The rolls of Scripture occupy naturally the place of honor. These are kept in a special wooden chest or "ark," which in this instance is incorporated with the larger tribune. You may see the four silver heads and the three spindles without heads projecting from the ark. When the service is over these will be carefully covered from sight. At the lectern Jesus is reading from another great roll. Note how richly it is adorned, first with the two carved silver heads and their pendent bells, and again with the stiffly embroidered cloth, which no doubt conceals a cylinder of brass or silver such as usually protects the volumes of great age or sanctity. These are all signs of the veneration the Jews paid to the scriptures, which were in their eyes the beginning and the end of their religion. That man was greatest among them who knew the Law most perfectly and who practised its precepts down to the last jot and tittle.

For the most part we can distinguish the people in the picture. One of them — very likely the man leaning over the balustrade — is the chief ruler of the synagogue. He is chosen by the congregation to have general oversight of the service, to see that everything is done decently and in order and to give the invitation to those who are to take part. Jairus, whose daughter Jesus raised from the dead, was such a ruler at Capernaum (Lk. 8 : 41). Associated with him are others, also called rulers, all of whom are chosen for their honorable state and their acquaintance with the Law, and who form the local Sanhedrim or court. You may see these men seated on the tribune and perhaps on the seats below. The " attendant " mentioned in verse 20 may be the one in the left foreground. The word is sometimes translated "minister." He looks after the house — as our janitors do — assists in the service, reads and expounds the lessons himself if necessary — for he is usually a "scribe" technically trained to expound the law; and in the smaller villages he no doubt performs all these offices regularly. He is also teacher of the village school which meets in the synagogue.

The other seats of honor, which are placed below the tribune and facing the people, are filled by those whom the Ruler designates; men of wealth or position in the community, especially scribes and Pharisees, and distinguished guests from abroad. These are usually asked to take part in the service, as Paul the famous Rabbi from Jerusalem was asked to preach at the provincial synagogue of Antioch in Pisidia (Acts 13 : 15). It was their love for "chief seats," among other things, that called forth Jesus' severe denunciation of the scribes and Pharisees (Mk. 12 : 38–39). In Tissot's picture we see one at least of these men, him with the white beard; a peculiarly unlovely specimen. The common people sit or stand in any part of the building, even behind the tribune, though the desirable places are in front where one can see and hear the speaker. Women have a special place assigned, in the gallery if there is one.

The service consists of a liturgy read or recited by a chosen leader, in which the congregation responds with "Amen." Then comes the reading of the Law by from three to seven men chosen from the congregation. These men are all scribes or priests if such are present. After each verse an Interpreter "targums" or translates the classic Hebrew of the text into the

Aramaic or the Greek or the Latin that the people understand. Following the Law, a section of the Prophets is read, always by one man. The reader if he is competent may "targum" the text himself; and this particular reader is expected to give some word of comment or exhortation in addition. In our scripture selection please notice that Jesus reads the prophets while standing, then makes his comment sitting. This is quite the usual manner. The concluding feature of the service is a season of free comment or discussion in which any one may take part. There is the utmost freedom of speech, always under the possible veto of the Ruler.

This simple institution of the synagogue played a wonderful rôle in the history of Israel. Originating in the time of the Babylonian exile when there was no Temple, the Sabbath assembly for the reading of the Law became the center of the Jewish religious and social life and kept alive those traditions of piety and worship that otherwise would have perished in a foreign land. After the Return, every community in Palestine established a synagogue; and wherever the Jews of the Dispersion went, in all countries under heaven, there they planted these democratic institutions, these rallying-places of Jehovah worship, "isles of safety" in the stream of a crooked and perverse world. The synagogue was Temple and school, "meeting house" and lecture-hall, club and courthouse and eleemosynary institution all in one. That was the one place to which all Jews turned. Paul in his travels always went straight to a synagogue on reaching any city. Jesus found most of his earliest audiences in them; and it is a wonderful tribute to their worth that he was a constant attendant even before he became a Rabbi (Lk. 4 : 16). The Nazareth synagogue was second home to him, nurse of his patriotism and his devotion to the community. Jesus began his work as a loyal supporter of his country's institutions, and no doubt expected always so to remain.

While the synagogue was the natural place for Jesus to deliver his message, he found its limitations. He met there the scribes and the Pharisees who speedily developed a keen hostility to the new teaching. It was doubtless this hostility, manifested through the rulers of the synagogue, that finally closed to him the opportunity of speaking at the regular services. And the growing fame of Jesus attracted such crowds that no synagogue would hold them. The open was soon the only auditorium large enough for him.

TISSOT: SERMON ON THE MOUNT

Matt. 5, 6, 7

Tissot, James (1836–1902)

Original: One of the series on The Life of Christ, painted during the artist's residence in Palestine, 1886–1895. Now owned by the Brooklyn Institute, New York.

Reproductions:

This picture has all the verisimilitude of a photograph; it shows us Galilee as it is today and perhaps as it was in Christ's time, Galilee the land of hills and valleys, of roads that carried all the world across her surface, Galilee of the Lake that gleams like a turquoise in its setting of opal hills. There is no

TISSOT: JESUS IN THE SYNAGOGUE

TISSOT: SERMON ON THE MOUNT

doubt whatever about the artist's intention, for there is only one view-point in the world that gives precisely this.

Jesus is standing on the edge of a broken crater that forms one of the two " Horns of Hattin." This volcanic mountain lies a little to the north of the modern carriage road that runs from Nazareth to Tiberias, and not far from where the oldest road in the world crosses it on its way from Damascus to Egypt. Since the sixteenth century this has been regarded as the place where Jesus delivered the Sermon on the Mount. One cannot help wishing that a less sinister spot had been pitched upon, for this old relic of infernal fires has also been blasted by the fires of Christian hatred and wet with Christian blood. Here on July 4, 1187, the Crusaders fought their last fight against Saladin. Almost where Jesus is standing King Guy pitched his tent, and on the slopes below us and to our right the terrible battle raged under a pitiless sun. Seven times Saladin stormed this hill; and here at last when the Christian power had been shattered forever he slew his prisoners, — the Grand Master of the Templars, Master of the Hospitallers, the Lord of Kerak, Guy of Jerusalem, and two hundred of the bravest knights. What a background for the Sermon on the Mount!

Below us the valley of Abu el-Amis sinks away to the lake. Where Tissot has shown us the multitude pressing up to hear the word of life, the modern traveler sees flocks of sheep and goats, the camels and the black tents of Bedouins. On the slope of the hill to the right Jesus is said to have fed the multitude with the seven loaves; and beyond it on the shore of

the lake lies Tiberias. The hill that begins to rise
to the left slopes gently for a mile beyond the picture, then ends in a great precipice honey-combed
with caves, where Herod the Great smoked out the
robbers. Below it by the shore is Magdala, that
gives its name to Mary Magdalene. The blue lake is
the Sea of Galilee, whose surface and precipitous
shores formed the theater of so much of Christ's
ministry. The hills beyond are the land of the
Gergasenes, where the demonized swine ran down the
steep shore into the sea (Matt. 5 : 1–20). Capernaum
lies nine miles away to the left at an angle of
forty-five degrees; Cana and Nazareth and Mt. Tabor
are behind to the right.

Tissot is accurate not only in his backgrounds but
in his costumes and his characters. We see here the
bright colors of the East; the long striped "abba-
yeh," or countryman's coat of raw wool; the "kaf-
fiyeh," or head-cloth that falls to his shoulder; the
"aghal," or roll that keeps the cloth in place; the
light-colored under-gown with its cloth belt. We see
the women with their single long garment and the
head-cloth reaching to the waist or lower. They
bring their babies with them, astride on their shoulder
or their hip. The people sit or squat on the stones
or on the ground. Easily they leave their work or
their villages, and walk miles and miles to get some
message for their souls; for religion in the East is not
a matter of convenience, it is the breath of life.
Of course in a picture like this we must not look for
fine detail. It is impossible to see individual types
of character or to discover their peculiar spiritual
needs; nor can we discover the effect of Jesus' teach-

ing except that every one is listening intently and that crowds and crowds are coming up from the populous shore. Tissot no doubt intends just this. He is saying: "See the magnetic power of this preacher who can thus draw all men unto himself!"

This type of picture has its value. It helps us to place the story in its setting; it makes us for the moment see the narrative as it unfolded itself, and feel the reality of it all as we might not otherwise be able to. Most artists give us a translation of the story into another language; Tissot always speaks the language of Palestine. If he fails to give us also the spiritual message we seek in the incident, that is not the fault of the language he uses, but of his lack of spiritual insight. Tissot is a painter but not an artist; or perhaps more accurately an artist but not a seer. For the seer's insight we must turn to the Italians or the Germans or the Pre-Raphaelites; but the limitation of these seers is that they never saw Palestine.

In comparing this out-door method of reaching people with the synagogue method, one discovers the special excellence of each. The synagogue furnished Jesus at once with a religious audience. All who were there were Jews and they had some sort of interest in the religious aspirations of the nation. On the other hand, the rulers of the synagogue were conservative and they would not long continue to invite one to speak who held in such contempt the scribes and Pharisees and the religion they professed. It is interesting to note that while at the beginning of the ministry Jesus is constantly seen in the synagogues in all the villages, as the work progresses there is less

mention made of the synagogue and at last none at
all. But out-of-doors is the natural habitat of the
East. Men prefer it for work and play. There are
the great natural amphitheaters where a man can
speak to thousands, there are breezes to temper the
sun, there are the inspirations of long views and
ravishing colors, there are the illustrations close at
hand — the flowers arrayed like Solomon, the birds
that know no care, and all the types of life that walk
through the immortal parables. And for audience
there is the whole mixed world of Palestine and that
demi-monde of harlots and publicans who would never
have crossed the threshold of a synagogue. Out-of-
doors was Jesus' opportunity.

On the other hand, the great crowds and the
spaces are inimical to the personal touch. Men
may hear the word in bunches, but they come into
the Kingdom one by one, each bringing his doubts
and his limitations and his problems. These Jesus
must deal with patiently and with infinite iteration,
or the seed that has sprung up will never bear fruit.
As one reads the gospels one is struck by the fact
that out of the thousands who flocked to hear Jesus
and to be helped by him, only a handful became his
permanent disciples, and twelve of these were personally chosen before the days of the great crowds.
It was to this handful that Jesus gave most of his
teaching and his companionship during the last third
of his ministry.

BLOCH: " COME UNTO ME "

Matt. 11 : 28–30

Bloch, Karl Heinrich (1834–1890)
Original: a fresco in the Castle Frederiksberg, outside of Copenhagen, one of a series on the Life of Christ, painted between 1866 and 1884.
Reproductions:

Bloch was a Danish painter and evidently used Danish models for this picture. It is interesting to note how the various artists give us Italian Madonnas or German apostles or Swedish Christs indifferently, and if they have a message at all are able to express it in any guise. That is because the fundamental needs of the heart and the truths men live by are as broad as the world and as deep as the soul. When Jesus says " Come unto me," he speaks to the undifferentiated substance of our common humanity, — or shall we say divinity? for it cries out not for temporal satisfactions but for the living God.

This picture is a symbol: each person stands for a type and represents a definite phase of spiritual life. Let us study these people in order.

The man at the right is a criminal. His hands are bound with chains and his face still betrays the fear of the hunted. He dares not touch the Master; he even approaches from behind as if afraid of being seen. He " feebly trusts the larger hope "; his hands are folded hesitatingly as if he felt that prayer and its answer never could be for him, that forgiveness and freedom were too wonderful to be true.

155

> " Weary of earth and laden with my sin,
> I look at heaven and long to enter in;
> But there no evil thing may find a home,
> And yet I hear a voice that bids me come."

This longing to enter in is his passport to that land of freedom. If he has faith but to touch the hem of His garment, the shackles will fall away.

A man past middle life has thrown himself upon his knees, and with a clutch almost of desperation draws himself to the Master's side. His eyes are closed to shut out the sight of this wretched world and to shut in the vision of help and healing that has drawn him here. Is his malady a sickness or a moral plague? Something at least it is that has caused him infinite wretchedness and has left him barely strength to stagger to the Fount of Mercy. With the touch even of the garments there comes something almost of ecstasy into the face, as if at last, after years of pain, the sufferer has found release;

> " And a gleam
> As of the dawn on some dark forest cast,
> Seems on thy lifted forehead to increase;
> Lethe and Eunoë — the remembered dream
> And the forgotten sorrow — bring at last
> That perfect pardon which is perfect peace."

There is peace, too, on the face of the old man who sits by the other side of Jesus. It is not the peace of sin forgiven or of sickness past, for this kindly patriarch has suffered little. He has toiled patiently along life's pathway, bearing without complaint the trials of the road and cheering the hearts of his fellow-travelers with his faith and courage. Now in his old age God has granted him a full vision of what life means. The ideal he has followed afar off has become flesh; Heaven has come down to earth, and he at last beholds its glory, " the glory as of the only-begotten of the Father, full of grace and truth." His face might well be the face of Simeon as he cried, " Now, Lord, letest thou thy servant depart in peace according to thy word; for mine eyes have seen thy salvation."

The three on the left are perhaps mother and daughter and son. Blessed mother, who has kept, through all her life of toil, the aspirations of her youth, and whose soul leaps up to greet this man of God. Do you see how her peasant face is trans-figured by this moment of realization? All she has willed or hoped or dreamed of good she has suddenly found to exist, not its semblance but itself. Her life has been but a broken arc; here is the perfect round. And with that joy come awe and self-abasement as she realizes how poor her life has been. But how fortu-nate for the daughter that at the beginning of her womanhood she can have this vision of the perfect life! All through her journey it will be her guide and stay; and in the burden and heat of the day as she pauses to raise her face to the sky, like the reapers on Esdraelon, she will never fail to see the snows of Hermon eternally white against the blue, and feel its coolness and its balm. And the mother has brought the lad with her. He is a little frightened, perhaps, and puzzled. He is too young to know what it is to see Jesus, but not too young to feel the pull of a great personality at his heart. Soon the spiritual life in him will come to consciousness; soon he will hear a

157

voice saying, "Son, give me thy heart." When that day of awakening comes, will he see again in memory this gracious figure with its hands stretched out to all the world — stretched out to him? And before the evil days come will he say those fateful words, "Speak, Lord, for thy servant heareth"?

There is only one discordant person in the picture. He stands alone in the background, untouched by the call. His hard face, in part concealed by his hard hand, reveals the epitaph of a dead soul, of one who has sinned away his day of grace, whose Will to Believe in the unseen and the eternal has perished under the impact of things that are seen and temporal. The call of the market-place has long since drowned the call of Heaven. Life's values for him are all minted with the superscription of Cæsar, and there is nothing left for God. To such as him Jesus addressed those pathetic words that are at the same time a judgment, "Ye will not come unto me that ye might have life!"

Thus Bloch has given us not the seven ages of Man, but seven aspects of the soul.

KOMMER TILL MIG I ALLE SOM ARBETEN OCH ÄREN BETUNGADE OCIAGWIL WEDERQUICKA EDER

BLOCH: "COME UNTO ME"

MILLET: THE SOWER

Chapter VII

THE PARABLES

No one has ever denied that the Parables of Jesus are pre-eminent. They are the work of a Master Teacher. Their chief virtues are three:

1. Each contains a single truth. Jesus never lost his grip upon the essentials of his idea, never was betrayed into complex argument or fine-spun philosophizing so that the main thought was obscured.

2. To embody this single truth he chose a concrete image, a thing or a person well within the experience of his hearers. Probably in most instances the subject of the parable was at hand as he spoke, so that he had only to point to the sower in the field or the merchant on the road or the laborers going into the vineyard.

3. He knew how to throw the whole into an attractive and rememberable form. Each was brief — so brief that no one can retell the story in his own

159

words so compactly; and usually the words took the form of that ancient parallelism that makes Hebrew poetry and proverbs so delightful. No other literature can rival the simple effectiveness of the short epigrams in the Sermon on the Mount, or the longer stories of the Sower, the Two Foundations, the Wise and Foolish Virgins, the Talents. All this is not the result of accident; it is skill that has become a fine art.

Only those parables are studied here that have found a specially happy artistic treatment. Pictures of other parables are listed in the introductory section. If it is available, many will enjoy Eugène Burnand's book of illustrations of the Parables; and the fact that the text is in French will be no drawback.

MILLET: THE SOWER
Matt. 13 : 1–23;   Mark 4 : 1–20;   Luke 8 : 4–15

Millet, Jean Francois (1814–1875)

Original: The theme was long in his thoughts; sketched first in his youth and modified gradually to its present proportions. A picture showing the same figure on a less ample background is now in the Quincy Shaw collection, Boston. The present canvas, exhibited in the Salon of 1850, is owned by the Vanderbilt family of New York. When exhibited it was criticised by some as the attempt of a Socialist to call attention to the ills of the peasantry! and it was praised by only one critic.

Reproductions: Taber-Prang, 1, 2, 13.

" Behold, a sower went forth to sow." There is something epic and elemental in this beginning of Christ's parable: a noun and two verbs, with the earth to stand on. In Millet's picture there is hardly

160

more: a man of unrecognized individuality but with the figure of a peasant strides out across the hillside and scatters the seed with a wide throw. The day draws to a close, but still the oxen against the sky plow on and the sower scatters on, for there is no end to the work as there is none to the unfenced plain. The one-act drama of toil is here universalized in its most primitive setting. This sower is only one of the unnamed millions who have gone forth to sow since long before Adam's date, and his landscape of sky and brown earth is the soil out of which every sower sprang and into whose exhaustless bosom he sinks again. Each individual is but a member in the eternally repeated sequence of man, work, bread. And we feel as we look at this figure moving so inevitably across the slope that some power of which he is not aware is driving him on. Can it be the primal instinct for life?

Mrs. Julia Cartwright says of this picture and its painter: "It is the first page in Millet's great epic of labor. . . . He thought of the serious meaning of the sower's task, of the great issues that hang upon the seed time, and of the new life that germinates in the grain that he casts abroad to supply the bread of the coming years. He remembered the old custom, still practised in his boyhood, of uttering a few words of prayer and sowing the first seed in the form of a cross. And as he meditated over these old memories the great picture grew into being. . . . In that solitary figure, with his measured tread and superb action, the whole spirit of the peasant's calling is summed up with a power and concentration of thought worthy of Michelangelo." And we might add in view of the present crisis, that Millet has also painted here the hardihood and devotion to duty that are immortalizing the peasant-soldiers around Verdun — indeed, the entire peasantry of France.

Now it is interesting to reflect that Jesus also was a peasant, and that like Millet he knew what it was to earn his bread by the sweat of his brow. He knew all the gamut of toil. From his shop-door in Nazareth he could look down upon the ruddy plain of Esdraelon and see the sowers going forth to sow. Elemental things attracted him as they did Millet, — the sowing and reaping and threshing, the grinding and the baking, the drawing of water, the casting of nets, the building upon the sand or the rock; and like Millet, he made all of these elemental acts carry a meaning.

In the sower Jesus saw not only himself but each individual among his followers till the end of time. He saw the infinite work involved in planting his kingdom of love in the heart of man, — the long hours from dawn till twilight, through the long round of the seasons and the long trooping of the years. He saw the barbarous lands far off where the good seed ultimately must be sown. He saw the workers fall by the wayside, and the never-ending procession of the generations take their places. And over all he saw the Lord of the Harvest yearning for yet more laborers and for yet more bread for the unborn children of tomorrow. He was saddened too by the wastefulness and the disappointments of the sowing, the failure of good seed on the rocky places, the loss through harpy birds and strangling thorns; and he knew the scant yield that comes from shallow soil

162

and faulty plowing. The sower in the parable, as in the picture, is not only a worker but a man of sorrows and acquainted with grief.

In the spiritual life, as in the picture, there is a compulsion that is deeper than our personal wills. We may think it is duty that calls us, or hope that beckons us across new fields of toil. Therefore in the morning we sow the seed and in the evening withhold not our hand, spurred by the thought that upon our faithful sowing depends our own fuller spiritual life, and that our sixty- or hundred-fold may feed other hungerers after righteousness. But this Will to achieve the higher life is the push of an elemental instinct; a manifestation of God's will that man shall not live by bread alone and that to each generation there shall be transmitted in fuller measure the spiritual harvest of the past. The epic of Millet's sower is thus seen to be a fragment of a cosmic Epos of the Spirit whose argument is the salvation of a race.

MILLAIS: THE EVIL ONE SOWING TARES

Matt. 13 : 24–30; 36–43

Millais, Sir John Everett, Bart. (1829–1896)
Original: Exhibited at the Royal Academy in 1865; privately owned in England.
Reproductions:

We have here the antithesis of Millet's Sower. In the former picture we saw toil that expended itself in giving bread to the world; it was a vision of sadness out of which would some day come joy. The English Millais gives us a picture of grotesque

163

joy out of which will come toil and disappointment for the world, hatreds and bitterness without end. One might imagine that the field here being sown is just the other side of Millet's hill; that only an hour ago while the bright sunset tints were glowing, the faithful peasant of the other picture had strode over this land, rejoicing in the rich soil and covering it in imagination with the gold of harvest. But now in the shadows an Evil One is undoing all the labor, sowing the tares that spring up with deceptive blade and refuse to disclose their worthlessness till the good grain is choked and the hollow seeds have scattered to every wind. The Evil One treads on the heels of the Good One. It is a parable of enmity.

See how Millais has suggested an evil mind. This old sinner with his Shylock face, his rough gabardine, his hair blowing unkempt about, looks furtively over his shoulder to make sure that he is not observed. He clutches his sack of tares and chuckles over the gorgeous mischief he is about to do. The eye gleams with wicked delight, and one can easily see how through his sowing there runs the thought of the good man beyond the hill-crest who will shed tears a month hence. Contrast the other Sower for a moment: the strong frank step, the unafraid sweep of hand, the confidence that in due season God will send his rain and sun and the harvest. Then look at this craven, this stealer of the children's bread, this sneaking libel on toil that ravens up life's means instead of increasing them. And lest we should not read correctly this picture of unholy joy, Millais has put in a wolf for hunger and a snake for craft. This old man is both these things, the snake that strikes

MILLAIS: THE ENEMY SOWING TARES

PUVIS DE CHAVANNES: THE PRODIGAL SON

unseen and the wolf that devours what men have provided for their living.

How good a symbol for the Devil is this? We do not have the feeling here, as in Hofmann's picture of the Temptation, that this is meant to represent a real personality; rather it is a disposition, a condition, a spiritual state. It is the essential quality of whatever evil in the world arises from human wills. It does not picture mal-adjustment merely; not the evils that spring from chance or from limitations or from natural forces which man has not learned how to rule. Rather it shows us " pure cussedness " — the intent to injure; the Old Adam that will not down; short-sighted selfishness that refuses to co-operate; revenge for fancied slights; murderous hatred; envy of another's good; — all fruits of the spirit of an unorganized and undisciplined life. Millais could hardly have pictured the Devil more accurately.

We do not have to fall back upon any mythical Evil One to account for these facts in our experience. All we need is to have some Nathan point his prophetic finger at our bosom and say, " Thou art the man! "

PUVIS DE CHAVANNES: THE PRODIGAL SON

Luke 15 : 11–32

Puvis de Chavannes, Pierre Cécile (1824–1898)
Original: One of his few easel-pictures, painted in 1879; privately
    owned.
Reproductions:

The Prodigal Son is such a universal type that he has been portrayed successfully in widely different ways. Tissot has given us the most extreme individuation in his four pictures of a young Englishman. In the first he shows us a young man setting out from his seaside home, a typical English globe-trotter down to his " sticks," his " luggage " and his travelling tweeds. In the second, the hero dines riotously with geisha girls in far-away Japan. In the third he lands back in England from a cattle-steamer, while the family in various states of mind are on the dock to meet him. The fourth presents the rehabilitated prodigal in college flannels coming across the homestead lawn from his boating. It is all modern and as true as life. These pictures would have been presented here but for the fact that they are merely illustrations: they translate into English the incidents of the prodigal's career but they make the most meager transcription of his spirit. In Puvis de Chavannes, on the other hand, the spectacular accompaniments of the story are not suggested, and the whole appeal is made on the basis of an inner experience.

In the present picture we cannot tell what country is given; it may be Palestine or China or France, — as a matter of fact, it makes no difference. Only it is a barren land, a hint, as it were, of the prodigal's wasted life; as the blasted tree speaks of his wrecked fortunes and the pigs proclaim his degradation. The youth is supposed to be taking care of the swine, but he has turned his back on them. Business more important than they is on hand and is going to be settled before the sun goes down. The wretched boy sits on a ragged rock, himself in rags, and in the intensity of his thought he hugs his naked breast and grips his legs together. He is a picture of want and irresolute revery.

But our main interest centers in that one burning eye! Deep-set and haggard though it is, a light of memory and of conscience redeems it and shows us that the soul is still alive. Before it are passing pictures out of his past, some faded and hideous, some sweet and appealing; but the wonder of it is that each of these pictures stands now in a different light from what it did before, as if a wizard had wrought on it with magic! There are the scenes of pleasure, one by one, the episodes of the riotous living, once so brilliant and altogether to be desired, but seen now from the distance of this field of swine, so garish and tawdry. Here comes the sequence of his loves, his charmers, who once through the glamor of wine seemed fit companions of the Graces, but now vampires all, — " a rag and a bone and a hank of hair." There is the dull old home with the dull old people in it; yet somehow those sober harmonies now begin to glow with the richness of remembered dreams, and in particular that father's face tugs at the heart and brings the hands instinctively to the bosom. How the hard knocks of life have laid bare the eternal values! The apples of Sodom that looked so fair in their baskets of tinsel have turned to ashes at the touch, and what once seemed only dross now gleams like gold. O son, son! Haven't you had enough of wilfulness and sin, the wages of which the devil is now paying you to the uttermost farthing? Hold fast, I pray you, to that picture of the old home till its outlines shut out every other sight, — and at the door the bowed and gray old father looking long, long, long, for you!

DÜRER: THE PRODIGAL SON

Luke 15 : 11–32

Dürer, Albrecht (1471–1528)
Original: a drawing.
Reproductions:

Dürer presents a moment subsequent to that in Puvis de Chavannes' picture. The prodigal has come to himself. He has held the memory of the old home steadily in mind till it has burned down into his soul and scorched the will into action. So he kneels among the pigs, and prays.

This picture is realism of the right kind. We are in a fifteenth century German village — likely enough a back-yard of old Nuremberg, whose quaintness even now travellers go far to see. Here are the long steep roofs with the drooping eyes of windows staring from the slopes. Here are chimney-pots and gables and towers, and an ample thatch-roofed barn on the right. Wheels. A harrow lying points up. A dunghill in which a cock scratches lustily. A split log hollowed into a trough. Pigs! — all sizes and in all stages of desire and satisfaction, one at least with both feet in the trough in order to get all the joy there is in feeding. The great boar beyond the prodigal looks sideways up to make sure that his keeper is not preparing to feed also, while the vicious one opposite prepares to see that he shall not! What a place for prayer! This poor fellow needed no sweet persuasion to draw him to the throne of grace, no glamor of the "long-drawn aisle and fretted vault," or

> "Storied windows richly dight,
> Casting a dim religious light."

DÜRER: THE PRODIGAL SON

RODIN: THE PRODIGAL SON

These for religious sybarites and saints surfeited with grace! Soul-hunger wrought this miracle. "God be merciful to me a sinner" unlocked the windows of heaven and brought the deluge of the blessing of forgiveness. Who shall say what thoughts and half-formed prayers brought him to this pass of decision? — but Dürer no doubt means to indicate by that intellectual and cultured face that consciousness of degradation had something to do with it. Like Ibrahim ben Adhem of the Muslim faith, he heard a voice crying, "Thou wast not born for this!" And that better self which he had so long kept locked in the dungeons of forgetfulness broke down the door and claimed its right to rule. This is proof that he is better than the swine, though fallen lower than they: for they are happy with the husks, while his soul is in torment till it finds its way back, not to the full table of the Father, but to the Father's heart. Surely the One who first drew the outlines of this parable knew all the depths of the human soul!

RODIN: THE PRODIGAL SON

Rodin, Auguste François (1840–   )
Original: A marble statue first shown in an exhibition of the sculptor's works in 1900; now, by his gift, the property of the State.
Reproductions:

One more interpretation of this prodigal's experience, this time by a Frenchman. With Rodin as with Dürer, the supreme moment is the "coming to himself." But Dürer conceives that moment to occur because the prodigal realizes his physical degradation: he, the delicately-nurtured son of respectability, brought so low that he envies the very pigs their happiness! Rodin, on the other hand, has nothing to suggest about swine, there are no externals whatever — not even rags to screen the prodigal's shame: he will have us understand that a naked soul is wrestling with God. This prodigal is the most profound and the most spiritual of all.

The statue is a marvel. The lines are executed with a haunting beauty while the face and pose express entreaty that is nothing less than passionate. One's dominant impression of it is of two arms straining to heaven in an agony of prayer. It is a true " De profundis." The soul has gone so low that it can go no lower, and the way back has been lost. " The pains of Hell gat hold " on him, and a cry has gone up that would rend heaven. It is a translation into stone of passage after passage of the penitential Psalms:

" Out of the depths have I cried unto thee, O Lord."

" Hide not thy face from me,
Lest I become like them that go down into the pit."

" O Lord, why castest thou off my soul?
Why hidest thou thy face from me? "

" Thy fierce wrath is gone over me;
Thy terrors have cut me off."

" Have mercy upon me, O God, according to thy
lovingkindness:
Wash me thoroughly from mine iniquity,
And cleanse me from my sin.
For I acknowledge my transgressions;
And my sin is ever before me.

Against thee, thee only, have I sinned,
And done that which is evil in thy sight.

.   .   .   .

Purge me with hyssop, and I shall be clean:
Wash me, and I shall be whiter than snow.
Create in me a clean heart, O God,
And renew a right spirit within me.
Cast me not away from thy presence;
And take not thy holy Spirit from me."

Is all this the language of the Prodigal? It can
be nothing else. It is the cry of an outraged conscience, the like of which has tortured every breast
since guilty Cain; it is the wail of the Eumenides as
they hunt the soul through all the mazes of subterfuge
till they bring it at last to bay. And although the
Father stands at the home-door with straining eyes
and outstretched arms, no power can turn our guilty
feet toward him till we are ready to sob out, " Father,
I have sinned! "

Rodin's Prodigal has reached that pass.

TISSOT: THE PRODIGAL'S RETURN
Luke 15 : 11–32

Tissot, James (1836–1902)
Original: One of the series on the Life of Christ, painted during
the artist's residence in Palestine, 1886–1895. Now owned
by the Brooklyn Institute, New York.
Reproductions:

The parable of the Prodigal would not be complete without some representation of the home-coming.
Artists have been less frequently drawn to this incident of the story, and when they have attempted to
portray it they have succeeded rather poorly. Some

show the riches and the comforts of the home; some
show the kindly indulgence of the father who is happy
that the wild oats have now all been sown; some
show the happiness of the restored wanderer; and
one (Burnand) shows him hiding behind a tree in the
lawn till he can overcome his shame and get courage
enough to approach the house. Tissot is the only
one, so far as the writer can discover, who has gotten
at the heart of the matter: and the truth he teaches
is that two souls have been suffering.

Here is the meeting — the boy and the old man.
It takes place in one of those Syrian city lanes where
the buildings overarch the way. Doors to several
houses open out upon the lane, and curious people
lean forth, Eastern fashion, to see the strange sight.
A grave old fellow stands at the extreme right and
shows by the position of his hands that he finds this
a moving spectacle. The two chief figures are dressed
in modern Eastern style, which may or may not approximate the clothing of two thousand years ago.
The Prodigal is on his knees with his arms about his
father's waist; the father is embracing his son's
head and trying in vain to kiss the ashamed and
repentant boy.

The figure of the old man is most appealing. He
is feeble and broken in spirit, but all the strength that
remains to him is here poured forth in self-effacing
forgiveness. It is as if the long strain were over for
him too, the anxious and lonely days, the endless
nights of wakefulness, the daily endeavor to picture
what good or what ill is today crossing the pathway
of the wayward son: — Now perhaps he is in Antioch,
now in Tarsus; now, alas! he may be in wicked

TISSOT: THE PRODIGAL'S RETURN

SOORD: THE LOST SHEEP

Ephesus where virtue, they say, is dead; now Euroclydon that wails across the bay from the rolling sea may be dashing him on the cruel Lybian strand, or the pirates be putting him up for sale in the slave-market at Delos! As the heart of Elisha went forth with Gehazi, so has the father's heart gone step by step out into the dark, following by some instinctive clairvoyance the erring feet down the broad road to sin. And just as the father's heart knows Sin to be worse than misery and want, so it assures him that no lever in this world or the next is so powerful to raise the fallen as Forgiveness. So while the boy is stammering through the speech that was to settle his status as a slave, the father pours the flood-tides of redeeming love into his soul, and the words so carefully rehearsed are swept away into the great gulf of forgetfulness.

Try, if you please, to invent a different ending for this story. Make the old man rebuff the boy at first; have him stand on his dignity and require of the rascal proofs of his change of heart; let him read him a sermon on wild oats before the forgiving kiss is bestowed; have him take the penitent at his word — as he richly deserves to be taken — and try him out with the slaves for a year or two, till the family pride, or outraged justice, is satisfied. Imagine, in short, *any possible ending but this*, and you have destroyed the noblest picture of redeeming grace ever created, and lowered God to the level of man's virtue. Heathen religions in plenty, and some versions of the Christian religion, furnish us with the alternatives suggested above, or worse; Christ alone shows us the suffering Father who saves by forgiving.

SOORD: THE LOST SHEEP

Luke 15 : 3–7

Soord, Alfred (–1916)
Original:
Reproductions: Taber-Prang, 1, 2, 4, 13.

The trouble with most " Good Shepherds " is that they are good for nothing. The theme has been handled over and over again from the time of the Catacombs down, but usually one sees the same type of picture, the figure of a pretty man holding a lamb in his bosom. To one who has seen shepherds in Palestine there is something particularly repugnant in such a representation. No real shepherd ever wore the elegant draperies that adorn these artists' models. No shepherd ever sported such ambrosial curls or posed so gracefully, or showed such an absence of character in his face. On the contrary, when you come upon a real shepherd in the shepherd's country, something is apt to grip your heart and your throat. Shepherding there is a man's job! There you see the rough jacket made of a fleece turned wool-side in; the bare bronzed bosom, the bare legs scratched with the thorns, the rough shoes of rawhide, the great club of oak with its knot on the end heavy enough to fell a bear; the high-stepping stride and the muscles like steel that endure the tramps over rocky country, the fearless eye that can face danger alone; and you often see a lamb in the strong arms. Such is the person Jesus had in mind when he said " I am the Good Shepherd."

Soord has presented something like the original parable, — not the one about the sheep-fold in John

174

10 : 1–16, but the parable of the Lost Sheep in Luke, which is a parable of rescue. This sheep is lost. No careful shepherd would have led his flock into such a pasture as this; the foolish sheep herself is responsible for the situation. Too much self-confidence, too adventurous a spirit, ignorance of the precipices and of the eagles circling high in the blue and waiting for things to die! Or was it sheer carelessness? Whatever the cause, here she is, clinging to the edge of nothing, unable to move, with the great gulf below and the eagles drawing nearer and nearer. Night and storm are shutting in. The situation is desperate.

A copy of this picture hangs in the room where the writer is accustomed to lecture to theological students. One day while the room was being used for a meeting of the Trustees, the President noticed that tears were rolling down the cheeks of one of the older members of the Board. As soon as opportunity offered he asked what the trouble was.

" It is that picture," said the man. " I have been looking and looking at it, and I see how truly it pictures me. I was just where that sheep is. I had lost my way. There was nothing below but the bottomless pit, and the eagles were coming down. Then Christ found me and saved me."

That was a simple statement of facts, but the facts were of transcendent importance for that individual: when he thought on them the fountains of the great deep were broken up! So simply and so forcefully may an artist picture the most profound truths of our experience.

BONIFAZIO: PARABLE OF THE RICH MAN

Luke 16 : 19–31

Bonifazio, Veronese I, or Veneziano (1490?–1540)
Original: 6′ 8″ x 14′ 2″, figures life size. Painted at the order of
Cardinal Grimani. Dives is said to be Henry VIII, and the
left courtesan Anne Boleyn, a reflection on that king's anti-
papal policy. Bought of the family of Grimani by Prince
Eugene and given to the Academy in Venice, where it now is.
Reproductions:

The parable of Dives and Lazarus is one of the most
vivid and searching that Jesus uttered. Bonifazio,
though not a great artist, has entered sympathetically
into the first part of the story, producing in this
picture a piece of sentiment that in spite of time retains much of its original effectiveness.

We are looking in upon a rich man's villa. The
house extends far to the rear and to the left, and beyond are the pleasure gardens. In the spacious
piazza some of the servants train a horse, one gives a
hound a drink, another worries a falcon, while others
are busy with household tasks. In the foreground
three groups catch our eye. On our left, Dives himself in dark red robe of richest material sits with two
courtesans at table. The banquet is over, but he
lingers over the wine and the music. He turns to
pay a compliment to the woman on his right, holding
out to her a golden bowl: the woman is a belle,
with peach-and-cream complexion and with a gorgeous dress of velvet rose, the sleeves of puffed satin.
The second group is a piece of poetic imagination. A
sweet-faced girl is singing to the accompaniment of
her mandolin, while a cellist and a flute-player fill
in the counterpoint. A little negro dwarf, sumptuously

176

and fantastically clad, holds the music book for them.
The second courtesan, whose face certainly belies her
trade, leans down gracefully to listen. She is by all
odds the most attractive character in the picture,
sweet, pensive, almost melancholy. The music has
touched a tender chord in her bosom, for she turns
away from her luxurious lord who still holds her
hand, and she looks far away at the days of her
innocence — the days that are no more. The face
and the position suggest the melancholy sweetness of
Wordsworth as he listened to the Highland Reaper
singing of

> " Old, unhappy, far-off things,
> And battles long ago."

All this is Bonifazio's translation of the " purple and
fine linen " and the " fared sumptuously," into the
Venetian dialect. There was many a Dives in Venice
in the sixteenth century.

Contrasting with this and in a way completing the
accuracy of this transcription from Italian life is
Lazarus the beggar. No more perfect beggar was
ever drawn. There may be more ragged ones and more
wretched ones, but none more psychologically correct.
Notice the approach on one knee, the gracefully in-
sinuated hand, the intentionally appealing eye, —
yes, even the soft and tearfully modulated voice that
is just low enough not to distract from the music and
just loud enough to form an accompaniment of pleasing melancholy, to be the proper foil to the joys of
the feast. Here is the antithesis mentioned in the
parable: " Thou in thy lifetime receivedst thy good
things, and Lazarus likewise evil things." Bonifazio

177

has given us a hint that some day the conditions will be reversed; for in the background to the right he has placed a burning building — type of Gehenna "where the fire is not quenched."

The artist was no doubt intent on painting a masterpiece for the good cardinal rather than preaching a sermon. Nevertheless the parable on which it is based carries its lesson of everlasting truth. It is this: Dives was sent to torment not because he was rich but because he ignored the responsibilities of riches. Lazarus may have been no saint, but as a human being he was entitled to help that he did not get, and God made the loss good to him. The parable is couched in the phraseology and the imagery of the day, and we are not warranted in building a theological structure upon such a slight foundation; but the ethical principle, which Jesus here elevates into a religious principle, is unmistakable and true. In the parable of the Last Judgment Jesus elaborates it still further and makes benevolence a cornerstone in his theory of life. Blessed is the heart that feels and the hand that serves, for of such is the kingdom of Love.

BURNAND: THE GREAT SUPPER

Luke 14 : 12–24

Burnand, Eugene (1850–   )
Original: Exhibited in the International Exposition at Paris in 1898; now in the museum at Winterthur (?).
Reproductions: Braun & Co., F. I. E.

This is not a great picture, but it induces revery; and the revery may outrun what is here given, just as the artist's fancy has outrun the gospel story.

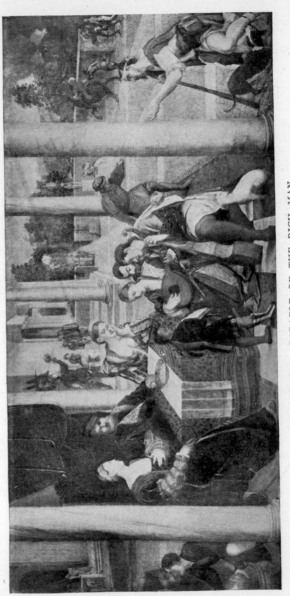

BONIFAZIO: PARABLE OF THE RICH MAN

BURNAND: THE GREAT SUPPER

The parable speaks of one servant who was messenger to the outcast, but here the children and the servants of the household are all messengers. This is more than Eastern hospitality; it is a parable of the Spirit of Christ.

See what we have. In the background through the trees gleams a grand house. Garlands festoon the walls, the windows stand wide open, and the Lord of the Manor looks forth with a kindly impatience because his hospitality has had to wait so long. Servants with baskets of good things on their heads are hurrying toward the festal hall. Under the trees by the house a table had been spread where a few of the early comers are being entertained. Nearer us a group of children stand, while a sweet-faced lady puts on their wedding garments. In the foreground to the right, a son in white bows graciously to the arriving guests and with voice and gesture speaks his father's welcome. And here you must observe that the figure in the window, tiny as he is with distance, is the true center of the composition. The servants hurrying on our right, the lithe contours of the son and the broad path itself all point toward him; and on our left, by gesture or by grouping, the figures lead our eyes to the same Master of the House. This is his feast, his invitation; it is his spirit that inspires all. The supreme joy also will be his.

The larger part of the picture is concerned with the procession of the poor, the maimed, the halt and blind, representatives of the submerged nine-tenths who never once have had an inkling of how the other tenth live. This group is not so much a study in wretchedness as in limitations. The people are poor

179

but respectable, they have clothing yet and character; but toil and poverty have kept them down below the level of opportunity. Take them one by one: — the blind old grandfather; the mother with the patient face and the almost broken spirit; her husband, suspicious of the rich whose freedom from toil he long has envied; the little girl and her bashful brother; the lame man whose only hope of getting there lies in the strong shoulders of his helpers; that woman's face beyond his, her eyes of curious joy peering from beneath the hand; and that last group, especially the young woman whose sensitive eagerness is so appealing. When the ordeal is over and they return to their obscurity, they will be happy to live this golden day over many times in memory!

But the sweetest part of the picture is the Children of the Home; that innocent one who leads the way, that grave young boy with the olive twig of peace, those two strong helpers of the lame — clean-limbed, clear-eyed, their father's joy and crown. Even the servant in the dark tunic has caught the gentleness of this house of hospitality, and points the timid ones to the waiting Master. Oh, the graciousness of this welcome! It is not the spirit of condescension but the true spirit of *noblesse oblige* that flows down from the open window through the children to the hearts of the poor.

Who does not stand condemned before this picture when he turns the parable upon himself? Where here are we? Is this our house in spirit, — humble though our actual roof may be? Are these children our thoughts and deeds searching the lanes of wretchedness and compelling the dwellers to come in?

Is ours the graciousness of the welcoming son, as we think of the riches and the opportunity of the Father's house? Or is that manor-house our church, towards whose doors the poor are flocking, and is the gospel feast there offered food indeed for the down-and-out? If all this were so, then the hungry would long ago have been fed, and the world's bitterness would have been healed. But instead we hear the hard voices of the wretched and the lonely and the sinful, rising from tenement and shop and our neighbor's door; and their words stand as our condemnation: " I was hungry and ye gave me no meat, naked and ye clothed me not, sick and in prison and ye visited me not."

HUNT: LIGHT OF THE WORLD

John 8 : 12; Rev. 3 : 20

Hunt, William Holman (1827–1910)

Original: Painted in 1854, his first success, and that a doubtful one in the estimation of the public! It has since become immensely popular. The original hangs in a chapel of Keble College, Oxford. A replica hangs in St. Paul's, London, on a pier in the south aisle.

Reproductions: Taber-Prang, 1, 2, 5, 6, 13, 18.

The emotional value of this picture cannot be expressed by any half-tone or photograph, for it lies to a large extent in color. Whether one looks at the original or at the more frequently seen replica the effect is the same; it is a romance, a poem, a symphony, a dream, in which the wizardry of pigment changes a plain mental image into pulses of living fire.

Imagine the grass as deeply green as mountainous

storm-waves at sea; the flowers and fallen fruit as lustrous as frost and light can make them. Imagine the cobalt blue of night and the radiance of stars tempered by the faintest imaginable flush of dawn. Imagine the soft and spotless robe of Christ illuminated and shadowed by the ruddy gold of the candlelight; the rich embroidery of the outer mantle shimmering partly with light from the east and partly with hidden fire of its own; the enormous brooch blazing with the dartled gleams of ruby and emerald, jacinth and chrysoprase. Imagine also the door, — not plain wood, but gray with weather and stained with the umbers and the chromes of iron-rust from the hinges and the nails; and the weeds all stark with autumn brown and " the sere, the yellow leaf." Then you must imagine the face with its fringe of chestnut beard and hair, its eyes of blue, and its coronet of gleaming gold and bramble ivy-green. If your soul is keyed to sensuous beauty, this picture sweeps all the strings.

But it is not color alone that has made this picture immortal — as it surely is immortal. There is a wealth of meaning in it that reveals itself in deeper and deeper levels as your thought and fancy play over it. It is a many-sided symbol that speaks now of poetry, now of myth, now of philosophy, and always of the spiritual life; while all of these aroused memories and depths and insights vibrate and echo within you not as sharply defined idea but as cadences of feeling. It is music mingled with memory and prophecy.

* * * * *

A pilgrim and a stranger stands before the door of my soul. I have closed the door in his face; or rather it has long been closed and bolted in anticipation of such a call. Not for a twelve-month have I opened the door; the grass without shows no footprint, and the rank growths of weed and ivy have flowered and cast their seed and withered undisturbed, and the bats cling by day and hover about the eaves by night. If the truth must be told, I have never once opened this door of my soul, and I do not intend to open it. There is nothing outside but the great world lying in darkness; and within I am at home. But I hear the knocking, knocking, — or is it my tell-tale heart beating, beating, as I stand in trepidation just within the door, my ear almost against it.

Though I do not open the door, I see as with clairvoyancy the person of my visitor. He is clad in a seamless robe spotlessly white, such as priests wear when they minister in holy places, such as the High Priest wears when he enters within the veil to make atonement for the sins of the people. Is he indeed a priest, and has he come to make possible for me an access to God? Shall I somehow find in him a Mediator, who would gather to himself all that I fain would be and cannot, and thus take my better self, in his own person, into the Holy of Holies and ask upon it the blessing of the Most High? My soul needs such a priest, for what I now am could not see God and live.

But there is another robe — too rich for the priestly office. None but kings should so clothe themselves in glory, the glory of tapestries of the thread of gold, with brede of pearl and pattern of woven jewels. None but kings should wear a brooch like this.

One side, like Aaron's breastplate, is studded with the twelve precious stones of the tribes of Israel; it is the Covenant of the Law. And on the other side flashes the circle of eternity with twelve precious stones of the foundations of the New Jerusalem; while between them, with an arm stretched out to each, is a Cross, binding the Old Covenant to the New and holding in place upon the person of the wearer the robe of sovereignty. Has this stranger also come to rule over me? And by what compulsion shall he bring my soul under his sway?

And I see crowns. One crown is gold, the circlet edged with rays and set with jewels. This must be an ancestral, an eternal crown, placed upon his brow by a royal Father in token of his right to rule. But the other is a crown of thorns, placed there by his enemies as a token of hate and a badge of suffering. Has he worn this wretched crown to remind me of the shame he once endured, to show how love can conquer hate, and through suffering lead the world's heart back to God? And lo, a miracle! The thorns have now lost their sharpness, the dead bramble lives again and has put forth leaves " that shall be for the healing of the nations."

I can feel the light the stranger carries beating through my door and into my brain. Its ray is golden on the garment and shows the utter purity of this robe of righteousness; but it smites all else like the fierce light of conscience and throws the shadows of the stalks of the dead past upon my door. It burns into my sight also the red apples that the trees have cast before my dwelling. Does the fruit belong to me — and this orchard that somehow I have not

184

seen till now? There are in my memory fragments of
a story of an ancestral orchard and of forbidden fruit,
of disobedience and a flaming sword, of a lost Paradise
and a curse of darkness that should blind the generations till a Sun of Righteousness shall arise with healing in his wings. The East is now flushing with
dawn; can it be He? And gleaming through the
silhouetted trees I see the shimmer of a river, as of
the water of life, clear as crystal; and through the
branches, stars of hope paling in the light they have
heralded. Is all this light and beauty for me? And
has the heart of this visitor led him to my door
while it is yet dark that I may not miss even the
first beam of the golden dawn of day?

I seem to see a tenderness and a love like this in
the stranger's face; a love that has known suffering,
a tenderness that penetrates a heart of adamant like
the imponderable ether, a patience that will knock
and knock till the stars are old, a silent will to rule
that, though it urge its claim with gentleness, will
no more be turned back than will the dials of time.
What shall I do with this strange and kingly pilgrim?

> " Knocking, knocking, who is there?
> Waiting, waiting, grand and fair!
> 'Tis a pilgrim, strange and kingly;
> Never such was seen before.
> Ah, my soul, for such a wonder
> Wilt thou not undo the door? "

" Behold, I stand at the door and knock. If any
man hear my voice and open the door, I will come in
to him, and will sup with him, and he with me."

185

HUNT: THE LIGHT OF THE WORLD

HOFMANN: CHRIST HEALING **THE** SICK

CHAPTER VIII

THE MINISTRY OF HEALING

PICTURES FOR STUDY

Hofmann: Healing the Sick
Keller: The Awakening
Keller: Raising the Daughter of Jairus
Zimmermann: Christ the Consoler

With Jesus, teaching and healing went hand in hand. He does not seem to have held a modern theory that one must prepare the way for a spiritual ministration by first providing a full dinner-pail and a dispensary. Jesus concerned himself primarily with sin and its elimination, and would gladly have left to others the secondary work of relieving misery. The Kingdom of God was for him not meat and drink, but righteousness and peace. But naturally he could not shut his eyes to the suffering that surrounded him. Professor Kent has given us a graphic picture of these conditions and Jesus' life in the midst of them in his *Life and Teachings of Jesus* (p. 97).

"Since the days of Alexander the vice of the East and the West had poured into Palestine. Wrong living and thinking had distorted the bodies and minds and souls of men. At every turn beggars, afflicted with all kinds of loathsome diseases, cried for help and healing. Oriental charity then as now was lavish; but it pauperized rather than permanently relieved the needy. The lot of the insane was especially pitiable. The current scientific explanation of most

187

types of insanity attributed it to malignant demons that took possession of those abnormally afflicted. The victims of insanity also shared this ancient theory, and it only added to the horrors of their hallucinations.

" Into this life Jesus entered, with a robust, wholesome body, with a mind that was clear and sane and that recognized many of the hidden causes that lay back of the guilt and suffering which confronted him. He was inspired by a divine pity and an intense passion not only to relieve but to heal and save the ignorant, shepherdless, suffering masses that crowded about in the eager hope that he could help them. Joyously, confidently, he met the human needs that appealed to him, for he knew that life and health and happiness were the good gifts that the heavenly Father was eager to bestow upon his needy children. Viewed in the broad perspective of history, it is incredible that a teacher and lover of men like Jesus could have lived and worked in the Galilee of his day and not healed men's bodies and minds, as well as their souls."

The best pictures on this subject also are by modern masters.

HOFMANN: CHRIST HEALING THE SICK

Matt. 4 : 23–25; Mark 3 : 7–12; Luke 6 : 17–19

Hofmann, Johann Michael Ferdinand Heinrich (1824–1911)
Original: A drawing.
Reproductions:

Hofmann has given us a sketch of what happened to Jesus every day of his Galilean ministry. The

only criticism one might make of the picture is that
the street is a little too clean, the houses a little too
architectural, the people a little too refined and self-
contained, a little too bent on participating in the
spiritual blessing that we are wont to associate with
the cures. Tissot gives us perhaps a more realistic
picture, the backgrounds drawn from actual life, and
the ragged men and women and children of the
crowd jostling one another in the attempt to be first
in the procession. The Gospels certainly give us a
vivid enough idea of this therapy; over and over
repeated one reads of " the crowd," " the multitude,"
" great multitudes," who throng him so that he
cannot so much as eat, and so that the question
" Who touched me? " sounds to the disciples absurd.
They speak of the demoniacs, the impotent man, him
of the withered hand, her with the issue of blood,
the one with the spirit of infirmity, 'the dumb devil,
the dumb and blind, the paralytic, the deaf, the
dropsical, those that had fevers and leprosies, " all
those that were sick," yea, even those who were dead.
Here is a clinic as varied as human ills; and that we
may not think the Gospel picture overdrawn, we have
precisely the same story of suffering and hope and
healing in the annals of our Medical Missions. " What
wouldst thou that I should do unto thee? " — " Lord,
that I may receive my sight! " The question, the
world over, calls out the fundamental human wish.
It is to relieve these primary wants and prepare the
way for more spiritual blessings that our medical
missions were established, and that Mr. Rockefeller
is devoting a hundred millions of dollars in China
alone.

189

It is interesting to consider why Jesus should have
done so much of this work. Certainly he did not
hope by this means to substantiate his Messianic
claim, — he fought out that question during his temptation. Nor did he regard this power to cure disease
as a special mark of divinity, for his disciples also
exercised the power. There seems to be no explanation except that his keen sympathy for men would
not let him rest in the presence of suffering till he
had done his utmost to relieve it. This work was an
injury to Jesus in two ways: it drew heavily on his
vitality so that frequently he had to go into "a
desert place," sometimes alone and sometimes with
the twelve, in order that by prayer to God and communion with his disciples he might regain his poise;
and it distracted the thoughts of men from the message he had for their souls. This latter aspect was a
serious danger to his mission. Indeed it would seem
that toward the latter part of his ministry, when he
realized that his time was short, he very largely gave
up his work of healing and bent all his energies to
his spiritual task.

And yet it is undoubtedly true that Jesus intended
healing and the general relief of suffering to constitute a large part of the work of his disciples. His
charge to the Twelve was, "Heal the sick, raise the
dead, cleanse the lepers, cast out devils." Even more
indicative of his emphasis on works of mercy is the
parable of the Last Judgment, in which the sole basis
of admission to heaven is declared to be the feeding
of the hungry and ministering to the sick and the
imprisoned. The love that prompts such service
Jesus felt to be the very heart of his gospel.

190

This picture suggests another line of thought: How are we to regard these stories of miraculous cure? Did every wonder happen just as the Gospels record it, whether or not it contradicts the laws which in this scientific age we are wont to regard as inviolable? Or are there degrees of probability and reasonableness discoverable in the various narratives? Every one must answer these questions for himself in the light of the demands of his intellectual and spiritual nature and of his general philosophy of life. The writer, however, has no hesitation in stating his own belief as follows:

1. Many of Jesus' cures, miraculous as they seemed to the bystanders and the Gospel writers, have been duplicated in our day. They result from the influence that mind can exert over the human body — an influence by no means understood but absolutely demonstrated to exist. Professor Holtzmann in his Life of Jesus (p. 193) refers to miraculous cures wrought when the Holy Coat of Treves was exhibited in 1891 — cures the validity of which was established by the "perfectly trustworthy evidence of German physicians of unimpeachable reputation." There were, out of thirty-eight cases of cure, eleven in which no other medical reasons whatever could be offered, and faith alone must have been the efficient instrument. These eleven included atrophy of the optic nerve of many years' standing, lupus, paralysis of the arm, complete loss of the use of arms and legs, St. Vitus dance, a serious abdominal complaint, blindness of one eye and paralysis of an arm consequent upon brain fever, chronic intestinal disorder, a cancerous tumor, caries of the spine, and a chronic inflammation

of the spinal marrow. " Facts like these," says Holtzmann, " which are not really open to question, will make Jesus' works of healing also seem not impossible."

2. There is another class of miracles, like raising the dead, which at present we see no way to explain, and yet which may some day be explained when we understand better the psychic nature and powers of man, and of such a wonderful personality as Jesus in particular. We must not reject these stories, but hold our judgment in suspense and wait for more light.

3. There are others, for example, turning the water into wine, cursing the fig tree, stilling the tempest, etc., which seem to be irreconcilable with the constitution and laws of the universe. In these cases — granted that science will not again revise her list of laws! — we must either reject the narrative as a mistaken interpretation of what took place; or regard it as a conscious allegory of some spiritual truth, or as a legend that grew up about an extraordinary personality. That there is some rational way of accounting for these narratives is not open to doubt, if we believe in a rational universe. In the meantime these three ways of viewing the records are in no way inconsistent with the highest possible interpretation of Christ's nature and mission, and certainly not with any reasonable view of scriptural inspiration.

KELLER: THE AWAKENING

Luke 8 : 40-42,   49-56

Keller, Albert von (1844–   )
Original: A preliminary study for the Raising of Jarius' Daughter.
Reproduction: In color, " Die Kunst Unserer Zeit," Vol. 19, p. 145.

This picture is introduced as a foil to the one that follows it. Both are studies in the same problem — and that a psychological one — and are by the same artist. Keller was exceedingly interested in hypnotism and spiritualism, evidently not for their bearing upon religion but because they furnished him with extraordinary problems in painting; and for twenty-five years under the inspiration of Charcot and others he made diligent researches into these realms. The theme of the raising of Jairus' daughter was the special one selected for exposition; for it he made more than a hundred preliminary sketches and studies, the present picture among them.

We are in some vaguely-sketched death-chamber that is filled with a brown gloom like that which might light the kingdoms of the departed. Spectators of some kind are dimly to be seen in the back of the room, but they are not there to be identified. They peer through the darkness like the vague presences seen through the delirium of fever; they are a part of the mystery and awe that surround the act. So is the night, and the palpitating flare of the torch that high up somewhere behind strikes down upon the chief actors. In the foreground lies the stiff and emaciated figure of a girl covered with the winding-sheet. A yard beyond the foot of the corpse stands Jesus, erect, but with head straining forward in the intensity of his effort, and his hands kinked into attitudes that suggest the " passes " of a hypnotizer. Through auto-suggestion, or other modes of occult procedure, he has kindled in himself the power necessary for the act; and now he emits an intense and silent energy of the will that shocks the dead one back to life. The corpse has raised its head in response to this magic summons.

The torch illuminates only the head and shoulders of Christ, his hands, and the bier. Seen in its original color, the effect is striking, not to say uncanny. Every element is calculated to our nerves to a nicety. The light sheds upon the green robe of Christ the luster of dragon-scales; upon the hands it glances and shimmers and corruscates until we can feel the electric thrills that run from the finger-tips toward the dead girl. We are attending a séance of the most dramatic kind; in fact, were it not for the halo about the head of Christ, we might think we were in the operating-room of some Madam Blavatsky!

Please consider, now, why we cannot accept this as an interpretation of the gospel miracle. Jesus was a wonder-worker; he did the most astonishing things " by the finger of God "; and the more we know of the mysteries of the psychic life, the more convinced we are that the divine power manifested itself in these cases through the channels of psychic law. If Jesus " knew what was in man," he knew instinctively how to discharge the God-given power in a way consonant with the soul-mechanism of the sufferer. Psychotherapy is not a discovery of the twentieth century; it is as old as man. We may admit all this, and yet reject this picture as a libel on

194

Christ. And we have a right to do it on the strength of a single phrase in the gospel account: " and he took her by the hand." Explain the power as we may, the thing that fascinates us in Christ is the personal touch. It is that that betrays the love and sympathy that are the basal substance of his nature. How often in the gospels he " put his hand on them," " he touched them "; not, we believe, through any psychic necessity, in order to establish rapport or convey " magnetism," but because whenever virtue went from him his heart went also, and the hand was the true revealer of compassion. All through the gospel he moves not as a wonder-worker but as a lover of mankind; not a " healer " but a friend, a binder up of broken hearts, a forgiver of sins, one who loved to the uttermost and gave his life a ransom for many. Jesus making passes is unthinkable; Jesus taking the maiden by the hand not only brings tears of joy to our eyes, but draws us to his feet in adoration.

Do you notice that this is a " preliminary study "? Keller himself, fascinated as he was with the psychological problem involved here, could not rest satisfied till he had restored to Christ the elements that alone make him our ideal — his love and personal sympathy. If you would know Keller's last word on this theme — yes, and ours as well — you must study his final picture that follows.

KELLER: RAISING THE DAUGHTER OF JAIRUS

Luke 8 : 40–42, 49–56

Keller, Albert von (1844–   )

Original: His masterpiece, painted in 1885; now in the Neue Pinakothek, Munich. For this picture Keller made the most exhaustive studies. He travelled all through Italy in order to acquaint himself with semi-tropical landscapes and southern modes of house architecture and of living. He looked everywhere for a sarcophagus of the right period and style, at last finding this one in Rome. The picture is also the outcome of long researches into the realm of hypnotism and spiritualism, but this final work betrays nothing of the uncanny side of such study. When the picture was first exhibited in the artist's studio, it caused a regular pilgrimage thither.

Reproductions:

This dramatic scene takes place on the porch of Jairus' house, against the background of a cypress-planted hillside. The architecture shows that Jairus was a rich man and that though a Jew he was sufficiently Romanized to build his house in the heathen style. Every detail suggests wealth: the elaborate bronze water-heater in the foreground, the numerous mourning wreaths, and in particular the beautiful sarcophagus with bas-reliefs of the Græco-Judaic mode, on the lid of which the little girl has been laid out. There are professional mourners here, also, in accordance with the customs of the East, a luxury that the poor could not afford. Jesus was not often called to homes of this sort.

These details are of course the creation of the artist, and are somewhat at variance with the scripture account. In Matthew and Mark we are told that the

KELLER: THE AWAKENING

KELLER: RAISING THE DAUGHTER OF JAIRUS

mourners were thrust out of the house, and that Jesus took with him into the room the father and mother, Peter, James and John; Luke does not compel us to think that the mourners were excluded. But the artist has kept the mourners and excluded the disciples, doubtless because he felt the greater dramatic possibilities of this arrangement. The religious value of the picture is certainly not affected.

There are three groups of people to whom we are successively attracted. First, Jairus and his wife at the left. These — as indeed all the people in the picture — are of Jewish type. The father is a strong-minded man of affairs, ruler of the synagogue at Capernaum. He had no doubt frequently seen Jesus at the service, and he must have been present when Jesus healed there the man with a withered hand. But his position would tend to keep him aloof from this wonder-worker; you may be sure that he would never have fallen down at the Master's feet and begged him to come to his house unless his need were desperate. His wife clings impulsively to him, and together they look upon this astounding scene with intense fascination and awe. Then there is the central group. Some near relative of the girl has thrown herself across the foot of the sarcophagus and covered her face with her left hand, while her right stretches out despairingly. One of the mourners is trying to comfort her. Behind, a young woman kneels beside her little daughter, — no doubt also a relative of Jairus or his wife. The woman has thrown out her hand in a wild gesture of joy as she realizes that the girl has been restored to them. Below, sitting on the pavement, holding her head and rocking to and fro while she utters her cries, is one of the mourners; above her a youth with a funeral torch. Three old women and three old men complete the number of professionals. Their faces well express the terror and awe that such an act would inspire.

The third group forms the focus of the picture. To it the hands are stretched out, thither all the eyes converge, even though the dynamic of the miracle seems to have hurled all the bodies in fear away from the spot. This composition gives a clear field in which to depict the two protagonists, while the dark curtain between the pillars serves as a foil for the two faces. Jesus in long red tunic stoops gently, almost tenderly, as he assists the girl to rise; and the girl, clad in the white winding-sheet of burial, sits up on the marble top of the sarcophagus and presses her hand, with his, to her cheek in the endeavor to find if she be really alive; her spirit " falters dreamily back into life out of the night of death," while her eyes are full of the mystery of an experience that she cannot fathom.

In this picture the artist has made us very fully aware of certain values. We feel the pathos and the tragedy of death that cuts off the hopes of youth in their flower; of wealth powerless to stay the hand of fate; of hearts breaking with their load of irremediable grief. In the figures of Jairus and his wife we feel the strength of the love that has bound this family together so closely, and that was the compelling power behind the father's search and behind his cry, " Come lay thy hand upon her that she may live! " What value did Jairus set now upon all his wealth? The touch of death upon one he loved brought out the true perspective in life, levelled the structures of pride and power his hands had reared, and showed Love standing out clear and alone, the one radiantly beautiful and supremely desirable thing in all the world. We feel that this tragic experience has been for Jairus a revealer of values; and we seem to see in his stricken face and in his embrace of the only remaining object of his love a hint that the eternal verities have found an echo in his soul.

Over against these emotions the artist has set Christ, the one who himself carried our griefs and whose heart was touched with the feeling of our woe. He is one who never resisted the God-given impulse to help when he saw human need. He has given back to Jairus his daughter for no other reason than pity for a breaking heart. Do you see how the artist has put nothing of vain-glory in the act? — no cause is being vindicated, no Divine Glory enhanced, no Messianic sign given; nor is there the self-consciousness of the popular preacher or the wonder-worker at whom all Galilee is agog. Simple love and pity are here incarnate and operative. He has come to the maiden's funeral couch just to set his seal on human affection. And how tenderly and beautifully he has done it! as if the privilege of thus restoring love to its own were a sacrament that made him and his Father one. This is one of the supreme lessons of the life of Jesus: that ministry to human need is a sacrament. It makes sacred not only the act but the doer, because through the act and the doer God himself is expressing his love.

ZIMMERMANN: CHRIST THE CONSOLER

Zimmermann, Ernst Karl Georg (1852–1899)
Original: Painted in 1888, exhibited in various German exposi-
tions, bought in 1892 by the Leipsic Museum, where it
now is.
Reproductions:

From the home of Jairus in Keller's picture we step
at once into a different atmosphere. This home belongs to the opposite pole of society. Instead of the
fair and silent valley for a background we are shut
in between the bare walls of a tenement. Instead
of marble pillars we have whitewash — and not
much of that. Instead of well-kept porches, utensils
of bronze, costly wreaths, hired mourners, we have
the minimum of household equipment, — an earthen
water-pitcher, an earthen bowl; and the cupboard
door hangs by one hinge. Instead of a marble couch
for the dead we have a pallet of straw for the dying.
Everything is different except the human need and the
divine Helper; those are constant, — as indeed they
have been factors in life ever since history began.

One cannot help wondering why Jesus came here.
Did that earnest mother go out, as Jairus did, and
finding him in the crowded market-place beseech him
" Come down ere my child die, " or did the soul of
Jesus, sensitive as any microphone to the pulsations
of pain, discern the voiceless cry of the soul within
the wretched house and respond of itself? Whichever
way the call came, we know that Jesus' response was
instantaneous; and if we understand at all the heart
of Jesus we must feel that he came more quickly to
this house of want than to the house of affluence.
Jairus had all the appliances of health and comfort

and the best physician in the city; this poor lad never saw a doctor or knew that poppy-seeds would ease pain. Jairus belonged to the Four Hundred, whose function was to be carried on the backs of the peasantry; Jesus belonged to the Million whose function it has always been to bear the burdens, to create bread for the world to eat, to furnish sons for war and shekels for the conqueror. Jesus' sympathies were all with the poor. If he could have gone to but one of the two homes, there is no doubt which he would have chosen.

There is another element here that no doubt had its influence upon Jesus' mind, as it has on ours: there is no father. You may be sure that were one living he would be here at this crisis. The man of the house is a boy of sixteen, and he is dying. Soon the other hinge on the cupboard door will break, the money-lender will carry off the two dishes, the landlord's steward will lose his patience, and then there will be two more widows on the street, two more "cases" to whom Jairus must dole out the synagogue's money. This is the endless story of the slum, no different in Capernaum in the year 28 than in New York in this present year of Grace.

The dear old grandmother realizes the situation, and to her it looks hopeless. She was young once, she once had a lover and husband, she had sons; but one by one her heart gave up its treasures, as now it must give up this last. Now to the burdens of age and an empty heart must be added the pang of hunger. There is no hope; it is "God's will," — as the fatalistic East says to this day. The hands are folded not in prayer but in resignation; there is no pain in her face because her spirit is too numb. She does not even see that the Helper has arrived.

The mother is still young — and it is *her* boy! Life is not yet hopeless; the heart is quick to catch the vibrant sympathy that radiates from this Healer's presence; the faith that can remove mountains stands up in her eyes.

"Her eyes are homes of silent prayer"

and her hands are clasped in an ecstasy of assurance that her supreme desire will be granted. She is pure mother — like yours and mine — whose hands have always toiled for others, as her heart has always borne another's sorrows. That is why she is a prophet and can foretell that help is nigh as soon as she hears Christ's step on the threshold. Is it possible for Jesus to resist that spirit — so like his own?

Jesus stoops over the boy to bestow the healing touch. The figure is gracious, the face is kindly, and one can almost say that Zimmermann's portrayal is adequate. But if one turns again to Keller's Jesus, one notices a difference. In Keller's conception there is an absence of self-consciousness, and a loving absorption in the work in hand that reveal the highest reaches of human sympathy. In Zimmermann's there is the slightest trace of posing, — a pause midway in the healing act just long enough for us to see it and to say to ourselves, "Look! He is about to do something." The suggestion is so slight that were Keller's picture not at hand for comparison one might never notice it; and perhaps it is ungracious to call attention to it. But it serves to show how hard it is to portray an ideal, and how super-critical one becomes when a painter attempts to show us our Christ.

Zimmermann has succeeded, however, in revealing the same supreme values that we found in the other picture. Love is here, and sympathy is here: the devoted love of motherhood that makes us know the truth of John's great generalization, " Everyone that loveth is born of God; for God is love "; the healing love of sympathy in its true sense of " fellow-suffering." Whether or not Christ will restore this dying boy to health, he has at any rate brought balm for wounded spirits, for he has himself taken upon his heart part of the burden and the pain. This is a divine act; but it is also a supremely human act. Indeed one might almost say that when we enter through sympathy into the fellowship of another's suffering we are at that moment the servant of God, his fellow worker in the eternal task of saving the world. For what is Salvation but that state in which love shares with its neighbor all his joy and his woe. In this matter, as in all other spiritual matters, " one is your master, even Christ, and all ye are brethren."

ZIMMERMANN: CHRIST THE CONSOLER

ROSSETTI: MARY MAGDALENE AT THE DOOR OF SIMON

CHAPTER IX

THE CURE OF SINNERS

PICTURES FOR STUDY

Rossetti: Mary Magdalene at the Door of Simon
Rubens: Christ in the House of Simon
Murillo: Mary Magdalene
Viti: Magdalene in the Desert
Hofmann: Christ and the Adulteress

The message of Jesus was primarily to the souls of men. It was the good news that God loves all his children and that if our vision of him has become blurred and our relation of fellowship destroyed through sin, we can be restored instantly by repentance. Contrast this idea with the cumbersome paraphernalia of any of the ancient creeds with their priesthood, their minute ceremonial requirements, their pilgrimages and sacrifices, and the immeasurable superiority of the gospel as a regenerative force is apparent. Combine with this the powerful influence of personality: on the one hand the proud disdain and self-righteousness of the Pharisees, whose attitude toward the common crowd is well voiced in John 7 : 49, " This multitude that knoweth not the Law be damned! "; and on the other that sympathy and penetration that could know all the worst in a fallen creature and still love him and associate with him. It is quite understandable how the down-and-out would turn toward Jesus, and through him to God,

205

and how the readiest jibe his enemies flung at him was " Friend of Publicans and Sinners."

Of all the " sinners " whom Jesus befriended none has won such favor with the artists as Mary Magdalene. One suspects that this favoritism is not founded in any special appreciation of her spiritual experience, but on the discovery that a pretty woman with long hair and a suggestion of laxity in morals made a popular appeal. At any rate, there are Magdalenes by the score, representing various incidents in scripture and some in legend.

There is some confusion about Mary because the New Testament accounts are not explicit. Lk. 8 : 2 says that out of her had gone seven devils; Lk. 7 : 37–38 says that Jesus was anointed by a " sinner " in the house of Simon the Pharisee; Mt. 26 : 6–13 and Mk. 14 : 3–9 say that Jesus was anointed at Bethany in the house of Simon the Leper by a woman; according to Jn. 12 : 1–11, Jesus was anointed in the house of Lazarus by his sister Mary. In the middle ages or earlier, the woman in each of these stories was regarded as the same person, viz., Mary Magdalene, and many legends sprang up to supply missing details. Mary also appears in the band of women that followed Christ and his disciples about Galilee (Lk. 8 : 2); she was present at the crucifixion (Jn. 19 : 25), and at the sepulcher (Mk. 16 : 1; Jn. 20 : 11–18). After the gospel narrative leaves her, legends carry her to Marseilles, where she becomes a marvellous evangelist and the patron saint of sinners.

ROSSETTI: MARY MAGDALENE AT THE DOOR OF SIMON

Rossetti, Dante Gabriel (1828–1882)

Original: A pen and ink drawing, 18 x 20″, begun in 1853 and finished in 1858. The theme occupied Rossetti's mind for many years more. For it he made many sketches in pencil, oil or water-color. Burne-Jones was his model for the head of Christ. The picture is privately owned.

Reproductions:

Rossetti has created here a scene not found in the gospels, the moment when Mary Magdalene is converted. The drawing is quite in Rossetti's style, with those mannerisms and shortcomings that make appreciation of his work so difficult at first, but expressing those poetic and spiritual insights that fascinate every one whose temperament is keyed to his.

Here are two houses opening upon a narrow lane. The one on our right belongs to Simon, who this day gives a dinner to the Prophet of Galilee. Across the way toward the end of the lane another house stands wide open, showing feasters within, and at the door musicians. Gaily-dressed and flower-decked revellers move thither: each couple kiss as they reach the threshold, then pass to the house of mirth. Beyond are a river and a high-road with its stream of toilers. Mary Magdalene and her lover were in the procession, passing the house of Simon; but catching sight of the face of Christ through the door, she has suddenly turned, she mounts the steps, stripping off with both hands the roses that deck her hair, in token that her days of vanity are done. A young woman, divining her intent, has sprung up the steps before her, and now bars the entrance with her hand. Mary's lover also interposes himself and half mockingly, with a hand upon her foot and knee, begs her to return. Those near her in the procession have turned round, disconcerted and displeased at the sudden discord in their mirth, while a beggar-girl offers them flowers from her basket. On the steps, faint reminder of Lazarus at the feast of Dives, or of the dogs that eat of the children's crumbs, sits another beggar-girl eating the morsels that have been thrown to her, and sharing them with the chickens. She wonders to see Mary go up to the house, knowing her reputation through the city. Simon also looks disdainfully at her, and the servant bringing a dish to the banquet throws a leer at one who is a far lower creature than herself. A white fawn crops the vine on the wall — mute reminder by its spotlessness and innocency that another creature here is far from innocent. The flowers growing beside the door hint at the two natures to be found within the house: the golden sunflower for the opulence and pride of Simon, the lilies for the modesty and purity of Jesus. They remind us also of the choice that has just confronted Mary, the pride and pleasure of the world or the whiteness of a redeemed life.

Our interest centers in two faces. Mary's is not without beauty; and her aspect is less sorrow and repentance than it is a proud resolve to rise into that region where her Lord is. She is oblivious to the jeers and the opposition: she sees One only, and to him will she go. And that Other, — it is a face of tenderness and sorrow, of reproach and of invitation, a mystic face such as only a poet and a dreamer could create — the only face that could turn the heart of such as Mary.

But there is no need to interpret further; Rossetti himself has shown us the heart of the Magdalene in a sonnet full of poetry and pathos, written to accompany the picture. It is the lover's remonstrance and Mary's answer, and it is at the same time the cry of one who has seen herself and the ideal:

" Why wilt thou cast the roses from thine hair?
    Nay, be thou all a rose, — wreath, lips, and cheek.
    Nay, not this house, — that banquet house we seek;
See how they kiss and enter; come thou there.
This delicate day of love we two will share
    Till at our ear love's whispering night shall speak.
    What, sweet one, — hold'st thou still the foolish freak?
Nay, when I kiss thy feet they'll leave the stair.

" Oh, loose me! Seest thou not my Bridegroom's face
    That draws me to Him? For His feet my kiss,
    My hair, my tears He craves today: — and oh!
What words can tell what other day and place
    Shall see me clasp those blood-stained feet of His?
    He needs me, calls me, loves me: let me go! "

RUBENS: CHRIST IN THE HOUSE OF SIMON

Luke 7 : 36–50

Rubens, Peter Paul (1577–1640)
Original: in the Royal Academy, Vienna, a sketch twelve by sixteen inches, on the basis of which the larger work, six by eight and a half feet, now in the Hermitage, St. Petersburg, was painted. The sketch was executed in 1618. It is drawn with clearer detail than the painting and is more satisfactory to study. Compare the Hermitage picture, reproduced in such works as Dillon: Rubens. Plate cxxxix.
Reproductions:

This is a superb conception, the work of a master mind and a master hand. Jesus and three of his

209

disciples are being entertained by Simon the Pharisee in his magnificent home. Three of Simon's friends have also been invited, — Pharisees all, who have no doubt made a special journey from Jerusalem with the object of studying this popular Rabbi at short range. Mary whose heart has made her bold is an uninvited and unwelcome guest. The subject is, of course, dramatic as far as Mary's act is concerned, for her presence throws into relief the chasm between her social status and Simon's, and her extraordinary act, though quietly done, is tense with emotion. But the artist has extended the tensity of the moment till it embraces all the guests. The picture is dynamic: force radiates from every figure and focuses itself on two objects, Mary and Jesus.

Study the composition a moment. The dark drapery hangs across the brightest light and leads the eye downward toward Christ, then serves as a foil to the glowing whiteness of his face. There is no profile in the picture so clean-cut as his. Almost all the other strong lines also center on him: the legs of his couch and his own leg lead the eye up; the line from the arm of the woman who holds the basket on her head, passes to the face and shoulder of the waitress in front, and thence by the line of heads to Christ; the old man's head and arm (extreme left) lead to the dish, and the line merges with the line of heads; the dark robe below the white beard (left center) points toward the other dark robe (right center), thence by the dark beards to Christ; the gaze of the three old men is strongly centered on Him; the dominant lines of Mary's figure flow upward toward Him; and Simon's white robe (extreme left) and the

curve of his chair-bottom close the loop and keep
all the force within the picture. Mary is the center
of a secondary group of lines: first, the beards and
facial angles of the central group of men point down
at her; then Simon's look and the line of his arm go
straight down to Mary on our left, as Christ's arm,
hand and leg lead down to her on our right. Mary
is the mediating personality between Christ and Simon;
as though Christ's desire to bless the Pharisee could
not pass over to him through the non-conducting
atmosphere of pride, but must flow down through
her.

Now note the psychology of the picture. The four
servants, even though their figures are necessary to
the composition, are not interested in the slightest
in what is going on. They are attending strictly to
their business. Simon is in a state of revolt. Never
before has a harlot crossed his threshold; but here is
one almost touching him, and making a fool of herself over his guest. Anger and disgust are on his
face. He is trying to move his chair away before
his ceremonial purity is defiled. His dog feels the
same way; he scents a taint!

Simon's guests from town are all cultured and
keenly intellectual gentlemen. The two under the
peacock are utterly astonished at Jesus' rebuke of his
host, but are convinced of his sincerity and fascinated
by his personality. The old man adjusting his
glasses is suspicious and hateful:

"What is coming to our nation, if a leader of the
people and a supposedly religious man, like this
Jesus, allows an abandoned woman to run after him
this way? It is disgraceful!"

211

The other guest, he without the beard, is listening in a rather blasé fashion to what one of the disciples is saying. We can hear the latter explain:

"This woman, you know, was a common streetwalker, though she belongs to a wealthy family. She was notorious all through this region till our Master cast out of her seven devils."

"How interesting," the guest will reply.

Between these two sits Peter. He has heard the story before, but his mind is trying to fathom the meaning of it and the Master's attitude toward sinners, so different from the attitude of the Pharisees. The disciple next to Jesus (is it John?) is having hard work to restrain his feelings: a great sob chokes him as he realizes the tremendous moral change that has come over Mary, and feels the beauty and significance of her act. These three disciples, you observe, are what the Sanhedrim later characterized them — "unlearned and ignorant men," if not uncouth.

One sees at a glance that intellectually Jesus belongs with the Pharisees. He is sensibly above the level of his disciples in refinement, in spiritual power, in beauty, in poise. He is not a whit disconcerted by this extraordinary act of Mary's; on the contrary, one might judge that it was an every-day occurrence with him. Nor is he ill at ease in this luxurious home even though he knows that he is being scrutinized by his enemies. He has divined Simon's self-righteousness, his repugnance to Mary, and he is interested merely in showing him the spiritual meaning of this act that shocks him.

"Look, Simon! Why do you not show me even the common courtesies due a guest? It is because

212

RUBENS: CHRIST IN THE HOUSE OF SIMON

MURILLO: MARY MAGDALENE

you never knew what it means to be forgiven. Your heart is cold. Here is a woman who has sounded the depths of sin and wretchedness; and this is the love she pours out upon the one who saved her soul."

There is an implication in these words that Simon cannot escape: this creature is more worthy than he! That is why Simon looks at Mary with such an insane hatred.

What is the sin that has chilled the heart of Simon? Rubens has held a peacock up aloft in the middle of the picture, against the sky so that all may see it. It is the symbol of Pride.

Mary is portrayed with great feeling and true perception. Her silk robe and dainty vase accord with the tradition that she was rich; but the entire absence of jewelry shows the true penitent. She lost all of the pride of life on the day when Jesus cast out the seven deadly sins. Henceforth her one purpose will be to minister to this prophet who has spoken peace to her heart. With what exquisite tenderness and respect she lifts the Master's foot. There is no paroxysm; her love is already chastened and disciplined. She does not press the foot to her bosom; her touch is more like a caress, and the kiss falls more lightly than even that lock of falling hair. Mary is wholly rapt and self-forgetful. Her face is not beautiful — indeed there is every reason why it should not be; but her act is beautiful because it is so utterly sincere.

Rubens has given us here a picture of human life that is true for all times and races. He has brought us face to face with cultured self-righteousness, devout ignorance, wanton sin, and a prophet of the living God. Over and over again this scene has been enacted: self-righteousness rebuked, devotion made more enlightened, the sinner saved. Our psychology and our metaphysics have not yet explained it all, but the facts are patent to any who will read the annals of rescue work — " Broken Pottery," " The Light of India," " The Dry-Dock of a Thousand Wrecks," or even James' " Varieties of Religious Experience." No truth on earth has been more completely verified than that ancient promise of Isaiah: " Though your sins be as scarlet, they shall be as white as snow."

MURILLO: MARY MAGDALENE

Murillo, Bartolomé Estéban (1617–1682)
Original: Royal Gallery, Berlin.
Reproductions: Taber-Prang, 1, 2, 3, 4, 5, 6, 10, 11, 12, 13.

This is a very pretty picture. The subject is represented in the flower of young womanhood, her sweet face set off with a wealth of exquisite hair, her eyes raised pensively to Heaven. The drawing is faultless, the coloring rich. Such a picture would make the reputation of any gallery. The only trouble with it is that the subject is not Mary Magdalene. Mrs. Jameson's judgment is well founded that the most distinguished painters have conspicuously failed to represent Mary adequately. " We have Marys that look as if they never could have sinned, and others that look as if they never could have repented." Murillo's Mary belongs to the former class.

We have in the character of Mary a most difficult subject for art. The Scripture represents her as hav-

214

ing once been possessed with seven devils. Just what that signifies in twentieth century medical terms we do not know; it may have been epilepsy or insanity or some moral perversity that was pathological. But the fact that the devils were seven rather than one indicates that she was sorely afflicted. The scripture also gives us no hint as to how the disease manifested itself in conduct. It has been customary, however, to identify Mary with the " woman who was a sinner " in the story of the anointing in Simon's house; and again to identify her (wrongly, we believe) with Mary the sister of Martha and Lazarus. As a result of this confusion an extensive tradition has grown up which because of its adoption by the western church has had an influence upon all. Mary is said to have been married to the governor of Magdala, her native village; but that when the devils got possession of her she became unmanageable, a perfect shrew about the house, and possessed with an ungoverned lust that so disgraced her husband that he divorced her. Her rich family tried to hush up the story of her sins, but they could do nothing to control her life; it was one continuous debauch broken by fits of remorse, made more conspicuous because of her social position. In this condition Jesus found her and cast out the devils. Murillo certainly knew this tradition.

Is there any trace of this evil life in Murillo's picture? Not a bit. We look in vain for any signs of epilepsy in this superb woman; mental derangement, if that were her trouble, has left no traces on the brow or in her soulful eyes. Passion less worthy than a love of Heaven could never have tortured her soul. There is nothing of the beast in her; she is an innocent creature whose life has been spent in contemplation or in deeds of kindness, a life saddened perhaps by the sorrows of others, but never touched by the poignancy of personal suffering. Remorse never stung her to despair, for what " her all but utter whiteness took for sin " would mostly pass for virtue in our sordid world. No, this Mary is not a Magdalene.

And when we look for the characteristics of Mary's redeemed life we do not find them. Where is that tempestuous recoil to virtue that drove her to follow Jesus all over Galilee (Lk. 8 : 2), and even to the cross and tomb (Jn. 19 : 25; Mk. 16 : 1)? Where the impetuous love that put fear to flight in the house of the Pharisee, and threw her at Jesus' feet in a paroxysm of repentance (Lk. 7 : 36–38)? Where is the self-sacrifice that lavished upon its ideal the box of spikenard, very precious? These feelings never swept through the breast of this sentimental creature; she is not capable of such depth of passion. She is just one of those contemplative saints who enjoy longing for the glories of heaven and who during the process are quite ready to serve as artist's model. Murillo has given us here a superb illustration for the " Sunday Supplement," an actress posing in some sacred drama.

But then, no other artist has succeeded any better. Domenichino's Mary (Pitti Gal.) is weakly sentimental. Gampietrino's (Brera) is inane. Van Orley's (National) is coquettish. Bellini's (Academy, Venice) has the " gazes." Metsys' (Antwerp Mus.) is mourning over lost spikenard. Carlo Dolce's (Uffizi) is too

216

prettily gotten up for the occasion. Correggio's (Dresden) is too self-satisfied. The task is an impossible one — to express at the same time sin and repentance, the distortion of demoniacal possession and the peace of salvation, fire that once flamed red with lust but that now glows with the pure whiteness of the empyrean, love once centered upon self but now pouring itself out in priceless sacrifice. Life shows us this transformation because life is mobile; but static art cannot give us hell and heaven in one face.

VITI: MAGDALENE IN THE DESERT

Viti (or Vite), Timoteo (1469–1523)

Original: Painted about 1508 for the Chapel of Ludovico Amaduzzi in the cathedral of Urbino; now in the gallery at Bologna.

Reproductions:

This picture is based on a late legend that identifies Mary Magdalene with Mary of Bethany. When the persecution mentioned in Acts 8 : 1 arose, their enemies put Mary, Martha and Lazarus in an open boat, without oar, sail, rudder or provisions, expecting that they would speedily perish. But a kindly Providence blew them the whole length of the Mediterranean to Marseilles in France. They were rudely treated by the pagans at first, but Mary preached to them with such wondrous effect that Christianity was securely planted among them and Lazarus became the first Bishop of Marseilles. Mary thereupon retired to the wilderness, where she did penance for thirty years, and though never seen by mortals was nourished by angels and visions. It happened that a holy hermit wandered into the neighborhood of her cell just in time to see her soul carried to heaven by angels. In the thirteenth century her supposed remains were discovered at St. Maximin, a little village twenty miles north of Toulon. Thereafter her fame became extraordinary in southern France. A convent to her memory was erected on the traditional scene of her penance — a wild spot between Toulon and Marseilles, — which survived till the beginning of the French Revolution, when it and its treasures of relics were destroyed. The church of the Madeleine, erected to her memory in Paris, is one of the finest shrines in Europe and the most costly memorial to her in the world.

Mary Magdalene is the type and patron saint of the repentant sinner. Pictures like this of Viti first became popular in the sixteenth century and were at the height of favor in the seventeenth. Mary is always distinguished from the other saints by her alabaster vase, symbol of her deed of love, though she may have also a book to show her devotion to contemplation, a crucifix as an emblem of faith, a skull for mortality and a scourge for penance. Viti gives us the vase and the book. He pictures for us the cave in the rocks that for thirty years was her home. Mary is clad in a long robe, crimson in token of Jesus' statement that "she loved much." Her hair is quite unbound — as the Magdalene's hair always is for no reason but tradition — and in this case it reaches to her feet beneath her mantle. Her hands are closed in prayer. Her pose and the look upon her face speak of meditation. She has an appearance almost of girlish innocence. It is hard to identify her with the passionate Mary of Scripture, or with the fiery preacher who converted the city of Marseilles. Surely her long penance has accomplished more than the salvation of her soul; it has transformed her very nature, put out the fires of youth, extinguished desire itself and left a pensive saint who waits in patience for whatever visions of bliss God may vouchsafe her.

This is a conception of sainthood quite foreign to our thinking but very much in vogue in the middle age, — as it is today in some parts of the world. Asceticism has always had its votaries. The great Indian epics that date a thousand years before Christ show us forests filled with hermits, who by their austerities were able to work miracles and even to control the gods. The Jews of our Lord's time had their sect of the Essenes in the region of the Dead Sea. Asceticism became a passion in the early Christian centuries, so that the desert cliffs of Judea were honey-combed with caves by the tens of thousands, and the Thebaïd in Egypt reckoned its hermits by the hundred thousand. Sometimes the austerities took unbelievable forms; as when St. Simeon Stylites lived for thirty-seven years on the top of a pillar a yard square, his neck loaded with an iron chain, his lips moving in continual prayer, his body wasted with continual fasting. The fame of his sanctity brought crowds to see him from the ends of the earth and made many converts. The history of sainthood throughout the middle age is filled with similar examples. Such a life was thought to atone for the sins of the past; and privations and bodily sufferings were meritorious in the sight of God and often brought a direct vision of Him. It is no wonder that the logic of such beliefs should lead Mary to an anchorite's cell. As her body had been the home of seven demons, so now, purified by self-mortification, it should be the abode of angels. As she had sinned beyond others in the days of her youth, so beyond others should her declining years bear witness to the genuineness of her repentance. There is both logic and poetic justice here. Granted only the views of life that the middle age held and we could think of Mary in no other terms.

But has this picture any message for us? — for us pampered children of the steam-heated house, the full table and the upholstered church? for us who are so tolerant of other men's beliefs and sins that we have snuffed out hell and given the sinner a college education? Do we believe that sin is deadly and must be atoned for by somebody? That the love that cannot immolate itself is worthless? That the plucking out of an eye may fill the whole body with light? Certainly we may hold these beliefs — indeed we should hold them. But it will do no good to snuff out hell unless we strenuously win heaven. No atonement for sin was ever made by self-flagellation, but rather by trying to live the Christ-life. Self-sacrifice for its own sake is suicide, but losing one's life for Christ's sake and the gospel's is finding it. The nobly ascetic life is not necessarily a life of privations, but rather a life surcharged with positive interests; given the dominance of an imperious ideal and all the lusts of the flesh and the pride of life will shrivel and die. Christ never denied himself — he was too busy; and the modern Christian can do no better than follow

220

VITI: MARY MAGDALENE

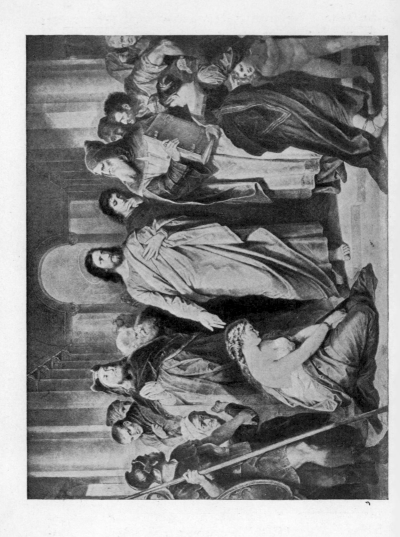

his Lord. We must therefore look upon Viti's picture as an allegory, or at best a half-truth that needs to be subsumed in a larger vision.

HOFMANN: CHRIST AND THE ADULTERESS

John 8 : 2–11

Hofmann, Johann Michael Ferdinand Heinrich (1824–1911)
Original: Painted in 1868, now in the Zwinger Gallery, Dresden.
Reproductions: Taber-Prang, 1, 3, 13.

The story of the Adulteress has a shady pedigree. It certainly was not in the original gospel of John where it is now found, for eight of the oldest manuscripts do not contain it; Eusebius says in his Ecclesiastical History that it was in the Gospel of the Hebrews; and there is a strong presumption that it was once in Mark's gospel but was dropped because it gave offense. The American Revised Bible brackets the passage and has a marginal comment on its textual irregularities. Yet the incident is undoubtedly historical, and it gives us a most important and precious insight into one side of Jesus' nature. It probably took place on the last day of Christ's public ministry as he taught in the Temple courts.

The encounter was " worked up " by the Scribes and Pharisees. They knew that Jesus had associated more or less with publicans and sinners — the two classes whom the Pharisees blasted with common condemnation. Their emissaries to Galilee had reported such facts about him as early as Mark 2 : 15–17. A few months previous to this, Jesus confessed that they had classed him as a glutton and a winebibber, a friend of the demi-monde (Mt. 11 : 19);

and as recently as yesterday he had allowed an abandoned woman to make a spectacle of him at Bethany (Mt. 26 : 6–7). Such a man evidently was himself bad and should be denounced before the multitude. The best way to discredit him would be to confront him with one of his "friends" and let him prove whether he would stand by the law of Moses or uphold sin. Nothing could be neater!

This canvas is not a great picture; it was painted earlier than "Christ in the Temple" and is inferior to it in color and technic. Still, Hofmann has presented the incident in an impressive way — more satisfactorily than any other painter. He has chosen the moment when Jesus says, "He that is without sin among you let him first cast a stone at her." Like many others, this picture has two foci. Jesus is shown to be the primary point of interest by being placed in the center in a commanding position. The perspectives of the Temple colonnade vanish to a point behind his head; the faces on the right turn toward him, as do those on the left; and there are numerous "eye-paths" established by arms and draperies to lead us to him. The Sinner is the secondary focus: the lines of Christ's robe and his arm point to her; four of the company are looking at her; the soldier's arm and the rift in the crowd behind the old woman draw our look down to her. The two chief accusers balance the picture about its major center, and by their prominence indicate that the quarrel is with them. Perhaps the composition is a little too formal, but it correctly emphasizes and interprets the story: two important persons are trying to entrap Jesus in regard to a woman.

222

We perceive in the faces of the two accusers the animus of the accusation. The Pharisee on our left is a perfect embodiment of the satirical prayer that Jesus invented, "Lord, I thank Thee that I am not as other men are." His hands are folded as if to symbolize a constant attitude of piety, — which means for him not the performance of works of mercy and charity, but keeping himself aloof from sinners. His countenance is hard, self-satisfied, devoid of passion. He would not stoop to mix up in this business at all were it not that he despised this teacher who is trying to overthrow the very base on which his righteousness stands. His companion on our right has a more enterprising temperament. He is the ringleader. He is actively malignant. It was his spies who caught the woman — they were doubtless well paid for it — and his wits have framed the charge. He has brought along his authority, the big book; his fingers are on chapter and verse — Leviticus 20 : 10. To give point to the law, at his elbow is one of his henchmen with his arms full of stones. As soon as the Master says the word, the ruffian is ready to carry out the sacred statute.

It is perfectly evident that neither of the accusers is interested in public morality, and a little further reflection will show that this whole proceeding is a bluff. For it is singular, is it not? that these zealous guardians of righteousness did not capture also the woman's partner in sin, for whom the law indicated the same penalty. Either they couldn't catch him, or he didn't exist! And there is no danger that the stones will be used. A Roman soldier is there to keep the peace, and in the Tower of Antonia, a bow-shot away, is a whole garrison lusting to run their spears through a score of these fanatics. Besides, the power the soldiers symbolize has decreed that sentence of death shall be given by the Roman Proconsul alone. Jesus may have come from the country, but he knows that little fact as well as the Sanhedrim does! No, there is no question of morals at stake; it is an endeavor to trap this demagogue into flatly contradicting the Law of Jehovah and proving himself to be an abettor of sin.

Hofmann has interpreted characteristically one or two other persons in the scene. Do you see John the disciple, between Christ and the chief accuser? His thought is busy neither with the indictment nor his Master's reply, but with the accused woman in the foreground. His heart has been touched. He is wondering what cross-currents of Fate, what hereditary taint, what weakness of will or strength of passion brought so fair a creature so low. His is the face of Dante as he muses in the second circle of Hell at the fate of Paolo and Francesca: "Alas! how many sweet thoughts, how great desire, led these unto the woeful pass." John will not swoon through pity, as Dante did; but he will live to absorb completely his Master's spirit and to write words about Love that show us the root of good even in the midst of so great a perversion as this. Jesus himself must have read this woman's heart through and through, or he could not have uttered those compassionate words, " Neither do I condemn thee."

But there are two others in this picture who do condemn, and that unsparingly; and they are both women! One would think that woman's sympathy would fathom something either of the passion or the weakness that leads to woman's fall, and would at least feel kindly toward the sinner even while condemning the sin. But it seems to be not so. Hofmann is true to the facts when he makes one spectator hasten away as from a plague, and the other raise a vicious hand to strike. The face of the latter tells the whole story: it is loathing coupled with satisfaction at loathing. And strangely enough this instinctive and active denial of sympathy to women who sin in this way is usually found conjoined with the noblest character and the keenest sympathy for other kinds of sinners. The good wife of the Vicar of Wakefield is a perpetual type. But Christ means to show that it is not his type.

Jesus holds the balance true, in this case as in all. He is a friend of sinners not because he condones sin but because he knows that friendship will redeem when condemnation will doubly damn. He sees that evil is often a perverted good. His method is not to extirpate the sinning instinct but to transform its aim, to sublimate it, attach it to some high and holy cause, and so redeem it by letting it lose itself in a life larger than that of self. Hofmann has painted into Jesus' face sorrow for sin, but greater sorrow for the deceit and hatred in these Pharisees; insight into the good in this fallen woman, and equally into the sin in her self-righteous accusers. There is no need to speculate about which of the sins here indicated is more heinous: the same voice that said, " Neither do I condemn thee," said, " Woe unto you, Scribes, Pharisees, hypocrites. . . . Ye offspring of vipers, how shall ye escape the judgment of Hell! "

Some one with dramatic insight has suggested that Jesus wrote on the ground, " Jonas defrauded a poor man of a pair of shoes "; " Eleazer stole a widow's house "; " Asaph brought false accusation against his neighbor ";—naming in each case one of the woman's accusers; and when each read in the sand the revelation of his guilt, in shame he withdrew from the presence of the righteous judge. This at any rate is the teaching of the incident: it is a graphic parable on the words " Thou hypocrite, cast out first the beam out of thine own eye, and then shalt thou see clearly to cast out the mote out of thy brother's eye "; and an equally graphic parable on the redemptive power of sympathy and forgiveness.

CHAPTER X

THE MARTYRDOM OF JOHN

The incident of John's arrest and death has usually been considered from the standpoint of John. It marks the end of a brave career, the fulfilment of John's own prophecy, " He must increase but I must decrease." But its true significance for Jesus lay rather in what it reflected of the dangers in the midst of which he worked. John had become a popular preacher whose power to sway men was phenomenal. Popular leaders are always looked at askance by autocratic rulers, who know full well the power of a multitude when welded into an instrument by the fire of an ideal. Every word John spoke was reported to Herod; and when John's denunciation of sin became specific, and when, according to Josephus, Herod began to fear that John would stir up a revolt, he clapped him into prison. The act was the answer of power to dangerous popularity. Now Jesus was treading the same road. He was as mighty a preacher as John, and he had come into the very center of Herod's domain, almost under the walls of his palace at Tiberias; and the same spies that had shadowed John now shadowed him. Herod was worried (Mk. 6 : 14–16; Lk. 23 : 8). Let there be the

227

slightest personal reflection upon Herod or the faintest suggestion that he was winning a following for political ends, and Jesus' dreams would all vanish in a dungeon. Between the Herodians and the Scribes and Pharisees, with whom Galilee swarmed, Jesus had a hard time. He now saw, as Holtzmann puts it, that " the preacher of righteousness, even though sent by God, is not protected by God against the arbitrary power and caprice of men. It is not God's will that the happiness of man on earth should correspond with his worth. From John's fate Jesus came to understand the fate which awaited himself."

The painters of course cannot suggest this wider significance. They look upon the incident as an act of wantonness on Herod's part, or an act of lasciviousness on Salome's, an act of revenge from Herodias, and a tragedy for John. In all these points of view there is truth and an opportunity for dramatic interpretation.

MASOLINO: THE FEAST OF HEROD
Matt. 14 : 1–12; Mark 6 : 14–29

Masolino: Tommaso di Cristoforo Fini, commonly called (1383–1447)

Original: a fresco in the baptistery of the chapel of Castiglione d'Olona, not far from Milan, executed about 1428. It was only recently uncovered from whitewash, and bears the signature of Masolino.

Reproductions:

This is an early and naïve story-telling picture. The architecture is fifteenth century Tuscan, the same as that in Fra Angelico's *Annunciation*. On the left is a loggia within which Herod and three guests sit at a table, while Salome followed by four men stands demurely in the court and asks her favor. Salome's face is innocent and finely cut. Herod is evidently taken aback by the request and the friar to his right is somewhat shocked. On our right is a colonnade surmounted by a terrace, the vaulting being carried on slender columns with Ionic capitals. In the near end Salome kneels and presents John's head to her mother Herodias. Note the latter's elegant profile and how the huge turban gives a barbaric air to her figure. Beyond her stand two maids. In the distance is a mountainous landscape where five of John's disciples are burying the body (head and all). Below at the end of the vista is perhaps Herod's pleasure garden. The artist is evidently not a master of perspective.

But the picture serves as well as any to make vivid to us the character of the incident, especially as it presents us with three points of view from which to survey it. Here are two different actors whose characters are to be pilloried by this event for all the future to look at; and we are reminded of another company to whom this piece of wantonness is a tragedy. On the right sits Herodias, glutting her eyes with the sight of her tormentor's head. Masolino has given us a very restrained picture of her joy, for according to St. Jerome, when Herodias saw the trophy she drew a pin from her head-dress and pierced St. John's tongue, the tongue whose judgments had been sharper to her than a two-edged sword. She is the malignant and baleful star of John's destiny, a type of those who in every age have been ready to send preachers of righteousness to their death if so be that it will still the accusing voice. Perhaps Masolino has meant to express by her calm attitude that this crime is nothing to her — as indeed it was nothing; but he has let us feel the horror of it in the person of the little maid beyond Herodias.

On the left we see an embodiment of the weak-minded voluptuary. His policy has been to get on with the least friction; would not play false with John, and yet would wrongly win. When John probes his sins he hesitates between penitence and desire. When Herodias clamors for John's death and the people applaud their prophet, Herod compromises on a long confinement. When Salome dances, the path of least resistance leads to a fool-promise. When the keeping of the promise brings him face to face with either a crime or the reproaches of his friends and the anger of a cruel woman to whom he is bound, he chooses the crime. From this time forth he will be a prey to fears; he will believe that every preacher who does mighty works is his old enemy risen from the dead. So between these two schemers the crime becomes a fact: she plotting actively to destroy her enemy, he twisting his way through the crooked paths of circumstance so that his pleasure will be least disturbed. To neither of these two is a prophet anything more than a pawn, to be sacrificed when greater interests are at stake.

But to many thousands in Israel this day of feasting and of sweet revenge is a dark day. John's disciples are overwhelmed. With fear and trembling lest Herod's wrath break out upon them, they beg the body of their master, bury it, and tell Jesus all. And Jesus sees in the death of this fearless preacher

MASOLINO: THE FEAST OF HEROD

PUVIS DE CHAVANNES: BEHEADING OF JOHN THE BAPTIST

the handwriting on the wall for himself also. "That fox" is already on his trail, and the Herodians — his spies and partisans — leaguing with the Scribes and Pharisees are soon to drive him out of Galilee.

PUVIS DE CHAVANNES: BEHEADING OF JOHN THE BAPTIST

Matt. 14 : 1–12; Mark 6 : 14–29

Puvis de Chavannes, Pierre Cécile (1824–1898)

Original: exhibited in the Salon of 1870 and characterized as an "outrage"; again in the Universal Exposition of 1889, after the artist was famous, and praised highly! Now in the Metropolitan Museum, New York, loaned by its owner, Mr. John Quinn.

Reproductions: In color: Seemanns three-color prints. No. 1409.

There is a vigor and a directness to this representation that accords with the swiftness of the scripture narrative: "And he sent and beheaded John in prison." Here are the three chief actors, — the wicked woman who is the cause of the tragedy, the skilful executioner, the obedient but unconquered prisoner. There is no fuss about it. There are no flowers from friends, no grave or coffin for John to look into, no scaffold, no headsman's block, no crowd of jeering or sorrowing witnesses, none of the glamor of public martyrdom with the ecstasy of angelic visions and an immortal name writ large upon the sky. Only a plain courtyard in a prison, only a tree-trunk and a wall, only a steel-hearted woman to see that the job is done; only a stride, a swing, a flash, — and a prophet dies as a dog dies!

But John dies like a prophet; he is still master of

231

his soul! He needs no cords to bind his wrists, or bandage for his face. His eyes look straight on along the path of duty. There is never a whimper or the faintest suggestion of relenting from that stern judgment he once passed upon the woman by the wall. Now, as then, "It is not lawful for thee to have her," and through all eternity it shall be the same! The hands spread wide are his oath of innocence of all wrong, for God to see. "I have fought a good fight, I have finished the course, I have kept the faith!" . . .

"But what went ye out for to see? a prophet? Yea, I say unto you, and much more than a prophet; for among them that are born of women there is none greater than John."

MOREAU: THE APPARITION

Matt. 14 : 1–12; Mark 6 : 14–29

Moreau, Gustave (1826–1898)

Original: A large water-color, first exhibited in the Paris Salon of 1876, together with another of Salome Dancing. Now the property of the State, in the Luxembourg, Paris.

Reproductions:

Even a casual visitor to the Luxembourg would be struck by this unusual picture: it expresses fully Moreau's exuberant imagination, his feeling for richness and for startling color. From one point of view the picture is ridiculous, for no castle of Herod's on the wild plateau of Moab ever looked like this! In another way it is quite true; for it suggests the barbarian lack of restraint, the autocratic power, the sensuous life that have always characterized the East.

Moreau's love of richness was almost an obsession. Note these marble pillars and walls, every inch sculptured or incrusted with arabesques. See this dancer clothed only in jewels, — and jewels such as today may be seen only in Shiva's temple-hoard at Madura! Look at that slave with the enormous sword, a mere wielder of the vengeance of his lord in whose sight he stands continually, himself likely enough the next victim of his lord's wrath. There are the guilty royal pair on their thrones of state; the one morose and hardly to be stirred even by this voluptuous dance, the other coldly satisfied that her daughter dances faultlessly, and that the reward she has asked will shortly be paid. The heart of the story lies in two faces, the sensuous face of Salome over against the calm and righteous face of John, — the one the vampire and the other the victim. But Moreau has here reversed the relations: John has become the tormentor. The picture is an allegory of remorse.

The birthday feast is over, the guests have gone. The order that John's head be brought on a charger has been given, and the executioner is even now groping his way to the dungeons beneath the castle. The king, autocrat though he is, is shaken by fear of the consequences of this murder of a prophet, and has asked for one more dance to drive away his melancholy. The little slave girl, crouching with her zither at the foot of the throne, strikes up again, and again the jewels flash and clash before Herod's eyes. Then suddenly, mingled with the vertigo of the dance there comes into the dancer's vision the very boon she has asked, at the precise moment when in the dungeon below the fatal stroke has fallen, —

the golden charger, now upright as it were a halo, the ascetic face, the piercing eye that transfixes her very soul, the clotted hair and the drip, drip of holy blood! No one else sees it; but for an instant the apparition hangs there for her and for us, a terrible incarnation of her deed. In vain she may cry

> " Thou canst not say I did it: never shake
> Thy gory locks at me ! "

The eyes will not release their hold till her sophistry breaks down and her conscience owns the crime. Then the lights and the blood will fade out, and in their place will grow a rooted sorrow that never can be plucked from memory.

The memory of sins committed may issue in two ways, in remorse or repentance. Shakespeare has taught the former lesson in Macbeth, where crime hardened the weak and vacillating king into a fiend, and drove to insanity the queen whose conscience could not be drugged to sleep. It was a Nemesis of Destruction for both. The lesson of repentance is taught by Paul, whose conscience was played upon by the memories of his share in Stephen's death, till they wrought in his soul the apparition of the Damascus Road. This was the Nemesis of Salvation. How the experience issued in Salome's life we do not know, for the scripture is silent. But we know that in this picture the vision sets before her life and death: death if it arouses only remorse and drives her to the opiate of further crimes; life if it leads her to hate the deed and to cleanse her soul through repentance. For though sins be as scarlet they may become white like wool.

MOREAU: THE APPARITION

FRA ANGELICO: THE TRANSFIGURATION

CHAPTER XI

THE TRANSFIGURATION

The wonderful experience known as the Transfiguration is a turning-point in the life of Jesus. Briefly put, the first period of his public ministry, marked by increasing popularity and increasing opposition, culminates in his controversy with the scribes and Pharisees (Mk. 7 : 1–23) when he definitely breaks with the traditions of his people and is branded as a heretic and a dangerous man. The second period is marked by his flight from the region of the Galilean Lake, and his wanderings on foreign territory, culminating in the declaration by Peter that he is the Messiah. In connection with this event, or shortly after, occurs the Transfiguration while Jesus is praying for strength to carry out a new purpose, the purpose to go to Jerusalem. To return to Galilee meant virulent hatred from the scribes and Pharisees and probably death at the hands of Herod; to stay on foreign soil meant an acknowledgment of defeat; to go to Jerusalem, the stronghold of his enemies, meant certain death. But his duty as Messiah was publicly to proclaim himself and his message at the Royal City, come what might; and from this time he "steadfastly set his face to go toward Jerusalem."

235

The Transfiguration is the reflected glory of that decision, interpreted by his disciples in this pictorial and mystic fashion long after his death and resurrection. This narrative, like the story of the Temptation, must be understood spiritually and symbolically.

No one knows the exact site of the Transfiguration. For many centuries tradition has located it on Mt. Tabor, a few miles due east of Nazareth, and therefore this mountain was in the mind of all the painters of the scene. The mountain today is crowned with two monasteries, one belonging to the Greeks and the other to the Latins. Their accompanying churches are the successors of those built by the crusaders, which succeeded others of the fourth century, which in turn represented the tabernacles that Peter proposed to build. Each sect of course claims to have the only and original site. However, the identification of Tabor with the Mount of Transfiguration is erroneous, the scholars having decided that the spurs of Mt. Hermon above Cæsarea Philippi meet the requirements better than any other spot.

The Transfiguration has not been a favorite subject with the artists. Aside from early mosaics, there are hardly more than a dozen representations that are at all well known. That is doubtless because there are no theological implications in the experience; it has never become the subject of dogma. However, if the artists had understood its true significance, had appreciated the heroism and the faith for which the glory stands, they might have made the world richer.

FRA ANGELICO: THE TRANSFIGURATION

Matt. 17 : 1–13; Mark 9 : 2–13; Luke 9 : 28–36

Angelico: Giovanni da Fiesole, called Fra (1387–1455)
Original: A fresco, 6′ x 5′, painted between 1437 and 1445 in
cell No. 6, Monastery of San Marco, Florence.
Reproductions:

In one way this is not a picture of the Transfiguration, but rather a subject for meditation. The
good Fra has made little attempt to reproduce the
details of scenery: Mt. Tabor is merely symbolized
by a little table of rock; and though Luke says
that Jesus was praying when his appearance was
changed, in the picture he is standing with his arms
spread wide. Moses and Elijah are symbolized by
two aureoled heads, that on the right being the
prophet and that on the left, with the horns composed of rays, the Lawgiver whose face also once
shone while he talked with God on Sinai. Peter
on the left and James in the center have heard the
voice and are fearful; John on the right is praying.
Besides them, two other mortals are present, both
adoring — as the artist would have us adore: on the
left the Virgin, or St. Clara; on the right St. Dominic
with his star and tonsure, founder of the Order in
whose monastery the fresco is. Christ stands calmly
in the center of the picture, his face passionless, his
eyes unmindful of the present, looking into the future.
About him plays a mandorla of light that throws his
figure into relief and produces with it the effect of a
cross upon a pedestal. In this symbol, therefore, we
are really contemplating the shadow of the crucifixion.

Let us meditate, as the Blessed Monk invites us

237

to do. We see before us three masters of religion, the supreme product of the Jewish race. Here is Moses who first introduced the Jacob-tribes to Jehovah in his Holy Mount, and bound them to him by a great oath and by the ever-expanding tables of the Law. Here is Elijah, the first, and by the Jews regarded the greatest, of the prophets, the one who had saved Israel from apostasy to Baal at time of peril, — type of Jehovah's prophetic and saving spirit. Here is Jesus, the master of both, with arms stretched out to unite them in a unity of meaning. He is the New Covenant of the Spirit which is to supplant the Old Covenant of the Letter given through Moses; he is that Prophet who is to incarnate all the ideals both of righteousness and of Messiahship that the prophets darkly saw through a glass. These two turn to him as their fulfilment and their crown. But Jesus, through his meditation upon both the Law and the Prophets and by his insight into the present, has discovered that he is also the Lamb slain from the foundation of the world, and the Suffering Servant who is to be bruised for our iniquities. Heaven's illumination shining upon the present therefore silhouettes a cross upon which is stretched the Man of Sorrows; yet strengthened for his sacrifice by the thought that all the centuries of Law and Prophecy are looking down upon him and claiming him for theirs.

Jesus needed the consolations of these great voices. Behind him lay the failure of his mission, — the multitude forsaking him, the leaders of his nation execrating him, a mere handful of the peasantry saved from the wreck by his personal friendship.

In his beloved Galilee he had not where to lay his head. Before him he saw only defeat and death. So the old struggle of the Wilderness had come back upon him, the temptation to run away from duty or so to modify his course as to win back the favor of the crowd. It is because the struggle within him was mighty that he had turned so fiercely upon Peter — "Get thee behind me, Satan! "; for the path of least resistance that Peter counselled was the road to Hell. But now through prayer the victory has been won again; and the glory of God and the voice out of the cloud proclaim that once more through accepting the Father's will he has shown himself to be the Father's well-beloved Son. In adoration of this calm face upon the living cross we therefore bow with these disciples, knowing that it is good for us to be here in this heroic presence.

RAPHAEL: THE TRANSFIGURATION

Mark 9 : 2–29

Raffaelo, Santi, or Sanzio (1483–1520)

Original: Painted by order of Cardinal Giuliano de' Medici as altar-piece for the cathedral of Narbonne, France, of which Francis I had made the cardinal Bishop. It was Raphael's last work, for he died (1520) when it was hardly completed. The canvas was exhibited above his coffin as he lay in state, and it accompanied the huge procession of mourners to the Pantheon where the painter was interred. Thereupon it was decided that the painting should not leave Rome, but should be kept as a memorial of the great artist. It was accordingly set up in the church of S. Pietro in Montorio. Napoleon carried it to Paris in 1797 with other artistic loot, but in 1815 it was returned to Rome, where it may now be seen in the Vatican Gallery. A marvellous copy of it in mosaic adorns St. Peter's church.

Reproductions: Braun & Co., F. I. E. T.

As one stands before the original, so dramatic, so rich in color, the first impression is that of contrasts. There are contrasts of light and shade: above, golden light, intensely luminous; below, shadows dark almost to blackness. There are contrasts of color: above, harmonies toned to the dominant note of glory; below, discords arising from harsh hues and unmediated juxtapositions. Contrasts in composition: above, graceful lines that adapt their curves to one another and to their central source; below, sharp angles that thrust their individuality into one another and refuse to blend. Contrasts in spirit: above, the peace of a self-sufficient and subtly-tempered will, that having subdued itself and all things to itself, has found the peace of self-surrender; below, the conflict of opposing wills that have no clear goal and are impotent

240

in their self-assertion. Below is the human need, above the divine help. Below is the mystery of suffering, the hereditary taint of sin, the darkness of ignorance and despair, the confusion of many tongues; above is the mystery of perfected character, the realized ideal of all the strivings and the prophecies of the past, the light of heavenly glory, " the silence of eternity interpreted by love." Here are two worlds: not earth and heaven, not this world and the next; but the world of the unredeemed over against the world of saved and perfected humanity. All history is telescoped into this single panel. Below, the procession of the generations, the whole creation groaning and travailing in pain; above, the parallel procession of the Redemptive Spirit, through Law and Prophet to the topmost pinnacle of the evolutionary process — man realized, man self-poised and at rest, floating in the eternal glory, mete companion for the Creator whose will and character he has embodied.

On this canvas Raphael has united two separate incidents that occurred at some distance from each other: the Transfiguration, which took place probably on one of the spurs of Mt. Hermon — the grand snow mountain of the Anti-Lebanon range that dominates all northern Palestine, — and the healing of the epileptic boy at the foot of the mountain, perhaps near Cæsarea Philippi. We will consider the latter incident first.

In the lower half of the picture there are two groups of people: the nine apostles on the left, and the afflicted family on the right. The family is indeed afflicted. The son is an epileptic, or according to Mark and Luke a " possessed " boy, who is often seized by a demon and thrown into the fire or the water. Raphael has pictured this unfortunate creature to the life, — the squat frame, the knotted muscles, the bulging eyes, the warped mouth, the spasmodic gesture. But he is only the culmination of hereditary evil. The father barely escaped the same infirmity and will no doubt lose his mind entirely some day. The boy's uncle (behind the father) is a simpleton, as his face and meaningless gesture indicate; and the aunt (beyond the uncle) is weak-minded. The mother's side of the house is more fortunate. Her family is evidently Greek, and she herself, kneeling at the boy's side, is an intellectual and refined woman, though worn by her heavy affliction. Her brother, just above, has an intelligent and earnest face, and her sister kneeling in the foreground has a beauty and a dignity that are impressive. The dim figure in the shadow of the mountain, perhaps the maternal grandfather, completes the family group. They are all drawn hither by their love for this afflicted boy and the hope of cure.

The disciples are evidently interested in this case, even excited about it, — all but Judas (upper left) whose gesture shows a scornful impatience with the whole affair. James the Less (on his left) is mildly remonstrating with him. Below Judas sits Philip looking at them, pointing at the mountain, and no doubt suggesting the advisability of going for the Master. Andrew is consulting his " Hippocrates " and has just come to a passage that promises help when the boy's spasm distracts him. Above him Jude looks earnestly at the boy's father and points to the mount. Thomas leans forward intently studying the boy. Next him sits Simon, regretting by his gesture the absence of the Master. Above this pair Bartholomew points to the boy and discusses his symptoms with Matthew, who leans forward full of compassion. It is a perfect picture of helpless ignorance and furor in the presence of a crisis.

Turning now to the mountain, we see to the left two figures who do not appear in the scripture. They are Giuliano de' Medici, father of the cardinal who ordered the picture, and the cardinal's uncle Lorenzo de' Medici, in the guise of Sts. Julian and Lawrence. This is a piece of artistic license which nevertheless has its symbolism. These saints may well stand for the church through the ages, — for us — who by faith are witnesses of the great event and who in the utmost reverence adore the glorified Christ.

The three disciples who accompanied Jesus to the mount are, as the scripture represents, very strongly affected. James is kneeling in awe and hiding his face. Peter though prostrated has yet the courage to look up through his fingers. James shields his face from the brilliancy of the light and thrusts out his other hand in astonishment. Floating in the heavenly glory are the two great personalities of the Old Testament who left their impress on the race as none others did. These are Elijah, on the left, type of the prophetic spirit whose function is to emphasize the direct access of man to God; and Moses, on the right, the Law-giver, whose table of commandments teaches that religion must eventuate in righteous conduct. "The Law and the Prophets" constitute the religion of the past, whose office is to support and to yield place to the fuller Revelation.

All of these figures are disposed about the figure of Christ with a skill and a beauty that Raphael alone commands. Discordant and confused as the lower half of the picture seems, it is nevertheless subtly related to its own center and to the upper half. Its leading lines and lights point upward in sinuous curves to Christ, as if subconsciously men knew that their true center was in him. Note in detail how this is so, from the book and Andrew's arm on the left to the father's fallen mantle on the right. " For there is none other name given under heaven among men whereby we must be saved." And just as truly the secondary lines point to human need. Either by look or gesture the disciples refer to the boy, while the boy is the actual as well as the logical center of the family group. By this means Raphael unifies the picture: he points to the boy as the problem and to Christ as the solution.

After we have examined all these details the eye comes back perforce to the Savior. He is the soul of the whole. From him radiates a golden glory that with the force of a breeze drives backward the robes of the sages, flattens to earth the garments of the three, and by its recoil sustains the body of Christ as in a field of force. How perfectly his figure is poised! He is not ascending, he is not supporting his weight; his garments, his toes and fingers, his hair, spread gently " like sea-moss in the water." By these subtlest of devices the artist conveys the sure impression that this is not a vision, nor yet a spiritual body, but the living Master himself, at one with all the universe, at home in the heart and purpose of God.

The face of Christ is an absolutely adequate embodiment of the meaning of the Transfiguration. The Master is not here dealing with men; he is not relieving human need, teaching with authority, nor denouncing Scribes and Pharisees. He is revealing to his chosen friends his inmost character in the presence of defeat and impending death. A study of the original or of a detailed reproduction will show what Raphael conceived the basis of that character to be: it is an absolute and loving surrender of his personal will to the will of his Father. Hence a beauty in this face that defies the most cunning phrases: it is the beauty of a perfect soul. And it is at the same time, in some marvellous way, " the face of that divine child of the Sistine, matured, perfected, transfigured." *

This picture is Raphael's masterpiece. It is not only a supreme composition and a supreme work of character-interpretation, but an expression of the deepest truth of life. And what is that truth? That man needs a Savior; and that to save us God in his love has given us Christ, a realization of transfigured and redeemed humanity.

*From H. T. Bailey: Twelve Great Paintings.

RAPHAEL: THE TRANSFIGURATION

SCHOOL OF REMBRANDT: CHRIST BLESSING LITTLE
CHILDREN

Chapter XII

LESSONS IN THE SPIRITUAL LIFE

PICTURES FOR STUDY

School of Rembrandt: Christ Blessing Little Children
Von Uhde: " Suffer the Little Children "
Hofmann: Christ and the Rich Young Man
Von Gebhardt: Christ and the Rich Man
Watts: " For He Had Great Possessions "

As Christ turned his back upon the failure of
Galilee and wandered through Perea toward Jerusalem, his mind full of his approaching end, he desired
to say to his disciples the few vital words that should
guide them when he was gone. Circumstances partly
favored him. First came the quarrel over who should
be greatest, then the experience with the insane prejudice between Jews and Samaritans, the question about
divorce, the incident of the rich man, the request of
James and John for preëminence, and the incident of
Zacchæus. These all pointed one way. It seemed
as if the whole world had gone crazy over wealth
and power. The disciples, dazzled by Jesus' now
plain statements that he was the Messiah and that
the kingdom was coming as soon as he should be
offered up, were reaching out after the plums; and
those who did not share the Messianic hope were a
few of them rich and selfish and the rest poor and
envious. Prejudice and hatred, lust and greed of
power seemed the dominant motives in the grand

scramble of life. Jesus therefore directed his earnest thought to showing how fundamentally these motives were out of place in his kingdom. In two instances he appealed to a little child, and in two he dealt at length with the problem of riches. By means of the child he showed that guilelessness, simplicity, an open mind, love, trust, are the saving qualities in character; and through his parable and his conversations with the rich man and with Zacchæus he taught that the love of money must be absolutely eliminated as a root of all evil. These two teachings Jesus evidently regarded as fundamental.

These two themes have fortunately found admirable expression at the hands of the artists, more especially the moderns.

SCHOOL OF REMBRANDT: CHRIST BLESS-ING LITTLE CHILDREN

Matt. 19 : 13–15; Mark 10 : 13–16; Luke 18 : 15–17

Original: In the National Gallery, London.
Reproductions:

This is surely just what happened. Jesus has sat down for a moment to rest after a period of strenuous teaching, and the mothers of the village have brought their little ones for a blessing. It is doubtless a bit of superstition on their part: they think that the laying on of hands and the utterance of some pious words by the Prophet will bring to pass for the baby all the good things they desire. Blessings like curses were supernatural things in those days. Isaac blessed Jacob by mistake, and when he found out his error

248

it was too late; words of power had gone from him and could not be recalled.

"Then Isaac trembled very exceedingly and said, Who then is he that hath taken venison and brought it to me, and I have eaten of all before thou camest, and I have blessed him? yea, and he shall be blessed. . . . And he said, Thy brother came with guile and hath taken away thy blessing."

These good women are the heirs of this world-old belief. They have heard that a Prophet has come to town; some of them perhaps have listened to his words and have felt the unsuspected deeps within them stir, as when God brooded upon the face of the waters; and with true mother instinct they long to secure for their children all the best things in life that they feel somehow are vaguely related to the good words the Prophet has spoken. Here they come with their hopes and their little ones, — good Dutch "huisvraus" to be sure, with wooden shoes, voluminous skirts of homespun, cupboard keys and the pocketbook hanging from the belt, kerchief tucked in the bosom, with babies in arms and babies under foot; a little timid in the presence of such greatness and goodness, but bold enough to approach in spite of the over-zealous disciples. Yea, and they shall be blessed! they and their little ones. In after times they will repeat over and over to the children the story of how the good Man of Nazareth came their way, once only, just before the Romans killed him; and how he took them up in his arms and blessed them. And when, a generation later, the armies of Rome shall compass Jerusalem about, the followers of this Jesus will flee beyond Jordan to these very villages, and find with these children, then grown to manhood and womanhood, a welcome and a home. So shines a good deed in an evil world long after the doer has passed on.

What is Jesus thinking about as he lays his hand on this little tot's head and looks at her in such an earnest way? Or is he not looking at her at all, but only thinking a blessing while his eyes are fixed on faraway deep things? There is something about a little child that opens up the vistas of spiritual vision, that removes boundaries and like the ocean rolls upon our spirit the music of the infinities. This is why Wordsworth, walking on Calais Beach on that " beauteous evening calm and free," turned so naturally from the great deep before him to the mystery of another deep beside him:

> " Dear Child! dear Girl! that walkest with me here,
> If thou appear untouched with solemn thought,
> Thy nature is not therefore less divine:
> Thou liest in Abraham's bosom all the year,
> And worship'st at the Temple's inner shrine,
> God being with thee when we know it not."

And perhaps that is why Christ asked almost as a privilege for himself that the little ones be allowed to come. He needed them. The child in the picture knows nothing of the blessing that is being given. Her hand grasps her apple, while the bashful finger and turned-away face show the most sublime unappreciation. But that makes no difference to the great Seer. He is resting his soul a moment on the unknowing heart of this little one, the heart that still beats true to God; that has not yet been seduced to love the things that are in the world, to hate like Jew and Gentile, to fight like Jew and Samaritan, to scramble for places on his right hand and his left, to worship Mammon and to anathematize God's prophets when they come to seek the lost. There is weariness in the face and the position of this Christ, a heaviness of soul that grows upon one the longer one looks at the picture, till one becomes uncertain who is giving and who is receiving. And when one recollects that it was only in this last period of Christ's life that his contacts with children are recorded, the thought becomes conviction that he found in their fresh and unspoiled spirits something that renewed his faith that men are the children of God, something that again opened to him the heavens that discouragement and failure were fast closing. `

Sometimes a child does that for us, in our home.

VON UHDE: "SUFFER THE LITTLE CHILDREN"

Matt. 19 : 13–15; Mark 10 : 13–16; Luke 18 : 15–17

Uhde, Fritz von (1848–   )

Original: 6' x 9', painted in 1884; exhibited at the Berlin Academy and at the Paris Salon of 1885; bought in 1886 for the Museum at Leipsic. A slightly variant treatment of the same theme is privately owned at Worms, Germany.

Reproductions:

"The art of painting," says Fromentin, "is perhaps more indiscreet than any other. It is an indubitable witness to the moral state of the painter at the moment when he takes his brush." One can believe Fromentin as one looks at this picture of Von Uhde's, a most touching revelation of simplicity and kindliness, and an insight as well into the heart of Jesus. This is Von Uhde's first religious picture; yet such is the sincerity and truth and directness of the conception, and such the technical manipulation of light to spiritual ends, that the painter himself feels that he has never surpassed it.

The picture is an apotheosis of childhood. It shows us the interior of what may be a village schoolhouse. The master has vacated his throne and now stands over there by the window looking modestly and reverently on while a greater than he exercises his function. The children gather round, caught by the net of kindliness this Fisher of Children has spread for them. One little tow-head has laid itself on his knee, happy in the love of a new-found friend; another bashful one stands in front and holds out a trustful hand; beyond, a mother is urging her little Gretchen to approach, and the finger in the mouth betrays Gretchen's feelings. In the foreground, the big girl in the wooden shoes is protecting her shyness behind the advance guard of a smaller sister! By the fireplace is seated one who is too young to come alone, and in the doorway are yet others in mothers' arms, waiting till the love of the children's Friend shall dissolve the parents' fears. These people are through and through German: this is the Fatherland to the life, — that Fatherland of simplicity and piety and of children that all the world loves. And Jesus loves it too, as he loved the peasantry of his own land and time; and he beams out upon it with a look of fatherly goodness and love that sums up to our hearts all that we too feel of goodness and love in our better moments.

The true message of the picture is revealed to us by what we might call the poetry of light. From the big window the sunshine floods the room, touching strongly each figure and symbolizing the joy and hope that Christ's presence brings. And at the same time it glorifies as with an aureole the golden hair of the little girl whose hand Christ is holding. Not only by the technical devices of composition, but by this visible token the artist draws our thought to this particular child, and lets us feel that the glory somehow interprets her. Look at her carefully. She is simple and unquestioning trustfulness; love brought her here, and in love she fain would abide. And this is all. Blessed creature, of such is the Kingdom of Heaven!

Did Jesus really mean what he said — " Except ye become as little children ye shall in no wise enter the kingdom of Heaven "? Did he mean to place innocence above virtue, helplessness above strength, ignorance above wisdom, inexperience and immaturity above ripened and disciplined years? Not at all. Look once more at the picture and you will see the precise thought of Jesus, for Von Uhde has caught it: this little child loves and trusts. This attitude toward God is the foundation of Christian character, the first step in the saved life. Seek this first and the other things shall be added unto you. This is the principle behind all those sayings of Christ, that seem so foolish to the worldly-wise — " Take no thought for the morrow "; " consider the lilies "; " behold the fowls of the air, your heavenly Father feedeth them "; " how much more shall your heavenly Father give good gifts to them that ask him." And yet our best philosophy tells us that if God is anything more than a bogy to scare wicked people with, he must be one who carries on his heart and secures through the operations of his universe the best good of all; that is, he is one to be trusted and loved. The noblest character is he who can look the universe full in the face and still trust, trust as absolutely as an unknowing child. To do this is to live by faith, to be religious. And if ever this old world reaches the land where the ransomed of the Lord dwell with songs and everlasting joy upon their heads, it will be because a faith like that of this little child has led them.

HOFMANN: CHRIST AND THE RICH YOUNG MAN

Matt. 19 : 16–26; Mark 10 : 17–27; Luke 18 : 18–30

Hofmann, Johann Michael Ferdinand Heinrich (1824–1911)
Original: Painted in 1889. Still in the painter's studio when he died.
Reproductions: Taber-Prang, 1, 2, 3, 4, 5, 6, 11, 12, 13, 16, 17, 18, 19, 20. Detail, Head of Christ, 1, 2, 3, 4, 5, 6, 18, 19, 20.
Fishel, Adler & Schwartz Co., artotype 14 x 18, $0.80; colored, $1.50; artotype, Head of Christ, $0.80; colored, $1.50.

This beautiful picture gives us a spiritual tragedy in briefest compass. Jesus is offering the young man a chance to leave his present life of ease and to serve the poor, and the young man is going to refuse.

While preaching one day in Perea as he journeyed to Jerusalem, Jesus noticed some rich people in the crowd. Immediately he adapted his message to them and spoke the parable of the Rich Man and Lazarus. The story was calculated to stir them deeply; Dives

254

VON UHDE: "SUFFER THE LITTLE CHILDREN TO COME UNTO ME"

in torment in the other world was not a reassuring object to contemplate. One at least of these men was moved so much that as Jesus was leaving he stopped him and asked what good thing he could do to escape such a fate. The answer was characteristic of Jesus. Having long since reached the conclusion that beliefs and ceremonies were of little worth beside a life of sympathetic service, he refers the young man to those commandments that have to do with human relations; and when the enquirer replies that he is perfect in that regard, Jesus puts his sincerity to the test: " Give your property away and join my disciples." This was an extraordinary proposition. The young man was ready to make some sacrifice but he was not ready to be a fool! And he went away sorrowful.

See how skilfully Hofmann has embodied the essentials of the narrative. The young man is very attractive. His beautiful clothes are spotless and in excellent taste; indeed one wonders whether this fine linen did not catch the eye of Jesus and suggest the description in the parable! The face though not strong is refined, the face of one delicately reared and accustomed to do conscientiously the works of the Law by which his religion assured him that he would be justified. It is easy to see how Jesus might love such a one, a youth of good impulses, of ideals, and to a large extent not responsible for the conditions that brought him to his present pass of selfishness. But it is also easy to read here the irresolute will, the habit of choosing the easier path, the superficial goodness that covers well enough the negative relations of life but does not extend in a positive and aggressive way beyond the pale of his own social set. He needs iron and a wider sympathy. Jesus divines it, and pronounces the conditions that alone will save the boy from the fate of Dives.

Notice how the eyes of Jesus are searching the young man's soul. They are kindly eyes, but they are the eyes of one who knows life. They see the issues that are involved here; not so much the difference it will make to the poor if the riches are divided, but the difference it will make in the life of this youth. It will mean no more fine clothes, no more fine dinners, no more gay companions, no more idleness, no more comfortable feeling of security in hard times, no more sense of power; but on the other hand it will mean freedom from the slavery to things, an opportunity to know what the great human needs are, a chance to invest life where its returns will compound themselves not only in blessings to the poor and the despairing, but in heavenly riches for himself through all eternity. Is this too strong a statement of the possibilities when one devotes culture and wealth to the service of God in man? Ask Francis of Assisi, ask Count Zinzindorf, ask the Earl of Shaftesbury and Henry Drummond and Wilfred Grenfell and Thomas Mott Osborne!

The antithesis in this picture is a constant one. On the one hand is poverty and wretchedness, crime and ignorance and degradation; on the other self-satisfied or proudly aggressive wealth. Between the two stands Christ with his hands pointing to the world's need and his heart wrestling with the youth of each generation, in the hope that some few among them may break their golden chains and go down to help. Now and then one sees the vision and responds; but usually they go away sorrowful, and Christ turns again with a sigh, saying, " How hardly shall they that have riches enter! "

VON GEBHARDT: CHRIST AND THE RICH YOUNG MAN

Matt. 19 : 16–26; Mark 10 : 17–27; Luke 18 : 18–30

Gebhardt, Karl Franz Eduard von (1838–   )
Original: Painted in 1892.
Reproductions:

In the Gospel of the Hebrews there is an account of this rich young man that throws light upon this picture. After telling the demand that Jesus made, the narrative goes on: " Then the rich man began to scratch his head, and the speech did not please him. And the Lord said to him, How canst thou say I have kept the law and the prophets — love thy neighbor as thyself? Behold, many of thy brethren, sons of Abraham, lie in dirty rags and die of hunger, and thy house is full of many goods, and nothing comes out of it to them." In Von Gebhardt's picture Jesus is apparently saying just this, for he has turned upon the youth with an earnestness that is almost fierce, and the young man has wilted under it. Jesus has based his demand squarely upon human need.

The general scene here given is novel and certainly attractive. We are in old Germany. The building where these folk have gathered is some kind of country storehouse or barn. Ladders hang against the wall; there is an old handcart; a pile of planks; bundles of straw spread on the earthen floor make

257

sitting easy for the heterogeneous company that has been beguiled here by the magnetism of a great Teacher. The people, though clad in the costumes of Luther's time, are in reality the people of the Parables, the homely every-day folks who work and suffer and hope. One would guess that these mothers had just brought their little ones to be blessed. Notice the good woman on the left, with her bag slung on her shoulder, peasant fashion, and her little boy asleep in her lap. See the dear old granny in the foreground hugging her knees; she is a worker still, judging by the bunch of keys and the work-bag tied to her waist. See the soulful face of the young girl next to Jesus: she is catching her first glimpse of the unfathomed abysses of the spirit. One motherless little fellow there on the right has no capital to begin life with but a torn shirt. Beyond him are the sick and the lame whose capital is now all spent or squandered, — derelicts for whom the community has not yet learned how to care; but yet not destitute of hope, since here they are, — hope dies so hard, especially with the wretched! In the center background stand the disciples and some of the able-bodied villagers, thoroughly interested in the great truths that are being discussed, especially that young man who leans forward and looks with such intensity upon the intruder. Can it be that he ever ran up against some sample of the rich man's righteousness!

"Intruder" we feel is the right word for this scion of aristocracy whom Jesus is addressing. He does not belong here. His brocaded and fur-trimmed mantle is out of place in a barn and next to home-spun. There was no doubt a little stir among the

company when he appeared at the door — the landlord's son, very likely — so that Jesus turned for a
moment to see the cause and thus gave the young
man a chance to make his speech. He may have
been sincere in his question; but Jesus seems to discover that at least he has not looked into his own
life very deeply. Else why this half-disdain in Jesus'
countenance, why the impatient gesture? Just the
contrast between him and the others shows that something is wrong: he has all he can use and more; the
others, some of them, sigh in vain for the necessities
of life. The issue is clear in Jesus' mind and his
expression of it is unequivocal: " Here are these
needy folks — your tenants, who till your soil and
create your wealth. There is no heaven for you till
you do justice by them! "

One does not have to be a Socialist to see the
righteousness of this demand. But it has taken
Christendom nearly two thousand years to get an inkling of the tremendous social reconstructions that are
implicit in that word. And the cause of the tardiness
of Christian insight and endeavor lies in the tardiness
of the Christian heart to love as Christ loved. The
fault is not all on one side by any means. It is
harder for the poor to love the rich than for the rich
to love the poor; but love each other they must if
either is to inherit eternal life. And when they begin
to love, the problem of wealth will disappear.

WATTS: " FOR HE HAD GREAT POSSES-SIONS "

Matt. 19 : 16–26; Mark 10 : 17–27; Luke 18 : 18–30

Watts, George Frederick (1817–1904)
Original: 55″ x 23″, exhibited in the Royal Academy in 1894. Now in the Tate Gallery, London.
Reproductions:

In looking at this picture one is reminded of a famous phrase of Dante, " One who made through cowardice the great refusal." Both elements in Dante's characterization apply to this sorrowing figure, for he has indeed made the great refusal and he made it through cowardice. He had not the nerve to face life without the armor of his riches. Life as a sporting proposition did not appeal to him.

This three-quarter-length figure offers us a narrow scope for study. The face is wholly hidden. We do not know the man's age, we cannot judge of his refinement, his uprightness, his intellectual power or any of his distinctive traits. We must refer to the gospels to discover the qualities for which Jesus loved him. That he is rich we judge by his raiment — the silk sleeves and turban, the velvet and fur of his mantle. That he is vain we discover when we count the rings upon his fingers and see the massy chain about his shoulder. But there is an atmosphere of indefiniteness about the whole composition, an absence of precision in character-expression that baffles us *until we come to the hand.* This is really the essential picture. It is a large hand, and it is alive; we can almost see it crawl! It is almost a passionate hand. But it is not beautiful. One feels that the spirit that animates it is as cold as a snake and as cruel as the rack. The fingers spread like talons; somewhat relaxed, to be sure, for this one moment of vain regret; but presently they will come together like a vise and never again will they open till they feel contact with some new object of desire. The man who owns it has shrunk to the compass of a silurian instinct. He has atrophied to a claw. This is natural law in the spiritual world.

We shall perhaps understand the picture more deeply if we follow Dante again. Descending with him through the frightful circles of the Inferno, we discover that in six distinct places punishments are meted out to those whom love of money has undone. The Circle of the Avaricious Dante found to be the most populous in Hell; yet though he thought he should have recognized many of the crowd, he failed to identify a single one. Virgil, his guide, tells him that the souls are in fact unrecognizable:

> " The undiscerning life that made them sordid
> Now makes them unto all discernment dim."

In other words, the love of money, failing as it does to appreciate the worth of personality, brings upon the soul the Nemesis of the loss of its own personality. The man is swallowed up of his passion. All that gives him distinctiveness as a soul, as a member of society, as God's image, dies out, and only the elemental function of grabbing remains. This is why Watts does not show us the man's face.

A little acquaintance with life indicates that poet and artist and seer are each correct. When the love of money takes possession of the soul, one by one the virtues leave and the vices arrive. First, the fountains of sympathy are stopped; then the pride of life looks out at the windows — one sees the " high-brow " and the " automobile face "; then arises the will to dominate rather than to serve; and last, that worst abuse of riches, " when it disjoins remorse from power." Jesus knew the whole tragic devolution of the type, and he sounded to his disciples the clearest notes of warning: " Lay not up for yourselves treasure upon the earth. . . . Ye cannot serve God and Mammon."

And yet, — who of us, alas! would not be rich!

WATTS: "FOR HE HAD GREAT POSSESSIONS"

Chapter XIII

THE BETHANY HOME

PICTURES FOR STUDY

Siemiradski: Christ with Mary and Martha
Rubens: Raising of Lazarus
Von Gebhardt: Raising of Lazarus

There is something restful in the name of Bethany. Whether the sound is a subtle psychologic palliative, or whether the memories of its ministry to the last weary days of Jesus mingle with the name, we feel that to rest in Bethany is to find Beulah Land. Nor is this thought belied when the traveler leaves the bustle of Jerusalem and seeks the little village still nestling in the folds of Olivet. The mountain interposes all its bulk between it and the city, and the buttresses that slope up from Kedron and the Fountain of the Apostles hold it in their embrace like the Everlasting Arms. As one lies under the old olive trees with which the slope is tufted, one feels the remoteness of the busy world and the nearness of the eternities. Below is the wrinkled and silent wilderness shuddering down to the Dead Sea. There is no sign of habitation but the tiny Arab village of Abu Dis on its little mountain top a mile away, and no sign of life but the specks of flocks that move like microscopic larvæ along the slopes. Southward the hills fade into the sky beyond the Hebron of Abraham; eastward the purple gulf where lies the "Asphaltic Pool" is backed by the precipitous scarps and level battlements of Moab, behind which the desert crouches. Wait till the shadows at your feet begin to creep eastward and the light turns golden and Moab begins to burn with the hidden fires of an opal; then you will believe that no corner of the earth is blessed with a beauty so ethereal.

But the little village of El-Azariyeh, whose name still betrays through its Arabic disguise the memory of Lazarus, has fallen from its high estate. Never was there a more wretched place, never more filth and squalor and poverty and impudence. From the moment you enter the first rubbish-choked lane that leads to the tomb of Lazarus till you emerge from the chickens and the flies that fight with you for the possession of Martha's house, you are enveloped in a swarm of women and children and boys, whose cries of "bakshish" and whose self-assumed, officious guidance make you wish that Jesus never had come to Bethany. First they open a little door that leads down to the tomb deep in the bowels of the mountain. Then to the "Castle of Lazarus" — a ruined tower that dominates the village, built last by queen Millicent in 1138 as a protection to her nunnery, but first by no one knows whom. Beyond the tower, they say, lay the house of Simon the Leper, and thirty yards to the east are the elegant though scanty vestiges of the convent that Millicent built for her sister Yvette, now doing duty as the home that Jesus loved. Over the traces of this grandeur and these memories are flung the forty hovels and the dung-heaps of El-Azariyeh. The whole is a parable of the mists and legends and the pious frauds through which we must grope our way back to Christ. But when we work ourselves once clear of these and come out into the open glories of the True, we see that majestic Figure coming up the trail from Jericho, we see Martha and Mary throw themselves at his feet, and we feel in our hearts that the silence and the beauty of that wondrous background of the wilderness against which he stands is but the reflection of his comfort and his power.

SIEMIRADSKI: CHRIST WITH MARY AND MARTHA

Luke 10 : 38–42

Siemiradski, Hendrik (1834–1902)
Original: Painted in 1885.
Reproductions:

This is Palestine. The old olive trees with their twisted hollow trunks are just like those that grow on Olivet. Through their wide inter-spaces you see the treeless hills of Judea, and the one-storied houses of stone that form the usual village The land falls off here to the right, as it does in the real Bethany when you look eastward from behind the houses, and the sun sloping down somewhat toward its setting throws the old glamor on field and tree. It is all in the picture, even to the hedge of prickly-pear, whose lobes you see behind the head of Christ.

So much the artist might have caught in a visit to the Holy Land; the rest came from himself. He inferred from the Bible that this was a home of wealth, and therefore he created this comfortable house, — not the palace that Veronese would have painted, but a wide-spreading villa of white stone; the leisurely approach with its pergola of vines and its seats for rest; the garden wall to shade the table there by the door; the mullioned window, small and rich, suggesting a noonday refuge from the heat in the dim, high hall. No wonder Jesus loved it, expressing as it did the hospitality of these generous hearts.

Martha has come down with her pot to draw water. She may have had enough already in her coolers, but this was a good way to call the attention of her sister to the duties still undone. No doubt she clanked the chain all she conveniently could and rattled the copper pail and perhaps spilled a little water on the curb so that she might utter an exclamation! But it was all no use; the pretty turban beyond the seat never stirred, the ears were deaf. And now Martha stands irresolute, poising her jar upon the steps and fidgeting with her dress, trying to decide whether to say nothing and go back to her kettles and her cakes or to give her lazy sister a piece of her mind. Ah, Martha, Martha, thou art anxious and troubled about many things. But thy guest would be pleased with nothing but figs for supper if he could only see thee here also, feasting thy soul upon his bread!

Did Mary know he was coming, and did she bring her harp out here by the rosebush and the seat, and spread the rug and place the water-pitcher, in the hope of waylaying his tired feet by these artless arts? What songs did she sing softly to herself as the moments sped, and what thoughts did she think before the moving speck on the far-away valley road became he? And with what pulses do you think she waited his approach and greeting? Let us not deceive ourselves. This sweet girl has lost her heart to the loveliest and the noblest of the sons of men. To look into his face, to hear his words, to sit at his feet, is to touch all the bounds of bliss. And this good man, who knows the hearts of all, knows this also; and he deals with her so tenderly, so wondrously, that almost without pain to her he transfers her love to something larger and worthier than himself, — to the poor whom her wealth can succor, to the suffering whom her sympathy can strengthen, to all those " little ones " of the " inasmuch," in loving whom she will still love him. Thus gently he disengages himself from bonds that are impossible, and leaves her sadly happy.

How sweet to her the memories of these lessons in which his gracious person merges with the truth he teaches, till all good seems easy and any sacrifice possible for his sake! And when the shadow of the great tragedy falls, then she begins at last to see dimly what it is he has done for her and why he did it.

RUBENS: RAISING OF LAZARUS

John 11 : 1–46

Rubens, Peter Paul (1577–1640)
Original: 8'7 x 6'5, painted about 1624. Now in the Kaiser Friedrich's Museum, Berlin.
Reproductions: Seemann Three-color print, No. 1448.
    Berlin Photographic Co., No. 5278: Photogravure $19\frac{1}{8}$ x $14\frac{1}{8}$," $5.00.

This theme has been frequently painted, doubtless because the church has seen in the incident the

supreme proof that Jesus was the Son of God. Other
miracles may be wonderful, but this one so far transcends the possible that it can be explained only as a
special fiat of omnipotence; its accomplishment removes the doer from the category of mere man.
Beginning therefore with Giotto we have the marvel
depicted with all degrees of realism and conviction.
But scholars of our generation, including some of the
most devout, are inclined to regard the narrative in
John as an allegorical expansion of Jesus' teaching, "I
am the resurrection and the life" (John 11 : 25–26);
and we must accordingly interpret the pictures in a
spiritual way in so far as the artist will allow it.

Rubens has treated the theme with considerable
realism. In accordance with the narrative he has
represented the tomb as a cave; in fact, the wall of
rock and the steps suggest the tomb that is shown
today in Bethany. Who the two men are we can
only guess, — probably disciples. One of them is
raising the grave-clothes from Lazarus' head as if he
were exhibiting him. The other is half crouching
with awe. The multitude of Jews who stood around
is nowhere hinted.

The picture is entirely Rubenesque: it is full of
dramatic power but lacking in spiritual depth. Jesus
stands like a professional wonder-worker, his arms
raised in rather theatrical style long after the occasion for gesture has passed. There is nothing especially attractive about his face; it gives the impression
of a man of commanding presence and personality
intent on doing a certain piece of work, and that
largely for the sake of exhibiting his power. One
of the sisters (Mary?) looks up at him with surprise

and admiration, as if the fact of the miracle appealed more to her than did the restoration of her brother.

The real beauty and power of the picture lie in the two figures of Lazarus and Martha. Lazarus is running up the steps of the tomb as if his spirit could not respond quickly enough to the divine summons. He is a picture of health, for the same power that has called him back from the grave has restored also his body to its full bloom of youth. It is interesting to observe that he pays no attention to his sisters, but fixes a gaze of love and gratitude on his benefactor. It is a beautiful expression, and appropriate enough from one point of view, but quite inexplicable from another: this look hardly belongs to one who has been lying in " Abraham's bosom " for four days, but rather to one who has been conscious of the darkness and the awfulness of the grave and whose only feeling on coming back to life is relief. When one considers deeply, it would seem that Keller, in his Raising of Jairus' Daughter (p. 196) had entered into the psychology and the true meaning of the experience of awakening more adequately than has Rubens. Rubens has transferred to Lazarus the expression that Mary should have worn.

Martha is wholly admirable. She has been suffering; her eyes are not yet free from tears. But the weeping turns to joy as the beloved face of her brother issues from the tomb. Wonder and awe at the miracle are swallowed up by the great tide of love that surges from her bosom. For the time being she has forgotten Christ: " My brother has come back to us! " is her one thought. In Martha therefore we see embodied a human affection that makes her

269

kin to you and me. In precisely this spirit would we clasp again our loved ones, restored after we felt they had been lost beyond recall.

VON GEBHARDT: RAISING OF LAZARUS

John 11 : 1–46

Gebhardt, Karl Franz Eduard von (1838–   )
Original: Painted in 1896; privately owned.
Reproductions:

We are standing in a continental cemetery such as one sees in old cities like Prague. There is a gateway of brick and stone; there are crowded graves with round-topped headstones, overshadowed by the green of deciduous trees and the darker evergreen of cypress. The grave of Lazarus is a shallow sarcophagus of white marble resting on a broad marble plinth. It is a grave such as few can afford, and the three great wreaths with their ribbons also speak of wealth. The emaciated young Lazarus is sitting up in his coffin and trying to recall what has happened, while three men and a woman are helping to unbind him. See the utter astonishment of the one who gazes into his face, and the kindliness of the old man at the head. The young man at the foot has turned to hear Jesus' words, impressed more with the doer than with the deed. The crowd of common folk compacted there at the gate dare not come nearer, but show on their faces with a realism that arrests our attention the whole range of emotions that such an event would produce, from interest to astonishment and fear and awe. The gaze of every one is riveted on Lazarus.

RUBENS: THE RAISING OF LAZARUS

The two sisters are kneeling at Jesus' feet. Martha is the one behind, wearing at her girdle the keys that are the symbol of her cares. She is too astounded for words. Mary, with rapturous upturned face, expresses with her eyes her eternal thanks and happiness. She is really beautiful, — her golden hair streaming down her shoulders, one hand raised in an involuntary gesture of wonder and the other grasping the arm of Jesus. The meaning of this experience for her and Martha is all expressed in this figure in terms of human affection. Hers is a love that gathers in one embrace both Lazarus her brother and Christ her benefactor. In this act she has poured out herself till nothing of self remains:

" Love took up the harp of Life and smote on all its chords with
    might;
  Smote the chord of Self, that, trembling, passed in music out
    of sight."

Such self-effacing love is Mary's. And such love in her case is too mighty to be called love: it is worship.

Jesus leans over her tenderly and lays one comforting hand on her brow while he points upward with the other. In this way Von Gebhardt shows us why Jesus performed the miracle, — it was because of love; and he indicates the source of Jesus' power, — it was his Father. The love of Jesus links our weakness and our mortality with the immortal source of life and power. His face, too, is the face of a sufferer, of one who has borne our griefs and carried our sorrows, even while his own sorrows are leading him to Calvary. Yet his faith rises superior to all these. Beyond his own cross he sees victory, and behind death, as behind life, stands love. Only because he apprehends this by a triumphant faith can he bring to our hearts the assurance of immortal love and life eternal. This is a human Christ, our Elder Brother; but it is also our Savior.

And thus it comes to pass that his words, " I am the Resurrection and the Life," have been repeated through the centuries over every Christian grave, and their music mingles in the ears of the dying with the music of the choirs of heaven.

CHAPTER XIV

THE APPROACH TO JERUSALEM

PICTURES FOR STUDY

Flandrin: Christ Mourns over the City
Giotto: The Triumphal Entry
Doré: Christ Entering Jerusalem

We now enter upon what is technically called Passion Week. Behind us are Christ's labors for the world at large, the rejection in Galilee, the sojourn in Perea till the Passover time should draw nigh, and his ascent from Jericho to the quiet suburb of Bethany. It is now Monday noon. There is time only for a midday refreshment in the home he loved, and then he must go forth to proclaim in his own unique way that he is the Messiah.

Today there are two approaches to Jerusalem from Bethany. You may take the carriage road that follows the contours of the Mount of Olives at an easy gradient to the southwest shoulder, above the " Hill of Offence." Here you reach the highest point of the road, and as your horses swing round the curve and head northward, suddenly the whole city bursts upon you, lying close at hand yet separated from you by the deep gulf of the Kedron. The other path, which has never become a road but which is still used, leads due west from Bethany up the steep sides of Olivet, past little Bethphage; then still hugging the slope, it ascends to the saddle where the Mosque of the Ascension now stands, a point some five hundred yards further to the north and some two hundred feet higher than the first-mentioned view-point. Here also the city comes suddenly upon you. From this point it was that Christ and his followers saw it.

It was a sight to set the imagination on fire. The little hill that had served David as his capital was nearest them and far below. Over it to the left rose the mass of Mt. Zion crowned with the High Priest's palace, the palace of the Hasmoneans and the houses of the aristocracy; and to the right the four great towers and massive walls of Herod's palace, the residence of Pilate the Roman Procurator. In the immediate foreground, so near that they could see each individual of the vast Passover throng that swarmed it, rose the huge pile of the Temple, its central building plated with gold, and its grand colonnades and porches gleaming with white marble. To the right of the Temple and dominating it frowned the fortress of Antonia, home of the Roman legions. And between these larger buildings lay the thrice-compacted houses of the people, climbing the steep hillsides or sinking with the valleys down to the Pool of Siloam. What passionate thoughts were his as Jesus looked at these symbols of his people's state: at the priestly palaces of the Sadducees, half Hellenized and wholly corrupt; at Pilate's judgment hall that summarized the despotism of an alien power; at Antonia where lay the ruthless instruments of that despotism; at his Father's house, beautiful as a dream to look upon, but surrounded by the powers of this world and desperately subordinated to, them. And helpless beneath them all lay the poor and the enslaved and the spiritually starved, who through fear might not come unto him to receive life. O Jerusalem, Jerusalem! ridden by priestcraft, wasted by cynical cruelty, seething with discontent and rebellion, thou knowest not the things that pertain to thy peace. When thy King cometh unto thee, thou wilt give him not a crown but the cross!

FLANDRIN: CHRIST MOURNS OVER THE CITY

Luke 19 : 41–44

Flandrin, Paul Hippolyte
Original: Painted in 1904
Reproductions: Braun & Co. I

No one but a modern could have conceived this picture, and none but moderns can understand it. It is an expression of the social failure of the gospel, the translation of Christ's lament into terms of industrialism and materialism and greed, the arraignment of civilization before the bar of conscience.

Christ stands on Olivet and with the vision of a Seer looks down the vistas of time. The Jerusalem of Caiaphas lying before him has dissolved in mist, and in place of the frowning city wall rises a compact tier of tenements. The dark flats are crowded like the rabbit-warrens of old Jerusalem, only there is no bright and wind-swept housetop for any family but the topmost one. Behind, where the temple of the Living God once stood, there is a murk of smoke and a reek of steam, and through the gloom come the pulse-beats of trip-hammers and the sudden spurts of white-hot flame from furnace doors. Some new god is being worshipped here, some

275

> " Moloch, horrid king, besmeared with blood
> Of human sacrifice, and parents' tears."

You can see the hosts assembling to serve him, the myriads of men who all day feed the flames and pour the metal; myriads of little children driving their task from dawn till sunset amid the rattle and roar of looms and gears. Once the seer holds out his arms and cries, " Suffer the little children to come unto me! " But his voice is lost in the din of ravenous machines.

Above where Herod's palace should have lowered, he sees the domes and towers of great cathedrals. But they stand deserted. No lights gleam from them; if there is organ music rolling through the lofty aisles no ear hears it but God's. There may be priests at the altar, but the people are not thronging thither for the Bread of Life; they are still tending their fires and their hammers, still fighting for the bread that perishes, still hating one another like the monsters of a pre-Adamic age.

> " There among the glooming alleys Progress halts on palsied feet,
> Crime and hunger cast our maidens by the thousands on the street.
> There the master scrimps his haggard sempstress of her daily bread,
> There a single sordid attic holds the living and the dead.
> There the smouldering fire of fever creeps across the rotted floor,
> And the crowded couch of incest in the warrens of the poor."

Meantime God's daylight dies, and the pall of night settles down unrelieved by stars. But still the

276

FLANDRIN: CHRIST WEEPING OVER THE CITY

Seer stands motionless above the city, his hands clasped in contemplation, his sad yet fascinated face still poring on the sights and sounds that strike upon his soul. Where are his disciples? Have they given up in despair the task of preaching love and good will? Is there no one to say, "See that ye despise not these little ones!"; no one to throw down the altars that smoke to Mammon and Belial? No one to repeat the old commandment, "Thou shalt worship the Lord thy God, and Him only shalt thou serve"; or that greater one, "Thou shalt love thy neighbor as thyself"? Yes, thank God, we know that there are some down there in the great city who care; there are a few who wrestle with Boards of Trade for a square deal, who clean up Bowerys and East Sides, who plead with Senators to pass Child Labor Laws in order that God's little ones may have a day of sunshine before they go to grind in the prison house; who preach an honest day's work for a day's pay, and no dynamite for the open shop. Yes, there are a few who care, — after two millenniums of the Gospel! But the artist who painted this picture has not shown them.

This is Paul Flandrin's judgment on Christianity in 1904. Had he painted the picture in the present year of Grace, he would have filled the air with bursting shrapnel, he would have wrecked the cathedral dome, piled the foreground with the shattered bodies of men, and pierced with bayonets a newly crucified Christ. And a fair maiden with stars in her hair would crouch behind the cross and hug a bag of gold!

GIOTTO: THE TRIUMPHAL ENTRY

Matt. 21 : 1–17; Mark 11 : 1–11; Luke 19 : 29–40; John 12 : 12–19

Giotto: Angiolo di Bondone, called (1266?–1337)
Original: Fresco in the Arena Chapel, Padua (v. note under Giotto's Baptism).
Reproductions:

Giotto has endeavored to give us here with all faithfulness the incidents of the scripture narrative. Jesus, a clear-cut, vigorous man, is riding on an ass, while the disciples follow as a solid phalanx, rather austere and determined in appearance. As the Master goes, some spread their garments in the way. You may see them performing this act most naïvely in the picture: the man on the right begins to free his arm from the sleeve of his mantle; the lady below is pulling hers off over her head; the one in front is unrolling his on the ground. This is almost as good as moving pictures! We read that others cut down branches and strewed them in the way, so Giotto shows us the process. The man in the palm tree on the left is certainly an adept at climbing, and the one in the slender olive tree is risking his life! Out from the arched and tower-protected gateway streams the crowd, interested but not excited. This is all vigorous realism.

This picture will serve as well as any other to turn our thoughts toward the event and its meaning. All four gospels give the story, and as we trace it from the earliest account to the latest we can see how a simple symbolic act becomes more and more complex. In Mark, Jesus is attended merely by his friends, perhaps twenty in number, who in their enthusiasm spread their garments in the way and strew the path with handfuls of straw plucked from the fields (Mk. 11 : 8, margin, Amer. Version). In Luke the band of disciples has become a multitude, and the Pharisees appear as critics. Matthew sees in the act the fulfilment of prophecy (Zech. 9 : 9), and adds that the whole city was stirred, that the children shouted in the temple, and that the cures of the lame and blind moved the chief priests to indignation. According to John the incident is a great popular movement in which the crowds that had assembled for the Passover, hearing that Jesus was coming up to the feast, streamed out to form a grand triumphal procession, carrying branches of palm trees — which probably never grew in Jerusalem. And John adds rather significantly (12 : 16): " These things understood not his disciples at first; but when Jesus was glorified then remembered they that these things were written of him and that they had done these things unto him." Which is another way of saying that it took time for a simple act to assume such triumphal proportions in the church's mind.

Mark, as usual, brings us nearest to the probabilities. Jesus has decided to show himself in Jerusalem as Messiah. To advance with big crowds and with shouting would be to stir up all those false conceptions of Messiahship that he had combatted all his life, to fan to a flame the fanaticism of the Passover enthusiasts and to call down upon them the legions from Antonia. Jesus needed to perform some act that should stamp upon the imagination of his disciples the significance of this final appeal to Jerusalem, and yet should be unobtrusive. He therefore deliberately turned the imagery of Zechariah to his purpose, rode upon the ass' colt, and accepted the joyful shouts of his friends as tokens of their loyalty and their hopes. Nothing further happened but a brief survey of the Temple courts and his retirement to Bethany with the twelve.

Simple as the facts are, they mark the beginning of a new act in the great tragedy. This was the first time that Jesus had allowed any one to make public proclamation of his Messiahship. He himself realized his call at his baptism, Peter had discovered it and confessed it before the disciples at Cæsarea Philippi, but Jesus had charged them to tell no man (Mk. 8 : 30). Now the time had come when Jerusalem must know it, even though the proclamation meant death to him. For his disciples' sake, therefore, he rides in symbolic triumph to the city, but for the peoples' sake he teaches daily in the Temple courts, and with all the fervor and the skill his soul and mind possess he offers himself to them as their Lord and King. The Triumphal Entry is the dramatic beginning of that final appeal.

DORÉ: CHRIST ENTERING JERUSALEM

Matt. 21 : 1–17; Mark 11 : 1–11; Luke 19 : 29–40; John 12 : 12–19

Doré, Paul Gustave (1832–1883)
Original: In the Doré Gallery, London.
Reproductions:

A comparison of Doré's picture with Giotto's throws light on both. In Giotto we have fact, in Doré fancy. Giotto portrays the outward and shows by pose and facial expression the significance of the event for the participators; Doré paints the inner aspect of the event, makes it a scene in a vast historic drama in which other ages and other worlds are involved. Both conceptions are true and can be reconciled with each other.

This picture is spectacular. We are evidently standing within the Temple courts and looking out through a grand triumphal arch, more beautiful than ever Rome decreed to her conquering generals. Beyond, the sunshine falls from a brilliant sky and whitens into a glory the houses of the city and the festal crowds upon the housetops. Within, the colonnades and towers have cast cool shadows, so that Jesus stands out clear and dark against the light behind. The vast multitude that John's gospel mentions is here thronging him and for a better view mounting the steps and even the pedestals of columns. All sorts are here: we see a Roman soldier on the right arguing with a priest, and within the shadow men and women of high rank. In the foreground are mostly women and children, some waving palm branches and some strewing them in the way. Some hold their little ones up to catch the Messiah's blessing; some are ready to throw great garlands about him. The attitudes and expressions of all indicate their reverence and self-abasement before the conqueror, their Messiah. On the far left we see the spirit of opposition, glances of suspicion shot his way, backs turned, arguments about what shall be done, — for " the whole world is gone after him." What can hatred accomplish against this hero, guarded by the loyalty of a mighty people!

Two features show Doré's interpretation of the

event, — Christ and the angels. Christ is advancing as in an ecstasy. He does not see the crowds, he does not hear their shouting. His eyes are fixed on far-away things; his hand is raised as if to greet the great events that the future holds. He is living in prophecy. Beyond this present people his view sweeps: he sees nation rising against nation and kingdom against kingdom, he hears the shock of earthquakes and the wailing that follows famine and pestilence, the terrors and the signs in heaven. But he knows that all these things must needs come to pass first, and that after those days the God of Heaven shall set up his kingdom that shall never be destroyed. In that kingdom he will be prince and regent. He shall see of the travail of his soul and shall be satisfied. In that glory the agony of the cross is forgotten, dissolved as a dream when one awaketh, casting no shadow against the perfect light of that Day.

The angels in the sky are Doré's externalization, for us, of Christ's vision. They are the answering glory that comes down to meet his triumphant faith. They are the seraphic guard that shall preserve him from all evil in the coming shock when the Prince of Darkness shall battle for his soul. They are reminders that

> " behind the dim unknown
> Standeth God within the shadow
> Keeping watch above his own,"

and that the death of his servant shall be but an incident in the onward sweep of his purposes.

Pictures like this make us realize the grandeur of the issues here involved, and the tremendous significance for all time of the life and death of Christ.

DORE: CHRIST ENTERING JERUSALEM

HOFMANN: CHRIST DRIVING OUT THE MONEY-CHANGERS

Chapter XV

FINAL LABORS FOR JERUSALEM

PICTURES FOR STUDY .

Hofmann: Christ Driving out the Money-Changers
Kirchbach: Cleansing the Temple.
Titian: The Tribute Money

There seems to be no reasonable doubt that Jesus came to Jerusalem partly to denounce the religious leaders of his nation who not only had through their emissaries made it impossible for him to continue his work in Galilee, but who by their personal greed and crimes and hypocrisies were destroying the Jewish religion. Knowing how utterly scathing his denunciation would be, he knew also that the rulers would not allow him to live long. But by contriving to keep himself always in the open by day, with the multitude whose cause he was championing, and by withdrawing each night to unknown places in the country, he managed to postpone his death four days! Never were days so filled with spiritual labor, and never did teacher show such defensive and offensive skill. By parable and argument and question, by direct denunciation and strenuous act, he taught his nation that the religion of the Sadducees and the Pharisees was an outrageous sham, and he demanded for the humble and the poor the right to worship God untramelled by the restrictions of priest and tradition. One has only to recall the incidents of Wednesday and Thursday to realize what a precious legacy of religious truth has come down to us from these days. To them belong the parable of the Vineyard, the incident of the Tribute Money, the question about the Resurrection, What is the greatest Commandment, the parable of the Good Samaritan, the Adulteress, warning of the Scribes and Pharisees, the widow's mite, the prophecy of the destruction of the Temple, the discourse on the Second Coming; and some scholars would also place here the parables of the Wise and Foolish Virgins, the Talents, the Last Judgment and the Wedding Feast.

One of Jesus' most significant acts, occurring on Thursday, was to drive the traders from the temple courts. These traders, or rather "grafters," were of two kinds, of which the first were bankers or money-changers. All Jews had to pay to the Temple an annual tribute of half a shekel (about 29 cts.), and that in Jewish coin. Since the Jews were scattered all over the world and brought all kinds of money when they came to the Passover, there was need of money-changers. The rate of exchange was excessive and yielded about $50,000 a year to the bankers, equivalent now to many times that sum in purchasing power. The priests did a general banking business in addition. The Temple revenues were so enormous that Crassus, in 54 B.C., was able to take loot to the value of $12,500,000. Then there was the traffic in sacrificial animals. These had to be bought of the officials of the Temple at a good round sum, or if brought from without must be examined by an official, who of course had his fee. The market was some-times cornered, and the price of a pair of doves, for

example, ran up from four cents to four dollars!
There is evidence in the Talmud that Annas the
High Priest was chief robber in the ring. No wonder
that Jesus attacked this great iniquity. It is noticeable that all the opposition of the Scribes and Pharisees to his teaching could not avail to bring about his
downfall; but when Jesus attacked the vested interests
of the Sadducees he was arrested within forty-eight
hours!

HOFMANN: CHRIST DRIVING OUT THE MONEY–CHANGERS

Matt. 21 : 12–17; Mark 11 : 15–18; Luke 19 : 45–48

Hofmann: Johann Michael Ferdinand Heinrich (1824–1911)
Original: A drawing.
Reproductions:

This picture is a piece of realism, valuable chiefly
as a basis of comparison with Kirchbach. Jesus is
coming out from the Temple proper into a porch or
colonnade, and driving before him the money-changers.
There is no suggestion of the sheep, oxen or doves
mentioned in John 2 : 14. Moreover Hofmann's
Temple is too humble an affair to represent the magnificence of Herod's building. But such as the details
are, they are specific and interesting. The scene is
vigorous. We see the general confusion caused by
Jesus' unexpected act, — the tables overturned, the
money spilled, the men's haste to get beyond the
reach of the Master's wrath. We see the anger and
resentment in the face and gesture of the man with
the money-bags whom Jesus has evidently just struck,
and the mild panic in the looks of the others. Jesus

is certainly in earnest and in command of the situation. His face is stern. "Take these things hence" (Jn. 2 : 16) is implied in his strong gesture. This is all good so far as it goes.

Nevertheless there is something lacking here. Hofmann has not apprehended the psychology of the situation. What was it that caused the panic in the hearts of those hard-hearted merchandisers? — Hardly a whip of small cords in the hands of an angry man. Any fanatic might attempt to clean out the Temple; but he would get about as far as upsetting his second table when somebody would lay hands upon him and hustle him out at the gate — if indeed the mob let him escape at all. Fanatics with small whips are too common in sacred places in the East to add anything to the scene but life and merriment. Something deeper must have happened. Some moral dynamic was present that far transcended the might of the whip, some power of indignation that in a small man would have been ridiculous, but in one who possessed the moral sublimity of Jesus was resistless. Jesus swept these men before him as the tempest drives the dust. His whip was the merest symbol of a might that was stronger than force, of the ultimate power of righteousness to drive wickedness into perdition. It is this phase of Christ's act that has escaped Hofmann; and his picture therefore fails to awaken in us the emotion of moral sublimity that the original act undoubtedly would have aroused. Kirchbach has succeeded better.

KIRCHBACH: CLEANSING THE TEMPLE

Matt. 21 : 12–17; Mark 11 : 15–18; Luke 19 : 45–48

Kirchbach, Frank (1859–   )
Original: Painted in 1887.
Reproductions:

In this striking picture our attention is arrested first by the Temple architecture. It is grandiose, spectacular, suggestive of a great civilization in which power has clothed itself in majesty. The lofty pylon in the background, shining white in the sun and suggesting heights beyond the limit of the picture, appeals strongly to the imagination and has even more dramatic force than the foreground. Yet the latter speaks of strength and beauty. Notice the giant column that stands out dark against the pylon and blossoms into a huge bell-capital, floreated with Egyptian motives. This and the background are reminiscences of the solidity, the strength, the barbaric richness of the land of the Nile; especially do we seem to hear the voice of Philæ and Esneh and Edfu, thoroughly Roman in spirit though they speak with the tongue of Egypt. All the rest of the Temple is classic: the engaged column, the round arch with its heavy decoration on face and soffit, the decorated pilasters beneath. Though Herod's Temple may not have looked like this, what matters it? The artist wanted a striking background for a dramatic scene, and he has given us just that. It is all grand-opera stage scenery, quite in the style of his master Munkacsy.

But Kirchbach has given us more than a grand background: he has added meaning. Although he

287

knew — or might have known — that the Temple in Jesus' day was only forty years old, he has presented here a time-worn structure that has evidently gone through sieges and conflagrations; otherwise why has he spoiled what ought to be a splendid flare on the edge of his two bell-capitals, and nicked the edges of his stones in the face of the building and elsewhere? He has suggested age as well as stability. He is trying to make us feel that here is a great and venerable institution, sanctified by generations of worshippers and protected by the sanctions of immemorial custom. All this on the one hand, and on the other,— a single man. This that is staged here is a heroic situation. With a sublime egoism Jesus stands in front of this embodiment of his nation's religion and challenges it in the name of God! That one figure is the dynamic center of the whole composition. He stands there as firm and unmovable as the great white pylon whose lines are only an echo of his own figure; and from him roll the waves of moral indignation that have swept the porch clear and strewn the wreckage on the borders of the picture. The building is a necessary background for Jesus; without it he would lose half his meaning.

The details of the actors in the picture are so obscure that it is difficult to make them out. On the extreme right is an old man, his wife (?) and son. Possibly the man is a money-changer for he has a table and a scroll. They are uncertain whether the Rabbi's wrath will reach as far as them. Between them and the Egyptian pillar is a group of Scribes and Pharisees no doubt discussing the legal ethics of the situation. Below them are three or four sheep.

Between us and the pillar two men are mildly struggling, the front one with the basket evidently reluctant to leave the Temple and the other one too frightened to return. The most dramatic action is in the foreground. An old man has landed in a heap on some pigeon crates, spilling the contents of his basket and freeing the pigeons. A dark figure is half trying to stop their flight, though too frightened to take his eyes from Jesus. The cause of the upset is the two struggling figures behind them, one courageously trying to bring back the frightened other one by force. Between the two pillars one sees in the distance the crowds going up into the Temple; in the foreground the angry or excited people who are affected by this incident. On the left of the picture is a panic-stricken group of four — a woman selling fish, another with eggs, an old man clutching money-bags and hustling away for dear life, and a younger man who as yet is holding his ground.

But where are the disciples? Possibly those who stand behind Jesus under the arch. One of them stoops over and speaks to the woman and her child as if to reassure them. The others are mere space-fillers. And who are these women and children, — why should they be here? Their attitude seems to be not one of fear of Jesus. On the contrary there seems to be a suggestion that they are looking to him for protection, and that for their sakes, somehow, he has cast these rascals out of the sanctuary. More than likely this was the artist's intention. It certainly was the fate of many a pious Israelite to be held up by these impudent dealers, because they could not compass the price of even a dove for sacrifice, and to

be sent home in any but a pious frame of mind.
This iniquity against the common man was precisely
what Jesus endeavored to stop. He was attacking
here a mighty vested interest with its grip on the
whole Jewish world. He was exposing graft that
began with the priestly retailer and wound its defiling
course up through the various ranks of priestly middle-
men till it coiled itself at last in the High Priest's
chair. This is the grand indictment that Jesus makes
of the rulers of his nation: those who should minister
to religion are filling their pockets; God's house of
prayer has become a den of thieves. And the wave
of indignation that breaks from him and engulfs
the evil-doers is not merely a zeal for God's house,
as his witnesses reported, but a zeal for the voiceless
thousands of his people whose only way to God, as
they thought, was barred by the greed of priests.
Jesus is here the champion of social justice.

KIRCHBACH: CLEANSING THE TEMPLE

TITIAN: TRIBUTE MONEY

TITIAN: THE TRIBUTE MONEY

Matt. 22 : 15–22; Mark 12 : 13–17; Luke 20 : 20–26

Titian: Tiziano Vecelli, called (1477–1576)

Original: Painted on wood, 2'8 x 2', probably in 1508 (Vasari says 1514). It was the property of Alfonso I, Duke of Ferrara, in whose study it formed a panel in a door, though the only evidence that it was painted expressly for him is the fact that on his gold coins was stamped the inscription, " Render unto Cæsar the things that are Cæsar's, and to God the things that are God's." From Ferrara it went in the beginning of the 17th century to Modena, whence in 1746 it was acquired by the King of Saxony and is now in the Dresden Gallery.

Reproductions: In color, Medici Prints, chromo-lithograph 20¾ x 15½", Italian, xlii. $9.50.

Seemann three-color half-tone, No. 33.

Berlin Photographic Co. No. 3004: Photogravure 25¾ x 19¼", $15.00.

The " Tribute Money " is acknowledged by all critics to be one of the noblest works of the greatest of the Venetians. Titian's contemporaries also regarded this head of Christ as the most perfect thing that Titian ever produced. It is painted with extraordinary delicacy, quite in contrast to the painter's usual " broad " style: one can almost count the hairs in some of the locks of Christ's head. And the story goes that he was led to take such pains because of the remark of some German travellers who visited him that no Italian could finish pictures like Dürer. Time has dealt not too gently with the once delicately transparent colors, but the picture is still one of the priceless treasures of the Zwinger Gallery.

This picture is a character-study. Two types are

291

in close opposition, the wise Master-teacher and the cunning Pharisee, and Titian has taken pains to emphasize the contrast in all possible ways. Christ's tunic is of rich red cloth of loose texture and his outer mantle of fine blue broadcloth, while the other's clothes are rough and coarse. The general form of the Pharisee is burly, — his face is tanned with weather, his arms are muscular and bronzed, his hand gnarled, his hair close-cropped; Christ is delicately modelled, with clear complexion, with hands that are full of nerve and grace, and with rich hair and beard — though this feature is lost in reproduction. The moment chosen by the artist is when Christ asks " Whose is the image and superscription? " for this moment better than any other brings to high light the characters of the two men.

Study the Pharisee first. He has a sly, sharp face, the face of one whose intellect is keen but whose morals are perverted. He has not brought this perplexing question to Christ because he wants light, but because he wants to entrap him. He knows perfectly well that paying taxes is a sore point with all Jews, since it is an acknowledgment of their political subjection, and if Jesus advises the paying of taxes the mob can easily be inflamed against him. He knows too that if Jesus says it is not lawful to give tribute to Cæsar, the next move of the Pharisees will be to denounce him to the Roman authorities as a seditious demagogue. He is going to impale Jesus on one horn or the other of this dilemma, and there is no escape. All this comes out in the face of this fox, — in the sharpness of the nose, the " bluffing wrinkles " on the forehead, the ready mouth, the insistent attitude that would hustle Jesus into an answer before he has time to think.

But Jesus is not to be hustled or bluffed. His face retains its serene and noble look; it turns full toward the inquisitor though his body turns not an inch — which is a gesture of disdain. Without the quaver of an eyelid his eye returns the ferret-look, and the wise spirit fathoms at a glance all the guile that prompts both the flattery and the question.

"Whose image? — Cæsar's! This heathen coin that you carry about on your persons is proof that you are slaves. You are Cæsar's already, in property and person. A denarius more or less counts nothing. The vital question is, Do you render to God the things that are God's?"

With such consummate skill he thrusts aside the casuistries of politics, and holds before these hypocrites the burning question of Religion. And in so doing he is following out consistently the principles established long ago in the Wilderness temptation: he will have nothing to do with politics, he will propound no theory of State; his business is to rebuke sin and lead men to God. That business he will prosecute without rest and without equivocation till his enemies silence his voice forever.

"Seek ye first the Kingdom of God and his righteousness" is thus the first and the last message of the Messiah to his people.

Chapter XVI

THE APPROACHING DOOM

It is possible to trace the movements of Jesus hour by hour from Thursday afternoon till his death, at least as far as the events are concerned; some of the exact localities are still the subject of dispute.

First comes the supper with the disciples. According to tradition the room in which they met was on Mt. Zion, not far from the palace of the High Priest, and now known to Christians as the Cœnaculum, though called by the Moslems the Tomb of David. We can trace its history back through the crusades, when much of the present structure was built (1342), to the time of Helena (4th cent.); and previous to that we have the testimony of St. Epiphanius (307–403) that when the emperor Hadrian arrived in the city in 135 A.D., he found Christians in possession of the little church of the Cenacle in which the apostles assembled after the Ascension. It occupied the site of the house of John Mark. This spot is therefore linked to two great incidents in the history of our faith, the Last Supper and Pentecost. If there is a " Mother Church " in Christendom it is certainly here.

Gethsemane is less surely identified, though the traditional spot cannot be far wrong. It is now a little garden, perhaps two hundred feet square, enclosed by a high wall (for purposes of defence!) and entered by a narrow door four feet high. A few tall cypresses and eight venerable olive trees, with trunks twenty to thirty feet in circumference, cast their shadows upon the flowers that the Franciscan brothers grow there with such care. The piety of the centuries has marked all the sacred places in the vicinity, — the rock where the disciples slept, the grotto of the agony, the column of betrayal. In the quiet of twilight it is not impossible to enter into the very spirit of the memories there enshrined, and to feel the tragic tensity of that hour. It is indeed a hard heart that comes away unsoftened.

JUSTUS OF GHENT: LAST SUPPER

Matt. 26 : 17–30; Mark 14 : 12–26; Luke 22 : 7–20; John 13 : 21-30

Justus of Ghent (born 1410?)

Original: On wood, 10′ square; painted between 1468 and 1475 for the brotherhood of Corpus Christi and paid for by the subscriptions of the Duke of Urbino and others. An altarpiece for the church of Sant' Agata at Urbino, now preserved in the Municipal gallery.

Reproductions:

There are three modes of conceiving and painting a Last Supper: as a dogma, as an incident and as a spiritual experience. Justus illustrates the first, Da Vinci the second and Von Uhde the third.

The picture by Justus is everything that a Last Supper should not be. It is not a representation of the gospel story, it is a piece of theology made tangible. The room here portrayed is not the upper chamber of the house of John Mark in Jerusalem but rather a church. The table is in the apse where the high altar should stand. Angels hover over the scene, one folding his hands in adoration, the other raising them most delicately and dramatically in astonishment at the miracle that has taken place. The disciples are most of them on their knees, as if at the altar-rail, and their hands are folded in prayer or otherwise indicate their perception of the mystical nature of the event. The one to whom Jesus offers the bread looks up with holy awe as if he were quite unworthy to partake. One can even discover by the looks on their faces that the three to our right have already received the Eucharist while those on our left have not. John the Beloved places on the table a flask; the man at his right holds a long taper; Judas, the last figure

297

on our left, grasps his money-bag and starts for the door. A rail separates the table from the rest of the church. Behind this the Duke of Urbino, with two attendants behind him, converses with a stately gentleman in a huge turban and brocaded robe. This last is a Persian ambassador named Zeno who had just come to the Duke's court to raise funds and troops for his master, the Shah of Persia, who was fighting against the Turks — old enemies of the Italian Christian states. The Duke did honor to the ambassador by introducing him here as spectator of the sacrament! On the table stands the chalice, patterned in conventional fashion. Pitcher and basin are in the foreground to remind us of our need of humility. Christ has also assumed an attitude of humility, yet with a look of supernal wisdom on his countenance; he holds in one hand a plate and in the other a wafer in form like the "host" of the Catholic mass.

What does this mean? It means that we are here contemplating a sacrament of the Church, one that has a vital interest for all succeeding generations; that the miracle of Transubstantiation has here taken place, by which the bread and wine of the supper have become in very truth the body and the blood of Christ; and that by the partaking of these elements a spiritual change is wrought in the soul of each partaker.

The history of this doctrine is typical of the transformation that so much of Christianity has undergone. The Eucharist was originally a simple act of breadbreaking performed at a family meal. Then it passed to the Christian synagogue and the other family groups of Christians, where the special act came at the close of the common meal or " love-feast." Soon it became the object of Greek speculative thought and absorbed certain mystic elements from the " Mysteries " of the Hellenic world. Controversies arose and schisms, men abandoning the true fellowship of communion for the antagonisms of theological strife and even for the sword and the stake! Out of the strifes the dogmas finally took shape. By 1215 at least the word Transubstantiation was used to describe the miracle of the Eucharist, and the Council of Trent, 1551, settled for the Catholic world the necessary belief about the Lord's Supper, viz. —

1. The Person of Christ, his humanity and his divinity entire, is wholly present in the elements of the Lord's Supper, in each element and in each particle of each. These elements are therefore legitimate objects of worship.

2. The effects of partaking of these elements are, first, a " spiritual and mystical union with Jesus by the theological virtue of Love "; and second, a " blotting out of venial sin and preserving the soul from mortal sin." The Holy Eucharist is not merely a food, but a medicine; it " cleanses with its purifying flame the smallest stain that adheres to the soul, and serves as an effective prophylactic against grievous sins." If this is true it is no wonder that a learned Catholic theologian should write (Cath. Enc., *sub* Eucharist): " The Church honors the Eucharist as one of her most exalted mysteries, since for sublimity and *incomprehensibility* it yields nothing to the allied mysteries of the Trinity and the Incarnation."

With these conceptions in mind, look again at the

picture of Justus and see how the feeling of mysticism
— even of "incomprehensibility" — is engendered by
the attitudes of all the characters, from the disciples
on the right to the angels and even to Zoroastrian
Zeno!

Protestants need not believe all that the Council of
Trent has laid down, and yet reverently accept the
Lord's Supper as a mystery. All spiritual matters are
mysteries, be they never so common. No one can
explain how we commune with a friend as we sit
silently in his presence; how much less can one
understand that interpenetration of the divine and
the human that takes place in prayer or in meditation
about the Holy Table. The symbol of the Eucharist
holds for all of us *whatever truth we can extract from it
and use.* It may not bind our intellects with the
same concepts, but it binds our emotions and our wills
to the great Person whose memorial it is.

> " Bread of the world, in mercy broken,
>   Wine of the soul, in mercy shed,
>   By whom the words of life were spoken,
>   And in whose death our sins are dead."

JUSTUS OF GHENT: THE LAST SUPPER

DA VINCI. LAST SUPPER

DA VINCI:. THE LAST SUPPER

Matt. 26 : 17–30; Mark 14 : 12–26; Luke 22 : 7–30; John 13 : 21–30

Da Vinci, Leonardo (1452–1519)

Original: A fresco painted in tempera on the refectory walls of the monastery of Santa Maria delle Grazie, Milan. It was painted in 1494–6 at the joint order of the Brotherhood and of Duke Sforza. The monastery has seen great vicissitudes, and the painting has suffered severely. In 1908 the most remarkable restorations ever undertaken were begun, by which the falling pigment was put back flake by flake.

Reproductions: Taber-Prang, 1, 2, 3, 11, 12, 13; Imperial Photogravure, $18\frac{1}{2}$ x $27\frac{1}{4}$, $1.00.

Braun & Co., F. I. E. O.

Fishel, Adler & Schwartz Co. Artotype, $9\frac{3}{4}$ x 18, $.80; colored $1.50.

In color, Medici Prints, chromo-lithograph 16 x $31\frac{3}{4}$, Italian No. iv. $12. — O. M. C. No. 268, half-tone.

The Head of Christ (drawing), Medici prints, Italian No. ii, chromo-lithograph; O. M. C. No. 75, half-tone.

Berlin Photographic Co. No. 191a: from $1.50 to $18.00.

As far as the conventional interpretation of the Last Supper is concerned, Da Vinci has said the last word. He has not given us the doctrinal or sacramentarian view, nor yet the extremely spiritual view, but rather he has pictured the scene truthfully as an incident, bestowing upon it all his power of psychological penetration and masterly execution. It is impossible to conceive of a more effective presentation of thirteen men about a table: all the pictures that came before Leonardo's were mere attempts, all that have come since are mere imitations. Leonardo is the genius of the Last Supper.

We must forever judge of this great painting through a glass darkly. Scientist and experimenter that Da Vinci was, he was forever trying something new with pigments and methods of painting, and frequently as in the present case the experiment was a failure. Restorers have done their worst, time and neglect have done worse yet, so that the beauty of what once was the master's masterpiece has gone forever. What is left is the artist's intention, his analysis of the incident: and that analysis is unsurpassable.

The supper takes place in a plain room hung with tapestries. Through the windows we catch a glimpse of a quiet and wonderfully beautiful landscape, while the central window also serves as a frame for the head of Christ. The near side of the table has been left free for service — and for us to view the scene, while the guests are grouped on the further side and the ends. The artist has chosen to depict the moment when Christ says, " Verily I say unto you that one of you shall betray me." These unexpected words have fallen upon the group like an electric shock; they have broken the company into four distinct groups, each distinguished by its peculiar psychologic state, and exhibiting in the several faces every emotion of which the situation is capable.

On the extreme left are Bartholomew, James the Less and Andrew, all speechless and dumbfounded over the announcement. Bartholomew stares incredulously, Andrew protests by holding up both his hands, James cannot believe his ears and reaches over to Peter to verify the word. In the next group, Judas, smitten by his guilty conscience, recoils from the Master and instinctively clutches his bag that has been his undoing, while in his agitation he upsets the salt cellar. Peter leans forward with breathless

DA VINCI: LAST SUPPER (DETAIL) THOMAS (L) JAMES (C) PHILIP (R)

DA VINCI: HEAD OF CHRIST

haste and whispers, " Tell us who it is of whom he speaketh." John in utter distress sinks back toward Peter. On the extreme right, Simon holds out both hands as if to show his utter innocence of any treachery, while Thaddeus gazes earnestly into his face as much as to say, " This is preposterous! He is certainly mistaken"; and Matthew says excitedly, " But he says it is one of us! " — pointing the while toward Jesus with both his hands. In the right center is the most vigorous and interesting group. Each one is bidding for the Master's attention and expressing his unmistakable protest. Emotional and self-distrustful Thomas, with finger raised almost in the face of Jesus, exclaims, " Is it I, Lord? " James, acting surely his part as a " Son of Thunder," explodes with a double gesture of horror; and Philip pours out his soul in a look of utter sincerity while his hands would lay open his naked heart for inspection. All this is passionate dramatic action; it dwarfs every other representation of the scene.

While these groups are separate they are all united to the central figure in subtle ways. By look or gesture or pose of body they lead our thought to that isolated one who sits unmoved in the midst of the confusion he has caused. His hands, too, are spread open in innocency, but the passivity of the gesture shows that he has surrendered himself to his fate. What his face was like we can only dimly guess. Yet in the Brera sketch we have undoubtedly a suggestion of the spirit which Da Vinci meant to breathe into this Christ. It is the face of a young man well under the prime of life, a beardless face whose unconcealed contours reveal every subtlest movement of the thought within. A Hebrew face, sensitive as the young Isaiah's to the whisperings of God. An intellectual face, keenly alive to the meaning of the issues that focus in this moment though they stream hither from the boundaries of space. A disciplined face, one that has subordinated to the higher Will the imperious forces of body and soul, and that can look tragedy in the eye calmly when it comes. An emotional face— the saddest face in history or in art — yielding itself for a moment only to the tortures of betrayed friendship, of spiritual teachings misunderstood or perverted, of work unaccomplished and purposes unfulfilled, of love poured out in vain. The moment will pass; the sinister cause of the shadow upon his spirit will remove himself to complete his work of perfidy, and once more the sunshine of self-forgetfulness will fill the room with cheer. "Let not your heart be troubled" will soon restore to these sorrowing disciples the comfort and the peace of one who has overcome the world.

VON UHDE: "TISCHGEBET"

Uhde, Fritz von (1848–   )
Original: painted in 1885 and exhibited in the Paris Salon; then bought by the State for the Luxembourg, Paris.
Reproductions: Seemann three-color print No. 3402.

Von Uhde has painted a Last Supper. It is a group of men, at least four of them past the prime of life, sitting about the usual table and looking at Christ with the varied expressions that his announcement would call forth. They are all German peasants, but more or less spiritually descended from the Italians of Da Vinci's masterpiece. It is an effective picture, but far less dramatic than its great predecessor. The subject of our present study is in no sense a Last Supper, yet it expresses what the writer believes to be the true and original intent of the Master as he partook of this final meal with his disciples. It is a poet's way of saying that if we really wish it, the spirit of Christ will be present at every meal, and that whenever we break bread and give to our children, we should remember our Lord.

The picture is a commentary on the old German " Blessing " at table:

" Komm Herr Jesu, sei unser Gast   " Come Lord Jesus be our guest
   Und segne, was du bescheret   And bless what thou hast
     hast! "   provided."

We are looking upon the large whitewashed living-room of a German peasant's home. It is not the home of want, but rather of self-respecting and hard-working poverty. Everything is neat and clean: there are no rags or broken furniture, but there are plain rough clothes and wooden shoes and forms bent with toil. Dinner-time has come. The family from the grand-parents down have come together, and as they are about to sit, Christ appears. With gracious bearing and with hand raised to bless he takes his place at the table in answer to the "blessing" the humble father of the house has just invoked. The young wife without apology has set their one dish upon the table, and now with earnest eyes seems to say that she has done her best for Him and for her loved ones. The pious grandfather looks across with awe at

305

the One he never hoped to see with living eyes; grandmother is too self-distrustful to look; and the dear
children gaze curiously as yours and mine would do if
a stranger should surprise them, bashful yet fascinated
and eager to add one more to the home circle. It is a
family idyll set to pastoral music.

An argument would be out of place here to show
that the sacrament of the Eucharist can be referred
for its origin to such a simple and necessary act as
eating a meal, and that the regular nightly supper —
when alone the household came together — was intended by the Master to be his memorial. There are
at least some passages that point that way (1 Cor.
11 : 17–26; Luke 24 : 30; Acts 2 : 42, 46; 20 : 7, 11).
There are those for whom the loss of the mystical
element in the sacrament would be a disaster; but
there are also those who find in the un-theological
interpretation of the rite a wonderful spiritual suggestiveness. Consider honestly whether the formal
partaking of a consecrated wafer at intervals of a
month or so — even though the wafer be by miracle
the actual body of Christ — can supply the spiritual
power needed in the hurly-burly of life, can nerve our
wills to endure the daily "strain of toil, the fret of
care," and calm our spirits to the daily contemplation of the eternal verities. With rare souls it
may indeed suffice. But how immeasurably more
beautiful it would be if when we gather with our little
ones about the table we could be conscious that
Christ is also our guest; that the seat of honor is for
Him; that His spirit of love and cheer is to dominate
the hour; and that when we parents give to our
children the bread we have earned we are doing it in

306

memory of Him and for His sake. Would it not hallow the table for our sons, without saddening it, if they could realize at least once a day that Christ is the bread of their life and that by his strength they are strong; and would our daughters not grow more surely into beauty and into service if memories of His love and tenderness mingled with the joys of home? Dogma and ritual split life up into the sacred and the secular; and while the formal ceremony of the Church may save the rite from becoming common and unclean, it emphasizes a distinction that does not exist. Jesus knew no division. All meals to him were sacred, for he made all serve his holy purposes. And today he will graciously come into our home, if we so desire, to hallow our daily breaking of bread and to become for us each day our Bread of Life.

BROWN: CHRIST WASHING PETER'S FEET

Luke 22 : 24–30; John 13 : 1–20

Brown, Ford Madox (1821–1893)

Original: Painted 1852, sold to a private owner for £200, and later acquired for the Tate gallery, London, where it now is. The color-scheme was considerably improved by the artist's repainting portions of it. The picture is a portrait-gallery of the Pre-Raphaelites. The man next to the left end is W. M. Rossetti; Holman Hunt holds his head in his hands; Dante Rossetti, the painter of the *Annunciation*, is just in front of Peter's head; and St. John, behind Peter, is Rossetti's sister Christina, who was also the model for Mary in the *Annunciation*. Brown writes of the picture: " I have retained such truth of surroundings and accessories as I thought most conducive to *general truth*, always intending, however, the documentary and historic to be subordinate to the supernatural and Christianic — wherefore I have retained the nimbus."

Reproductions: Photograph by Fred Hollyer & Co., London.

In color: Medici print, chromo-lithograph, 14¾ x 17", English Plate xxxvi, $12.

Seemann three-color print No. 1382.

The early church understood that the act of foot-washing was obligatory upon Christians, like the celebration of the Eucharist. Just when the rite fell into disuse is not clear. Augustine says that it was observed on Maundy Thursday by the church of his day; St. Bernard recommends it as a "daily sacrament for the remission of sins." It is still sometimes performed, as by the Pope, and the emperors of Austria and Russia; and at the Greek Easter every year at Jerusalem the Patriarch, in the presence of a huge concourse of people, mounts a stand erected for the purpose in front of the Church of the Holy Sepulchre, and washes the feet of twelve carefully

VON UHDE: "TISCHGEBET" (Grace Before Meat)

selected and previously bathed beggars. The performance is a travesty on the original act, but it serves to show that at least one portion of the Christian church recognizes the importance of Christ's lesson of humility and service. Since the Western Church never accepted the act as a sacrament, Art has largely passed the incident by; its grand lesson has been lost — as far as the painters are concerned.

Brown has given us the most helpful representation of the scene. The picture shows only nine of the disciples, and they are sitting in various attitudes of absorbed attention. The face of John, at the right, indicates a breathless interest. Toward the left is one who clutches his head in both his hands as if it were utterly impossible to comprehend an act so strange. Judas at the end of the table, red-haired as tradition represents, is putting on his sandals again after washing. His look would indicate that Satan is "entering into him"; he will leave the company, for the words of Christ, "Now are ye clean, but not all," will make him feel very uncomfortable.

Peter is the center of interest. When Jesus began to perform this menial act, Peter's indignation flared up, as his vehement words show, "Thou shalt never wash my feet!" But when Jesus briefly explained that Peter could have no part with him if he had not the humility to let his Master's will be supreme, Peter's vehemence flew to the other pole: "Not my feet only, but my hands and my head!" indicates that nothing should stand in the way when it came to his being reckoned among Christ's friends. This moment of the collapse of Peter's pride is the one Brown has indicated. Peter does not understand the meaning of the act yet; he only knows that it is his Master's will, and he accepts it; at the same time he venerates the one whose character is so incomprehensible and lofty. See the folded hands, the head sunk on the breast, and yet the eye still burning and intensely fixed, — as if the fire within were hot, though the will had submitted.

True to the creed of Sincerity, which he shared with the Pre-Raphaelites, Brown has painted Christ with absolute literalness. Jesus is here doing the work of a slave, and he looks the part. He has laid aside his outer mantle that lends such dignity to the human figure; he has girded himself with a towel, and with it he wipes Peter's foot, holding it over a copper basin that in the original is the most beautiful piece of color in the whole picture. Christ's head, like Peter's, has sunk upon his breast. But a spirit emanates from him that contrasts mightily with Peter's. Peter exemplifies suppressed pride, Christ is incarnate humility. Jesus owned the rightfulness of the terms Master and Lord which the disciples had given him, but he knew that he was most notably their master in his contempt for personal dignity. Dignity Jesus had in superb measure, as, for example, Kirchbach conceived him to have in his " Cleansing the Temple." But the dignity came from the profound moral principle he was embodying; it had nothing to do with any comparative scale of desert as between himself and his fellows. Yet his disciples had carried their jealousies over " chief seats " even into this solemn hour and place, and only this striking act-parable could teach them the futility — yes, the downright wickedness of it all. Jesus therefore as-

sumed the garb and the spirit of a servant to teach
that service is better than "place"; nay, that if one
have not truly the spirit of service he has no part nor
lot with Christians. All of this is summed up in the
attitude Brown has given to Jesus. It is his sermon
on the text, "The Son of Man came not to be
ministered unto but to minister, and to give his life
a ransom for many."

HOFMANN: CHRIST IN GETHSEMANE

Matt. 26 : 36–46; Mark 14 : 32–42; Luke 22 : 39–46; John 18 : 1

Hofmann, Johann Michael Ferdinand Heinrich (1824–1911)
Original: three-quarters life size, painted in 1890; privately owned,
Berlin.
Reproductions: Taber-Prang: 1, 2, 3, 4, 5, 6, 10, 11, 12, 13, 18,
19, 20. Detail, Head of Christ, 1, 2, 4, 5, 6, 12, 13, 18.
Fischel, Adler & Schwartz Co. Artotype 13 x 18", $0.80,
colored $1.50.
Berlin Photographic Co. No. 2037: from $1.50 to $18.00. In
color, 20¾ x 15", $15.00. Detail, Head of Christ, No. 2443:
from $1.50 to $3.00.

Hofmann has mingled in this picture the ideal and
the real in a most appealing way. In the dim background rises the city wall crowned with some large
building. Below in the blackness we feel the presence
of the Kedron valley that separates Olivet from the
city, and on the hither slope we see the reclining
figures of the three beloved disciples. So much is real.
Now the artist begins to create. He has transformed
the "garden" into bare rock and in this way symbolized the relentless fate that has brought this Holy
One to such an undeserved doom. He has made to
grow here only one living thing, and that a thorn-
bush for tomorrow's crown. In the figure of Christ

he has given us a most beautiful picture of ecstasy, of the moment when the struggle is over and the words " Not my will but thine be done " have sealed the victory of his faith over his personal will. The light about his head is the outward sign of the glory of that moral achievement, and the light that streams from heaven to illuminate his upturned face is the smile of the approving Father.

Hofmann has given us a thoroughly emotional treatment of the incident. We feel the beauty of it, the serene self-surrender of it, the transfiguring glory of it; but as usual with Hofmann we fail to catch the deepest significance of the experience. That experience was the most terrible that Jesus ever passed through. He had had moments of anxiety before, moments of storm and stress, moments of personal danger. He had undergone forty days of conflict in the wilderness so severe that it had to be pictured in symbolic language. But never has the scripture said of him that he was in agony or that his sweat seemed like blood. Such language hints at a spiritual struggle too intense for description. After the crisis of such a struggle had passed, traces of it would still mar the face and no doubt the raiment of the sufferer. But you will observe that Hofmann has omitted such realistic touches as this. They would not make a pretty picture. He has toned down the facts, reduced the agony to the mere contemplation of opposing wishes, lighted the victorious face with something of self-satisfaction and turned it toward us a bit so that we may enjoy it. We are carried away with the picture till we begin to think; then its beauty becomes pretty sentimentality.

The struggle of Jesus in Gethsemane was the endeavor to harmonize his personal human will with the fate that now seemed to be his Father's will. It was to accept a course of events the good purpose of which he could not fathom it was to avoid not the tortures of the cross but drinking the cup of failure bitterer than death. If he died, what would become of that sublime vision of a regenerated social order that apparently he alone had seen? What would become of his disciples who had hardly absorbed as yet the first principles of the Kingdom of Righteousness? From the distance of the Mount of Transfiguration a martyr's death had seemed to have a place in the great scheme of things, but now when death was at hand the tragedy to his cause seemed irreparable. Death simply could not be! Yet the outcome of the struggle was a victory of faith over sight, a surrender of his entire personal interests and the interests of the Kingdom into the Father's keeping. Henceforth he could face death or life with the calm consciousness which had been his in former days, " I do always the things that please Him." His attitude toward the Father was precisely what Tennyson has declared ours must be toward him who by this midnight victory showed himself to be the "Strong Son of God" and our Master and Lord.

> " Strong Son of God, immortal Love,
>   Whom we that have not seen thy face,
>   By faith, and faith alone, embrace,
> Believing where we cannot prove;
>
> Thou seemest human and divine,
>   The highest, holiest, manhood, thou:
>   Our wills are ours, we know not how;
> Our wills are ours, to make them thine."

313

BACON: CHRIST IN GETHSEMANE

Matt. 26 : 36–46; Mark 14 : 32–42; Luke 22 : 39–46; John 18 : 1
Bacon, F. W.
Original:
Reproductions:

In Bacon's picture the point of view shifts from the personal spiritual conflict of Jesus to his relationship with his disciples; and it brings to the fore the constant and pathetic struggle of Jesus to find help and comfort in the companionship of even those who loved him best.

The narrative tells us that Jesus left most of his disciples somewhere in the garden and took Peter, James and John apart with himself. Then again he separated himself even from these: " Abide ye here and watch with me." But in the brief moments of his first prayer the three fell asleep. Bacon here pictures the return of Christ to the little group. He shows us the faithless ones sitting upon a bench that the owner of the garden has built there. Their backs lean against the great scarp of rock that forms the background of the garden terrace. The lantern used to guide their feet in the pathway of broken stones up Olivet throws its beams upward, and distorts the faces of the sleepers and the near asleep into queer grimaces of astonishment or of unconcern. The eyes of James, the nearer one who sits almost bolt upright, are open but " their sense is shut." He is in a maze. Faintly he has seen Christ's sore trouble of soul and faintly heard the groaning of the prayer, as in a dream; and faintly now, with Christ's rebuke, dawns the sense of duty vaguely undone, and the half-resolve to do it, at least at a more convenient season. But

314

HOFMANN: CHRIST IN GETHSEMANE

it is all unreal, and when the Master returns to his praying, this brief thread of reality will be woven indistinguishably into the dream-texture. John who has sunk upon his brother's bosom is unfeignedly and solidly asleep. Sorrow and anxiety have overcome his delicate spirit. Peter yonder is also well under the spell of the night. But somehow the shadows on his face suggest that he has not quite forgotten the travail of the hour. Pain is still knocking at the door of consciousness, though the soul has not yet arisen to let it in.

The pathos of the picture is centered in the face of Christ. With reproach and sorrow and pity he looks out from eyes that show at once the depth of his nature and the intensity of his need at this hour, — a glance that would melt a heart of stone but that cannot pierce the barrier of sleep. The pathos arises from our sense of the failure of friendship. Jesus had chosen these three from the eleven because they were the earliest and the truest of his friends. He needed to feel their presence and their sympathy as he fought the temptation to run away that assailed him. He had not concealed from them the bitterness of his soul as he threw himself on the ground in their presence. Now he returns to lean for a moment on their love, and satisfy himself that though insight fails, love is sure, when, lo! this revelation of obtuseness, of inability or unwillingness to enter into the fellowship of his suffering.

But it is wonderful to see how soon this personal disappointment changes to solicitude. Their spirit is indeed willing, but their flesh is weak. Within this hour will come their testing-time, their temptation to

315

deny him, to run from danger, to think of their own safety rather than their loyalty to him. Jesus therefore counsels them to watch and pray that they yield not. His love for his friends enables him to enter sympathetically into their coming crisis, though theirs for him is inadequate to the great test. So leaving them to their sleep of sorrow, he goes back to his lonely wrestling, to his agony of blood, to his victory.

We may not fathom the spiritual processes by which Jesus was able to bring his will into harmony with God's. There are souls that seem to need no mediator, but by a sort of interfusion allow the infinite spirit to penetrate their being. Some accomplish it through the agency of human sympathy, as Jesus tried in this instance to do. But for most men there is probably no mediation comparable to that of Nature. The visible universe, in its infinity, its harmony in complexity, its unerring obedience to law, its beauty, stands as a symbol if not an actual incarnation of God. So Bryant found it in his "Thanatopsis"; so Wordsworth and Shelley and all the later seers of our English tongue. Who shall say that Jesus, finding human friendship a broken reed, did not return to find comfort in the stillness of the night, the deep blue of the Syrian sky, the calm and impartial luster of the Pascal moon, the dew that distils silently like His grace, the patter of the olive leaves above His head, responsive to every breath of the night wind? This at least is suggested by Sidney Lanier in his exquisite *Ballad of the Trees and the Master:*

" Into the woods my Master went,
Clean forspent, forspent.
Into the woods my Master came,
Forspent with love and shame.
But the olives they were not blind to Him,
The little gray leaves were kind to Him:
The thorn-tree had a mind to Him
When into the woods He came.

Out of the woods my Master went,
And he was well content.
Out of the woods my Master came,
Content with death and shame.
When Death and Shame would woo Him last,
From under the trees they drew Him last:
'Twas on a tree they slew Him — last
When out of the woods He came."

VAN DYCK: THE ARREST OF JESUS

Matt. 26 : 47–56; Mark 14 : 43–52; Luke 22 : 47–53; John 18 :
1–11

Van Dyck, Anthony (1599–1641)
Original: an early work, now in the Prado gallery, Madrid.
Reproductions: Berlin Photographic Co. No. 3251, Photogravure
18¼ x 13¼", $5.00.

The confusion and hurly-burly of the arrest are here
best represented. It is night. Dark shadows fill the
foreground, for the moon is nearly hidden by angry
clouds. Only the light of one blazing cresset illumines
the scene, flaring upon the upturned faces and the
leaves that overhang the company, and glancing from
the halberds and the steel armor of the centurion.
The band rushes forward with common impulse to
seize the guilty one. This is the most vigorous kind
of realism.

We can identify a few of the characters. The

317

commander of the band is of course the man with the armor on the extreme left. One does not have to be an antiquarian to see that this is not Roman armor; it merely serves to dignify the wearer and make legal an arrest that would look otherwise like a private lynching. The next man, with a black beard, is one of the rabble; he is excited and keen on the chase. The one who holds the cresset, and the soldier beyond him, are enjoying the fun hugely. The old man who follows so hard upon Judas is full of animus; he is quite in sympathy with the priests who desire to capture this dangerous demagogue. He has brought a rope. Beyond him another vigorous fellow raises both arms in the endeavor to throw a bight of the rope over Christ's head. Judas the leader of the rout presses forward to give his kiss. Beyond Jesus we see one or two dim forms and one frightened face. These are probably disciples, who would save their Master if they knew how, but are utterly taken aback by this sudden irruption of force. We must not overlook Peter, in the darkness of the left hand corner, delivering his valiant assault upon the ear of the High Priest's servant. Peter must have been terribly excited, or such a blow on such an exposure would have severed the head from the trunk!

Van Dyck has brought out the true significance of the event by means of masterly composition. Do you see with what tremendous force the men on the left are dashing into the action? Their vigor and abandon are indicated by the lines that cross at right angles or nearly so, lines of opposition, of struggle; but the leading of the action is forward. With Judas, however, the impact has lost some of its force: some of

VAN DYCK: THE ARREST OF JESUS

GEIGER: THE KISS OF BETRAYAL

his drapery curves backward, and the shadow that precedes him is perpendicular while the line of shadow that drops downward on the right side of Christ slopes the other way and acts as a buttress to his figure. The motion has stopped! Nay, it has reached a barrier that it may not pass. One feels the situation to be like that of the great seas that the north-easter drives upon the rocks at Scituate; they strike and rear aloft their arms of power a hundred feet above the granite precipices, then thunder back again baffled into their own seething mass. Christ is that barrier. Judas cannot prevail against him; the hands will sink and, as John asserts, the rabble will draw backward and fall to the ground. As we look at the face of Christ we can see why. It is the face of one who is past all fear and whose calm soul looks indifferently upon any fate. One so rooted in the Father's will is not to be stampeded by any Temple rabble or even by the eagles of imperial Rome. "Whom seek ye? — I am he." With a dignity that befits his Messianic character he surrenders himself to the now chastened band; henceforth they may lead him where they will, for "as a sheep before her shearers is dumb" so will he not open his mouth.

Van Dyck has placed aloft for us a pretty symbol. A dove has been frightened from her nest by the lights and the shouting, and a night-hawk trusses her with his talons. It is innocence seized by cruelty.

GEIGER: THE KISS OF BETRAYAL

Matt. 26 : 47–56; Mark 14 : 43–52; Luke 22 : 47–53; John 18 : 1–11

Geiger, Caspar Augustin (1847–   )
Original: painted 1886, life size.   Privately owned in Munich.
Reproductions:

Here are two character-studies. Judas is more difficult to portray, especially since the artist has chosen not to show us the traitor's full face; but his characteristics are surely hinted. First notice the effusiveness of his act; it is not a kiss merely but an embrace and that of the most strenuous kind. This in itself is a hint of insincerity.

> " Ever note, Lucilius,
> When love begins to sicken and decay,
> It useth an enforced ceremony."

Then observe the treachery in the pose of Judas. Somehow the artist has conveyed the impression that Judas was crouching or trying to conceal himself, and that suddenly he darted upward but not with sufficient courage to carry him his full height, so that to kiss the face he had to stretch his neck and elevate his chin. There is something uncanny about this approach from below, suggesting the snake in the grass, or the Evil One himself who lieth in wait. And last, study the face of Judas — what you can see of it. It is mostly wrinkles. It is one of those mobile faces that forever over-expresses itself, the face of a gusher or a bluffer. It is a danger-signal to all who can read character, for whatever sentiment it expresses, you know it is a lie. Perhaps also the pointed and scant beard, the pointed nose, the hair in pointed tufts, help out the suggestion of Mephistopheles, and make us feel that we have here an exhibition of treachery incarnate.

The crisis reveals Christ's character too, and that by acts and looks that are instinctive. His whole nature recoils from the traitor's touch as from a viper. See how his body leans backward, how the hands become electric with life, and the fingers almost tremble with their repudiation of the loathsome embrace. See too how the disciplined and immobile face endures the kiss, while the eyes transfix the guilty soul of Judas. Yet there is no hatred in the look. Jesus can still address him as " Friend " (Luke 26 : 50). The body may recoil because of deeply-buried instincts that act independently of the will; but the soul of Jesus, calmed by his struggle with himself and by a fresh grasp upon the Father's love, can now show Judas that the old relation of friendship may still exist as far as he is concerned. Jesus is here loving his enemy even in the act of treachery that makes him an enemy. Love of this kind is not an emotion but an ethical principle, the active willing that the highest good shall be to another, regardless of that other's deserts. Such love is a function of the Will and not of the feelings; it may therefore be commanded. " Love your enemies " is a perfectly feasible principle of action, if one has only reached the spiritual plane that Christ occupies in this picture.

Chapter XVII

TWO FAITHLESS ONES

PICTURES FOR STUDY

Prell: The Corruption of Judas
Harrach: Peter's Denial
Armitage: The Remorse of Judas

The treachery of Judas doubtless had its roots in the past, perhaps existing from the first as a rift in his moral nature which his association with Jesus could not obliterate. But until the anointing at Bethany there is no indication of it on the surface. Then, in Luke's picturesque language, "Satan entered into Judas." It would seem that the treachery was not the result of weakness or of pressure from without, but was actively malignant. He took the initiative in going to the Chief Priests and driving a bargain with them, and from that time he "sought how he might conveniently deliver him unto them." Brief as the scriptural account is, the villainy of the deed has seared it into the memory of all time, and in Jerusalem itself the various phases of his act are marked for show. The bald hill that rises south of the valley of Jehoshaphat they still call the "Hill of Evil Counsel," for there tradition says the covenant of crime was sealed. By the entrance gate to Gethsemane is a pillar to show where the kiss was given; and over against the Valley of Hinnom, once the site of the King's Gardens, but polluted by Solomon's idolatries till

> " Tophet thence
> And black Gehenna called, the type of Hell," —

overlooking the grim scarps of the chasm still writhes an ancient olive tree to perpetuate the memory of his hanging.

It is rather unfortunate that Peter, the only one of the disciples who showed even a scruple of courage, should be singled out by the gospels for so much blame. No doubt it was Peter's own penitence that prompted him to tell the story to Mark — for he is the acknowledged source of Mark's Gospel — and the other gospel writers took the cue from him. Peter deserves praise for most of his conduct, and sympathy rather than blame for the rest. He and his cock have become precious reminders to the church of the necessity of watchfulness and fidelity. Very early the incident was enshrined in a church on Mt. Zion, built over the grotto in which Peter "wept bitterly." Within a few years the French Fathers have acquired considerable sections of the slopes of Zion, have unearthed innumerable remains of the city contemporaneous with Christ, including the street-stairs on which he descended to Siloam, the foundations and mosaic pavements of the High Priest's house with the inscription "KORBAN" on the threshold of the tithing-room, and this little church of *St. Pietrus Gallicantus*, or "St. Peter of the Cock-crow," mentioned by medieval pilgrims. Thus in an unbroken strain the challenge of Peter's bird rings down through the ages to our time, and still greets us from the spires of our New England churches, lest we forget!

PRELL: THE CORRUPTION OF JUDAS

Matt. 26 : 1–5, 14–16; Mark 14 : 1, 2, 10, 11; Luke 22 : 1–6

Prell: Hermann (1854–   )

Original: life size, painted in 1886; bought in 1894 for the Dresden Gallery.

Reproductions:

We have here the most vivid possible presentation of the temptation of Judas. It shows us the conflict that Judas is waging in his own mind, a conflict that undoubtedly was acute and covered a period of some days at least, but that we almost never attempt to picture to ourselves. We have been so accustomed from childhood to think of Judas as an out-and-out traitor that the steps by which he became one are quite overlooked in the final catastrophe. Prell has shown us one of those moments-before.

The landscape on which the artist has staged the scene is a powerful psychologic aid. It represents a solitary valley somewhere outside the city, a barren and depressing place; a somber and sinister landscape with its precipices of rock and its tree or two, especially the one on the edge of the further cliff just high enough to hang a man from! Why are these two important and richly dressed persons out here laboring with this poor wretch? Something secret is on foot, and something evil. In the left distance are three tiny figures approaching: the decision must be made before these men come near enough to identify the conspirators. And when the great Pascal moon peers at them over the hill as if to discover something, one feels like running to cover before the shame of it is revealed! This is mind-manipulation: the

325

artist, through his setting, has strung us to the proper pitch.

The rest of the picture is character-study. Two priests are present as the tempters. One of these, on the left, is apparently the arch-schemer. He has furnished the wits for the job, and a good part of the active malignity. His face is full of cunning, his eye is clear and sharp. No doubt he has been doing the preliminary arguing to show how Judas will prove himself a blessing to his country if he can bring about the arrest of this troubler of Israel. Following the lead of his own instincts, he has pictured the honors that will come to such a public servant, the praises, the friendship of the powerful and the rich, the salutations in the market-place and the chief seats in the synagogues. But as we look at his face we loathe him! He is a spider, a snake in the grass, a cowardly briber of other men to do his dirty work for him. See the spidery hand stretched out cautiously to arouse Judas from his revery and call his attention to the silver argument his partner is presenting. Such a touch would make an honest man creep. It is not a grasp, not an assurance, not a sign of cooperation, but an insinuation, a feeler, a translation into actual terms of the subtle suggestion in that wicked eye. He is an incarnate Devil of Seduction. No one's honor is safe within the radius of his touch.

The crowning argument is now forthcoming: it is furnished by the rich old toad who holds the silver. This is a regular allied " drive " on Judas. The way for the advance has been carefully prepared by forty-two centimeter guns — by the overpowering weight of fine silks and jewels, high position in the church,

326

social prestige and the fact that all of this dignity has condescended to present in person the needs of its high associates and to assure Judas of their eternal friendship. Now the advance is on. Ten infantry corps have already cut the barbed wire and taken the first line of trenches; and now while General Lucre is observing carefully the effect of the charge and figuring how many more divisions will be required to carry the citadel, he is feeling with a thumb and forefinger among the reserves at his girdle. This campaign is being calculated as exactly as Kitchener's against Khartoum: not a man nor a gun more than necessary will be used. And how revolting it all is, — this gross person, this utterly sordid face! It makes one shudder to think that he is a priest and is doing this villany in the name of religion. He has just one redeeming trait — wit enough to let his money talk for him. He is a practical psychologist, knows the dynamic power of an idea when kept in the focus of attention; so he just holds the silver in the corner of Judas' vision and lets the eloquence of its brightness altogether persuade him. He and his partner make a capital cuttlefish, with a couple of tentacles stretched out to suck the soul out of their victim.

What a contrast between these tempters and Judas! Judas is an unkempt, ragged fellow, not a bit above the part he is destined to play. He is here in the toils. The forces of good and evil are at deadly interlock within him, — or is it the conflict of boldness with prudence, the questioning about which path leads to larger gain for him? One hand pulls at his beard and the other at his rope-belt, as if — using a fanciful symbolism — his wisdom and his purse were

327

at loggerheads! Whatever the exact nature of the battle within, we see that the "genius and the mortal instruments" are here in council, and that his state of man is suffering the nature of an insurrection. And we can predict the outcome so long as that handful of coin remains motionless. Oh, the pity of it! the downright stupidity of it! to sell one's soul for thirty pieces of silver!

Perhaps it was not silver that tempted Judas. Perhaps it was none of the arguments we have suggested. One writer assures us that Judas meant merely to force Jesus to assert Messianic power and destroy his enemies rather than be himself destroyed; in this way Judas thought he would be doing the world a service. When it was too late he saw that he had miscalculated. Another writer maintains with more plausibility that Judas did not believe that Jesus was the Messiah; and seeing that Jesus was bound to perish anyway, took this way of making himself solid with the authorities. On this basis, cowardice and not greed was the motive. But whatever the motive, it is inconceivable to us how one who had preached repentance and the Kingdom of Heaven with Jesus, cast out devils in his name and followed him faithfully through perils and privations, could now so utterly fail. It makes us tremble to realize that the human nature we all possess in common with Judas can have concealed within it such pitfalls, such structural faults, that without apparent cause and without warning can yawn and swallow us up. Bunyan's remark, "But for the grace of God, there goes John Bunyan!" seems to be the only appropriate one as we contemplate this catastrophe.

PRELL: THE CORRUPTION OF JUDAS

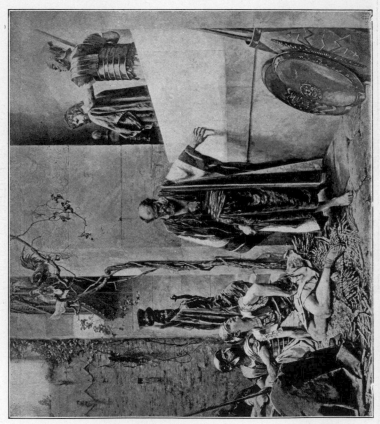

HARRACH: PETER'S DENIAL

Matt. 26 : 69–75; Mark 14 : 66–72; Luke 22 : 55–62; John 18 : 15–18, 25–27

Harrach, Ferdinand, Count von (1832–   )
Original: 6′4″ x 7′2″, painted in 1879 and bought immediately for the museum at Breslau.
Reproductions:

This picture illustrates particularly verse 61 of Luke's account: " And the Lord turned and looked upon Peter."

We are standing in the courtyard of the High Priest's palace. In the left background is the boundary wall of rough material finished with a coping of dressed stone. In the center are the piers of a large entrance, the lunette of the archway being filled with a wooden grill. Running toward us from one of the piers is a parapet of large stones, behind which a narrow passage leads to the entrance from some hall of the palace behind us. The quality of the masonry and the fine alabaster-like veining on some of the blocks indicate the magnificence in which the High Priest lives. Dawn has arrived, and with it the chill that makes a fire of coals grateful. The soldiers of the guard who are temporarily off duty have stacked their shields and spears in a convenient corner and are sitting on a heap of matting thrown on the flagstones of the court, warming themselves and discussing the prisoner and the incidents of the arrest. A maid just going in with a jar of milk on her head is pointing a crooked finger at Peter. What she is saying seems to amuse her and interest the soldiers, but Peter fails to see the joke. The cock in the grapevine over

329

his head, greeting the dawn so joyously, has taken the joy out of him; and the look that Jesus casts over his shoulder as the guard leads him to another phase of his ignominy, crumples Peter's bravado and brings over him the full realization of what he has done.

It has been a hard situation for Peter. In spite of John's assertion that there was " another disciple " present — introduced to explain how Peter gained entrance to the palace — the probability is that he was the only disciple who had the courage to follow the Master even afar off. The presence of a miscellaneous rabble emboldened Peter to press in with them to learn if he could what fate awaited Christ. There in the courtyard he stayed with the other hangers-on, while the maids coming and going furnished unofficial bulletins of the progress of the trial. We must remember that Peter did not know whether the arrest of the Master would involve also the speedy arrest of his followers; and more particularly, Peter had a half hour ago amputated the ear of one of the High Priest's servants under highly complicating circumstances! If the other disciples should escape, on him, at least, the officers of the peace had some just claim. Worse yet — a cousin of the victim of Peter's sword, no doubt itching to get his hands on the villain, suddenly confronts the quaking disciple and says point-blank, " Did I not see thee in the garden with him? " Under these circumstances Peter deserves credit for not taking to his heels! He does the next best thing — begins to curse and swear. This is very interesting for the soldiers; there is prospect of fun ahead for them. But suddenly the prisoner passes along the gallery, bound and guarded. The cursing

Galilean stops in the midst of his oaths, falters along the wall to the porch, and disappears. A burst of laughter from the soldiers, a loud guffaw from the crowd, a shrill " I told you so! " from the maid, and the incident passes from all minds but Peter's. This was a turning-point in Peter's career.

Peter's faithlessness belongs to a different category from that of Judas. There was no treachery in it, no premeditation, no active purpose to betray; only a temporary lack of nerve, a down-curve of courage in the presence of personal danger, a recrudescence of the primitive instinct of self-preservation such as the recruit feels when first under fire. But the tears of repentance that followed washed out the guilt, and purged at the same time the elements of weakness that had prevented Simon from always being Peter. Henceforth Peter is all " Rock." Exceeding boldness, as at Pentecost, takes the place of fear, and upon Peter Christ may henceforth safely build his church.

ARMITAGE: THE REMORSE OF JUDAS

Matt. 27 : 3-10

Armitage, Edward (1817–1896)
Original: painted 1886; now in the Tate Gallery, London.
Reproductions: Photograph by Hanfstaengel, New York. In color: Seemann print No. 3427.

" I have betrayed innocent blood! " Could a more terrible cry ring in the ears of any man? It is not only the cry of personal conscience, but the voice of the race imbedded deep in the structure of our nature, the reverberation of ancestral voices proclaiming a law that runs unbroken from the jungle to the man-pack, the tribe and the state, that the unit must be loyal to its own. And just because this voice is racial it comes with an authority absolutely resistless, like the condemnation of a great cloud of witnesses testifying at the bar of God. No man can hear that voice and live.

The terror of such a cry rings from the picture before us. Judas has come panting into the presence of these great ones; the veins and cords of his neck are swelling with the intensity of his effort; the mouth is open for breath as well as for speech; the eye bulges, the cheek is haggard. He clutches the neck of the empty bag as if he would strangle it and keep it from testifying against him, while with the other hand he thrusts the thirty pieces into the faces of his one-time friends. The handle of a knife stuck in his girdle adds a suggestive threat of some desperate action. Judas is going mad. He cannot, it is true, save his victim, nor can he save himself, but he can at least lighten his torment of soul to the extent of the crushing weight of this silver. " I have betrayed innocent blood! innocent blood! "

But the raised hand and the imperturbable face of the Chief Priest put a chill even upon the fever of remorse. Not so easily is the load rolled off. The deed has been done, the money has been earned; the irrevocable has arrived. Before the face of Judas yawns a great gulf fixed, so that those that would pass from hence to the sweet heaven of virtue where the will is free may not. The priest stands for the eternal fixity of things done, for the adamantine wall of the city of Dis. To be sure there is no virtue in his face, but that is another affair. His gesture and his look are merely the reflection of the inexorable.

The other two priests represent the human side of this transaction. They are the " great ones " whose friendship Judas was supposed to earn; they are the Sanhedrim whose word of praise was to enroll Judas on the rostrum of fame. Look at them now! In the face of one, scorn and loathing — half pity for the wretch who was so simple as to be caught with such cheap bait, and so moral that he can suffer remorse. In the face of the other is that self-righteous and sublime unconcern that raises its brow and says, " Depart from me, I never knew you." Riches and Power found and used their tool; now they cast it away. Its very name will be forgotten; the placid surface will close where it sank and smooth out every ripple. This enviable power of oblivion is attained at a great price: it is the supreme product of a life of selfishness. Such a life, if history is correct, lived Annas and all his house. So in this picture Caiaphas coolly turns his back on the creature that has gratified his dearest wish.

There is a vulture in the sky beyond the wall. Do you see how the light, striking against the nose of Judas, has transformed it into a vulture's beak? So here are two vultures: one that has preyed upon his own kind to his infinite undoing is hurrying to his doom; and the other, who even now scents the carrion on the tree of hanging, is hurrying to the feast. Thus the dead bury their dead lest the whole world become corrupt.

History has pilloried Judas as the arch-traitor of the race. The heinousness of his sin, the absolutely unforgivable quality of it as far as man's sense of justice can see, is reflected in the punishment that Dante has meted out to him in the Inferno. In the lowest pit of Hell, frozen into the lake of ice whose waters are the tears of humanity, is Satan, a huge shaggy monster with three faces and great bat-like wings. In each mouth he crunches a traitor: Brutus and Cassius, traitors against the divinely appointed State, and Judas, traitor against God's Son, as Satan himself was traitor against God, Judas as chief of the three is placed in the central mouth, the one in the crimson face of hatred — for his sin was against love, and the little love he once had has now all reverted to hate. His head is mangled by the teeth of Satan in memory of the crown of thorns his treachery brought on Christ, and his back is lacerated by Satan's claws in repayment for the scourging. No other seer has produced so terrible a symbol of the enormity of the sin against redeeming love, and of the execration that has followed the traitor and will follow him through all eternity.

ARMITAGE: THE REMORSE OF JUDAS

GUIDO RENI: "ECCE HOMO"

Chapter XVIII

THE LAW'S INJUSTICE

The trial of Jesus has always been admitted to have been a travesty, but historical criticism has somewhat lessened the severity of the charge. The facts of the case come out most clearly in Luke. In this account, Jesus is taken to the High Priest's house and there kept till daybreak, suffering in the meantime the abuse of the irresponsible soldiery. At dawn the Sanhedrim convened in the council chamber near the Temple and there merely examined Jesus for the purpose of getting from him incriminating evidence that would weigh in a Roman court. This they finally obtained in his qualified admission of Messiahship. Then they adjourned to present the case to Pilate in due form. The charge was one of sedition. " We found this man perverting our nation, and forbidding to give tribute to Cæsar, and saying that he himself is Christ, a king." (Luke 23 : 2.) This was a serious charge of which a Roman Procurator was bound to take cognizance. Pilate was shrewd enough to see enmity behind the charge, and probably innocence in the prisoner, whom he doubtless took to be mildly insane. Through fear of trouble that these High Priests might make for him at Rome, he received their testimony at its face value and passed the sentence they desired. The only failure of the law was in not acquitting the prisoner on moral grounds in spite of the evidence. Pilate's scourging was the usual method of getting evidence out of a prisoner. All the rest of the shocking proceeding was the outcome of irresponsible hatred.

The sufferings of Christ have been regarded as the most powerful argument in moving a sinner to repentance: "All this he suffered *for you*, and because of your sin." The Church has therefore caused these events to be pictured in all their gruesome details, over and over, with all the power her greatest artists could command. There are at least seventy pictures of the trial with its attendant cruelties and forty of the incidents of the Via Dolorosa. About sixty artists have painted the Crucifixion, while more than that number have given us "Depositions" and "Pietàs." The name of hardly a single artist of note previous to the eighteenth century is omitted from this list.

MUNKACSY: CHRIST BEFORE PILATE

Mark 15 : 1–20; Luke 23 : 1–25; John 18 : 28–19 : 16a

Munkacsy, Mihaly (Michael) (1846–   )

Original: For many years Munkacsy cherished the plan of painting this picture, and made many sketches for it. The final piece occupied a year's time and was finished in 1881. It was too late for exhibition at the Paris Salon of that year, but all Paris came to see it in the artist's studio. It was then exhibited in various cities in Europe, when over two million people paid to see it. In 1886 it came to New York.

It was bought by Mr. John Wanamaker of Philadelphia,
and is now in a permanent exhibition hall in that city.
Reproductions: Taber-Prang 1, 2, 3, 4, 13.
　　Braun & Co., I, E; detail of Christ, either head, or three-
　　quarters, or full length, I.

Munkacsy has conceived this incident as part of a
great drama. It looks like Grand Opera, the closing
scene when all the actors assemble for the impressive
finale. The " stage-princes " are here with their "grand
manner," their exaggerated gesture, their consciousness
of the audience; and the director has arranged the
properties and grouped the personages so that the
audience shall have an unobstructed view. The
curtain has just risen.

The scene is set for the Pretorium, or Judgment
Hall of Pilate. On the " bema " sits the Procurator
himself. Below on benches are the various judges,
who to be sure have no jurisdiction in a Roman
court, but who represent the legal talent of the nation
and lend dignity to the scene. To the left is the
rabble that has pressed in to add the weight of its
clamor to the evidence. Caiaphas is making a virulent speech: one can see that he is depending for his
effect more on noise and gesture than on solid argument. He has the self-assurance of a Pharisee as
well as a Pharisee's intolerance and obstinate prejudice.
Notice the other Pharisees, for each is a character-
study. Below Pilate are two: the farther one utterly
malignant, the nearer one beginning to fear that a
mistake has been made. Next Pilate's hands is a
judgment-warper who hopes to make Pilate look at
him and take a tip on a point of law. Another stands
up behind Caiaphas, his back against the wall, and

337

looks down with curiosity and contempt on the prisoner. Under Caiaphas' raised arm three doctors of the law whisper about the case. Last and most impressive of these " judges " is he on the front seat, a banker, self-complacent embodiment of the vested interests, a sort of Pharisaic " Uncle Trusty " who believes that this innovator who has upset the money tables in the Temple has shaken the very foundations of society! He is certainly a masterpiece.

Now follow the minor characters. See the bunch of usurers behind Christ — very likely victims of his recent cleansing zeal. See the scoffer who leans over behind Uncle Trusty in order to get a jeer squarely into the face of the prisoner. Another has climbed a bench and stretched out an arm toward his scoffing friend. On the left, held back by the soldier's spear-shaft, a fanatic throws up his arms in a hired paroxysm of zeal and shouts, " Crucify him! " Every face carries its message, gives its judgment of the prisoner, and that judgment is always unfavorable. Christ has only one friend here — that sweet-faced mother by the arch-pier, a " Madonna lost in the Sanhedrim." She is a foil to the chaos and the hatred of the mob, an embodiment of the Christian idea; powerless now, to be sure, but bearing in its heart the power that will regenerate the world. She will teach her little child to be a Christian, and through children the world will grow into righteousness.

Pilate sits conspicuous against the background of his judgment seat. His robe is white and purple-bordered, the toga of a Roman senator. Behind him are the symbols of the power of Rome, the wreath, the fasces and the letters S. P. Q. R. that throughout the world proclaim the supremacy of the Senate and the Roman People (*Senatus Populus Que Romanus*). Pilate has a strong face, yet in this instance it is "miserably full of indecision." Mechanically he hears the arguments, but his thought is busy with the bearings of the case upon his personal fortunes: "If I release, what trouble will these High Priests make for me? If I condemn, what about Justice or a possible appeal to Cæsar?" His nervousness betrays itself as his fingers rise mechanically to keep count of the arguments in his brain. The politician, the trimmer, the time-server, the responsibility-shirker, is here worming his way through the possibilities, while the justice of the Senate and the Roman People waits in the background.

Christ stands in the center of composition, white against the background of his enemies. He is haggard from the physical strain and loss of sleep; yet with courage, dignity, calm forbearance, he looks his judge in the face and mutely demands justice. The loudly iterated charges of Caiaphas, the shouts of the mob, have no power to shake his sublime consciousness of his mission. Principles from which he will never swerve have brought him here, and they will carry him hence to an end that Pilate is powerless to change. His searching glance in reality reverses the relations that he and Pilate sustain — as Van Dyke has pointed out. He is in reality Judge, and Pilate is on trial. Pilate is measuring himself against a great ideal of Law, which in spite of their faults the Romans had established throughout the circle of the lands; he is being weighed in the balances and found wanting. And the Roman governor, like the traitor Judas, will be written "Guilty" on the judgment-rolls of eternity.

RENI: "ECCE HOMO"

John 19 : 1–5

Reni, Guido (1575–1642)
Original: in the National Gallery, London.
Reproductions:

This mode of representing the sufferings of Christ appears to have been quite in favor in the seventeenth century. Guido Reni is the patron saint of such art, and is himself responsible for several " Ecce Homos," though before his day greater painters like Titian had set the fashion. They all express the physical agonies of Jesus and for the most part convey little hint of the spiritual. The thorns stick into the flesh, the blood drops, the tears flow, the eyes turn to heaven in an agony of entreaty, and the mouth drops open as if praying that the torture might cease. In these days we do not find the contemplation of such suffering particularly helpful; thoughts are suggested that are somewhat remote from our conceptions of religion.

There is no denying that the thought of Christ's suffering has been a powerful stimulus to the religious life of the past. Latin Christianity is full of it, and even Greek Christianity found inspiration in it. Hymns to the suffering Savior have sounded from many a monastery cell and have echoed sweetly down even to our own time. Take for example the wonderful hymn of Bernard, redolent of the midnight vigil and of modes of thought characteristic of his age, but of such beauty that every country and every Christian sect claims a share of it.

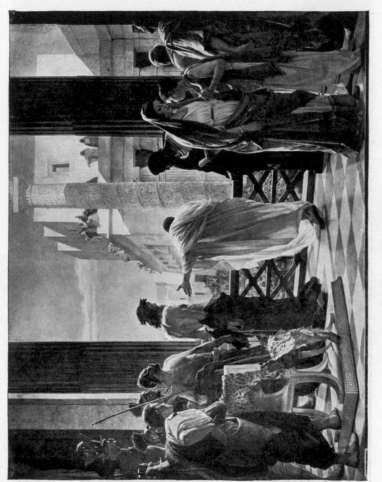

CISERI: "ECCE HOMO"

MUNKÁCSY · CHRIST BEFORE PILATE

> " O Sacred Head, now wounded,
>   With grief and shame weighed down;
>   Now scornfully surrounded
>   With thorns, thine only crown.
>   O Sacred Head, what glory,
>   What bliss till now was thine!
>   Yet though despised and gory
>   I joy to call thee mine."

This hymn is one section of a long poem beginning "*Salve mundi salutare,*" addressed to the different members of Christ, "a most devout prayer of the Abbot St. Bernard, which he made when an image of the Savior with outstretched arms embraced him from the cross." There is a still earlier hymn by Theoctistus of the Studium, Constantinople, less widely known but scarcely less beautiful in Neale's translation. It is found in some of our hymnals under the first line, "Jesus, name all names above." This hymn evidently arose under the same need as Bernard's, and serves to show how all the harrowing details of suffering may be blended in thought with one's highest spiritual good.

> " Jesus, crowned with thorns for me,
>   Scourged for my transgression,
>   Witnessing in agony
>   That thy good confession.
>   Jesus clad in purple raiment,
>   For my evil making payment:
>   Let not all thy woe and pain,
>   Let not Calvary be in vain."

Christ's sufferings have received various interpretations through the Christian centuries. The dominant thought from Anselm to Calvin seems to have been that they constitute a payment made by Christ on our behalf to cancel the debt to God created by our sin. On this theory, every stroke of the scourge and every laceration of the thorns was just so much spiritual coin paid into the heavenly treasury and credited to our account. To contemplate these sufferings is therefore to realize the enormity of our sins, our absolute insolvency of righteousness, and at the same time to acknowledge the love and sacrifice that could lead one to suffer so in our stead. Our own day has seen a change of emphasis from the commercial and legal aspect of the Atonement to the vital and the ethical; and with the change has come the necessity of reinterpreting such pictures as this — of translating them into symbols of the solidarity of the spiritual universe, by which when man sins God must suffer also, and must redeem us by causing us to know his suffering and so to repent. Such pictures and such hymns, therefore, are still rewarding to those who can be persuaded to think upon them.

CISERI: "ECCE HOMO"

John 19 : 1–16

Ciseri, Antonio (1821–1891)

Original: completed shortly before his death. and considered his masterpiece. Now in the National Gallery of Modern Art, Rome.

Reproductions:

This is a beautiful and striking picture, worthy to rank with any great historical painting of the last century in regard to technique, truthfulness and insight. No one who has seen the original will forget

342

it, — the glowing sky, the brilliant Temple, the rich and archæologically accurate costumes, the "sea of upturned faces," the dramatic tensity of this moment when the turn of a hand determines the life or the death both of the victim and the nation.

The term " Ecce Homo " — " Behold the man " — usually suggests to our minds the tortured upturned face of Christ wearing the crown of thorns, the Guido Renis and Carlo Dolces that are supposed to be aids to devotion. Ciseri reverts to the larger application of the words in their setting, shows us Pilate and his prisoner and the mob to whom the words are addressed. Undeniably the scene is well staged. Half the background and more is filled with the mass of the Temple, Egyptian in general motive, to suggest the permanence and dignity of the theocratic institutions on which the Jews prided themselves. Between it and us rises a column of victory adorned with a spiral band of sculptures like that on Trajan's column in Rome. In the foreground where we are standing, tall pillars of the Roman mode indicate the palatial quality of Pilate's Judgment-hall. Other symbols of his power are here. On the left, the bronze eagle of the legionary standard, the plumed bronze helmets of two soldiers of his bodyguard, and not the least, the curule chair on its Greek-bordered base, cushioned with a leopard's skin, — simple, but indicative of the judicial power of life and death which alone the Roman wielded.

Pilate's dignity is also shadowed in his friends. Note the self-possession and the power of that Roman patrician behind the chair, by his position and his pose a personal adviser to the chief. By the right

343

hand pillar stands a dark-haired man with the garb and beard of a philosopher, his roll still in his hand. He will doubtless charm Pilate's leisure by reading and discussing selections from Plato and Cicero and Epicurus. He loses none of his dignity when we learn that it is Ciseri himself. Beyond the pillar two other Romans, an older and a younger, study intently the passions of the crowd. This is a new experience for one of them at least. Pilate's wife has turned her back on the bloody prisoner and the noisy mob, anxious for her husband and heartily sick of this wretched business, while her maid supports her hand with apparent sympathy. In their faces we see the only spark of feeling for Christ that the picture affords.

The prisoner stands near the balustrade in full sight of all. He wears the thorns with which the soldiers crowned him; his back is lacerated with their scourging; his hands are bound with a knotted rope, one end of which his keeper holds, a burly Gaul of gladiator build who also carries the reed with which they smote the King. Christ is utterly wretched, yet he bears himself like one who foresees the end and has prepared for it. Pilate, resplendent in diaphanous robes, leans over and presents him to his subjects. For the moment Pilate subordinates himself, effaces himself by pointing to Christ and addressing the people; his friends likewise efface themselves by giving all their attention to the objects of Pilate's thought. There are therefore just two objects left for us to contemplate, the Man of Sorrows and the mob.

This is the real picture, these two. Over against one another they stand, the silent and bleeding

MUNKACSY: HEAD OF CHRIST

Detail of "Christ Before Pilate"

MUNKACSY: PILATE
Detail of "Christ Before Pilate"

Messiah and the howling crowd that was to constitute
his kingdom! Look at the faces through the balustrade and tell whether citizenship in a kingdom not of
this world is for them! Look also at their dignified
rulers who have climbed to the roof of their Temple
and are undignifiedly waving their arms and hounding
the crowd on to cry, " Crucify him! " The moment is
big with decision. A nation's fate is hanging in the
balance. But clamor and hatred are tipping the beam,
with direst consequences. The nation that rejects
its heavenly king in favor of an earthly will ere long
reject the earthly also, the white wonder of this
Temple will dissolve in Titus' fervent heat, and forever
they who would not have this man to rule over them
shall be a People of Dispersion, kingless and homeless,
because they knew not the time of their visitation.
This is the insight Ciseri gives us: the nation is seal-
ing its own doom.

TIEPOLO: CHRIST BEARING HIS CROSS

*Matt. 27 : 31–32; Mark 15 : 20–21; Luke 23 : 26–32; John 19:
16–17. See also mention in the Gospel of Nicodemus.*

Tiepolo, Giambattista (1696–1770)
Original: A large canvas over five yards square, figures life size,
in the Church of S. Alvise (St. Louis), Venice.
Reproductions:

The " Via Dolorosa " or the " Way of Pain " is
still marked by appropriate memorials in the streets
of Jerusalem. It begins with Pilate's Judgment-hall,
at the place where the sentence was pronounced and
where Jesus was scourged, mocked and crowned with

thorns. The second station is the Arch of the "Ecce Homo," where Pilate showed Jesus to the people. The third marks Jesus' first fall under the weight of the cross; the fourth, his meeting with his mother. At the fifth, Simon of Cyrene was pressed to help carry the cross. The sixth is the station of St. Veronica. At the seventh, where streets cross and one of Hadrian's magnificent columns still looks down, Jesus is said to have fallen a second time. The "Daughters of Jerusalem" meet him at the eighth station. Tradition says that as the procession reached the foot of Calvary, Jesus was compelled to take his cross again. Soon he fell utterly exhausted and had to be carried the remaining distance. The place where he fell this third time is the ninth station. Within the Church of the Holy Sepulchre are the others, all on Golgotha: the tenth where Jesus was stripped of his raiment; the eleventh where he was nailed to the cross; the twelfth where the cross was erected; the thirteenth where Mary stood and where the body was taken down; and last, the fourteenth, the tomb. Along this route for fifteen centuries faithful pilgrims have gone every day on their knees, repeating their prayers and living over again the sufferings of their Lord.

Tiepolo has here pictured the Ninth Station. The Holy Women of the eighth are visible in the left center, Mary standing and the Magdalene kneeling; St. Veronica has followed him thither from her Sixth Station, and is here kneeling on the right and gazing with pity at the face upon her handkerchief. The other details are tremendously realistic. Beginning on the left are the two guarded thieves, one of them a Hercules and the other of similar stamp but older,

Though both of them are brutal men, the latter seems to have some glimmerings of pity for the helpless young victim who has fallen, yet his face and figure are of one who is being led out to die. In the center behind the cross are the coldly indifferent figures of the priests — notably one in a white robe and turban. On the right the procession winds up the ramp of Calvary. First a splendid horse on which Caiaphas is riding to the spectacle; beyond him a trumpeter, blowing a blast for some unknown reason. Nearer, a young fellow carries a sign that will soon be nailed above Jesus' head, I. N. R. I. (Jesus of Nazareth the King of the Jews). Men with banners and pikes are marching ahead, the centurion Longinus leading on horseback. Aloft on the summit of the hill of rock workmen have erected two crosses and are now impatiently waiting for the third to arrive. Between us and them are the symbols of the Roman power: the eagles of the Legion, the statue of the Emperor, the banner blazoned with S. P. Q. R.

The foreground of the picture is filled with the group about the cross. Jesus on reaching the first step of the rocky slope has fallen, so that one of the executioners and Simon are obliged to lift the burden from him. These helpers are giants, but not unkindly; in fact we see very little hatred and brutality in the picture — except in the face of the white priest! The situation calls for pity. Looking at the two hands of Christ and the position of his body upon the rock, one can see that he is utterly helpless, and the face is expressive of the utmost exhaustion. We have here, therefore, a story-picture, a vivid and dramatic presentation of what took place,

It is a religious picture only in the sense that the chief personage in it is our Savior on his way to execution.

MAX: JESUS CHRIST

Max, Gabriel Cornelius (1840–   )
Original: painted in 1874, a replica in 1878.
Reproductions:

Weird enough one would call this picture; at first sight one prefers not to contemplate it. Yet when one comes to understand it, it enshrines a beautiful tradition and a noble truth.

As Christ was bearing his cross along the Way of Pain, mocked and jeered at by the rabble, a good woman named Veronica, of whom the world knows only this single deed, was struck with pity at sight of his bleeding and dust-stained face. Pressing to his side she gave the Savior her handkerchief that he might wipe off the bead-drops of his agony. When he returned the piece of linen to her, his face was imprinted on it, and there it remains to this day, a miraculous token of his gratitude. Max has painted both the cloth and the face, — the hair bedraggled and clotted with blood, the cruel crown still in place, the sad features overspread with a death-like pallor. At first glance the eyes seem to be shut. But as you look steadily at them you will discover that the lids grow transparent, and out of the depths of the shadow the soul looks at you appealingly, as if to call to your memory the words of Lamentations: "O all ye that pass by, look and see if any grief is like unto my grief!" Only a painter of Max's peculiar temperament could have conceived such a face.

We may dismiss the tradition as a mere attempt to

348

TIEPOLO: CHRIST BEARING HIS CROSS

MAX: JESUS CHRIST

give reality to the word "veronica," which means "true likeness," and we may discount as a pious fraud the handkerchief with its bloody imprint, so carefully preserved since 700 A.D. at St. Peters in Rome. But the teaching embodied in the parable is true: the blessed spiritual reward of human sympathy. One can picture Veronica of the legend taking her handkerchief home with reverent care and putting it away among her treasures. Now and then as her heart prompted she would spread it out before her and live over again the hour that brought her face to face with that gentle sufferer. One can imagine how her heart would burn within her, until as she looked and mused, the eyes would open, as they open in this picture, and look straight into her soul. His recognition, his fellowship, would thus become her reward for sympathy.

This is always the reward for sympathy — friendship. The act of sympathy is a stirring of the soul with feelings like those one sees in another. And when that other recognizes the community of experience, the two souls flow out toward each other and merge in fellowship. Community of experience, whether of work or play, of pleasure or suffering, points toward friendship provided only 'the will-to-friendship be present. When Veronica entered into the fellowship of His sufferings, Christ became her friend. So may we enter through meditation and prayer and find that the dead past may be transformed into a living present; and out of the pages of the Book, as out of this picture, the soul of the Master will shine upon us. Sympathy is the spiritual gateway to friendship, whether human or divine.

349

Chapter XIX

THE DEATH OF THE CROSS

PICTURES FOR STUDY

Rubens: Christ Between Two Thieves
Fra Angelico: The Crucifixion
Munkacsy: Christ on Calvary
Carrière: Christ on the Cross

The crucifixion of Christ is one of the tremendous facts of the world. Its historicity is established beyond question, and by the unanimous consent of Christians of all creeds and ages, the event is freighted with tremendous significance not only to the individual soul but to the destinies of the world. But when we come to ask precisely what that significance is, we receive various assurances. These answers constitute the Doctrines of the Atonement that the Church has advanced from time to time.

The older theories went on the assumption that the death of Christ was efficacious with the powers of the other world. Origen asserted that the Devil had a claim on mankind and that Christ paid the lien and freed us. Anselm argued that Christ's death satisfied God's outraged honor because of his law broken; and Grotius asserted that it satisfied God's sense of justice. Our Puritan forefathers accepted the medieval satisfaction theory in one form or another, and Milton gave it literary expression (Par. Lost, xii: 395–401, 416–419). Pictures that represent the " Descent into

351

Hell " suggest the first or mythological theory; those that present in some form the contemplation or the adoration of the Cross or the crucifix — by far the larger number — presuppose some form of the satisfaction-theory.

Modern theories of the Atonement assume that God is always yearning over man, and that man must do the changing. The spectacle of Christ on the cross moves man's heart in two ways: it shows the triumph of character over failure and death, and it shows that the way to salvation is through loyalty to God's will, through the complete surrender of ourselves to a life of love and service, come what will. This spectacle of the cross has proved to be the greatest spiritual lever in history. Through it men have seen that God was in Christ reconciling the world to himself. This conception has not yet been clearly expressed in art, though one could interpret in this way such pictures as Carrière's " Christ on the Cross." Indeed, one may read it into most of the pictures of the Old Masters, and thus find spiritual help by translating the doctrine into modern terms.

No artist has attempted to give the Crucifixion its actual physical background for the reason that no one knows where the crucifixion took place. From the gospels we gather that it was outside the city at some little distance, and that it was near one of the roads. Whether it was north, south, east or west from Jerusalem is not stated. Apparently the early Christians gave the matter no thought, so that when the true site was discovered in the fourth century by imperial order, there was no evidence of its authenticity except an alleged miracle. Nevertheless the rocky hill of Golgotha and the near-by tomb, now enclosed by the Church of the Holy Sepulchre in Jerusalem, have maintained unbroken to the present day the tradition established by the empress Helena. This quarter-acre of ground has been literally the most fateful spot on earth. Toward it the millions of pilgrims of all ages have pressed, for its possession seven crusades and the Crimean war were waged, and the faith of Christendom has embraced it as the one undoubted witness of the Great Sacrifice. No other site rivals this in probability, for Gordon's Calvary outside the Damascus gate may be dismissed as a mere guess. Indeed the writer, after repeated visits extending over a series of years, and after considerable investigation, finds himself drawn more and more forceably to the Golgotha of tradition, hallowed as it is by the memories of sixteen centuries of worship and by the blood and tears of Christendom.

RUBENS: CHRIST BETWEEN TWO THIEVES

Matt. 27 : 33–56; Mark 15 : 22–41; Luke 23 : 33–46; John 19 : 16–37

Rubens, Peter Paul (1577–1640)
Original: painted for the Recollet church, Antwerp, in 1620; now in the Museum, Antwerp.
Reproductions: Taber-Prang, 1, 2, 4, 5.

" Struggle " is the word that describes this picture. It is an embodiment of physical agony, unilluminated by a single ray of spiritual meaning. The impression is conveyed largely by the lines of composition, which nearly always meet one another at right angles. Note, for instance, the angles made by Christ's two arms, by his arm and the thief's, his arm and the spear,

the left thief's two arms, the centurion's arm and
spear, his body and the horse's head, the horse's head
and the Magdalene's arm, her arm and the ladder, the
ladder and the executioner's body or the nearer thief's
leg, the thief's legs and body, his body and arm.
There is not a graceful curve or an oval in all the
picture — except in the figures of John and the
Virgin; all is opposition, shock, tension; pent-up
energy is being discharged. Even though Christ is
dead there is no relaxation in his muscles; he is
apparently suffering still. A great picture, a powerful
picture, but without the saving grace of religion in it.

All the figures are Rubenesque, titanic. The thieves
have struggled so that they have nearly freed themselves. They are still shouting and cursing. Since
the central victim is already dead and the Sabbath
draws nigh, a soldier climbs the ladder and with his
iron mace starts to break the legs of the near thief
that the shock may kill him. His only concern seems
to be that he may not get kicked off the ladder.
Another soldier is piercing the side of Christ with his
spear in order to verify the death. This is Longinus,
about whom so many legends have clustered. He is
said to have been blind in one eye, but drops of
blood from the wound fell upon the eye and restored
its sight; whereupon he became a convert and a
missionary. This spear has been adopted as one
of the symbols of the passion, it came to have
miraculous properties, and as a wonder-working relic
it figures in the legends of Parsifal and the Grail.

Of all the mourners, Mary Magdalene is the most
passionate. She has seen the soldier thrust with his
spear, and her sympathy brings her hands out in

RUBENS: CHRIST BETWEEN TWO THIEVES

FRA ANGELICO: THE CRUCIFIXION

instant protest, while her grief-stricken face implores the tormentor to desist. She has been embracing the foot of the cross; you may see her right hand raised beyond it. John is the only weak figure, here, though the Virgin comes painfully near to weakness. She is graceful enough, and her face fairly beautiful, but Rubens has put her up here for our admiration. Her grief is self-conscious and stagy. If she really had felt a sword pierce her bosom, as the prophecy suggested it would, she would not assume this pose of almost injured innocence. Really, the Magdalene's passionate grief and protest is the most finely human thing here. If there is any religion in the picture it is suggested by this intense love of hers for the one who had opened heaven to her.

FRA ANGELICO: THE CRUCIFIXION

Matt. 27 : 33–56; Mark 15 : 22–41; Luke 23 : 33–46; John 19 : 16–37

Angelico, Giovanni da Fiesole, called Fra (1387–1455)

Original: a fresco in the chapter-house of the monastery of S. Marco, Florence; painted about 1442–3 at the request of Cosimo de Medici. It was never wholly finished, and has been seriously injured by restoration, notably the central figure and the group of women.

Reproductions:

The decorative quality of Fra Angelico's Crucifixion is at once apparent. It is a lunette framed below with portraits of seventeen of the most illustrious members of the Dominican Order, and above with lovely Renaissance foliage out of which as from windows the Prophets and a Sibyl flutter their scrolls of prophecy to call men's attention to this fulfilment.

In the picture itself we have a minimum of realism. The three crosses with their occupants are highly conventionalized; the torture of crucifixion is hardly hinted, though in the face of Christ we have a marvellous suggestion of resignation and self-sacrifice. Of the original witnesses only four are presented. The Virgin (No. 7) is being supported by John the Beloved (No. 9) and by Mary Magdalene (No. 8) who kneels before her in a grief-stricken attitude. There are no soldiery, no priests or mob. The ordered company below, the calmness, the adoration, also proclaim that we have here not merely a decoration but an object of thoughtful contemplation that should impress us both with the fact of the great Sacrifice and with its significance for all time. And when we begin this contemplation we discover that we are in the presence of a dogma, a symbol. The key-note is struck by the Pelican at the apex of the frame, and the accompanying inscription over the Savior's head: " I am become like a pelican in the wilderness." The pelican is the symbol of self-sacrifice, for the bird was said to lacerate her own breast with her talons in order that her brood might drink her blood and live. The unusual elevation of the cross proclaims also the world-wide scope of the redemption: "And I if I be lifted up will draw all men unto me." At the foot of the cross is a skull, the one that gave its name to the " Place of a Skull " on which Christ was crucified. It is the skull of Adam, who according to Jewish tradition was buried here. When the blood of the second Adam trickled from the cross it fell upon the skull of the first Adam and caused his resurrection and redemption from Hell. " For as in Adam all die, even so in Christ shall all be made alive." Fully translated, then, the picture means: Christ our Sacrifice and our Redemption is the proper subject of the world's adoration.

That world, for Fra Angelico, meant largely the saints of the Church. One of the thieves may stand for the vast world of the unregenerate to whom Christ is foolishness and a stumbling-block. But the elect are the proper Kingdom of our Lord, and of the elect those who stand in some special way related to the painter's own Florence and his beloved monastery are the representatives he would naturally first think of. These are all given. The one standing by the foot of the left cross (No. 5) is John the Baptist, patron saint of Florence, he who once pointed to the "Lamb of God that taketh away the sins of the world." The one kneeling on his right (No. 4) is St. Mark, pointing to his Gospel wherein the veracious record of the crucifixion may be seen; he is the saint in whose honor the monastery was built where the painter lived and where the picture is. The kneeling figure at the right of the cross (No. 10) is St. Dominic, founder of the Order of monks who inhabit this monastery. Of the two left-hand figures, the one who weeps (No. 1) is St. Damien, and he who looks at Christ (No. 2) is St. Cosimo, the patron saints of the Medici family which in the person of Cosimo de Medici has built this building.

We shall appreciate something of the grandeur of this conception if we examine in detail the other members of the assemblage; for they represent the world of thought in which Fra Angelico lived, and they summarize the history of the Christian Church.

Two of them are martyrs. On the left (No. 3) St. Lawrence stands with the gridiron on which he was roasted. He was a deacon in Rome whose special care was the poor, the orphans and the widows. During the persecution under Valerius he was summoned to produce the treasures of which he was custodian, and to abjure his faith; whereupon he gathered together all the poor of his flock and presented them as his treasures, " more precious than all the wealth of the empire." He suffered martyrdom in 258 A.D. On the extreme right (No. 20) kneels Peter Martyr (1205–1252), a Dominican monk of such fiery zeal that he became head of the Inquisition in Italy. Two "heretics" slew him with an axe as he was returning to Milan; whence the clot of blood that he always wears on his head. These two saints may well stand for Christian devotion, the one zealous for the poor, the other for the purity of the faith. They represent the two great activities of the medieval church.

Now follow four great Fathers of the Church. Ambrose (No. 11) is earliest (340–397), the young patrician prefect of Upper Italy, so judicious, so temperate, so beloved, that by acclamation of both Catholics and Arians he was called to be Bishop before he had been baptized! But receiving the call as from God he entered the church and became the best-beloved of all the Latin Fathers. A wise administrator, a powerful orator, a fearless preacher of righteousness, daring even to repulse the emperor Theodosius from his cathedral door and excommunicate him for his cruel treatment of the Thessalonians. A poet and liturgist also, if to him may be ascribed the " Te Deum." How well these high qualities are reflected in his face (see the detailed picture). He stands in the full regalia of his office and bids St. Jerome have faith in the cross.

Next (No. 12) comes Jerome (342?–420), most learned of the Latin Fathers. He kneels, an old man in penitential garb that recalls his austerities at Chalcis; before him his palmer's hat that shows him to have come from the Holy Land. Indeed from 386 A.D. till the end of his life he lived in a cave in Bethlehem adjacent to the holy Grotto of the Nativity, and there he poured forth his polemics against the heresies of his time and finished his translation of the scriptures, from the Greek and Hebrew to the Latin. The " Vulgate " is his great gift to the world.

Augustine (354–430) stands behind Jerome, clad in his robes as Bishop of Hippo in Africa (No. 13). He holds a book and quill in token of the writings that make him greatest of the Fathers. Converted under Ambrose, he became the first unifier of Christian thought, and till Thomas Aquinas arose, his writings were the supreme authority in theology. He died while Genseric the Vandal was besieging his city. It was he who taught the Church how to grasp the scepter from the dying hand of Rome and with it create the Papal empire of the middle age.

Thomas Aquinas (1224–1274) is the last of this group (No. 19). He is the great scholastic, the Father of Moral Philosophy. So great was his fame as a theologian that he is called the " Universal Doctor," the " Angelic Doctor," the " Second Augustine." His contribution to the Church was the application of the philosophy of Aristotle to Christianity, and the creation, in his *Summa Theologiae*, of the first complete theological system. He represents the Church at the flood-tide of its intellectual power.

The rest of the company are the great Monastics of the middle age. Of these, two are of purely local celebrity, monks who went from Florence to found Orders: St. Romualdo (No. 17, 976–1027), a Benedictine abbot, founder of many monasteries and of a new order whose members lived solitary, — he himself having once spent seven years in solitude and absolute silence; and his contemporary St. John Gualberto (No. 18, 999–1037), one who was before his conversion a man of blood and who here appropriately weeps at this bloody reminder of how he once crucified the Lord afresh. He is the founder of the famous Vallombrosa monastery of Benedictines near Florence. The remaining four names belong to the world at large, men of extraordinary power both as organizers and as mystics. Chronologically they are as follows:

St. Benedict (No. 15, 480–543), he with the reverent mien and the staff, founder of monasticism in the West. He retired from the wicked world at fourteen years of age, founded twelve cloisters, and then made himself famous by devising the rules that brought order and discipline and useful work into the more or less lawless brotherhoods of monks. Rapidly his new Benedictines rose to influence. They became and still are the most learned of all the orders, and their zeal caused them to be for five hundred years the chief agents of the spread of Christianity and learning in the West. By the year 1354 they could boast of having given to the world twenty-four popes, two hundred cardinals, seven thousand archbishops, fifteen thousand bishops, fifteen hundred and sixty canonized saints, twenty emperors and forty-seven kings!

St. Bernard (No. 16, 1091–1153), founder of one hundred and sixty monasteries, the "mellifluous Doctor," one of the most beautiful characters of the middle ages, was during his lifetime the Oracle of Christendom. By his learning, profound judgment and stirring eloquence he ruled the thought and life of his time from his little cell at Clairvaux. He is best known to history as the preacher of the Second Crusade (1146), when he emptied France and Germany of their manhood for an expedition that failed utterly. Out of this failure of his hopes arose the beautiful hymns of the celestial country, now the possession of all the world.

At the foot of the cross kneels St. Dominic (No. 10, 1170–1221), the fiery Spaniard who founded the Order of the Preaching Friars (Dominicans) to which Angelico belonged. To their zeal was committed the conduct of the Inquisition, which on the one hand saved the doctrines of the Church from pollution and on the other drove the heretics into Protestantism. For centuries they were the great rivals of the Franciscans, dividing with them the control of the Church. The figure of Dominic is the finest in the picture. The hands are raised in wonder and adoration, and in the face are blended in a wonderful way sorrow and an intellectual comprehension of the mystery of the Atonement. Truth and passion reach their culmination here.

St. Francis of Assisi (No. 14, 1182–1226) closes the list. Tender-hearted monk that he was, calling the flowers and birds his brothers and ministering to the lepers in the gutter, he cannot bear the sight of the suffering Savior, but kneels weeping and presses his hand to his head. In the other hand he carries his crucifix. You may see the rays of light that issue from the " stigmata " — the five wounds of Christ that were given Francis as a special favor of Heaven. Francis is the most remarkable religious genius of the centuries, most blameless and gentle, who turned his back upon his property to " wed Poverty " and to found the glorious Order that bears his name, bound by the triple vow of Chastity, Poverty and Obedience. The Franciscans became the great missionaries of the later middle age. In less than fifty years they numbered 200,000; and such was their zeal in caring for the sick and dying that in the fourteenth century 124,000 of them fell victims to the great Plague. Through their lay-brothers also they became the great civilizing and moralizing force of their time.

These brief sketches of the saints who kneel here will serve to call up the grand pageant of the Church that for fourteen centuries to Angelico's time had marched past the Mount of Calvary, — men of learning and of power, administrators, thinkers, men of action, mystics, philanthropists, finding their inspiration in this central fact of history and laying at the foot of the cross their wondrous contributions to the Redeemer's Kingdom. It is partly this perspective of history, with its conjuring power of great names, and partly the sincerity with which they all adore this symbol of their faith, that makes Fra Angelico's Crucifixion one of the world's great religious paintings. It is the painter's " Te Deum " sounding sweetly

FRA ANGELICO: THE CRUCIFIXION

10   (DETAIL)   11   12   13

through the ages in tones that only his pure soul could create, parallel line for line with that of Ambrose:

" The glorious company of the Apostles, praise Thee;
The goodly fellowship of the Prophets, praise Thee;
The noble army of Martyrs, praise Thee;
The holy Church throughout all the world doth
    acknowledge Thee;

.   .   .   .

Thine adorable, true and only Son."

MUNKACSY: CHRIST ON CALVARY

*Matt. 27 : 33–56; Mark 15 : 22–41; Luke 23 : 33–46;
John 19 : 16–37*

Munkacsy, Mihaly (Michael) (1846–)
Original: 20′ x 30′, painted 1883–4; owned by John Wanamaker,
    Philadelphia.
Reproductions: Taber-Prang, 1, 2, 13.

One discovers in this scene the same grandiose effects that mark the *Christ Before Pilate.* There are the same Grand-opera characters, the same largeness of manner, the same staging for effect, the same dramatic quality. One must admit also that there is nobleness of conception, dignity and reverence in presentation, and at least the opportunity for religious meditation because of the faithfulness of the picture to the spirit of the incident and the details of the narrative. What is given is frankly an illustration, it is an endeavor to make clear the facts; and it is therefore far removed from the Fra Angelico on the one hand and the Carrière on the other.

In the crucifixion company we may detect three groups of people: the Jewish authorities with their satellites, the Roman soldiers and executioners, the group of friends. These all show characteristic emotions.

Take first the group of Jews in the left foreground. Of the two walking, one seems to be Caiaphas; at least he bears resemblance to the Caiaphas of the other picture, and he is still talking! He is bolstering up his conscience with arguments to show why this heretic should have been put out of the way. His companion is willing to listen, but the scene has made an impression upon him; he is not wholly convinced that some other method of procedure would not have been better. Another prominent Sanhedrinist is riding; his parting look suggests mingled hate and satisfaction. Behind Caiaphas are two other dignitaries who are struck by the awfulness of the scene and by the agony of Jesus' cry, " My God, my God, why hast Thou forsaken me! " The miscellaneous rabble behind the ladder are all brutal; as they had shouted " Crucify him! " so now they gloat over the accomplished deed. The runner on the extreme left is going to be the first to tell the news in Jerusalem. The young man in the exact center of the foreground is an embodiment of our own attitude: the painter expects that we will look and feel as this one does — astonished, awestruck. Those who have seen the original will testify that the painter was not far wrong.

The Romans also are differentiated by their attitude toward the event. A mounted centurion on the left center, holding the spear, is struck by the Savior's cry, but his look suggests the anxiety of an executive officer that all the details of the execution shall be duly performed. On the contrary, the centurion nearer the cross is the open-minded one mentioned in scripture, who exclaimed, "Truly this man was the Son of God!" One hand is raised to his head, the other is extended in a gesture of awe. Other soldiers in the rear are merely suggested; the one in the right foreground has been detailed to guard the crosses till death overtakes the victims; the chief executioner with the ladder is a perfect picture of brutal indifference.

The group at the foot of the cross portrays the poignancy of grief. John standing at the right is too numb with pain for any expression; he is just stolid. Mary or Salome, to the left, looks up with a gesture of anxious pain as Christ utters his cry; Mary the Virgin has thrown herself on her knees and embraces her son's feet, almost swooning with grief; while the Magdalene, her long golden hair falling loose behind, buries her face in her hands.

The Savior in this picture is wholly occupied subjectively. He is not noticing the mourners or the crowd, but his face is upturned as if in prayer. The look corresponds with the words he uttered in the semi-delirium that preceded death, when the soul was losing its grip upon reality. In the gathering darkness and in the numbness of dissolution he could think of nothing but the words of a penitential Psalm (Ps. 12 : 1) uttered by his people always in times of dire distress. These words have no theological implication whatever. They merely show that the Scripture was his one ray of comfort, as it has been to thousands of saints since his time.

All this is realistic, dramatic. We feel as if we had been present at the crucifixion, and as we look at the picture the emotions that such an experience would engender are faintly ours.

CARRIÈRE: CHRIST ON THE CROSS

Carrière, Eugène Anatole (1849–1906)
Original: 88 x 51", painted in 1897 and presented by a group of
admirers and friends, in conjunction with the government,
to the Luxembourg Museum, Paris.
Reproductions: Braun & Co. F. I.

This is a nineteenth century "Stabat Mater"
painted by a true artist and a seer. It expresses one
of the meanings of the crucifixion, that event so rich
in significances — and a truth about life that is
spiritual and profound.

In style the picture is characteristic of the artist;
there is no definite outline. The background is a
shadow that partly absorbs details and that gives
place in spots to a luminous mist that conceals quite
as effectively. What place and time are here presented no one can say. It may be Jerusalem two
thousand years ago, or Rome in the middle age, or
this may be a crucifix hanging in the dim aisles of
Notre Dame. It is all of these in one, for the picture
is timeless and spaceless; it is a universal. By the
mist and shadow the artist has also obliterated individuality. One cannot discern whether the figure
standing by the cross is a man or a woman. As a
matter of fact, it is the Virgin Mary; but by envelop-
ing the figure in gloom and allowing only her soul to
express itself, the artist has painted you and me.
The features of Christ are likewise dissolved in vapor,
for he too is no longer an individual, but a spiritual
experience. This is the work of a genius.

Examine Christ more closely. His body is formed
of a vague luminosity the intensity of which varies
from shadow to brilliancy. The figure hangs a dead

weight, suspended from the lacerating nails of the cross. The head has dropped sidewise against the arm, with the vaguest suggestion of thorns crowning it. The features are in shadow: only one thing can surely be made out, and that is that Christ is at peace. Compare any picture of a dead Christ you ever saw and you will find nothing like this. It is the face of a righteous man who has suffered all the agonies that hatred and malice can devise, but who has accepted them as his way of life. In self-sacrifice he has found the consummation of his ideal, for he has proved that love can endure — yes, conquer — hate; and he knows that this spectacle of love will draw all men unto himself.

Contrast now this peace with the pain of the Virgin. Her robe is black like her grief. Her pale hands clasped convulsively together are pressed to her lips that they may keep back a sob. The eyes, whether open or closed we know not, together with the brow and the crouching posture, suggest a mental agony that is intense, the stupor and the desolation of one who realizes nothing but the grief that crushes her. Truly the sword has pierced the soul of this woman, of this Mother, — for it is *her son* who hangs here. This is the passionate grief that only a mother can know, an instinctive cry of the heart and the flesh for one who came forth from her and is gone forever. That cry arose to heaven over the dead Cain, and ages before that in the caves and lairs of the evolutionary forebears of mankind. It is the cry of the eternal Parent.

Why has Carrière brought these two figures into juxtaposition? Before answering this question, observe that the cross is not raised on high, but that Christ is almost on a level with his mother, and that he has no halo. This means that the artist has given us here two aspects of the human soul, two moments in spiritual evolution, by which we can trace the ascent of man to the divine. We have here nature over against super-nature; instinctive devotion over against self-sacrifice; the pain of unaccepted evil over against the immortal peace of one who wills *even this*, because the ends of man and God are being served. This symbol is a hint at an understanding of the problem of evil, a suggested way of life, by which the pangs of the mortal and the finite may be swallowed up in victory when by faith we let our finiteness be subsumed into the Infinite Good. So may we learn how

" God's greatness flows around our incompleteness, —
Round our restlessness, His rest."

The supreme lesson of the Crucifixion is that man, through voluntarily accepted suffering, may participate in the redemptive purposes of God.

CARRIÈRE: CHRIST ON THE CROSS

RUBENS: DESCENT FROM THE CROSS

CHAPTER XX

THE DEAD CHRIST

There is no doubt that Mariolatry gave an impetus to the painting of Descents from the Cross, Entombments and various forms of the Pietà. The sufferings of Mary are the touch of nature that makes her kin to us all; through her experience of the pains of life she keeps her sympathy with mortals even though as Queen of Heaven and Mother of God she is far exalted above them. This power of pity and sympathy in Mary make her particularly susceptible to entreaty; she can be moved when her dread Son remains obdurate. Hence it was that the Flagellants in the later middle age carried her worship into every corner of Europe as they flogged themselves in public while they sang the " Stabat Mater," the song of Mary's grief. Hence it is that by gazing upon such works as a " Descent " or a " Pietà " the faithful are led to throw themselves upon her mercy, knowing that she can understand their plight. Such works are also calculated to move the beholder to pity for her; and pity, like any of the tender emotions, shades off into religious feeling. Protestants will find in them less stimulus to devotion than do the pious of the Latin and Eastern Churches. They are for us interesting studies in pathos, but to the theology that underlies them we are strangers. So are we strangers to the philosophy of the "Descent into Hell." But even this weird theme has a background of truth that can be translated into the language of today. On the whole, therefore, the period between the crucifixion and the resurrection, though it has inspired about seventy representations by the greater artists, is barren of spiritual helpfulness to our generation.

RUBENS: DESCENT FROM THE CROSS

Matt. 27 : 57–61; Mark 15 : 42–47; Luke 23 : 50–56a;
John 19 : 38–42

Rubens, Peter Paul (1577–1640)
Original: the central panel of a triptych painted in 1612 as an altar-piece for the Guild of Arquebusiers in the cathedral at Antwerp; still in the cathedral.
Reproductions: Braun & Co. F. I. E.

The "Descent from the Cross" has been one of the most admired religious paintings of the world. Technically it is superb. The brilliantly lighted white center against the black-green background, the grand masses of dull red, are wonderfully impressive, even when seen across the great cathedral; and the suffering here depicted is far above the level of Rubens' later picture which we have studied. Here there is restraint, nobility, pathos. The horrors of the crucifixion have passed away, and only the dull pain of memory mingles with the veneration due to the body of so precious a friend.

The friends of Jesus are removing the body from the

370

cross before nightfall, in order that the Sabbath may be unpolluted. Joseph of Arimathæa, who begged the body of Pilate, stands half way up the ladder on the left. On the right hand ladder is Nicodemus. Two strong men have mounted other ladders and having released the body are now lowering it in a winding sheet. That the body is heavy is indicated by the strength exerted by the older man, who holds the cloth in his teeth while he braces himself against the crossbeam. John, too, who receives the body from below, finds that he is handling no phantom. In such details lies the realism of the picture; this is what actually took place.

The body of Christ is a piece of masterly work. There is no doubt about Christ's being dead. All his members hang limp: the head drops heavily forward, the eyes are dead eyes, and in the original the color is livid. And do you observe how the illusion of motion is created? — by the straight tensity of the upper part of the winding sheet that falls almost perpendicularly, merging by degrees into the folds and upturned portions below. The body has slid into the arms of John; and the affectionate way in which all these mourners and helpers receive the burden shows how precious a burden it is.

Among the three Marys it is easy to distinguish the Virgin because of her greater dignity and sorrow. She does not touch the body but follows its every movement with a quick sympathy. Mary Magdalene receives the feet, as she does in so many pictures, just as in many of the crucifixions she embraces the feet. In this way the artists picture her passionate sorrow and her sense of unworthiness because of past

371

sins. As in Rubens' *Crucifixion*, the Magdalene is the most human, the most delicate and the most beautiful portion of the picture.

The religious value of such a picture lies in its power to revive personal memories. Death is one of the most solemn realities in the world; it is the door by which one passes from the seen and temporal into the more immediate consciousness of things unseen and eternal. Death is therefore a religious experience for him who dies and for those who follow with love the departing soul. No one who has performed the last rites for a loved one will fail to be touched by this pictured service or to feel again in less poignant form the solemnity of that hour. There are few spiritual lessons to be learned in the House of Mirth, but many and faithful are the counsels our hearts receive as we stand between the eternities and watch the iron doors close.

TITIAN: PIETÀ

Titian: Tiziano Vecelli, called (1477–1576)
Original: 11′6″ x 12′6″, painted in 1576 as payment for his grave in the church of the Frari, Venice. Because of a dispute the picture was never finished and the painter specified that he should be buried at Cadore. He was, however, buried at the Frari by order of the State, and the picture was given its final touches by Palma Giovine, who added the inscription, "*Quod Titanus incohatum reliquit, Palma reverenter absolvit, Deoq[ue] dicavit opus.*" It was placed in the now suppressed church of Sant' Angelo, Venice, whence it was removed to the Academy.
Reproductions:

The background of this superb composition is a structure of stone, simple, dignified, classic, and

typifying the Church Universal (1 Peter 2 : 5; Eph.
2: 19–22). The apex of the roof is filled with a huge
keystone in three parts to suggest that the Father,
Son and Spirit are the crown and guarantee of the
integrity of the whole; while the triangular boss on the
central voussoir proclaims the trinity of the perfections
of the Godhead — truth, beauty and goodness. Below the keystone hang five drops, or guttæ, like those
found on classic buildings, but standing here for the
five wounds of Christ on the cross.[1] In the angles of
the pediment two angels proclaim the gospel to every
creature. Above, on the roof, seven crystal lamps are
burning, the spirits of the seven churches to whom the
Beloved Disciple wrote in the Apocalypse, the bright
and shining lights set aloft where their testimony
cannot be hid. Within the gilt mosaic semidome of
the niche, a pelican strips her breast that her young
may be nourished with her blood. This is an ancient
symbol of Christ and his sacrifice (John 6 : 53–56).
As a part of this architectural setting Moses stands
upon our left, bearing his three symbols: the horns
on his head — the idea of which arose from a mis-
translation of a passage in Exodus; the tables of the
Law; and his rod, " the potent rod of Amram's son."
Below on the pedestal a lion glares at us, possibly
standing for the wild beast in us that the law must
subdue; and in front a little angel stoops to raise a
vase of spikenard with which to anoint the body of
Christ. On the other side stands a strong and graceful figure, the Hellespontine Sibyl, crowned with
thorns and pointing to the cross which she holds,

[1] For many of these details the writer is indebted to H. T. Bailey: *Twelve Great Paintings.*

while she speaks to the little angel hovering near. The Sibyls are heroic figures that come down to us from classic antiquity. Plato knew of one, but the number increased in later writers to eight, ten, or even twelve, and in the early Christian centuries their Sibylline Books were received by Christians with almost scriptural authority. Michelangelo has shown five of them on the Sistine ceiling, and established their character for all time. They are the Spirit of Prophecy, not as limited and personalized by any specific prophet, but as existing at large in the constitution of the spiritual universe. Any one of them may stand for " all prophecy " — as the Hellespontine here does; and for her, all prophecy points to the cross. So that she well may rebuke the little angel with his torch which is a symbol of death, and bid him look to her symbol of Christ's passion in which a death has brought life to the world, and death itself has been swallowed up in victory. As the heraldic supporters of this arch that represents the divine plan of Salvation — keyed by the three stones of the Holy Trinity, lighted by the seven messages to the Churches and blazoned with the symbol of self-sacrifice — these two figures stand for Law and Prophecy, the two avenues by which hitherto the divine plan has been revealed to mankind. But they and the architectural structure they support are now the background for the full revelation given in Christ.

The center of our interest is the group in front of the niche. Mary Magdalene the forgiven sinner, clad in green, utters a cry that is at once the expression of her passion and a warning that no one shall break in upon the grief of this holy place. The Virgin in

374

TITIAN: PIETÀ

CISERI: THE ENTOMBMENT

blue robe, her face bathed in tears, holds in her lap the form of her dead Son, in "whose feet and hands are wound-prints, and his side." The whole structure of the Church enshrines these two, the central treasures in the penetralia of its faith. Joseph of Arimathæa, who has begged the body for burial, comes reverently on his knees, takes the dead hand in his and looks into the face of the departed Savior as if reverence were hesitating to bestow the kiss that love impels. The whole group constitutes a symbol of that mysterious dispensation by which one who is the object of such transcendent human devotion is at the same time the Lamb slain from the foundation of the world. The finite and the infinite here coincide and coalesce.

But there is another meaning which fills this picture with the most tender sentiment and pathos. We recall that Titian is painting this *Pietà* as a payment for his burial. The hand that for three generations has dominated the art of the world has not yet begun to falter nor has the fruitful brain lost its power to conceive grandly and with power. But the tale of the ninety-nine years bids the master prepare for the great change. Thoughts like those that Michelangelo has expressed in his sonnet now take possession of him:

> " Painting nor sculpture now can lull to rest
> My soul, that turns to His great love on high,
> Whose arms to clasp us on the Cross were spread."

And he pours out upon this canvas his last prayer. The picture is intensely personal. The grand sweep of line that starts with Moses falls along all the figures and ends in a little tablet that leans against the pedestal of the Sibyl. Looking carefully there, as the painter thus bids us do, we discover that the tablet half conceals an escutcheon on which are the arms of the family of Titian; on the tablet itself Titian and his son kneel humbly before a little group of the " Christ of Pity " resting in his mother's arms; and looking once more at Joseph of Arimathæa we discover that the face is the face of Titian. The old man, clad in scanty sackcloth rather than in the rich robes he is wont to wear, is bringing into the divine presence his century of achievement, his immortality of fame, and laying it all at these blessed feet. It is his final act of worship before that swift-approaching day when by the power of the living Christ he shall stand in His presence and give account of the deeds done in the body. The grand plan of salvation that avails for the world, avails for him!— and in this last hour his spirit cries, in language that voices the final prayer of all the redeemed:

" My faith looks up to Thee,
Thou Lamb of Calvary,
Savior divine."

CISERI: THE ENTOMBMENT

*Matt. 27 : 57–61; Mark 15 : 42–47; Luke 23; 50–56a;
John 19 : 38–42*

Ciseri, Antonio (1821–1891)
Original: painted in 1869, an altar-piece in the church of the Madonna del Sasso, Locarno.
Reproductions: Taber-Prang, photogravure $15\frac{1}{4}$ x $21\frac{3}{4}''$; 50 cts. plain, $1.50 colored.

This picture is an artist's commentary on Lam. 1 : 12 — " Is it nothing to you, all ye that pass by?

Behold and see if there be any sorrow like unto my sorrow! "

One golden afternoon in 1898 the writer was wandering alone over the heights above Lake Maggiore, when he was attracted by an old monastery crowning a conical hill that rose some eleven hundred feet behind the city of Locarno. Straightway he became a pilgrim and began to climb the zigzag path, conspicuous from a distance by what looked like a succession of white milestones of enormous size, but in reality were little shrines containing pictures of the Stations of the Cross. Crude though they were, they suggested the depth of piety that had constructed this laborious way and the monastery on the summit, and dedicated it to Our Lady of Sorrows, called now from the eagle's nest of her shrine, "Our Lady of the Rock." There is no need to tell of the deserted cloisters, the hideous wax effigies of the Last Supper, the Nativity and the like, that stared from unexpected grottoes and divided one's mind between awe and mirth. But the church itself was the climax of wonder, its inner walls covered with a thatch of votive offerings that wretched folk had left in hope of cure or in token of the same: chromos, faded flowers, ostrich eggs, samplers and mottoes in all kinds of stitches, models of ships and what not, mirrors framed in gilt tinsel, tufts of hair, shreds of rag,— all the flotsam and jetsam of petition or of thanks thrown upon this hospitable rock by the wrecked voyagers of life, each bit eloquent of suffering and release through the intercession of the Blessed Virgin. One great tablet of marble told how the Queen of Heaven had stayed a plague that was devastating

Locarno, and the grateful city had vowed this acknowledgment.

Out of the mass of this holy bric-a-brac flamed Ciseri's glorious picture. The late sun streamed upon it, upon the pallid limbs of the Christ, upon the Virgin's upturned face of sorrow and her cerulean mantle; it kissed the bared shoulder of the Magdalen and lighted into a glory the golden stream of her hair that had fallen forward in the ecstasy of her passion. And it seemed then as if the picture were the final and perfect expression of that profound sorrow of the Mother that makes her eternally akin to every sorrowing heart. This is the Mary whom the poor can pity and love, the Mary who can pity and love in return. This is the embodiment of all the tender sympathy which man longs for in the Divine, but which a frigid and inexorable theology has driven from the heart of God. Finding only justice in the Father of the creeds, and only exalted perfection in the Son whose chief function is to endure the Father's wrath, and only ecstasies for solitary saints in the descending Holy Spirit, the yearning heart of the world has turned toward Mary the eternal Mother, whose fellowship in its sufferings makes her ever ready to pity and intercede. This is the true philosophy of the worship of Mary.

The other figures in Ciseri's picture are only accompaniments to Mary and her Son. Yet they all enhance the beauty and interpret the sorrow of these central ones. One discovers that Ciseri has a feeling for subtilty and suavity of line as well as for harmonious color: that he can express dignity as well as grace, the gravity of age as well as the charm of

378

youth. Nicodemus, just past the prime of life, leads
the sad procession, his face almost as ruddy as the
orange under-robe he wears. Joseph of Arimathæa
shares with him the major burden, his snow-white
beard contrasting so richly with his dull green mantle,
and it in turn with the cream-colored head-cloth.
The faces of these two have a strong portrait quality;
they are full of character. John who carries the
shoulders of the Savior has the face of a poet — large
eyes, full features now grief-stricken, and ruddy locks
that hang upon the shoulder. Behind the Virgin
walks Mary the wife of Cleopas, and last of all Salome.
And while the majestic bearing of Christ's mother
makes us feel that the message of the picture is her
grief, we almost forget her in admiration of the beauty
of the Magdalen, — the sunlight on the foot, on the
white under-robe, on the mantle of old-gold and the
rippling luster of her tresses.

The head of Christ is the center of composition.
While it follows somewhat the traditional features, we
see in it a dignity and strength that few representations of him possess. One feels that here was a great
man, one absolutely worthy of the wealth of love that
is being poured out; and this feeling in turn adds to
our own sorrow that one so good and great should
have been cut off in his prime. These feelings, you
observe, are all modern rather than medieval. There
is positively no theology in this picture. This is not
the entombment of the Second Person of the Trinity,
with the Queen of Heaven for chief mourner; it is the
burial of a beloved son and the grief of a stricken
mother.

PIGLHEIN: THE ENTOMBMENT

Matt. 27 : 57–61; Mark 15 : 42–47; Luke 23 : 50–56a;
John 19 : 38–42

Piglhein, Elimar Ulrich Bruno (1848–1894)
Original: painted in 1888; now in the Neue Pinakothek, Munich.
Reproductions:

Outside of Jerusalem is a burying-place that looks like this. Going northward from the Damascus gate about half a mile, you turn in at a little entrance opposite the English Bishop's house and suddenly there yawns before you a deep excavation in the rock, like a quarry, the sides precipitous and the way to its depths hewn carefully in the solid rock. Descending, you come to the level floor of the chasm. The rocks tower above so that you see nothing but the blue sky overhead and hear nothing of the world outside. The solemnity of death settles over your spirit, especially as you turn to a half-effaced facade sculptured on the western wall and realize that here is the entrance to royal tombs. In the floor at the back of the excavated vestibule you find a rolling stone cut from the wall; it still runs in its groove like a millstone on edge and closes the inner entrance. Passing down a few steps and stooping to enter the little aperture, you find yourself in a dark fore-chamber perhaps eighteen feet square. You light your candle and perceive that you are in a palace of death; through doors you enter the four large mortuary chambers and from there you may look into still other tiny ones, each of them a little sepulchre where bodies could be laid and the whole sealed up. Benches of stone surround the rooms, and niches in the wall may still be seen where lamps were set. There are thirty-one of these little tombs within the palace, room enough to accommodate Queen Helena, her son Izates and most of her forty-eight grandchildren. This good woman was queen of Adiabene beyond the Tigris, but becoming a proselyte to Judaism she came to Jerusalem about 44 A.D. at the time of the famine mentioned in Acts 11 : 48, when Saul and Barnabas brought relief from Antioch. She too employed her riches in relieving the poor, buying grain from Egypt and figs from Cyprus. By her order this mausoleum was constructed and adorned above with pryamids and columns, so that it became the best known landmark in the region. It is the finest extant example of a Jewish tomb of the best class. In principle it is like Joseph of Arimathæa's, — rock-hewn and closed with a rolling stone. In such a tomb, though of humbler proportions, the body of Jesus was surely laid.

Piglhein, inspired by his studies in Jerusalem, has shown us the descent into such a sepulchre. We see the rocky stairs, the precipitous walls, the Dantesque masses above, and the shadows, deepest at the sculptured portal of the crypt. It is a royal burial. The King of a lost cause is being carried to oblivion; three faithful ones bear cautiously the sacred corpse, another passes down before them with the winding-sheet and the spices, and the inner circle of the beloved waits in the gloomy depths of the canyon, while the Magdalen throws herself on a ledge and petitions the dead eyes for one more look. It is all so hopeless. It is like the descent into Hades such as Homer and Virgil have depicted, or like the " savage

way " by which Dante went down among the lost.
One feels the abysmal shadows gathering, as if the
next turn would confront one with the gate and its
inscription,

" Through me the way is to eternal dole;
All hope abandon, ye who enter in."

This was the meaning of Christ's death to those who
loved him: it was tragedy unrelieved and irremediable.
They all descended with his body into the valley of
a great shadow; and the sun fell from the sky when
the adamantine portals closed upon him.   Piglhein's
picture is a transcription of their hopelessness.

FRA ANGELICO: THE DESCENT INTO LIMBO

1 Peter 3 : 18–20; Ps. 16 : 10; Apostles Creed

Angelico: Giovanni da Fiesole, called Fra (1387–1455)
Original: a fresco in cell No. 31, convent of S. Marco, Florence.
Reproductions:

The notion that Christ descended into Hell is
perpetuated by the so-called Apostles Creed. The
particular clause that affirms it is a late comer; it was
not found in the fifth century, while the other clauses
were present at least in the third. It rests upon the
two passages in scripture cited above, though the
verse from Psalms probably means " Thou wilt not
allow my soul to enter Hades," and so should properly
be excluded from the case.   Peter is seemingly explicit,
but when one inquires exactly, his meaning is impossible to determine. The oldest belief was that
upon his death Christ went to Hades, the land of

PIGLIIEIN: THE ENTOMBMENT

FRA ANGELICO: DESCENT INTO LIMBO

dead men, and remained for three days. Later came the idea that he went down to show Satan that his power was broken and that he and his rebel crew had no longer exclusive jurisdiction over Hell. After several centuries of controversy the church of the middle age established the belief that Christ descended into a place called the "Limbo of the Fathers," where all the saints of the Old Testament were waiting till the great salvation should be consummated. These spirits were "in prison," to use Peter's phrase, but not suffering; they had merely not yet entered upon their higher bliss. And when Christ announced to them the full accomplishment of his mission on earth, they joined at once the ranks of the believers and went with him to heaven.

The Protestants after Calvin have believed that the words "He descended into Hell" are a figurative expression for the "unutterable sufferings of Christ's human soul which he endured in the last moments of his vicarious dying"; whereas more "liberally minded" people see in the phrase some support for their belief in a "second chance" for the wicked.

In his illustration Fra Angelico takes us into the Limbo of the Fathers. He has pictured the scene with more than his wonted vigor. Christ bursts through the gateway of Limbo with a rush and a gladsome sprightliness that show his intense satisfaction with what he is about to do. He is walking on the air — almost dancing, in fact. His garments flutter gaily behind with the wind of motion; his flag of victory flaps merrily over his shoulder. A mandorla of light surrounds him, the rays of which have power to smite down all opposition. It is this power of living light that has knocked down the door and pinned flat under it a poor devil who tried to buttress it. You can see the head and horns emerging at one end of the fallen door, while a snaky tail wriggles through the keyhole! The other devils have beat to cover; one is gibbering behind an angle of rock to the right and another has taken to the roof. There are great cracks in the floor, caused by the earthquake that occurred when Christ yielded up the ghost. Dante reports that the bridges across Malebolge, the lower section of Hell, were some of them broken by the shock, and there was an enormous landslip from the upper to the nether circles.

The joy with which Christ comes to these spirits in prison is equalled by theirs in receiving him. Adam leads the happy band, hastening with great strides to clasp the long-wished-for hand. Eve follows, her hands clasped upon her bosom. Abel in hairy skirt presses on beside her; and "time would fail me to tell of Gideon and Barak, Samuel and the prophets, who through faith subdued kingdoms, wrought righteousness and turned to flight the armies of the aliens." They are all here in this glad procession.

It is upon the bridge of the eleventh of Hebrews that we must pass from the picture with its mythologic terrors and uncertainties to the sure land of spiritual truth. "All these, having had witness borne to them through their faith, received not the promise, God having provided some better thing for us, that apart from us they should not be made perfect" (Heb. 11 : 39–40). The "Harrowing of Hell" means that salvation before Christ came could never be perfect. Salvation is completed manhood, it is the evolutionary process consummated, it is frail humanity raised to the nth power, till its insight and will, without losing their identity, merge with the Divine. In this divine process, ideals play a leading part. Not till Christ showed what Man and God are and what the perfect relation between the two should be, could any individual rise to more than a far-off glimpse of salvation. Read the various Old Testament accounts of Jehovah, his variable character, his low ideals that reflect the civilization of the primitive peoples who created him, and then ask yourself whether likeness to that kind of deity would produce a satisfactory salvation for you. The Old Testament worthies, the best of them, were in Limbo. They needed the larger vision. And there is no reason to doubt that they had to await the revelations time had in store before they could understand the height and depth of the love of God and the riches that are for all time in Christ Jesus our Lord.

The " Descent into Limbo " means that the completion of Christ's work opened to man the possibility of a new and a higher spiritual life, into which all who ever lived may enter. It marked a node in human evolution.

CHAPTER XXI

EASTER MORNING

PICTURES FOR STUDY

Unknown: The Resurrection
Ender: Holy Women at the Tomb
Burnand: Peter and John
Fra Angelico: " Noli me tangere "
Burne-Jones: Morning of the Resurrection
Von Uhde: Easter Morning

Nothing is more certain in this world than that without the Resurrection there would have been no Christianity. Christ's death on the cross put an end to all the hopes of the disciples: " We trusted that it had been he which should have redeemed Israel," was the despairing eulogy pronounced over a vanished cause. All the pictured glories of a Messianic Kingdom faded into the murk of night when the Messiah cried, " It is finished." The dreams dissolved; grief brought back the chill of waking reality; and instead of twelve thrones on which they should judge the twelve tribes of Israel, the disciples faced the disgrace of disillusionment and the pangs of hunger — for they had given away all their possessions before they left Galilee, expecting to receive houses and lands a hundredfold in the new kingdom. " I go a-fishing " is Peter's laconic abdication of his Chancellorship.

But the unexpected and the transcendent happened: the disciples received indubitable proofs that Jesus was alive! All had visions of him, and their hearts

387

burned within them as these contacts shed a dazzling meaning on his past promises and teachings. Their spirits caught fire again, and with revived and transfigured hopes they went out to conquer the world: first with the idea that the Kingdom was imminent, coming on the clouds of heaven; then, when the Lord delayed his coming, with the idea that man's vocation was to fit himself for membership in that heavenly kingdom; and then tardily but surely, with the idea that "the kingdom of God is within you," here and now, and must be won by spiritual endeavor. Transforming and being transformed, these grand ideas have been steadily operative in human life from Easter dawn to the present. They are the "*élan vital*," the divine life in the soul of man, the essential energy of that spiritual evolution decreed from the foundation of the world, by which God brings man to himself. It is no wonder, then, that Paul believed that if the resurrection were vain his preaching was vain, and that Easter day has been throughout all the ages the grand Allelujah of the Church Universal.

UNKNOWN: THE RESURRECTION

ENDER: HOLY WOMEN AT THE TOMB

UNKNOWN: THE RESURRECTION

Matt. 28 : 1–15; Mark 16 : 1–11; Luke 24 : 1–12; John 20 : 1–18

This picture was formerly attributed to Taddeo Gaddi (1300–1366), but is now assigned to the " Unknown painter of the Spanish Chapel."

Original: a fresco in the Spanish chapel of S. Maria Novella, Florence, a Dominican church erected in 1320 and decorated in the middle of that century. The vaulted ceiling is divided into four triangles, of which this is one, each illustrating an incident of sacred history: (1) the Resurrection, (2) the Ascension, (3) the Descent of the Holy Spirit, (4) the Ship of Peter. On the wall below each is a fresco presenting a related event: (1) the Passion of our Lord, (2) the Dominicans carrying out the great Commission, (3) the outpouring of wisdom upon Thomas Aquinas, the great Dominican theologian, (4) the triumph of the Church under the guidance of the Dominicans. These frescos illustrate the truth that the event of primal significance in the world, the one from which all others depend, is the Resurrection.

Reproductions:

This early fresco is an attempt to paint the events clustering round the Resurrection. Following the then prevailing custom, several moments of time are presented, and presented against a varied though conventionalized background. In the pinnacle is the resplendent figure of Christ borne on the clouds, holding in his hand an image of victory and carrying the resurrection banner — forked, with a red cross on a white field. Below is the open tomb, a sarcophagus of white marble with an inlaid colored pattern. Two angels are seated on it, one of them calling to it the attention of the three holy women who advance on the left with their vases of ointment. Beyond these women rise the walls and towers of Jerusalem. In the immediate foreground are the figures of five

389

sleeping soldiers, while among them sits a turbaned priest who is giving them the bribe. On the right appears a garden of tufted trees and flowers in which the Magdalen adores the risen Lord.

This is wholly a narrative picture. Its significance lies in the story told. There is no symbolism, no theology, and no attempt at character interpretation. We are asked to take the gospel account at its face value, remember the facts, and believe that somehow they are of the greatest importance for our soul's welfare. Just what that importance is makes little difference, for St. Peter and St. Thomas Aquinas in the other frescos have taken care of all that, and the Dominican Order will give us all the practical instruction necessary to keep in the fold. Only believe. This is a comfortable way of taking religion, and it answered very well till the Renaissance and the Reformation.

ENDER: HOLY WOMEN AT THE TOMB

Mark 16 : 1–11

Ender, Axel Hjalmar (1853–   )
Original: an altar-piece in the church at Molde, Norway.
Reproductions:

Molde is a city of fishermen, lying almost under the Arctic circle. The writer remembers a quiet Sunday spent there some years ago, — the gray skies, the leaden fjord opening out to the Arctic sea, the violet mountains to the south, and to the east the jagged peaks of the " Troldtinder " above the Romsdal. He remembers the morning walk up the sloping streets among the wooden houses; and although much of the detail of Molde has faded from memory, he still carries with minute distinctness this glowing picture within the little wooden church. We sat long before it, surprised and delighted to find here in this remote corner of the world so sincere and beautiful an Easter message, and withal so Norwegian. It is a fragment of the gospel with which Olaf smote the warlocks of Eyvind Kalda and the berserks of Raud the Strong. It is the " Peace-cry " that drowned the blows of the hammer of Thor and conquered the Norseland for Christ.

We are within the great cave of the sepulchre. Two Marys and Salome have come to anoint the body of Christ, but to their amazement they find the body gone and a young man in white apparel sitting by the empty grave. The color effects are wonderfully fine. The near woman has an undergarment of light-salmon silk with a woolen over-robe of terra-cotta. Mary the Virgin, in the center, has a cotton dress of dark blue with a woolen head-cloth of straw color. The woman just entering has a skirt of terra-cotta, an upper garment of blue and a straw-colored head-dress. The angel is pure white, with the loveliest golden hair and a face as Norwegian as it is strong and fine. The light of dawn streams through the archlike entrance, but the shadows in the rear of the cave still form a solid background for the brilliance of the angel. It is striking, rich.

Ender has painted these women with great force and truthfulness. They are barefooted like peasant women the world over; they are strong creatures, big limbed, and the two nearer ones at least have un-tutored faces that show the class to which they belong. And see how genuine they are in their emotions: the

Magdalen, half bold and half afraid; Mary, astonished but eager to hear the message, Salome still busy with her sorrow and unaware of the angel's presence. And the line of the three faces leads you down gently but surely from the sorrow of Salome to the heart of the Resurrection message,

" Till you find the deathless Angel seated in the vacant tomb."

And on the lips of this deathless angel is the one immortal truth which all the legends of the Forty Days vainly try to enhance, " He is not here, he is risen! " This is the great light that lightens every tomb, that flames with celestial radiance against the background of our deepest sorrow: " Christ is risen! " and because He lives, our Elder Brother, we shall live also.

The joy of this truth finds beautiful expression in an old Greek hymn by John of Damascus of the eighth century, written in the monastery of Mar Saba in the desolate canyon of the Kedron above the Dead Sea. Here is the second stanza:

" 'Tis the spring of souls today:
    Christ hath burst his prison,
From the frost and gloom of death
    Light and life have risen.
All the winter of our sins,
    Long and dark, is flying
From His light to whom we give
    Thanks and praise undying."

Now transplant this nature-figure to Norway. Let the " winter of our sins " be that long Arctic night unbroken except by the stars of hope. Then let the

Easter-tide arrive! Then they who live in Molde see the unconquered sun burst from underground and day by day mount the heavens till in the light of its perpetual radiance the ice dissolves from the fjords and the flowers spring up again in glad resurrection. Easter-time means to the Northland the world's rebirth. No wonder, then, that the Norwegian Ender chose the Resurrection for his theme: it is his Nature-saga and his Christian message in one.

BURNAND: PETER AND JOHN

John 20 : 1–10

Burnand, Eugène (Contemporary French)
Original: in the Luxembourg Museum, Paris.
Reproductions: Taber-Prang, 1, 2, 13; Braun & Co. F. I. E.

What Sidney Lanier calls " the heart of Haste " is beating in Burnand's now famous picture. Peter and John are running at top speed; yet even so, desire outdistances them. Some resistless impulse drives them on, or rather some supreme attraction pulls them, some spiritual gravitation like that which seizes upon a comet when a mighty sun wheels in from the celestial spaces and draws the wanderer into swift perihelion. So these two turn their backs upon the golden dawn, brilliant though it glows with promise of a new day, and fly to the Sun of Righteousness that has risen from the tomb of Golgotha.

It is interesting to see how this illusion of motion is produced. John's hair ripples backward, the body bends forward, and the folds of his garment accentuate the forward thrust. Peter's long locks flare in the wind; they belly and tug like flame-pennons; his cloak tosses behind, his mouth opens for more breath, and the hand presses back a heart that would beat through the bars of its prison. There is no need of legs to show that they are running; on the contrary, legs would hinder, with their necessarily static position. The runners are leaving the wind behind as it is.

It is evident that "that other disciple" is outrunning Peter. He has youth in his favor. His hands are pressed to his bosom, but not to help out labored breathing; they are clasped as if in prayer or as if already grasping an expected joy. For him, running is a mere reflex of which he is not conscious; all his thought is projected far ahead, even as his eye is fixed on that gate in the garden wall. Poor old lumbering Peter is divided between the ecstasy of anticipated bliss and the fear that his lungs and heart are not equal to the strain. Peter will see John's little lead widen, and he will have the added pain of fearing that John will see a vision that will not stay for him.

It is wonderful, too, to see how the artist expresses anticipation, in its old Latin meaning. Anticipation is the present experience of a future event, the reaching out and grasping of that which is not yet here. See how these disciples reach out with their spirits. John fixes his eyes on the goal — strains his eyes, rather — that he may not lose sight for an instant of the spot toward which his feet are speeding, while his imagination already pictures the wonder and awe that will be his when he stands within the empty tomb. Peter is running by faith and not by sight. He cannot make out the gate, though he knows it is there; but grasping the substance of things hoped for he presses on toward the prize. There is also in

FRA ANGELICO: CHRIST APPEARING TO MARY MAGDALENE

BURNE-JONES: MORNING OF THE RESURRECTION

Peter's face a look not arising from the strain of running; it seems almost like fear that perhaps the report may not be true, or that should he meet his risen Lord he would be ashamed to face him after the cowardice and the oaths of that hour in Caiaphas' courtyard. Or is it rather eagerness to make amends that so crowds the face with lines? — a yearning to embrace the feet that he is not worthy to touch, and cry, "Lord, thou knowest all things, thou knowest that I love thee!" Surely it is this last, and love is the power that draws these two with such swiftness. Like the great Florentine after his vision of the mystery of heaven, these also confess:

" Now my desire and will
That Love is turning which moves the sun and the other stars."

FRA ANGELICO: "NOLI ME TANGERE"
John 20 : 11–18

Angelico: Giovanni da Fiesole, called Fra (1387–1455)
Original: a fresco in a cell in S. Marco monastery, Florence.
Reproductions: The Medici Society, O. M. C. No. 258.

This beautiful story is told only in John. It is the story of tears changed to joy, the garment of praise given for the spirit of heaviness. The Angelic Brother has caught the mood perfectly, at least as far as the medieval conception of Jesus allows one to catch and interpret an intensely human experience.

There is something here that reminds one of Angelico's *Annunciation*, the first picture in our series. There is the same stillness and seclusion, there are the sprinkled flowers in the grass, there are the distant garden fence and the thick hedge of the trees to insure the privacy of the scene. For the arches of the cloister we have the rocky archway of the tomb, and we have two figures, this time another Mary and a different heavenly visitor.

Mary has turned from her weeping at the door of the tomb and has seen this man standing near. He has a garden tool over his shoulder, but all the signs of his spiritual nature are suppressed. To him she makes her passionate plea. Then that one word, " Mary," spoken in answer, sets all her pulses beating, and with a swift instinctive gesture she kneels at his feet and would embrace him but for the kindly warning. Fra Angelico has given us this moment in the action. Jesus is saying to her, " Touch me not! " The position of the Savior's feet shows that he has stepped suddenly aside, and his deprecating gesture and look indicate that his caution was needed. The two faces interpret the situation in the same way: Mary is all surprise and joy and love, Jesus is serenity and something of aloofness or at least other-worldliness. No doubt Fra Angelico felt that these were the two attitudes to express. He did not, of course, believe with Renan that the Magdalen loved Jesus as only a woman can love a man, but he knew her passionate devotion to the Master's cause, and her long and faithful following of him all over Galilee and even to his cross. Devotion and love of some kind she surely had, and her reward was that Jesus granted her a special vision. But in this picture, Jesus' regard seems to be for himself rather than for her. He is anxious to preserve himself from all earthly contacts, as if a taint would attach to his spiritual essence if he allowed a woman to touch him.

396

The gospel narrative, it is true, lends color to this view; but it seems strange that Jesus should have mingled so freely with the despised, the outcast and the loathesome during his ministry, and now should shun the grateful touch of one whom he had saved from perdition. Fra Angelico could explain this change satisfactorily: Christ had become something different by the fact of his resurrection; the days of his humiliation were over, the era of his triumph had arrived. He was about to resume the glory that he had with the Father before the world was. Under these conditions it is inevitable that he should act as here represented. But to us it seems incredible that while Jesus should deal so patiently with the doubts of Thomas, even to allowing him to touch his wounds, he should rebuff the devotion of Mary in this summary way. It is easier to believe the story to be apocryphal than to believe this of Jesus.

BURNE–JONES: THE MORNING OF THE RESURRECTION

John 20 : 11–18

Burne-Jones, Sir Edward Colley (1833–1898)
Original: painted in 1886, privately owned in England.
Reproductions:

Burne-Jones has expressed the mystery and awe that surrounded the vision of Mary.

Mary has thrown a great cloak about her and in the gray dawn has come to the tomb. It is a grotto in the rock made by the bending of the strata but deepened by the hand of man. At its mouth is the beautiful sarcophagus of stone, now sacred forever as

having been the casket of the world's greatest treasure. Mary has found two shining ones sitting the one
at the head and the other at the foot. Love and
grief have made her bold. In spite of them she has
looked within, she has stopped awhile to weep, while
the shining ones look on in silence. They disturb her
not, even by so much as a rustle of the great pinions
that fold themselves into the spaces of the grotto, or
by the flicker of the flames that glow like a star upon
their foreheads. But now of a sudden they start,
and by that act recall Mary's fancy from the past to
the present. The angels raise a fold of their garment
to their lips, half in token of silent awe and half to
cover their faces in humility before One whom they
recognize to be above all Thrones and Powers. One
of them points vaguely, and Mary following the finger
turns a timid and startled face upon the visitor. A
strange figure is approaching through the misty light.
It is the owner of the garden, or the gardener, who has
come to bid her begone. She steadies herself with
her hand against the low arch and catches up her
cloak as if to hide in it. The figure comes nearer.
It changes its appearance. She cannot take her eyes
from it, while her heart falters between courage and
fear. It stops and looks at her. Its mild eyes penetrate her soul deeper and deeper, till the slumbering
memory begins to stir. Is it a waking dream or a
reality? She cannot tell, and what she does or says
she does not know. It is something mystic, ineffable
and full of awe.

This is the moment presented by the artist.

Why has this visitor come? Look carefully at him
and you will see. He has come because love has

JESUS, PETER, AND JOHN

summoned him. Note the sweet humility of his
figure, the grace, the quietness, the half-stoop of
shoulder, the forward-bending head, the deep-set eyes
that rest so steadily upon the timid one, yet with such
reassuring kindliness. He has come because she loved
him and prayed for him to come. He is the answer
to her prayer. Never can this Christ say to her,
" Touch me not! " for his thought is not of himself
but of her. Let her soul embrace him if it needs;
there is no taint in love, for God is love. This meeting is not a rebuff, rather it is his fulfilment of Mary's
heart's desire, his assurance that he lives and that she
may love him still.

Let us follow the mystic dream beyond the moment
given. The vision will stay awhile, the look will set
her heart-strings quivering with richer and richer
music, the form will shape itself in clearer outline till
at last it links itself with a sound once so familiar
on His lips and so dear to her: " Mary! " All the
chambers of her soul echo that word, till the memories
of sight and voice and act and passion fuse in one
bright picture of remembered joy: " Master! " She
has seen the Lord!

The sun rises, the angels vanish, the gardener stoops
over his flowers, the nearby city awakes to its traffic
and its sin; along the dusty road a shepherd leads
his flock to pasture; and as he raises his eyes he sees
a woman in white returning from Joseph's garden as
in an ecstasy.

VON UHDE: EASTER MORNING

John 20 : 11–18

Uhde, Fritz von (1848–   )
Original:
Reproductions:

Von Uhde differs from all others in his point of view and his message. Easter morning means for him the Christ of Comfort. Where Angelico sees only the transfigured other-worldliness of Christ and Burne-Jones lets us feel the mystic passions that tremble in Mary's heart, this artist shows us the utter humanness of even a risen Christ.

To do this he has thrown away practically every shred of the gospel data — only the garden is left, and that is less a garden than a solitary pathway in a glade. Gone are the angels, the rock-hewn grotto, gone are the usual signs by which we recognize the Magdalen — the beauteous and dishevelled hair and the half-bared bosom. Even the conventional dress the history-painters use has been discarded. We have only a poor German peasant girl crying alone in the forest. She is not "weeping" in theatrical fashion and showing at intervals a tragic face to excite our pity. She is just crying as if her heart would break.

Jesus, the friend of all the broken-hearted, while wandering like a pilgrim through the pathways of life, has heard her sobbing and has come to comfort her. Gentle inquiry is on his face, kindliness and tenderness envelop his form. He touches her on the arm; he speaks her name; and there flows in upon her grief a healing balm as from some fountain of Nepen-

400

the, a balm of friendship and of sympathy, the only balm man's heart ever knew or ever will know.

In this act of sympathy Christ is intensely human. He is the same Christ now as before the great change. The one who took the little daughter by the hand and said, " Arise!" the one who wept at the tomb of his friend and comforted the sister with the words of his transcendent faith, is here continuing the ministry to which God called him. Through all eternity and in all worlds he will be Mary's friend. She may not always see him but she can feel him at her side and know that he cares.

And what is true for Mary is true for us. We may universalize this picture of Von Uhde's, though we cannot universalize Fra Angelico's. This brotherly Christ is the one we know and love; our great comforter not only in the hour of our supreme sorrow but in all the ills of life.

> " The healing of His seamless dress
> Is by our beds of pain;
> We touch Him in life's throng and press,
> And we are whole again."

For the picture of such a one we turn in vain to the old Masters, prepossessed as they are with their creeds and cabined by the canons of an imperious Church. Only a modern, who can translate God into wholly human terms as the Son of Man, can make our hearts burn within us by picturing our Friend. To such a Christ we can say, with Tennyson:

> " Thou seemest human and divine,
> The highest, holiest manhood, Thou."

401

Chapter XXII

THE TRANSCENDENT CHRIST *

PICTURES FOR STUDY

Girardet: The Walk to Emmaus
Rembrandt: The Supper at Emmaus
Raphael: The Charge to Peter
Von Uhde: The Ascension

Paul, the earliest writer in the New Testament, gives us a categorical and probably authentic and exhaustive list of the various appearances of Jesus after his death, and clearly implies that they were not physical but spiritual, in the form of visions. " He appeared to Cephas; then to the twelve; then he appeared to above five hundred brethren at once, of whom the greater part remain till now [57 A.D.] but some are fallen asleep; then he appeared to James; then to all the apostles; and last of all to me also." (1 Cor. 15 : 4–8.) This list omits all reference to the appearances mentioned in the Gospels except those to Peter (Luke 24 : 34) and the disciples. The oldest gospels — Mark and the Gospel of Peter — indicate that all the appearances were in Galilee amid the scenes of their common labors. Luke places his all near Jerusalem, and crowds them and the Ascension all into the limits of Easter Sunday. John combines both the Jerusalem and the Galilean cycles. Only in

---

* For a remarkably clear and reverent treatment of this most difficult subject, the reader is urged to turn to Prof. Chas. F. Kent's "Life and Teachings of Jesus," pp. 298–310.

Luke and John do we find stories of the physical reappearance of Jesus. These stories, which the pictures of this chapter illustrate, apocryphal though they be, are witness to the intense desire of the primitive Church to make more certain and vivid to others the vivid certainty of their own hearts that Jesus still lived.

GIRARDET: THE WALK TO EMMAUS
Luke 24 : 13–35

Girardet (Contemporary French)
Original: painted 1904 and exhibited in the Paris Salon.
Reproductions: Braun & Co. F. I.

It is still possible to walk from Jerusalem to Emmaus. Taking the Jaffa road that runs in general northwest, after fifty minutes we break off from the carriage-way and descend steeply to the bottom of the valley of Sorek. Crossing the stream we come shortly to a spring. It was here that Jesus appeared to the two disciples. Thence the path winds in a narrow gorge, across terraces of rock, through slopes of olive and pomegranate trees, by fragments of buildings in the Græco-Roman style, and at last emerges on a lofty hill whence we may see the Mediterranean. Here lies Emmaus, near the junction of ancient Roman roads, and on the direct route from the sea to Jerusalem, traversed in past centuries by countless pilgrim feet and by the armies of Richard and Saladin. This was the home of Cleopas and his son, St. Simeon, who became the second Bishop of Jerusalem. The Holy City is just three-score furlongs off, as Luke says, or by foot, two and a half hours.

Girardet has pictured for us this "Way of the

Disciples," — the trail over the gaunt hills of Judea, treeless and covered with scant herbage between the stones. He has shown us Cleopas and his friend, clothed in the Syrian garb and talking earnestly about the theme now uppermost in the heart of every disciple. Jesus walks between them and a little to the rear, his raiment white to indicate the difference that exists between him and the others. In fact, one is inclined to wonder whether this diaphanous robe, the somewhat vague outline of the figure, and the fact that the two men are ignoring him in their conversation are suggestions from the artist that we are looking upon a vision. It may be his endeavor to interpret the incident in twentieth century terms, to indicate that this appearance was subjective, induced by the vivid experiences the disciples had just had and by the spiritual presence of Christ as they recalled the words of scripture that spoke of the Messiah. Perhaps some such enlightening experience as this lay at the bottom of the Emmaus tradition.

Another truth may be found also in the "Walk to Emmaus": our eyes are usually holden to the true significance of events until some Providence or some prophet opens them for us. This is particularly true of our personal lives. We live mostly in the dark; we make our decisions, we suffer our defeats and failures, we move on to the next task as chance throws it in our way; we walk ofttimes through a land of thorns and briars, not knowing whither the trail issues. Then there falls a lightning-flash of illumination, some simple happening that lights up the whole path we have been traveling, shows the reason of each detour and the lesson of each defeat; and we see how through it all God has been leading us by the hand. Sometimes it is a wise friend that points it out to us; sometimes it is a verse from the Good Book or a line from the poets that furnishes the Pisgah retrospect. But however and whenever it comes, our hearts burn within us as the panorama of life takes shape before our eyes, with its pathways running surely to their goals and the duties lying plain before our feet; and we know that it is good for us to be here. It is precisely this experience that Cleopas and his friend had. The darkness of the present dissolved in the light of a new insight; the tangled web of Scripture became a divine pattern; and the Kingdom, which they thought had vanished forever, now for the first time became possible of achievement because they had realized at last its true meaning. This is what we call inspiration; and whether or not we can visibly trace its source, it always comes from the Master of Life.

REMBRANDT: THE SUPPER AT EMMAUS
Luke 24 : 13–35

Rembrandt: Harmenszoon van Rijn (or Ryn) (1606–1669)
Original: now in the Louvre, Paris.
Reproductions; Braun & Co. F. I.

The day is far spent; the disciples, loath to part with the stranger whose insight is opening to them a new heaven and a new earth, have persuaded him to be their guest. They now sit within at the simple evening meal, and listen still with rapt attention to one who spake as never man spake. The light falls golden from the window, illuminating vaguely the

406

GIRARDET: THE WALK TO EMMAUS

REMBRANDT: THE SUPPER AT EMMAUS

simple lines of the room, — the door, the unorna-
mented pilaster, the tall recess in which the stranger
is framed. It touches into life the raised hands of the
younger man, the earnest face of the servant, Cleopas
thoughtful and fascinated; and then, reinforced by
the reflection from the white cloth, it throws the
central figure into strong relief against the dim wall.
That face, etched by the brilliant light, is one of
Rembrandt's great creations.

Strangely enough, it is a face of sorrow. One can
easily believe that this man has been in hell, for the
traces of suffering have not yet been obliterated by
the heavenly life. And yet there is something more
in the face than memory of the past. There seems
to be a present sorrow, and a wistfulness, as if the
future of his hopes were not yet assured; as if the
words he had spoken to them on the way were still
echoing in his soul: " O foolish men, and slow of heart
to believe." As in a former time he is marvelling at
their unbelief, for to his own soul the leadings of
Providence are so luminously clear. And as he looks
down the centuries that should be so rich in faith,
to distant times that ought to comprehend at a glance
the grand perspective of God's plan, he hears only
the jarring of the creeds, and the " melancholy, long,
withdrawing roar " of Faith,

> " Retreating to the breath
> Of the night wind, down the vast edges drear
> And naked shingles of the world."

This is the message of Rembrandt: The death and
resurrection of Jesus are not the consummation of his
work, but only the commencement. Set free now from

the limitations of time and place, he must begin that vaster work which stretches out before his vision till the last syllable of recorded time, the task of bringing a Universe to God! The weariness and pain of it are at this moment uppermost; yet even now he fixes his eye on that far-off divine event toward which he knows the whole creation moves; and breaking the bread of life to these two doubting ones, he vanishes to renew the task with others who need him. And these two will rise at once, return whence they came, and begin their part in the salvation of the world.

RAPHAEL: THE CHARGE TO PETER

John 21 : 1–23

Raphael: Raffaelo Santi, or Sanzio (1483–1520)
Original: one of the cartoons for the Sistine chapel tapestries. See the account given under " The Miraculous Draught."
Reproductions: .

As in the former cartoon we have studied, Raphael is less concerned to give us an accurate transcription of the scene than to interpret the spirit of the incident. Though the gospel says that Jesus met the disciples on the shore of the sea of Galilee, Raphael has no-where hinted this background, unless the blank space to the right is meant for the lake. The big catch of fish that had so astonished the disciples has been omitted, there is no fire of coals or miraculous break-fast; only a smiling landscape, a hill covered with trees and buildings, and a glorious church tower. Eleven disciples occupy the foreground. Eight of them have no special excuse for being here; two of them (James and John?) have caught in Christ's question to Peter a slight disparagement of their own love, and are raising their hands, James in protest and John in avowal of complete devotion. The true message of the picture is confined to the left half where Christ is speaking to Peter and pointing to the sheep. It is this group we must study.

Peter holds in his hands two huge keys. These are they that were given to him, figuratively at least, in Cæsarea Philippi just before the Transfiguration (Matt. 16 : 18–19). They stand for the confession that Jesus is the Messiah, a truth which like a key unlocks the treasure of the ancient scripture and makes it for the first time understandable, and which at the same time opens up, explains, gives significance to the whole course of Jesus' life and teachings. The confession is a key that unlocks also the future. Lacking the truth that Jesus is the chosen of God there can be no Church; but founded upon it the Church is unassailable. We need not decide whether this foundation stone is Peter or his confession; it is both. Peter and his keys, the man and his conviction are one; he and all succeeding men of like conviction make up the Christian Church. They are the conscience and the loyalty of men writ large and expressed in an institution. They henceforth are to constitute the norm of truth by which the world will be judged and Hell and Heaven will be peopled. And the gates of Death shall not prevail against it.

Peter in this cartoon is hugging his conviction, but Jesus is telling him that convictions will never save the world. Man needs a motive power to drive his convictions into life. Jesus may even point to the flock of sheep behind him, symbolizing the world that needs to be fed, the other sheep that are not yet of his fold. If Peter's keys are worth anything, they ought to unlock the true fold for these. But Peter may possess this second conviction that his keys are given him to use and that the need of using them is great, and still remain inactive. The will must be touched from another source. That source is his love for his Master. Peter needs the spur of a revived and intensified personal devotion. Therefore Christ confronts him here with the splendor of his spiritual character fully revealed, and asks the question that alone can set Peter's heart on fire, " Lovest thou me?" If Peter does really love his Master, then he will love supremely the things his Master loves, and the high potential of that overmastering passion will drive him to the ends of the earth. Christ here shows that profound knowledge of the human soul that made him the leader of men he was; he knows that love is the only power that never faileth, that melts down the barriers of past sin, and floods with the sunshine of new life the hidden germens of character. In this solemn moment, then, when the fate of his Church is hanging in the balance, when Peter the leader has not yet forgiven himself for his recent cowardice and has not caught the vision of his next duty, Christ with his thrice-repeated question at once absolves Peter of his past and fires him with immortal enthusiasm. Henceforth the love of Christ will constrain Peter, and he will become the true shepherd and bishop of the souls of men.

RAPHAEL: THE CHARGE TO PETER

VON UHDE: **THE ASCENSION**

VON UHDE: THE ASCENSION
Luke 24 : 50–53   Acts 1 : 1–11

Uhde, Fritz von (1848–   )
Original: painted about 1893.
Reproductions:

There are very few satisfactory " Ascensions." This is perhaps due to the artist's endeavor to make a spectacular picture, to show a super-radiant Christ rising amid clouds and angels to reassume the glory that was his before the world was. Such attempts place the emphasis wrongly. A true Ascension should picture not so much what the event meant to Christ — for we have no means of determining that, — but what it meant to his disciples. And assuredly the glimpse of heavenly glories into which their Master and friend was received could assuage for only a moment the sense of loneliness and personal grief which must have been theirs. The ascension was in reality less a revelation of bliss than a realization of infinite loss.

Von Uhde has conceived of the incident in this human fashion. The cloud that is to receive Christ out of their sight has no miraculous brilliancy; it is just vapor, blowing up from below in patches that fitfully conceal the treetops. We feel the upward and onward drift of the cloud that like a Fate is bearing Christ forward to some untried form of life of which he knows only that the Father is there. And we cannot surely say whether Christ is treading the air or merely ascending Olivet a few steps in advance of his friends. Of one thing we are certain: Christ is leaving them. He is passing on to a larger work in which his

411

spiritual rather than his bodily presence shall be the operating force. They are staying behind to cherish a great memory and to work out the problems involved in the Great Commission. They show by look and gesture that life is henceforth to be desolate. Not yet has Pentecost come with its revelation of hope, with its Comforter who shall bring to their remembrance the true meaning of their Master's life. This parting is for them a second tragedy the outcome of which they cannot yet see. Their anxious question, "Wilt thou at this time restore the kingdom to Israel?" shows us how difficult it was for them to shake themselves free from the idea of an earthly Messianic kingdom: not only will he not restore it, but he will withdraw from their sight altogether, for in no other way can he teach them that the Kingdom of God is within the soul. So Von Uhde has pictured here on their faces not so much wonder and ecstasy — though perhaps the young woman on the right and the one near Jesus express that — but longing, yearning, entreaty and almost despair. And Christ, true to his character of lover and inspirer of men, turns his face toward them in affectionate farewell and encouragement; he stretches one hand forth to them in blessing, while with the other he reaches up to clasp the Father's hand.

Yet who can doubt that because of this experience the spiritual life became more real to these simple and noble-hearted people, and the resolve more unshaken to follow their Friend into the heavens. It is as if they had been pursuing an ideal; they had followed it faithfully up and up the steep slopes of life till it seemed as if it were within their grasp. Then while they reached out to seize it, it disclosed a new depth of meaning and silently passed beyond the limited and the earthly into the realm of the limitless and the heavenly. The ascension is a parable of the infinite progression of man toward the divine, an illustration of Browning's truth that " man's reach should exceed his grasp "; and of Tennyson's noble figure that the Gleam of Merlin may not be overtaken short of eternity. Yet to that infinite quest Christ calls us by the very fact of his ascension, though the pursuit take us from earth to the heavens and from the shore to the fathomless reaches of the great deep.

> " O young mariner,
> Down to the haven,
> Call your companions,
> Launch your vessel,
> And crowd your canvas,
> And e'er it vanishes
> Over the margin,
> After it, follow it,
> Follow the Gleam."

CHAPTER XXIII

THE LAST JUDGMENT

PICTURES FOR STUDY

Fra Angelico: The Last Judgment
Michelangelo: The Last Judgment

Our conception of the Great Day is a heritage from
the eschatology of the Jews. Primarily, of course, it
takes its shape from the words of Jesus in such passages as Matt. 24 : 29–31 and its parallels in the other
gospels, and in the parable of the Judgment in Matt.
25 : 31–46; but the imagery Jesus used was part of
the familiar thinking of the Jews of his day. One
has only to turn to the word " Eschatology " in any
of the religious encyclopedias to discover what a maze
of beliefs was evolved between the second century
B.C. and the year 100 A.D.; so that one wonders not
that the New Testament contains so much of it but
so little. The early church was powerfully influenced
by these ideas, and through the centuries till the
Renaissance and almost to our day they have dominated the imaginations and the theologies of men,
have lighted the whole future of the personal life with
the lurid flames of their burning. Religion for most
men of the middle age consisted in the endeavor to
escape the judgment of the " Dies Irae."

To Dante we owe a description of the realms of
the saved and the lost so vivid that after his day
men were virtually compelled to think of the future

415

life in his terms; and Art, when it undertook to paint the Judgment, borrowed its imagery from the Divine Comedy. Orcagna blazoned it on the walls of Santa Maria Novella at Florence; he or Lorenzetti terrorized with it the mourners at the Campo Santo in Pisa. Fra Angelico received the great tradition through Orcagna, Signorelli drew upon it for the frescos at Orvieto, while Michelangelo drew from all these sources and from Dante direct. Only two great painters since the sixteenth century have ventured upon this theme, Tintoretto and Rubens, partly no doubt because there was nothing new to offer and partly, it must be confessed, because the interest of man in this particular incident has died down. The conception needs re-translation into modern terms; but no artist has yet ventured to translate it.

FRA ANGELICO: THE LAST JUDGMENT

Matt. 25 : 31–46

Angelico: Giovanni da Fiesole, called Fra (1387–1455)

Original: 3′5″ x 6′11″, painted about 1429 during his stay at Fiesole, for the Camaldolese monks of Santa Maria degli Angeli; now in the Academy, Florence. The extreme right end was painted by an assistant. The picture has wonderful charm of detail and the finish of a miniature.

Reproductions:

" Pax ibi florida,	O sacra potio,
Pascua vivida,	Sacra refectio,
Viva medulla,	Pax animarum.
Nulla molestia,	O pius, O bonus,
Nulla tragoedia,	O placidus sonus,
Lacryma nulla.	Hymnus earum."

Berenson, in the *Florentine Painters of the Renaissance*, says: " In the weaker personality [Fra Angelico]

416

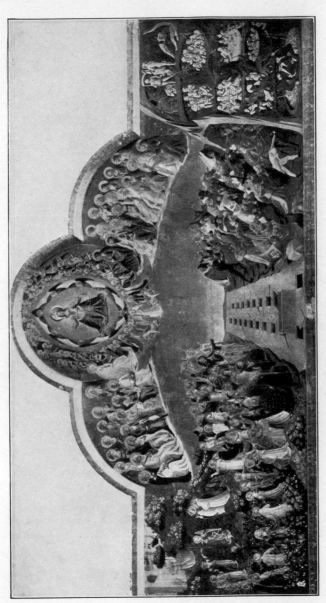

FRA ANGELICO: THE LAST JUDGMENT

FRA ANGELICO: CHRIST IN GLORY
Detail of the "Last Judgment"

the significant, vaguely perceived, is converted into emotion, is merely felt and not realized." This picture of the Last Judgment perfectly illustrates what Berenson means: the theme is significant to the last degree, one of the greatest incidents in the spiritual life of man; but the artist has not visualized the full implication of the idea with fidelity to the known facts of the spiritual life, and he has taken refuge in a symbolism that is wholly unsatisfactory to the intellect. The emotional values of the theme, however, take full hold of the painter, and up to the limit of his power they are expressed with wonderful sincerity and brilliancy. But Fra Angelico is not a modern; the picture is a medieval kindergarten rhapsody.

The picture is divided into three sections, each in turn subdivided. Above in the three-lobed portion — suggestive of the Trinity — sit the Judge, his twenty-eight associates and his angelic guard. Below to our right is the troop of the wicked hurrying toward their eternal doom; to our left the blessed partaking of the preliminary joys of heaven. Down the center stretches a double row of empty tombs like those still to be seen in Florentine cemeteries.

In the central lobe, Christ is seated on the throne of his glory. From him stream the rays of a mandorla so brilliant that they conceal all but the faces of the eight miniature angels who look in upon him from its edge. His hands show plainly the prints of the nails, for by his wounds shall the righteousness of his sentence be justified. His right hand is extended in welcome to the blessed, but his left is turned down for the wicked in token of rejection. Round about this mandorla, rejoicing in its lesser rays, is a troop of the angelic host in the Fra's most entrancing style, exquisite butterfly-souls with the faces of children. Most of them adore the Savior with extended or folded hands, but some of them are clad in armor and form a celestial bodyguard in vindication of that scripture the devil once quoted in irony, " He shall give his angels charge over thee." At the lowest point of this glory stands a beautiful angel with the cross; it is the supreme symbol of that sacrifice by which the world is judged. And on either side are the archangel trumpeters of the Resurrection whose blasts have just emptied the tombs.

Nearest the angels on our left sits the Virgin Mother, occupying in the picture as she does in Catholic theology the chief seat in heaven. In symmetry with her on our right is John the Baptist. The twenty-six witnesses of the judgment are those who by their deeds or their writings have pointed men to heaven: In the front row next Mary, Peter with his keys, chiefest of the apostles; then Moses holding up the two tables of the Law that should have been schoolmasters to bring the world to Christ; then Elias with his pen and prophetic scroll. Most of the others carry books and quills to show their testimony, so potent in shaping the destinies of men. Some have palm-branches indicating martyrdom; several are tonsured, to show that the monastic orders have been among the great witnesses of Christ; and on the ends, St. Francis of Assisi with lilies, and St. Dominic, the founder of the painter's order. These all are in the highest heaven of bliss, and their felicity seems to consist in satisfaction that their testimony is at last vindicated.

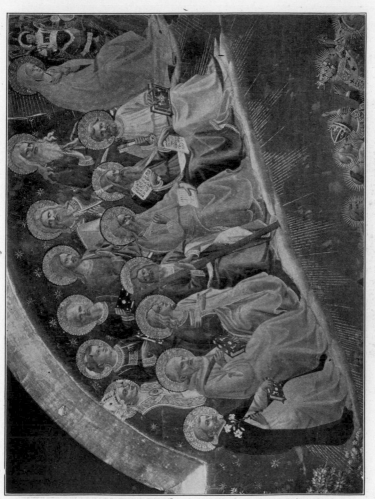

FRA ANGELICO: SAINTS IN HEAVEN

Detail of the "Last Judgment"

FRA ANGELICO: SAINTS IN HEAVEN
Detail of the "Last Judgment"

Turning now to the lower group on our right. The landscape consists solely of iron rocks, the near portion of which arches up to form hell-gate. A crowd of wretched souls is being hustled along by a crowd of demons who have all the characteristics of their profession, grotesque faces, flaming eyes, claw-toes and various instruments of torture. These harry their victims in various ways suggestive of the various sins committed. But just here the good Fra's imagination begins to break down. He has not found it possible to picture souls in torment, and therefore he has given us a miracle-play of the most childish sort. This is a masquerade ball; or it is a troop of school-girls being teased along by naughty boys who pull their hair, trip them up, make faces at them and otherwise prove to be genuine nuisances. It is impossible for the twentieth century to regard this group seriously, for it does not even remotely suggest the infinite spiritual pangs of those who have spurned their Highest Good. Some writers have argued that Fra Angelico's pure soul could not express sin or suffering because he had had no contact with either. It is true that he had to call in an assistant to paint hell itself on the extreme right, with its caldrons full of souls and its bogy-devils. But the real trouble lies in the medieval conception of Sin and Hell. Sin was not necessarily a failure of character but a failure to comply with technical requirements. A perfectly good man would go to Hell if he had not been baptized. How then could even the best of painters paint a Hell that should represent a spiritual condition such as we understand Hell to be? The best he could do would be to represent physical tortures more or less realistically. This Fra Angelico has done, and the result is Bogy-land.

When one considers the condition of the blessed, one finds it superficially more satisfactory but fundamentally as childish. Fra Angelico has lavished upon these happy souls all the resources of his art, has poured out his own spirit here in anticipation of the glad day when his eyes also shall see the King in his beauty. Beneath the radiance of high heaven the saved ones gather fresh from the tomb, and turn their eyes first to adore Him who is the author and the perfector of their salvation. How wonderfully they scintillate; the very garments are woven of the colors of heaven and their coronets are fashioned of light supernal. " They that be wise shall shine as the sun, and they that turn many to righteousness as the stars forever and ever." They are literally Christ's jewels. All sorts are gathered here, many individuals no doubt being intended to represent historic characters. Popes and bishops are conspicuous by their miters, one has a sword — perhaps a Crusader — one has a pilgrim's hat and beads; but monks and nuns are most conspicuous, as if the laity had small chance to enter heaven.

As our eye moves to the left, we discover a change in the interests of the blessed; having adored, they turn to the pleasures that await them. Angels mingle with the throng. Embraces follow. Some of the shining ones act as ushers to lead the new-comers to the celestial garden-party already going on in the pastures of the blessed. The chain is forming down below: monks and angels alternate, the bald tonsures of the monks showing white through their crowns

420

FRA ANGELICO: THE LOST

Detail of the "Last Judgment"

FRA ANGELICO: THE BLESSED

Detail of the "Last Judgment"

of flowers. All hold hands at first and then break off in couples at the upper end for the minuet. How daintily the last angel leads the enraptured monk in his first dancing-lesson! Heaven is surely a happier and livelier place than he ever dreamed in his cell!

This is but preliminary to the bliss beyond, for there in the margin glows the celestial city, Jerusalem the Golden. The painter has wisely not tried to picture its glories, for " eye hath not seen, ear hath not heard, nor hath it entered into the heart of man to conceive the things that God has prepared for those that love him." Bernard of Cluny caught a far-off vision of it, and the song he made of it is his eternal glory :

> " O one, O only mansion!
> O Paradise of joy!
> Where tears are ever banished,
> And smiles have no alloy;
> With jasper glow thy bulwarks,
> Thy streets with emerald blaze;
> The sardius and the topaz
> Unite in thee their rays;
> Thine ageless walls are bonded
> With amethyst unpriced;
> Thy saints build up its fabric,
> And the corner-stone is Christ.
> O sweet and blessed country,
> The home of God's elect!
> O sweet and blessed country
> That eager hearts expect!
> Jesus, in mercy bring us
> To that dear land of rest;
> Who art, with God the Father,
> And Spirit, ever blest."

Two thirds of Fra Angelico's picture is an attempt to visualize this great poem; but the attempt is a failure. The poem is a stimulus to our imagination; its noble ecstasy snatches us away to celestial heights and depths of bliss. But the picture limits us to its own interpretation; it says to us, "This is precisely what heaven looks like." The wings of fancy are clipped and the joys of the vision of God that should prostrate us with their divine excess are frittered away with childish games and tinsel crowns. Contrast for a moment Dante's heaven: "the souls floating like stars amid the harmonies, the mingled splendors, the mystic roses radiating and vanishing in the azure, the impalpable world in which all the laws of earthly life are dissolved, the unfathomable abyss traversed by fleeting visions like golden bees gliding in the rays of the deep central sun." Or take that ineffable vision in the Apocalypse, of the Son of Man "whose voice was as the sound of many waters; and he had in his right hand seven stars, . . . and his countenance was as the sun shineth in his strength. And when I saw him I fell at his feet as one dead." One is tempted to quote about Fra Angelico what that racy Frenchman, Hippolyte Taine, said about Milton: "When he was arranging his celestial show, he did not fall as one dead!"

The garden-party heaven of Fra Angelico is the exquisite dream of a child. This half of the picture is as great a travesty on Heaven as the other half is on Hell, but it is more seductive. When we first look at it we feel like Bunyan: "Which when I had seen, I wished myself among them." But when we consider the suitability of such occupations for men and women of intelligence for fifty million years, we would pray rather to be excused!

FRA ANGELICO: THE HEAVENLY DANCE

Detail of the "Last Judgment"

MICHELANGELO: THE LAST JUDGMENT

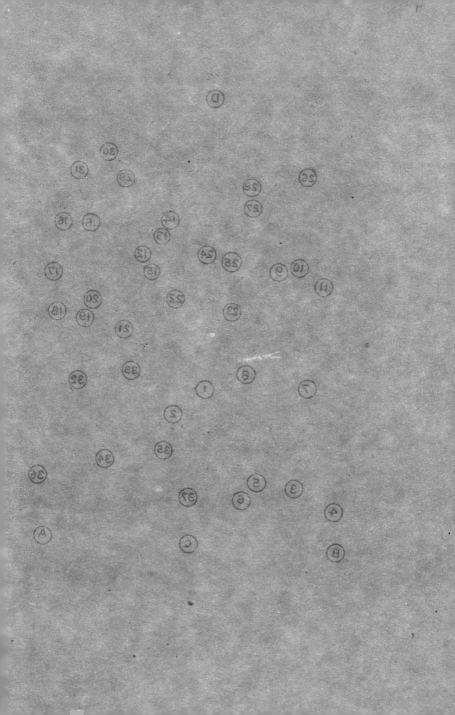

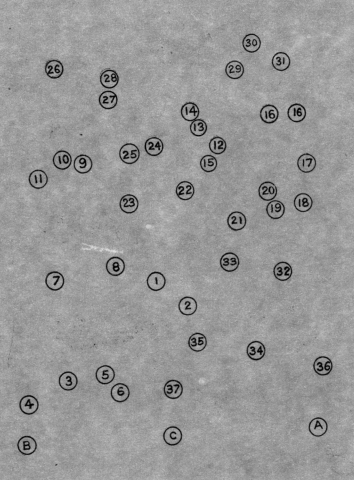

MICHELANGELO: THE LAST JUDGMENT

Matt. 25 : 31–46

Michelangelo: family name, Buonarroti (1475–1564)

Original: the largest single composition in the world, 50′ x 66′. It occupies the end wall of the Sistine chapel, Rome, built by pope Sixtus IV in 1743. Under pope Julius II Michelangelo had covered the ceiling with frescos that represent the highest reach of his genius; and now after thirty years, at the age of sixty, he was commissioned by pope Paul III to paint the Last Judgment. The work occupied seven years. The scores of figures are all conceived in titanic form and were originally all nude — with the possible exception of the Virgin. The immoral court pretended to be scandalized and induced the pope to have Daniele da Volterra add draperies. The whole is now so blackened by time and the smoke of candles that its beauty is gone; only its energy and its terror remain.

Reproductions:

If Fra Angelico's *Last Judgment* is a translation of Bernard of Cluny's "*Urbs Beata*," Michelangelo's is the "*Dies Irae*."

" Dies irae, dies illa,	" Day of wrath, that day of mourning:
Solvet saeculum in favilla,	See fulfilled the prophets' warning,
Teste David cum sybilla."	Heaven and earth in ashes burning."

The dominant note of the one is bliss, of the other terror. In the one our hearts sigh for the joys of the blessed, in the other we tremble at the righteous punishment of the damned. The two are poles apart in conception and in spiritual power, proceeding as they do from natures so utterly diverse and from experiences with life that are diametrically in contrast. In the one we share the vision of a gentle

423

eremite, in the other we hear the thunders of a tempestuous Titan. Neither is wholly true or wholly false, and the world is richer for both.[1]

In our first plate, the entire end of the Sistine chapel is presented. At the right (A) is the door by which one enters the great hall and feels the grip of the tremendous frescos of the ceiling. The other door (B) leads to other apartments of the Vatican. Between them is the altar (C) at which the pope officiates on high days. As we turn to face this largest of all pictures, we see the lunettes of the vaulting above, and over the central corbel the prophet Jonah (D) as he turns himself in astonishment and thankfulness at his great deliverance. He is the symbol of the resurrection of Christ, which was the first act in the triumphant life of the Savior that is to find its dénouement in the Judgment. And Jonah is also a reminder that Nineveh repented at his preaching before it was too late. We stand in the presence of the eternities. Above us on the ceiling stretches the past, from the creation of light to the coming of the prophets; on the walls are spread the parallel histories of Moses and Christ; and before us, the Great Day in which the heavens shall pass away as a scroll and the elements shall melt with fervent heat. And the epic sweep of it all has been embraced by the genius of one man.

We shall begin our study with the angels of doom (4). Seven angels with trumpets announce the arrival of the Great Assize, with blasts that wake the dead:

[1] The Latin quotations are from the *Dies Irae* of Thomas of Celano, 13th century, and the translations are by W. J. Irons, 1853.

In studying the picture, locate the particular persons on the first plate by means of the numbers, then identify them on the detailed plates.

424

" for the trumpet shall sound, and the dead shall be raised " (1 Cor. 15 : 52).

" Tuba mirum sparget sonum Per sepulcra regionum, Coget omnes ante thronum."	"Lo! the trumpet's wondrous swelling Peals through each sepulchral dwelling, All before the throne compelling."

With this group of seven are two other angels with the Doomsday Books (2): " And I saw the dead, the great and the small, standing before the throne; and the dead were judged out of the things which were written in the books according to their works." (Rev. 20 : 12.)

" Liber scriptus proferetur, In quo totum continetur Unde mundus iudicetur."	" Lo! the Book exactly worded Wherein all hath been recorded: Thence shall justice be awarded."

In response to this dread summons, the earth (3) writhes and yields up its dead. Numberless forms break through the ground, some clothed with flesh, some mere skeletons " desiring to be clothed upon." It is like a second creation when man is being reformed from the dust of the ground that he may give account of the deeds done in the body. " And the sea gave up its dead: and death and Hades gave up the dead that were in them: and they were judged every man according to their works." (Rev. 20 : 13.)

" Quantum terror est futurus, Quando iudex est venturus, Cuncta stricte discussurus! "	" Death is struck and Nature quaking, All creation is awaking, To its Judge an answer making."

The artist has probably pictured Purgatory in the little shelf of rock on the extreme left (4) beneath

which a man is struggling to rise. And he may have
intended to show in two other figures (5, 6) how the
sins of life still cling and try to drag the soul into
Hell, even at the bar of the Judgment; for demons are
contending for their bodies, one wrapping himself like
a serpent about his victim. A side entrance to Hell
is close at hand. This may also be a reminiscence of
Bible passages like these: " But Michael the archangel, when contending with the devil he disputed
about the body of Moses " (Jude 1 : 9); " But as for
me, my feet were almost gone, my steps had well-nigh
slipped " (Ps. 73 : 2). " He brought me up also out
of a horrible pit, out of the miry clay " (Ps. 40 : 2).

Above the quaking earth the forms of the just are
rising into the heavens (7). Heaven is also coming
down to help, in the form of mighty wingless angels
or of saints and loved ones. A wife lifts up her
despairing husband: those whom death has separated
rush into each other's arms. Whatever joys heaven
contains are symbolized in the few figures of this group
and in the few embracing groups on the extreme right
(16). Elsewhere the thunders of the judgment roll.
One beautiful symbol is expressed by him who is
raising two others by means of a rosary (8). It is a
reminiscence of James 5 : 16, " Pray for one another;
the effectual fervent prayer of a righteous man
availeth much." And it finds an echo in the Idylls,
where the dying Arthur begs of Sir Bedivere,

> " Pray for my soul. More things are wrought by prayer
> Than this world dreams of."

The saints in heaven are grouped on both sides of
the central Judge. Michelangelo may not have in-

MICHELANGELO: THE LAST JUDGMENT
Detail, lower left corner, The Resurrection

tended that each person should be a historic character, but we can recognize enough to show that on our left, in general, are Old Testament personages and on our right New Testament and post-Biblical ones. The huge figure clothed in the pelt of an animal (9) is Adam, from whom this deluge of humanity has proceeded. He looks with startled eyes upon this " second Adam " who not only has redeemed part of humanity, but who now blasts the rest with his curse. Abel cringes beside him and grasps his arm (10). Eve the mother of mankind (11) protects with an arm one of her daughters who hides trembling in her garments. On our right the titanic Peter (12) holds out his keys in testimony that he has locked and unlocked in strict accordance with the charge once given him. Behind him Paul looks on astonished (13) and John (14), the apostle of love, raises a hand in protest against a judgment that he cannot fathom. Only Dante (15), peering between the bodies of Peter and Paul, has the intellect to reconcile in an all-embracing unity eternal punishment with eternal love, for his eyes have seen written over the gate of Hell,

> " Giustizia mosse il mio alto fattore,
> Fecemi la divina potestate,
> Lo somma sapienza e il primo amore."

> " Justice moved my high Creator,
> Created me divine Omnipotence,
> The highest Wisdom and the primal Love."

In the forefront of the circle of heaven are the martyrs, conspicuous by the signs of their martyrdom. They are calling for vengeance. " I saw underneath the altar the souls of them that had been slain for the word of God and for the testimony which they held: and they cried with a great voice saying, How long, O Master, the holy and true, dost thou not judge and avenge our blood? (Rev. 6 : 9–10.) " These are they that came out of great tribulation." (Rev. 7 : 14.) Here are St. Andrew (17) with the huge cross on which he drank of his Lord's cup; St. Sebastian (18) holding the sheaf of arrows he has plucked from his breast; St. Catherine (19) with the wheel whereon she was broken; an unnamed one (20) with the hatchels wherewith he was carded; St. Simeon Gelotes (21) with his saw. St. Bartholomew (22) holds up to Christ's view the knife with which he was flayed, while from his left hand depends his skin to which the face still clings. St. Lawrence (23) shoulders the gridiron on which they roasted him, and looks appealingly at the judge. All these show upon their faces surprise, awe, appeal for vengeance, but no pity. The righteousness of the judgment has silenced every tongue.

Christ himself (24) is the most extraordinary conception in the picture. His face is beardless, as in early Byzantine representations. He has the frame of a giant and the pose of Jupiter wielding his thunderbolts. In spite of the threatening gesture and the awed saints' movements of self-protection, there is no anger in this calm face. The " vials of the wrath of God " are indeed being poured out, but they are vials prepared from the foundation of the world. This is not a personal vengeance; the sentence is the utterance of an almighty executive who carries out the decrees of a moral universe. The vengeance of the martyrs "who from the altar call" is subsumed in a vaster and more righteous retribution; for the guilt of the damned lies in their rejection of God and of his offer of salvation. They have sinned the unpardonable sin against the Holy Ghost. Even Mary (25), who would have pity if pity could be found, turns a calm face away, yet herself remains close by the side of her Almighty Son as if sanctioning the decrees of justice. Those who see here a wrathful deity have been misled by the resistlessness of the gesture without giving careful scrutiny to the face: for the face is as impersonal as Fate, and the power he wields sweeps through him from the remotest limits of time and space.

It is no wonder that in the presence of such primeval forces the saints can only fear their own involution in the general ruin. Fra Angelico's redeemed ones may well adore and tread their joyful measures in heaven's meadow; but in Michelangelo's dread day, when men are calling on the rocks to fall on them and hide them from the wrath of the Lamb, they dare not hope. The tender pleading of the *Dies Irae* is but an overtone to the thunders of crashing worlds; and in this canvas the anxious faces of the saints echo the same strain:

"Quid sum miser tunc dicturus,
Quem patronum rogaturus,
Dum vix iustus sit securus?

"When shall I, frail man, be pleading?
Who for me be interceding,
When the just are mercy needing?

Rex tremendae maiestatis,
Qui salvandos salvas gratis,
Salva me, fons pietatis!"

King of majesty tremendous,
Who dost free salvation send us,
Fount of pity, then befriend us!"

Moreover there are tongues more eloquent than theirs
to plead for them, — the wounds of Christ still visible
in his feet and side, the cross (26), the thorns (27),
the nails (28), the column (29) where were given the
stripes by which we are healed, the ladder (30), the reed
and sponge (31). These recall to the Judge the depth
of his own mercy for sinners, and the fact that some
have trusted in that mercy.

" Recordare, Jesu pie,   " Think, kind Jesus, my salvation
 Quod sum causa tuae viae; Cost thy wondrous incarnation!
 Ne me perdas illa die!   Leave me not to reprobation!

Quaerens me sedisti lassus, Faint and weary thou hast
           sought me,
Redemisti cruce passus: On the cross of suffering
           bought me;
Tantus labor non sit cassus!" Shall such grace in vain be
           brought me? "

And it is precisely these tokens of his dying grace that
are the sinners' condemnation. They look on him
whom they pierced, and that sight sears their eyeballs
with the terrors of outraged love. It is from these
they flee as well as from the heaven that spurns them.
This is not vengeance but Nemesis.

As it is possible to feel the upward movement of the
saints, so one senses the falling of the lost. From
above they are being beaten and cuffed by the seraphic
ministers of Nemesis, while from below they are being
seized and dragged down by demons. The souls are
tumbling pell-mell in a cataract of terror. "Surely
thou settedst them in slippery places; Thou castedst
them down to destruction. How are they become a

desolation in a moment! They are utterly consumed with terrors" (Ps. 73 : 18–19). Conspicuous in the upper row are personifications of the seven deadly sins (32) first catalogued by Thomas Aquinas. They are wonderfully drawn, and when the faces are visible they exhibit not the childish annoyance of Fra Angelico's reprobates but genuine spiritual suffering. Notice that solitary one in whose ears the trump is being sounded (33). Spirits of evil are dragging him down by the feet; but the face, half hidden by his hand, is contorted not with terror but remorse. The irrevocable has set its seal upon it. There is no room for repentance now though he seek it carefully and with tears. Such a face as this stares at one from the very circles of Malebolge.

" Confutatis maledictis, Flammis acribus addictis."	" Cursed, confounded, Doomed to flames of woe un- bounded."

J. A. Symonds says of this figure: " Nothing could express with sublimity of a higher order the sense of irremediable loss, eternal pain, a future endless without hope, than the rigid dignity of this not ignoble sinner's dread."

While the spirit of Dante hovered near the painter of this mighty fresco, the imagery of Dante has been withheld till now. In the lowest plane, the lost are arriving at the shore of Hell (34). Over the river Acheron the bark of Charon has ferried them, and now they disembark, blaspheming God. Dante has given us the full tale, though he describes the embarkation on the hither side:

"And lo! coming toward us in a boat an old man white with ancient hair, crying, 'Woe to you, wicked souls! Hope not ever to see heaven!' . . . Thereat were quieted the fleecy cheeks of the ferryman of the livid marsh, who *round about his eyes had wheels of flame.* . . . But the souls, bitterly weeping, drew back all of them together to the evil bank that waits for every man who fears not God. Charon the demon with the eyes of coals beckoning them collects them all; beats with his oar whoever lags behind (35). As in autumn time the leaves fall off, first one and then another, till the bough sees all its spoils upon the earth; in like wise the evil seed of Adam throw themselves from that shore one by one at signals, as a bird unto its lure."

And here Virgil offers an explanation to Dante that shows why in this picture the wrath of the Son of Man is not necessary to drive the wicked into Hell: "They are eager to pass over the stream, because divine justice spurs them on, so that fear is turned into desire." (Inf. iii: 82–85, 97–99, 106–117, 124–126.)

Dante has furnished the painter also with the figure of Minos (36) the infernal assayer.

"There standeth Minos horribly and snarls; examines the transgressors at the entrance, judges, and sends according as he girds him. I say, that when the spirit evil-born cometh before him, wholly it confesses; and this discriminator of transgressions seeth what place in Hell is meet for it; girds himself [with his tail] as many times as grades he wishes it should be thrust down. Always before him many of them stand; they go by turns each one unto the judgment;

432

they speak, and hear, and then are downward hurled."
(Inf. v: 4–15.)

Here again the symbolism of Dante interprets
Michelangelo; for Minos is not an arbitrary judge,
nor yet the administrator of heaven's justice; he
represents the condemning power of conscience. Each
soul confesses to him its sin, and as in a dial it sees
in him its self-registry of punishment. Thus Michelangelo removes the last suspicion that the Great
Judgment is a revelation of God's wrath. It is the
vindication of the moral integrity of the universe even
by the finite conscience of the sinner.

The drama of the Great Day ends with the mouth
of Hell (37). It is by no accident that the entrance
yawns immediately over the High Altar. Stern
moralist and fearless preacher that he was, Michelangelo has here flung the terrors of the Judgment full
in the face of the Pope. For like Bunyan he sees that
there is a way to Hell even from the gate of Heaven;
and like Savonarola, the inspirer of his youth, he fears
not man. Within the span of his life he had seen
Pope Sixtus IV adopt secret assassination and shameless duplicity as integral portions of the Church's
policy. He had hung his head in shame at Innocent
III, the celibate father of sixteen children, and the
arch criminal even in that age of shameless scandals,
in which absolution for any crime could be bought of
the Holy See. He had seen cardinal Borgia buy his way
into the papal chair with such spiritual blood-money,
extorted on the ironical explanation, "God desires not
the death of the sinner, but rather that he should pay
and live!"; and he had seen him as pope make the
name of Borgia the most detested name in Europe.

433

The painter had seen Leo X attempt to subjugate the world by splendor and extravagance, to supply the means for which he sold indulgences and in consequence lost the half of Europe. Under Clement VII he had seen the Church descend to its nadir of disgrace, the pope a terrified refugee in the castle of Sant' Angelo, and the priceless spoils of Rome torn from her churches and palaces by the rabble of German and Spanish armies. And Paul III, intriguer and hypocrite, the very pope who was now commanding him to decorate this private chapel of villainy, was endeavoring to bolster up his spiritual honor by excommunicating Henry VIII for an illegal marriage, while at the same time he was scandalously aggrandizing the fortunes of his own illegitimate son! As the painter hurled from his brush the forms that constitute this grand Assize of the Ages, there must have rung in his ears the words of his forerunner Isaiah: "How is the faithful city become a harlot. . . . Thy princes are rebellious and companions of thieves; every one loveth bribes and followeth after rewards. . . . Woe unto them that call evil good and good evil, that put darkness for light and light for darkness, that justify the wicked for a bribe." And as Paul III stood before his altar on Christmas day, 1541, when the picture was unveiled, unless he had abandoned all belief in the doctrines it was his sacred duty to uphold, he must have trembled as he looked straight into the jaws of Hell.

MICHELANGELO: THE LAST JUDGMENT

Detail, lower right corner, The Lost, The Shore of Acheron

HOFMANN: HEAD OF CHRIST
Detail of "Christ and the Rich Ruler"

Chapter XXIV

THE FACE OF CHRIST

PICTURES FOR STUDY

Hofmann: Detail of Christ and the Rich Young Man
Raphael: Detail of the Transfiguration
Fra Angelico: Dominicans Receiving Christ

It is impossible to paint a satisfactory picture of Christ. The difficulty lies not so much in the artist's inability to suggest ideal traits as in the many-sidedness of the ideal. Christ was the sanest and most wholesome man that ever lived; he was at the same time so completely filled with the spirit of God that the keenest analysis fails to tell where the human leaves off and the divine begins. He touched life throughout its vast orbit; he entered into all the relationships that men sustain with one another, and that man and God may enter. He knew what work with his hands involved; he knew the duties of a son, a brother, a wage earner; he was friend, teacher, physician, wedding guest, mourner, father-confessor, preacher, denouncer, temple-cleanser, pilgrim, fugitive, wonder-worker, prophet, law-giver, social lion, friend of the demi-monde, story-teller, reformer, visionary, mystic, Jewish Messiah, martyr, Son of Man, Son of God! What single portrait can compass this range? The problem reduces itself to the adequate embodiment of a single trait or two, the presentation of only

435

an aspect of his personality; and we shall find ourselves attracted now to this picture and now to that, as our appreciation of life varies and our affections shift with our growing insight and character.

If we glance over the pictures we have studied, we shall realize afresh the partial quality of them all and yet the essential perfection of many of them within the limits set. There is Correggio's *Holy Night* for simple babyhood, Hunt's *Finding of Christ* for healthy boyhood, Cornicelius' *Temptation* for moral purity and idealism, Keller's *Raising of 'Jairus' Daughter* for love incarnate, Rossetti's *Mary at the Door of Simon* for mysticism, Rubens' *Christ in the House of Simon* for intellectual superiority, Hunt's *Light of the World* for patience and moving tenderness, Rembrandt's *Christ Blessing the Children* for soul-weariness, Von Uhde's *Suffer Little Children* for friendliness, Titian's *Tribute Money* for worldly wisdom, Da Vinci's sketch for unmitigated sorrow, Brown's *Washing Peter's Feet* for humility, Bacon's *Christ in Gethsemane* for reproachfulness, Munkacsy's *Christ before Pilate* for keen penetration and almost fanatical consciousness of a mission, Carrière's *Christ on the Cross* for the peace of self-sacrifice, Michelangelo's *Last Judgment* for power and the irrevocableness of Fate. These are all facets of the flawless jewel; we must turn the crystal slowly and meditatively, holding it up to the light of our spiritual experience, in order that each plane may flash its message to us. The whole we can never grasp in one act of sight; it comes to us as a synthesis of insights, and we realize it as an unvisualized emotion. So with all things that have an infinite element; they must be apprehended

436

by the imagination as symbol and experienced by the heart as feeling.

> " The great Idea baffles wit,
> Language falters under it,
> It leaves the learned in the lurch.
> Nor art nor power nor toil can find
> The measure of the eternal Mind,
> Nor hymn, nor prayer, nor church."

We love pictures without fully appreciating what they mean; for we can love the ideal and the infinite even though we cannot comprehend it. And so it comes about that while men's intellects have never been able to agree about what Christ was, their hearts through all ages have united in the love of this consummate personality in whom the ideal of every several man is realized.

> " But Thee, but Thee, O sovereign Seer of time,
> But Thee, O poets' poet, Wisdom's tongue,
> But Thee, O man's best Man, O love's best Love,
> O perfect life in perfect labor writ,
> O all men's Comrade, Servant, King, or Priest, —
> What *if* or *yet*, what mole, what flaw, what lapse,
> What least defect or shadow of defect,
> What rumor, tattled by an enemy,
> Of inference loose, what lack of grace
> Even in torture's grasp, or sleep's or death's, —
> Oh, what amiss may I forgive in Thee,
> Jesus, good Paragon, thou Crystal Christ."

HOFMANN: DETAIL OF CHRIST AND THE RICH YOUNG MAN

Some observations on this face were made in analysing the whole picture in chapter twelve. The detail

cannot be torn wholly from its context; it still refers
to some one standing near, and its message is primarily
for him. But the face may stand in general for Christ
as Moral Influence. The spiritual quality of the
character is revealed in the large eyes. No doubt
also the beard and long hair subtly suggest an other-
worldliness, or at least an aloofness from the physical
toil of the world which seems to be essential for poets
and dreamers and seers generally. We all confess that
it would be impossible to express spirituality in a
smooth-shaven Christ with the close-cropped head of
a German captain. Flowing hair has become indispen-
sable to our ideal. But our insistence upon it lays
us open to the charge of apotheosizing effeminacy
as in the present case; for however adorable this
Christ may be, he is certainly not one to set the world
on fire. The qualities of incisiveness, strenuousness,
iconoclasm, generalship, or even moral sublimity are
absent. He is pleading here for the acceptance of a
moral ideal, and if the young man will not accept
it he has no recourse but to turn away with a sigh.
There is moral purity here, idealism, entreaty, a touch
of pain or disappointment, but not the sterner qualities by virtue of which he cursed the Scribes and
Pharisees, overturned the tables of the money-
changers or faced the rabble in Gethsemane. It is
the face of the good and gentle Christ, the friend of
children, the comforter of the sorrowing, the patient
teacher of those who hunger and thirst after righteousness. This is a partial Christ, and one not likely to
become the ideal of the twentieth century.

RAPHAEL: HEAD OF CHRIST
Detail of "The Transfiguration"

FRA ANGELICO: HEAD OF CHRIST

Detail from "Christ as Pilgrim"

(See Front Cover)

RAPHAEL: DETAIL OF THE TRANS-FIGURATION

There is a decided gain in spirituality in this creation of Raphael's. We feel it in the upturned face and the unconverged eyes. Turn in quick alternation from the Hofmann to the Raphael and back again, and see how their respective traits grow in vividness by contrast. The Hofmann becomes more troubled and anxious, the Raphael more peaceful. The eyes in the Hofmann become more critical if not hard; in the Raphael they are liquid, dreamy, — revelations of things ineffable. There is a difference in volitional attitude also. Hofmann represents the Master dominating, though never so mildly, the weaker personality of another. In Raphael, Christ has surrendered his will to one greater than he. There is a gain of poetic ecstasy in the Raphael, an increment of mysticism, a suggestion that he is experiencing something too lofty for us to enter into, something parallel in a way to the experience of Mary of the *Immaculate Conception*; though while her personality has almost disappeared in the solvent of her emotion, Christ retains something of his masterful quality. We have here a man with his heart fixed on God, manhood merging into divinity. None but Raphael had the vision necessary to conceive such a face, and the technique necessary to embody it; and this representation must therefore always remain one of the great creations of art.

FRA ANGELICO: DETAIL OF DOMINICANS RECEIVING CHRIST

(See colored reproduction on the cover)

Angelico: Giovanni da Fiesole, called Fra (1387–1455)
Original: painted about 1440, a fresco in the lunette over the guest-room door, monastery of San Marco, Florence.
Reproductions: In color, Alinari, Florence.

The full picture from which this detail is taken is one of Fra Angelico's most characteristic creations, full of the beauty of tender color and the charm of sincerity. In placing it over the guest-room door he reminded his brethren not only of the duty of entertaining strangers but of responding to all the other calls of mercy of which this is an example.

Two brothers of San Marco are here welcoming a pilgrim to the hospitality of their convent. They are unaware of the true nature of their guest, but they come forth eagerly to bid him enter for Christ's sake. The pilgrim carries a staff, and as the nearer monk reaches out his hand of welcome, the two arms make with the staff the secret sign of the cross. It is the password by which all the poor and the travel-stained may enter " In His Name." The picture breathes the spirit of another epoch. This may not be so apparent in a small print, but as one stands before the original one feels unmistakably the glamor of a by-gone age, of monastery stillness in the virgin forest, of vigils and *Ave Marias* and midnight visions, of cloister walks and the calling of the bells of prayer, of simple tasks in the *scriptorium*, copying breviary or gospel, and simple works of charity before the convent door.

" Far off the noises of the world retreat;
The loud vociferations of the street
Become an undistinguishable roar.

.   .   .   .

The tumult of the time disconsolate
To inarticulate murmurs dies away."

The face of Christ is utterly other-worldly. The cruciform nimbus gives it a sort of unearthly setting, and the hair falling at first so smoothly, then breaking into ringlets of spun gold, adds to the impression of unreality. Notice that his eye does not look into the welcoming eye of the monk, but is elevated somewhat under a heavy lid, as if he were pursuing a vision and had stumbled by chance upon this hospitable inn. It is the face of one whose citizenship is in heaven; the face of a pilgrim and a stranger who can tarry but a night.

" Do not detain me, for I am going
To where the fountains are ever flowing.

There the glory is ever-shining, —
Oh, my longing heart, my longing heart is there:

I'm a pilgrim and I'm a stranger;
I can tarry, I can tarry but a night! "

We have only to ask ourselves a few foolish questions in order to discover the quality of this pilgrim. Would he make a good business partner? Could he invent a telephone, or navigate a submarine, or promote a Steel Trust, or engineer a political campaign? Would he do for a doctor, a lawyer, a farmer, a college professor, an *Atlantic Monthly* contributor, or even a

441

book-agent? It is absolutely impossible to fit him into the world of our feverish activity, this Western world throbbing with business and politics and all manner of vanities; though he might become an Eastern Buddha or a Rishi in the forest of Dandak, or even some modern saint like the elder Tagore, who sits in the door of his whitewashed house at Bolpur and sends great thoughts, like wireless calls, out over the Gangetic plain. This Christ stands aloof from all the interests of this world; he is a dream-Christ from a land of heavenly dreams.

But perhaps this is nearer the essential Christ than we have suspected. It may well be that some vision of other-worldliness is precisely what Christ brought to men and still longs to bring. There was plenty of business in the Roman empire of the first century, plenty of politics, of materialism, of feverish pursuit of vanity. But Christ dabbled in none of these things. He called men away from the world that was too much with them, bade them trust the Father for daily bread, and seek first the shadowy though intimately real Kingdom of God. And his message today is of like import. He still

" calls us o'er the tumult
Of our life's wild restless sea,"

and the face with which he looks at us in the night watches, when if ever we climb out of our frenzied life and for a moment try to look at it under the aspect of eternity, is some such face as this, radiant with the light of a celestial country and eloquent of things unseen and eternal.

LIVES OF THE ARTISTS

ANGELICO, Giovanni da Fiesole, called Fra.

Born in 1387 in the hamlet of Viccio, 20 m. from Florence. Nothing is known of his early life. An entry of the year 1407 in the chronicles of the monastery of San Domenico at Fiesole reads: "Brother Joannes Pietri da Mugello, of Viccio, who excelled as a painter, and adorned many tablets and walls in divers places, has accepted the habit of a clerk in this monastery." His name was now changed to Giovanni; not till after his death was he called "Il Beato" — the blessed — or "Angelico." After residence in monasteries at Cortona, Foligno and Fiesole, he and his brother monks found a permanent home in the San Marco monastery of Florence which Cosimo de Medici built for them.

His first work in the new monastery was the Crucifixion in the chapter-house, "the great frontispiece to the book of the painted cells." Then followed his thirty-two scenes in the corridors and cells, beginning with the Annunciation and ending with the Coronation of Mary, "so that the series embraces the whole *catena* of the mystery of Christ's love." This work occupied six years. Angelico had no idea that any but the monks would look upon his work — as indeed they did not for four hundred years, till 1867, when the monks were disestablished by the government and the monastery became a museum.

In Florence, Angelico enjoyed the friendship and the inspiration of the great geniuses of his day; he was in touch with the tremendous commercial life of his time, yet was uninfluenced by it; his vow of poverty, chastity and obedience protected him from passion, ambition and discouragement.

In 1445 he was summoned to paint in Rome by Pope Eugenius IV. Part of his work here has perished, but the little chapel of St. Niccolas V. in the Vatican shows his most mature work. He died in Rome in 1455.

Vasari, in his Lives of the Painters, tells us that Fra Angelico was an ideal monk who painted wholly to the glory of God, and who never began a picture except after fasting and prayer,

" To Fra Angelico was reserved the glory of fixing in a series of imperishable visions, the religious ideal of the middle ages just at the moment when it was about to disappear forever." — *M. La Fenestre.*

> *Best short life*, Edgcombe Staley: Fra Angelico. London, Geo. Newnes, 19—. Contains also 64 half-tone reproductions of his paintings.
>
> *Appreciations*, Masters in Art Series: Fra Angelico. Boston, Bates & Guild, 1903. Contains also biography, bibliography, and 10 half-tone plates.

ARMITAGE, Edward.

Born in London, 1817. Studied in Paris under Delaroche from 1835, and exhibited in the Paris Salon of 1842. In 1843 he won first place in a competition for the decoration of the houses of Parliament. In a similar competition he was successful in 1847, following which he executed a succession of historical paintings and frescos for public buildings. During the Crimean war he went to the front in order to paint battle scenes. After 1860 his subjects became largely Biblical. He was elected to the Royal Academy in 1872. Being of independent means he could work unhindered at favorite themes, and he painted gratuitously many frescos for public buildings and churches. He died in 1896.

BACON, F. W.

Contemporary British School.

BLOCH, Karl Heinrich.

Born in Copenhagen, Denmark, 1834; died 1890. A genre and historical painter. He entered Copenhagen Academy of Art when he was fifteen years old and took all the prizes. At first he specialized in the peasantry of Zeeland and Jutland and acquired a reputation for humorous pictures; but after his residence in Rome from 1859 to 1865 he painted mostly historical subjects. From 1866 to 1884 he painted twenty-three scenes from the life of Christ for the chapel of the Castle Frederiksberg, Copenhagen, among which is " Come unto Me." His work is characterized by facile technique and genuine dramatic effect.

BONIFAZIO, Veronese I, or Veneziano. Family name not known.

Born probably about 1490 and perhaps in Verona. The first notice of him tells of his admission to a brotherhood at Verona in 1523. At the age of eighteen he settled in Venice and became a pupil of Palma Vecchio. Many important commissions were given him by the Republic. He was a fine landscape painter and skilful in representing rich garments. In his paintings we discover a frank worship of wealth; his characters whether saints or sinners are all as rich as princes. After a long life of steady work he died in 1540 and was buried in S. Alvise in Venice.

BROWN, Ford Madox.

Born at Calais in 1821, the son of a British naval officer. Early he showed talent, and was given the best art education possible in Flanders. A series of family tragedies culminating in the death of his wife in 1845, and his own ill health, prevented much productive work; and when he finally began to exhibit, his work became the subject of much derision. Nevertheless it brought him Rossetti as a pupil in 1848, and thereafter he became the inspirer of the Pre-Raphaelite Brotherhood, though never himself a member. Brown was in advance of his time. But though the art-critics scorned him, his pictures began to sell, and he tardily secured the recognition that should have come much earlier. He was engaged upon a series of mural paintings for the Town Hall of Manchester when he died, in 1893. His salient qualities are invention, composition and color. To him we really owe the startling change that came over British art in the middle of the nineteenth century.

Best life, F. M. Hueffer: Ford Madox Brown. Longmans, 1896.

BURNAND, Eugène.

Born in 1850 in Moudon, Switzerland. Studied architecture in Zurich, and drawing and painting in Geneva; then in Paris, under Gérôme, and in Italy. He began to exhibit in the Paris Salon in 1875 and since 1890 has been a member of the National Society of Fine Arts. His earlier paintings were mostly Swiss

445

landscapes of great beauty; in his second period he turned toward religious subjects, of which the State has bought two for the Luxembourg, — the "Disciples at Emmaus" and "Peter and John Running." Such pictures are the expression of his genuine religious character and represent his endeavor to humanize and make real the character of Jesus. His later work as an illustrator expresses the same qualities. In 1908–9 he published a series of illustrations of the Parables, clean-cut and reverent work. His drawings for the great French authors place him in the front rank of illustrators.

BURNE-JONES, Sir Edward Coley Burne, Baronet.

Born in Birmingham in 1833. His mother died at his birth; his father was a small tradesman of Welsh descent, of a deep and simple piety but rigid in his ideas about books and poetry. "No one ever more literally hungered and thirsted after beauty than did the lonely child in his dreary home in the grimy streets of Birmingham." Until he was twenty-three he never saw a good picture. His father wished him to be a clergyman. He entered Oxford at nineteen, with this in view, but on the first day he met William Morris and the face of things was changed. Together they read Ruskin and the Morte d' Arthur and had their dreams of beauty and romance. In 1855 he saw two pictures by Rossetti that set him on fire and determined him to be an artist. Leaving Oxford without his degree he went to London and studied under Rossetti. Morris followed in 1857, and later these two formed the Wm. Morris Co. for the production of stained glass, tapestries, etc. To these two may be attributed the great impulse given in the last century to decorative art, for Burne-Jones had an unrivalled gift for decorative design and an inexhaustible imagination. Many exquisite windows in English churches, and some in America, are from his hand. Trips to Italy in 1859 and with Ruskin in 1862 made a deep impression upon his art. In 1881 Oxford gave him a degree, in 1890 he received the French decoration of the Legion of Honor, and in 1894 Queen Victoria made him a Baronet. He died in 1898.

Burne-Jones was in spirit a Pre-Raphaelite, though he was not a member of the Brotherhood. His artistic creed is stated by himself in a letter to a friend: "I mean by a picture, a beautiful romantic dream of something that never was, never will be, in a light better than any light that ever shone, in a land no one can define or remember — only desire."

> *Best short life,* with appreciations and 10 plates, Masters in Art series: Burne-Jones. Boston, Bates and Guild, 1901.
>
> *Authoritative life,* Lady Burne-Jones: Memorials of Sir Edw. Burne-Jones, 2 Vols.

CARRIÈRE, Eugène.

Born at Gournay, France, in 1849. Leaving his childhood home in Strassburg, he went to Paris and entered the École des Beaux-arts in 1870. He exhibited first in the Salon of 1876, was made Knight of the Legion of Honor in 1889, and received numerous other prizes and honors. His work has an intensely personal quality and the traits of tenderness and gentleness. His themes are frequently poor people or children or the sick. The peculiar atmosphere of the *Christ on the Cross* is characteristic of him. He died in Paris, 1906.

> *Best life,* G. Séailles: Eugène Carrière, l'homme et l'artiste. Paris, 1901.

CISERI, Antonio.

Born at Ronco, a village above Ascona in Italian Switzerland, in 1821, the son of a decorator. He studied at the Academy at Florence and there became marked for his skilful portraits. His greatest reputation was made in portraiture, the most famous men of Italy — King Victor Emmanuel, King Humbert, Cavour, etc.— having sat to him. While still very young he was made Professor in the Academy, and for many years also conducted private schools of art in Florence. His historical pieces are almost all religious, and possess great charm of color, with a somewhat theatrical composition. He died at Florence in 1891.

CORNICELIUS, Georg.

Born at Hanau, Germany, in 1825. After brief schooling he worked in a jewelry factory, then changed to a pottery where he painted the designs. At fifteen he painted his first portrait. Then he began his art studies in the Academy; traveled to Antwerp in 1848 to copy pictures in the galleries, to Dresden in 1851, Paris in 1852–3 and Italy in 1869 and later. In 1888 he was named Professor by the Prussian crown-prince. Died in

1898. He had a special interest in religious painting, and excelled as a colorist and a portrayer of spiritual experiences. His best-known paintings are all religious in theme.

> *A good account,* with many illustrations is K. Siebert: Georg Cornicelius, sein Leben und seine Werke. Strassburg 1905. There is no biography or criticism in English.

CORREGGIO, Antonio Allegri da.

Antonio Allegri, one of the half-dozen most famous painters of the world, was born in 1494 in the little village of Correggio, near Modena. The town was the seat of a local lord under whose patronage Allegri grew up. The boy studied in Modena and Mantua, but never traveled so far from home as Bologna or Rome. His education was finished in his teens, and all contact with other art than his own then ceased forever. Evidently he had no ambition for the great world of wealth and fame, for he returned to his obscure birthplace in early manhood, where he died in 1534 when only forty years old. Almost nothing is known of the facts of his life. The tales of his lack of education, his poverty and miserliness have all proved to be false. To his contemporaries he was practically unknown and it took the world a hundred years to discover that he was a genius.

J. A. Symonds writes of him (Sketches and Studies in Italy and Greece) that he did not try to handle subjects with a pregnancy of intellectual meaning. He conceived the universe under the one mood of sensuous joy. His figures are uniformly beautiful and real, all created for pleasure rather than for thought or heroic action. " Gazing at his frescos the thought came to me that Correggio was like a man listening to sweetest flute-playing, and translating phrase after phrase as they rolled through his fancy into laughing faces, breezy tresses and melodious tenderness. When he attempts to depart from the fairy-land of which he was the Prospero, and to match himself with the masters of sublime thought or earnest passion, he proves his weakness. Within his own magic circle he rules supreme, no other artist having blended the witcheries of coloring, chiaroscuro and faunlike loveliness of form into a harmony so perfect in its sensuous charm."

Best short biography, with critical estimates: Masters in Art

448

series, Correggio. Boston, Bates and Guild, 1901. Contains also bibliography and ten half-tone plates.

Most authoritative biography, Corrado Ricci: Antonio Allegri da Correggio (translated by Florence Simmonds). New York, Scribner, 1896.

CRIVELLI, Carlo.

Crivelli was born between 1430 and 1440 and died after 1493. His earliest picture is dated 1468 and his latest 1493. The fact that he attached the word " Venetus " to his name on all his paintings shows that he was a native of Venice or neighborhood, and was proud of the fact. Practically nothing else is known of his life. His pictures show that he was influenced by the Byzantine tradition that came to Venice through her commerce with the East, and by the Paduan school that delighted in plastic ornament of the Classic type. (Note the pilasters and other architectural features of the Annunciation.) Most of his active life was spent in the hill towns above Ancona; probably at Ascoli between 1473 and 1486. This isolation from art centers accounts for his never having changed his methods or materials of work.

" On the whole a striking and original genius." — *Crowe & Cavalcaselli.*

" He had a special gift as a designer of decoration. Almost every square inch of his canvas attests the inexhaustible richness of his invention — an invention fed no doubt by the rich products of Oriental looms, of which Venice was the emporium. . . . Crivelli wrought only for the church." — *Monkhouse: In the National Gallery.*

Best short life, Masters in Art Series: Crivelli. Boston, Bates & Guild, 1908. Contains appreciations, 10 plates and bibliography.

DORÉ, Louis Christophe Gustave Paul.

Born in Strassburg in 1832, the son of a government engineer. He began to sketch as soon as he could hold a pencil. When he was fifteen his family moved to Paris, and immediately he began to contribute sketches to various illustrated magazines. He first exhibited in the Salon in 1848, a pen-and-ink landscape; then an oil painting in 1855. His first picture to attract attention was "Paolo and Francesca," in 1863. His fame as an illustrator, however, was already made, for from the first his wealth of imagination and facility of hand had been astonishing. It has been stated, probably without sufficient evidence, that his drawings in fifteen years numbered 40,000! His most famous illustrations were for Balzac, Dante, Don, Quixote, the Bible, Paradise Lost, Idylls of the King, Ancient Mariner and Poe's Raven. He won the Cross of the Legion of Honor in 1861, but never realized his ambition to become a great historical painter. As a painter he excels in conveying ideas of distance, of multitude and of movement. After a temperate and laborious life of uneventful dreams, he died in Paris in 1883.

Interesting Biography, with 138 illustrations, B. Jerrold: Life of G. Doré. London, 1891.

DÜRER, Albrecht.

The third of eighteen children, born in Nuremberg in 1471, the year when Caxton set up his printing press at Westminster, and the Pope sent Savonarola to the stake. "His life was coincident with one of the stormiest periods in history — a struggle between light and darkness; and he was the Luther of Art." Albrecht was first taught goldsmithing by his father, but protesting that he wanted to paint, he persuaded his father to bind him out to Wolgemut, the artist-engraver, for three years. 1490–4 were his "wander-years." Returning to Nuremberg he set up as master-painter and engraver on wood and copper. In 1505 he journeyed to Venice, whither his fame as an artist had penetrated, and returned with new inspiration in 1507. He now began his period of great painting, while he carried his wood-engraving to still greater perfection. To this period belong the two sets known as the Great Passion series (12 cuts) and the Little Passion (37). His copper plates too became famous (e.g., Prodigal Son). In 1512 the Emperor Maximilian visited him and gave him a large commission. The emperor died in 1519 before certain promised sums had been paid, and Dürer started for the Netherlands to get on the right side of the new Emperor Charles V. He traveled a year from city to city, paying his way by selling his prints, and being received everywhere with the greatest marks of respect. He returned in 1521, but his health was not good thereafter. His city of Nuremberg had become Protestant during his absence, and he embraced the new faith; for he had great admiration for Luther and Melancthon. He died in 1528.

Dürer was thoroughly Teuton, expressing the old northern delight in the grotesque, its instant sacrifice of grace to truth, its love of pure craftsmanship and its quaint mingling of austerity and playfulness. "He has every gift in art except the Greek and Italian gift of beauty or ideal grace. In religious painting he has profound earnestness and humanity, and an inexhaustible dramatic invention. In portrait he is equally the master of the soul and the body."

Best short account, with appreciations and 10 plates, Masters in Art series: Albrecht Dürer. Boston. Bates and Guild, 1901. Another monograph on his engravings is found in the same series, 1904.

ENDER, Axel Hjalmar.

Born near Kristiania, Norway, in 1853. Studied at the art school in Kristiania, at the Stockholm Academy, and at Munich. He has spent considerable time in Paris, but lives mostly in Kristiania. He is classed as a genre painter with national motives. The Molde altar-piece is his most popular work.

FLANDRIN, Paul Hippolyte (contemporary French school).

Born in 1856, son of Jean Hippolyte Flandrin, who was one of the most famous mural painters of modern France.

GEBHARDT, Karl Franz Eduard von.

Born in the parish of St. Johannis, Estland, Russia, in 1838. Studied in Petrograd Academy and at Karlsruhe. In 1860 he came to Düsseldorf, Germany, where he still lives. His work has brought him numerous honors, among them a Professorship in the Düsseldorf Academy in 1875. Among his best-known works are the frescos of the life of Christ (6 scenes) painted for the chapter-house of the ancient gothic Cistercian monastery at Loccum — a work that extended over many years; and the frescos in the Friedenskirche at Düsseldorf. His special distinction lies in his deep and sincere religious feeling, which he embodies in figures clothed in the costume of the age of Luther, the period of Germany's greatest religious fervor. His avowed aim is to restore to Germany the religious spirit of the Reformation. He and von Uhde have both been very successful in translating the Gospels into modern speech.

Best account: There is nothing satisfactory in English. His pictures, especially the Düsseldorf frescos, are reproduced in " Die Kunst Unserer Zeit," Vol. 17, pp. 433–449. Munich, 1908. For his life and full description of pictures (in German), see A. Rosenberg: Eduard von Gebhardt. Künstler-Monographien series. Bielefeld, 1899.

GEIGER, Caspar Augustin.

Born at Larringen in 1847. Studied at the Munich Academy and under private teachers. He has lived for a long time in Venice, and since 1889 in Munich.

GENTILE di Niccolo di Giovanni Massi, of Fabriano.

Gentile, of the family of Massi, takes the name by which he is best known from his native village of Fabriano, a little hill-town of Umbria. He was born between 1360 and 1370. How he got his training we do not know. His first journeys away from home took him to Brescia, and then to Venice, where he spent some years in adorning the Ducal palace and making altar-pieces for the churches. His work there has wholly disappeared. Jocopo Bellini became his pupil there and followed him to Florence in 1422. In Florence he had a shop near the church of the Trinita, and being a contemporary of Fra Angelico, they must have seen something of each other's work, doubtless to the enrichment of both. About 1425 Pope Martin called Gentile to Rome to help adorn the recently restored church of St. John Lateran. All this work also has perished. The artist died in Rome probably in 1428, though perhaps in 1432.

" Gentile shows great minuteness, careful fusion of tone, absence of shadow, bright contrasts of color. While Fra Angelico's work appeals to the spiritual, Gentile's appeals to the sensuous and splendor-loving elements in the spirit of his age." Michelangelo used to say of him, " He had a hand like his name."

Best account, Crowe and Cavalcaselli: History of Painting in N. Italy, 3rd vol.

GHIRLANDAJO, Domenico di Tommaso di Currado Bigordi, called.

He was known as Ghirlandajo because as an apprentice to a goldsmith he made the golden " garlands " so popular as ornaments for young ladies. Born in 1449, he was a contemporary of Botticelli, Leonardo da Vinci, Mantegna, Signorelli and Perugino, all of whom outlived him. Michelangelo was a pupil of his.

Nothing is known of his early training in art except that while a goldsmith he was perpetually drawing. He became the best all-round draughtsman of his time, and was said never to need rule or compass. Among his earliest pictures were certain frescos in the church of Ognissanti, Florence, made for the Vespucci family, of whom one was Amerigo, for whom America was named. In 1475 he painted certain frescos in the Vatican library. His most celebrated ones are in the choir of Santa Maria Novella, Florence, and depict the lives of the Madonna and St. John (1485–9). He died of the plague in 1494 at the age of only forty-four, and was buried in S. M. Novella.

Ghirlandajo was a man of prodigious industry, extraordinarily rapid and sure. By instinct he was a portrait painter; contemporary Florentines in whatever picture of ,his they appear are always natural and are the strongest portion of the canvas. His compositions are balanced and dignified. Symonds called him a powerful but prosaic painter, deficient in the finer sense of beauty and of poetic inspiration.

Best short account, with appreciations and 10 plates, Masters in Art series: Ghirlandajo. Boston. Bates and Guild.

Fuller account, G. S Davies: Ghirlandajo.

GIOTTO, Angiolo di Bondone (nicknamed Angiolotto or Giotto).

Born in 1266 (?) in the little village of Colle, 14 miles from Florence. He kept his father's flocks on the slopes of the Apennines, where according to Vasari he amused himself by drawing sheep with a sharp stone upon a rock, till the painter Cimabue found him and took him to Florence to make a painter of him. This happened when he was ten. Giotto was a genius. His fame soon spread. His skill is shown by the story of his drawing a perfect circle with a full sweep of his arm, a feat that gave rise to a phrase to express the impossible — " rounder than Giotto's

O." His title to fame rests on his abandoning the purely conventional and symbolic art which Italy had inherited from the Byzantines: painting natural backgrounds instead of golden ones, portraits instead of sour typical faces, and telling a story with naturalness and simple dramatic power. This was nothing short of a revolution in art. His great works are (1) the fresco decorations in the church of St. Francis at Assisi, (2) frescos in the Arena chapel, Padua, (3) frescos in Santa Croce church, Florence — covered with whitewash from 1717 till recently. In his day he enjoyed the greatest fame; popes and kings were his patrons, and his own city of Florence proudly pensioned him for his "excellence and goodness." Florence also commissioned him to build the Campanile, which stands today as one of the noblest architectural monuments in the world. Dante was his friend, and during his exile staid with him at Padua. He died in 1337 and was buried in the cathedral of Florence.

Best short account, with appreciations and 10 plates, Masters in Art series: Giotto di Bondone. Boston. Bates and Guild, 1902.

GIRARDET, Eugène.

Born at Paris of Swiss parents in 1853. Studied under Gérôme, and became famous as a painter of Oriental scenes (*Halt in the Desert, Arab Café at Biskra*, etc.).

HARRACH, Ferdinand von, Count.

Born at Rosnochau, Silesia, in 1832. Studied at the Weimar Art School. Served in the wars of 1866 and 1870, lived one year in Italy, then settled in Berlin. He has been a member of the Berlin Academy since 1874.

HOFMANN, Johann Michael Ferdinand Heinrich.

Born in Darmstadt in 1824. Studied in various important Academies in Europe, then in 1862 settled in Dresden. In 1870 he was appointed Professor in the Dresden Academy of Art. He is classed as a historical and portrait painter, though his fame rests upon his religious pictures, of which the chief are Christ and the Adulteress (1868), Christ and the Doctors (1882), Christ in Gethsemane (1890), Christ and the Rich Young Man.

He has been a prolific illustrator of the life of Christ, and these drawings have found wider use in Sunday schools than those of any other artist. Hofmann is never profound, but he is always clear and simple; and his portrayal of the face of Christ, while effeminate rather than strong, has elements of beauty that make a strong appeal. He died in Dresden in 1911.

HUNT, William Holman.

Born in Cheapside, London, in 1827. He early showed talent for drawing, but his father strenuously objected to an artist's career for his son and at twelve years of age sent him to work in a warehouse. The boy's artistic ambitions would not down. He began to take drawing lessons at night, and when he was seventeen he won his father's consent to educate himself as a painter. His struggles were equalled only by his perseverance. Millais, younger than himself, became his first friend, and in 1848 these two, with Rossetti, formed the Pre-Raphaelite Brotherhood (see sketch of Rossetti's life, p. 469). Their pictures, in which they fought the existing artistic tradition, brought on them no end of abuse, but Hunt persisted in his creed practically without change through a long and very busy life. His first success was the "Light of the World," bitterly criticised till Ruskin came to the rescue. Then, following a boyish ambition to paint religious themes realistically, he went to Palestine in 1854. Altogether he spent many years in the East, divided among four trips between 1854 and 1886. Honors were long in coming, partly because of his frequent sacrifice of beauty through his devotion to truth, and partly because his work was too intellectual to be appreciated at sight. The churchmen of England were slow to appreciate his art, for theological reasons; the Light of the World was bought by a printer, and the Finding of Christ by a brewer! But toward the end of his life he was given the Order of Merit, 1905. He died in 1910.

> *Most complete account:* O. von Schleinitz: Wm. Holman Hunt (in German), with many half-tone plates, in the Künstler-Monographien series, Leipsic. — Good appreciation found in Percy Bate: The English Pre-Raphaelites, pp. 25-30.
>
> *An Autobiography:* Pre-Raphaelitism and the Pre-Raphaelite Brotherhood.

JUSTUS OF GHENT.

Born at Ghent in 1410. Little is known of him. He was probably a pupil of the Van Eycks and is supposed to have assisted them in some of their most celebrated pictures. It is probable that a series of paintings executed for the library of the Duke of Urbino is his.

KELLER, Albert von.

Born in Gais, Switzerland, in 1844. He worked for a time in Paris, then settled in Munich, where in 1886 he was named Professor in the Academy. Numerous medals and honors have been awarded him. He is classed as a historical and genre painter, with a special taste for scenes and portraits from fashionable life. Each of his pictures is an experiment in pictorial effect or in color or in psychology. (There is no biography or criticism in English.)

KIRCHBACH, Frank.

Born in London in 1859 of German parents, his father being an artist. He studied in Dresden, Munich and Paris. In the latter place he came under the influence of the Hungarian artist Munkacsy, with results that are evident if one compares his "Cleansing the Temple" with Munkacsy's "Christ Before Pilate." In 1889 he was made director of art in the Institute of Frankfort, Germany. His first painting was exhibited in 1881 and he received Honorable Mention in Paris in 1895. His paintings are mostly historical, the best known being illustrations of the Niebelungenlied in the castle of Drachenburg on the Rhine (near where Faffnir the Dragon lived).

LEROLLE, Henri.

Born in 1848 in Paris. Studied under local masters. Was awarded a first class medal at the salon of 1880. He has painted five religious themes with noteworthy results. His favorite subjects are large landscapes with few figures, and his effects of evening light are unusually fine.

LONG, Edwin.

Born at Bath, Eng., in 1829, the son of a hairdresser. He was entirely self-taught, copying from the works that interested him in the galleries. His first exhibit in the Royal Academy was in 1855. To perfect himself he visited Spain, and later Egypt and Syria, whence he secured numerous subjects for pictures. He was fond of the romance of history, and many of his canvases show his archæological and poetic interest. He was elected an Associate of the Royal Academy in 1875, full member in 1881. He died in 1891. Though very popular in his day through his expression of the poetry and sentiment of the past and because of his religious bent, the critics do not rate his artistic talent high. One has styled his work " imposing scene-painting, full of empty rhetorical passion." His " Anno Domini " is one of his most satisfactory larger canvases.

MASOLINO, Tommaso di Cristoforo Fini, commonly called.

Masolino was long confused with Masaccio (Tommaso di S. Giovanni) since both lived in the same city in the first half of the fifteenth century.

He was born in Florence in 1383. About 1427 he was employed in Hungary. Immediately on his return he was commissioned to paint the chapel which Cardinal Branda Castiglioni had just erected in Castiglione d' Olona. Practically nothing else is known of him. It is probable that the frescos in the Brancacci chapel in Florence, formerly attributed to him, are by others.

MAX, Gabriel Cornelius.

Born at Prague in 1840, the son of a sculptor. Studied at the Academies of Prague, Vienna and Munich. First exhibited in 1867 at Munich the picture called " The Christian Martyr " — a young girl crucified. It caught the public instantly, and the artist has enjoyed a steady fame since. He traveled all over Europe, won many medals, was made Professor at the Munich Academy in 1879. Many of his best paintings are on religious themes. His interest is largely in the psychologic, the weird and the poetic. For this reason he has been called a " Soul-painter."

MERSON, Luc Olivier.

Born in Paris in 1846, the son of a distinguished art critic. He became a painter of historical-religious themes, though in a somewhat eccentric style. His honors consist of a Grand Prix at

Rome; medals 1869, 1873; Legion of Honor 1882. He is a man of wide reading, who frequently gets his inspiration from the visions his reading evokes. The works by which he is best known in this country are both given in this book; and his title to consideration lies in his faculty for humanizing scriptural characters.

MICHELANGELO BUONARROTTI.

" Michelangelo's genius is the fountain-head from which all great painters since have drunk." — *Delacroix.*

Born in 1475 at Caprese, Italy, of honorable ancestry. He was early apprenticed to Ghirlandajo, and assisted him till he became a better draughtsman than his teacher. At the age of sixteen he procured an introduction to Lorenzo de Medici and became one of his household in Florence. There in his garden-collection of antique sculptures, Michelangelo found his calling, and in the learned society of the Medici court and in the fiery preaching of Savonarola he found his inspiration. After Lorenzo's death and the expulsion of the family from Florence, Michelangelo went to Rome in 1496, where he carved his " Pietà," then returned to Florence where he made himself famous with his " David " and his cartoon of " The Bathing Soldiers." From now on, his name stands first in the list of artists. Pope Julius II called him to Rome in 1505 and ordered him to execute a mausoleum and to rebuild St. Peter's church on a scale grand enough to contain it. These two gigantic tasks, absolutely suited to Michelangelo's genius, were destined the one never to be completed and the other to be performed largely by other hands. The statues of *Moses* and the *Bound Captive* are the only relics of the " Tragedy of the Tomb," the former remaining in his workshop forty years till the tremendous plans were at last abandoned. In 1508 Julius set him to work upon the ceiling of the Sistine chapel in spite of the artist's protests that he was a sculptor. The result was a stupendous product of genius, the whole vast design with its 343 major figures conceived and executed by Michelangelo almost singlehanded in four years!

Under Leo X, Michelangelo spent most of four years quarrying marble! With 1520 begins the work of the Medici chapel of San Lorenzo, Florence. Designs and work for this monument occupied him for fourteen years, but by another irony of fate this too was never completed. He was now fifty-nine years old, had outlived all his contemporary artists — Raphael, Leonardo, del Sarto, Correggio; yet he was destined to live thirty years more, see the extinction of Florence, the humiliation of his country at the hands of Spain and the establishment of the Inquisition. With the election of Pope Paul III he was commanded to execute the *Last Judgment* for the Sistine; this occupied him from 1534–1542. His last great work was to erect the present dome on St. Peter's. This last period of loneliness was lighted by the pure love of the Marchioness Vittoria Colonna, who became to him a solace and an inspiration. Michelangelo died in 1564 and was buried in Santa Croce, Florence.

"Sculpture is Michelangelo's domain. . . . His works are sublime rather than beautiful. Power is more strongly expressed than order, and awe is commingled with our admiration. The *Il Pensieroso* and the *Moses* represent the art of sculpture carried to its highest pitch of grandeur." — *Guillaume.*

"All of Michelangelo's works betray a struggle — the struggle of sublime ideas striving to surge up into being from the wonderful depths of his mind. . . . There can be no calm enjoyment of such works. They irresistibly involve us in their passion and make us sharers in their tragedy." — *Lübke.*

Best short life, with appreciations and plates, Masters in Art series: Michelangelo. Boston, Bates & Guild, 1901 (2 numbers).

MILLAIS, Sir John Everett, Baronet.

Born in Southampton, England, in 1829. Entered the Royal Academy school when only eleven years old, and while yet a lad learned all that schools could teach. When he was seventeen he first exhibited at the Academy. His real inspiration came from his friendship with Rossetti and Hunt, with whom in 1848 he formed the Pre-Raphaelite Brotherhood (see life of Rossetti). His first picture thereafter (*Lorenzo and Isabella*, 1849) evoked a storm of criticism, but his second (*Christ in the House of his Parents*, 1850) called forth even worse ridicule, largely because the critics were more aware of the innovations than the excellencies of the work. For ten years Millais held strictly to the principles of the Brotherhood, but then began to modify his style toward the popular and the luxuriant. The change was a distinct loss to art, for instead of sincerity and originality came commonplaceness in idea and composition. He now developed a skill in portraiture that soon made him the most popular and expensive portrait-painter in England. He had an instinct for popularity. Life for him was fortunate: he was handsome, rich, accomplished, could make a success of whatever he chose to do. Yet he would undoubtedly have been a better artist if he had been less blessed. Materialism killed the divine fire. He became a member of the Royal Academy in 1863, received honors and degrees too numerous to mention, was made a Baronet in 1885, was elected President of the Academy in 1896, but enjoyed the coveted honor less than six months. He died in 1896 and was buried in St. Paul's.

"At his worst Millais was simply a mediocre painter with a curious instinct for what would prove popular; at his best he was one of the greatest artists, and quite the most original, that England has produced."

Best short life, with appreciations and 10 plates, Masters in Art series: Sir John Millais. Boston, Bates and Guild, 1908.

Authoritative life, by his son, J. G. Millais: Life and Letters of Sir John Millais. 1909.

MILLET, Jean François.

Born in 1814 in the hamlet of Gruchy, perched on the cliffs of Cape La Hogue, near Cherbourg, France. He was the son of a peasant, and his mother worked in the fields with the rest of the family. His uncle, a country priest, taught him to read French and Latin. He was a youth of poetic soul, but till he was eighteen he knew only the unremitting toil of the farm; then his father, impressed by his passion for drawing, took him to a teacher in Cherbourg. "You will be damned for keeping him at home so long," exclaimed the artist. Noting his talent the Town Council gave him a pension of 400 francs that he might study in Paris. There he arrived in 1837 and began the battle with poverty, little teachers and ridicule. His fellow students called him the "Wild man of the Woods"; landladies and bullies and thieves made life wretched, and his shyness kept him even from asking his way in the streets. Only one thing held him in Paris — the great Masters in the Louvre. For years he kept going by selling pastel portraits at five francs, or even painting sign-boards. Some little notoriety came to him as a " painter of naked women," till a chance remark overheard on the street made him resolve to paint no more of that kind. Then his true work began, to paint the toil of peasants; but it meant for years the direst poverty — six drawings for a pair of shoes! In 1849 his "Haymakers" was admitted to the Salon, and sold. Moving to Barbizon on the edge of the forest of Fontainebleu he lived there twenty-seven years and painted the whole cycle of peasant life. The public took to his new style very slowly, and pictures brought him only a pittance that afterward sold for hundreds of thousands of dollars! He began now to fail under constant work and worry, and only when it was too late did recognition come. In 1868 he was awarded the Cross of the Legion of Honor, and in 1873 the State, anxious to repair its past neglect, commissioned him to adorn the Pantheon. But he was no longer able to work, and died in 1875.

Millet's art and the man are one. He painted the world that he knew, with its toil and its sadness and its unadorned beauty. The mainspring of his art is character: to discover in each person he portrayed the essential character and then to manifest it in every detail of his picture. He often remarked, " Nothing counts but what is fundamental." Henly writes: " From his hillsides and his park-like expanses of plain he speaks with the very voice of the ground. In a solitary figure he résumés and typifies the fortunes of a hundred generations of patient toil. He is a Michelangelo of the glebe; and his shepherds and his herd-women are akin in dignity and grandeur to the prophets and sibyls of the Sistine frescos."

Best short account, with appreciations and 10 plates, Masters in Art series: Jean-François Millet. Boston, Bates and Guild, 1900.

MOREAU, Gustave.

Born in Paris in 1826, son of a government architect. Became a pupil of the École des Beaux-arts. First Salon picture 1852. Various medals and honors, including the decoration of the Legion of Honor in 1875. His subjects were drawn largely from ancient history, myth and legend. He was a painter of extraordinary imagination, many of his canvases having the atmosphere of dreams and a tinge of melancholy. He died in 1898. Practically all of his sketches and paintings were given by his will to the State, and in 1903 were housed in a special building, also given by him.

" Moreau was a highly intelligent, learned and lyrical man who had a deep affection for art. He not only loved painting, he was passionately fond of music, poetry, occult science and mythological symbolism." He was rich, and chose to live in solitude with his dreams. " Moreau's imagination, nourished by the most noble poetry and by the taste for archaism and symbolism, was completely admirable. His color was brilliant and impressionistic, and his work less that of a painter than the expression of the thoughts, researches and dreams of an intellectual person."

MUNKACSY (pronounced Moon'-ka-chee), Mihaly (Michael)

Born in 1844 in the fortress of Munkacs, Hungary. His mother died soon after his birth, his father joined the army of Kossuth to fight Russia, and died in prison. Michael, aged four, the youngest of five orphans, was cared for by an aunt. Her house was plundered at night by marauders, and all were murdered but this boy. A poor uncle took him and apprenticed him to a carpenter, where he worked unremittingly for six years, growing in stature but with his mind a blank. As he mastered his trade he developed a strong desire for an education. Some students taught him to read and write, and he began to be interested in history and poetry. His first attempt at art was as a house painter! His first drawing was on the smooth side of a plank he had planed. Soon he showed such skill in decorating trousseau chests that he gave up everything else for this, painting flowers, then figures. Working from twelve to fifteen hours a day at wages of one dollar a week, he broke down in health, and " Uncle Reok," who now had a small fortune, took care of him. Recovering, he became acquainted with a portrait painter named Szamosky, and knew at last that he was meant to be an artist. His first painting was a group of the entire family of a tailor, for which he received a winter coat!

462

In 1863 he went to Pesth and made a living by drawing peasants, gypsies, etc. Then to Vienna, where the professors prophesied ill of him. In 1866 he nearly went blind. Next he landed in Munich with $10 in his pocket! Gradually he acquired a market for his pictures and moved to Düsseldorf. His first real commission came from an American; the result was "The Last Day of a Condemned Man." This was exhibited in the Paris Salon of 1870, and made him famous. Soon after he married a rich and titled widow of Luxembourg, and thereafter lived like a prince in Paris. In 1879 he won the Cross of the Legion of Honor. His most important pictures are *Milton Dictating Paradise Lost*, *Last Hours of Mozart*, and the two huge canvases we here study.

> *Best life* (in English), in "Christ Before Pilate," edited for the New York exhibition of 1886–7 by C. M. Kurtz.—(In German), Ilges: Munkacsy; with many illustrations. Künstler-Monographien series, Bielefeld.

MURILLO, Bartolomé Estéban.

Murillo was born in Seville in 1617. His parents died before he was eleven, and little is known of his early years. Studied art with his uncle and soon outdid him. He had a desperate struggle with poverty, walked to Madrid and was befriended by Velasquez, then court painter. For three years he grew in mastery under this guidance, then returning to Seville he obtained his first commission from a Franciscan monastery. From now on his rise to fame was rapid: fully occupied with orders from religious bodies and nobles, admitted to the highest circle of society and worshipped by the people. In 1648 he married a lady of noble house and his home became a resort for the distinguished. Only once did he leave Seville till the time of his death in 1682. Murillo was a very devout Catholic, as his pictures imply. He painted the Immaculate Conception some twenty times.

> *Best short life*, Masters in Art Series: Murillo. Boston. Bates & Guild, 1910. Contains also appreciations, bibliography and 10 plates.

PIGLHEIN, Elimar Ulrich Bruno.

Born at Hamburg in 1848. Studied at Weimar and Munich and in 1879 traveled to Palestine to make ethnological and archæological studies. Thereafter he painted a remarkable panorama of the Crucifixion, 1700 square meters in area, which proved to be his masterpiece. This was burned in 1892. He became Professor (1880) and Honorary Associate (1888) at the Munich Academy, and died in 1894 at Munich.

PRELL, Hermann.

Born at Leipsic in 1854. Studied at the Dresden and Berlin Academies, and at Rome from 1880. His chief title to fame is his skill in fresco, especially shown in the Rathaus at Worms (1884), Hildesheim (1886), and the Albertinum at Dresden (1889).
Life (in German), Rosenberg: Prell. 115 illustrations. Bielefeld, 1901.

PUVIS DE CHAVANNES, Pierre Cécile.

Born at Lyons, France, in 1824, the son of a mining engineer. Educated at the college of Lyons and at the Lysée Henri IV, Paris. A journey to Italy during convalescence from a serious illness brought his first acquaintance with the great masterpieces of art, and led him to change his proposed career from mining to painting. Finding no Paris masters to suit him he began a long process of self-education in art, with a few comrades of like mind. His first Salon picture was in 1850, but no second was accepted till 1859, his attempts in the meantime being much ridiculed. His exhibit of 1861 showed that he had a genius for mural decoration, and to that form of art he devoted the rest of his life. The list of public buildings decorated by him is a long one, including those at Amiens, Marseilles, Poitiers, the Pantheon and Sorbonne at Paris, Rouen, and the Public Library at Boston, Mass., the last-named panels being executed in 1895-7. He worked till he could no longer hold a brush, and died in 1898. His one great friend and inspirer was Princess Marie Cautacuzene, whom he loved for more than forty years, though he married her only in 1897 and followed her to the grave two months after her death.

He was the most famous mural decorator of the present age. " For forty years he persistently pursued his ideal, seeking ever more and more for the serene decorative line, dignified gesture, immobile attitude, clear, calm, lovely color; painting anecdote less and less; making his landscapes ever more and more simple, his figures more and more abstractions, his symbolism higher and finer."

Best short account, with appreciations and 10 plates, Masters in Art series: Puvis de Chavannes. Boston. Bates and Guild.

RAPHAEL, Raffaelo Santi, or Sanzio.

Born in 1483 in Urbino. His father was a painter of saints, though on account of his father's death his first teacher was Perugino. His talent was precocious, for even before he was twenty he had modified the medieval tradition of his teachers and outstripped them in execution. In 1504 he went to Florence, the great center of Renaissance art, where Leonardo and Fra Bartolommeo were at the height of their fame, and Michelangelo had just set up his statue of David. Raphael here learned the exceeding beauty of the human face and form, and he dropped his medieval " soul-painting "; henceforth " he finds in the most perfect human beauty the means of representing the divine." Some of his most famous Madonnas date from this Florentine period.

In 1508 he was summoned to Rome by Pope Julius II, at the suggestion of Bramante, greatest living architect, who was building St. Peter's. At this time Michelangelo, the greatest living sculptor, was engaged in painting the Sistine ceiling. The three were a notable trio. Raphael was now 25 years old. His first work here was the apartments of the Vatican called " Stanze." Although other masters had decorated many of these rooms, the Pope was so well pleased with Raphael that he had the old work stripped off, and transferred the whole space to this new genius who threw old masters and new alike into the shade. In three years the first salon was complete: he had made himself the greatest master of fresco that ever lived. This work occupied him and his assistants till 1517.

On the death of Bramante, 1514, Raphael was appointed chief architect of St. Peter's. Countless other works—buildings and paintings—occupied his attention till one wonders how a single brain could plan so much. In this crowded period he designed the Tapestries and painted the consummate Sistine Madonna. His reputation was now so universal that the representatives of foreign princes crowded his studio and begged him to paint for their masters. The most he could do was to sketch the composition, paint a few strokes and turn the rest over to his pupils to finish. The artist worked at fever heat, in fact worked himself to death. Struck down by fever while engaged upon the Transfiguration, he died in 1520, aged thirty-seven. The grief was universal. In accordance with his will he was buried in the Pantheon, Rome.

"Of all artists since the Greeks, Raphael had the most perfect feeling for true beauty. . . . A genius of which grace was the essence, moderation the principle, and beauty the guiding star. Raphael was in truth the greatest of artists because the most comprehensive. . . . Bred in a devotional school of art and transferred to an atmosphere charged with classical ideas, he retained enough of the first while he absorbed enough of the second to make him a painter of works Christian in spirit and Greek in elegance." — *C. C. Perkins.*

"He had a nature that converted everything to beauty. Thought, passion, emotion, became in his art living melody. We almost forget his strength in admiration of his grace." — *J. A. Symonds.*

Best brief account, with appreciations and 10 plates, Masters in Art series: Raphael. Boston. Bates and Guild.

REMBRANDT, Van Rÿn.

Older lives of Rembrandt have proved to be largely fictitious. The facts, few as they are, were made known by Michel in 1893. (Rembrandt: His Life, Work and Times.)

Born at Leyden, probably in 1606, the fifth son of a miller. Early he showed a bent toward art and was sent to teachers; but after about three years he determined to study by himself. At Leyden he accordingly remained from 1624 to 1630. He was now ready for work in Amsterdam, and Amsterdam, the rapidly growing, prosperous and art-loving metropolis, was ready for him. His first Corporation picture, the *Lesson in Anatomy*, was painted in 1632. In 1634 he married the now famous Saskia, " much of whose short married life must have been spent in sitting to her husband." Saskia left some property, which in an unexplained fashion brought about the financial ruin of the painter, if not a serious moral degeneration. About 1658 he had to give up his palatial house, and for the rest of his life shifted from lodging to lodging, with only his artist's tools and a few bits from his studio. His melancholy life ended in 1699 at Amsterdam.

Rembrandt was primarily a portrait painter, a keen analyst of character who had the power to enter sympathetically into the soul-life of the most diverse types of his people — and he never passed beyond the limits of his own age and nation. Fromentin asserts that he had a dual nature: he was on the one hand a realist and accomplished technician, and on the other an idealist and dreamer who expressed ideas and emotions through the manipulation of light. His works show an unreconciled mixture of these two natures.

" Rembrandt belongs to the breed of artists which can have no posterity. His place is with the Michelangelos, the Shakespeares, the Beethovens. An artistic Prometheus, he stole the celestial fire, and with it put life into what was inert, and expressed the immaterial and evasive sides of nature in his breathing forms." — *Michel.*

Best short life, with appreciations and 10 plates, Masters in Art series: Rembrandt. Boston. Bates & Guild, 1900.

RENI, Guido.

Born at Bologna in 1575, son of a musician. His father wished him to follow music, but art claimed him. He was apprenticed to a Flemish painter at the Bologna palace on condition that if the boy failed to make satisfactory progress he should return to his music. But Guido made good. At twenty he entered the studio of the Carracci, then in their heyday. Here he learned something but suffered somewhat, and left them in 1598. He had now developed a manner of his own and was fast becoming one of the famous painters of Italy. Removing to Rome he gained the patronage of the powerful, including Cardinal Borghese, for whom he painted the *Aurora,* and Pope Paul V. But wranglings with officials and the enmities of lesser artists disgusted him and he returned to Bologna. The Pope however commanded him to return, and this time he received all the attention and flattery

467

heart could wish. His chief work at this time was the decoration of S. Maria Maggiore. Commissions now arrived from Bologna, Genoa, Mantua and Ravenna, and his pictures commanded prices hitherto unheard of. But Guido gambled and lost; his debts together with his arrogance brought him into trouble; and in the last fifteen years of his life he fell from the high esteem in which he had been held. He died in 1642.

" Guido Reni was an admired, fortunate, worldly artist, who accommodated himself to the tasks of his day, and aimed not at nature but at making an agreeable effect upon the spectator's mind; and having once hit upon a taking type he repeated it constantly, painting not living beings but combinations of pleasing contours." — *Taine.*

RODIN, François Auguste.

Born in Paris in 1840, his father a clerk. He showed no precocity in art, but drifted into a free drawing-school at about sixteen. Here he gradually found himself. He was very religious as a boy and found great inspiration in the church services when music and art added their emotional appeal. He made three vain attempts to enter the School of Fine Arts. To earn a living he became assistant to a maker of architectural decorations in plaster, till he was twenty-four years old, but lost no opportunity of improving his mind and hand. His first work submitted to the Salon in 1864 was rejected. He now became sculptor's assistant, 1864–70; after the Franco-Prussian war he went to Brussells, where he began to win some recognition, and to travel in order to study the French and Belgian cathedrals. In 1875 he went to Italy to study Michelangelo. Returning now to Paris, he exhibited in the Salon his " Age of Bronze." The foolish charge that the statue was cast from the living model brought him into prominence as the first sculptor since Greek times to follow nature absolutely. Within three years the bronze cast of it was bought by the State. Next came his St. John. From 1880 his reputation was assured and speedily became international. He is probably today the greatest living sculptor. His great works are the Gate of Hell, Citizens of Calais, Balzac the Thinker, the Hand of God, and Victor Hugo. In 1916 he gave to the government his entire collection of statues and the building in which they are housed. He lives at Meudon, outside of Paris.

Best account, Frederick Lawton: Life and Works of Auguste Rodin. 1907, many plates. Cuts of 107 of his statues and sketches are found in Grautors: Auguste Rodin, in Künstler-Monographien series (German).

ROSSETTI, Dante Gabriel.

Rossetti was born in London in 1828 of Italian parents. His father, a scholar and poet, had been expelled from Naples because of his patriotic poetry, and took refuge in England. Dante showed poetic and artistic gifts when five years old. His schooling was finished (Kings College) at fourteen. His impatience for results hampered not only his art studies but his whole subsequent career. Out of sympathy with the conventional art instruction then in vogue he went as a pupil to Ford Madox Brown; but refusing to "drudge" over matters of technique, he left Brown and joined Holman Hunt. These two, with Millais, aged 21, 20 and 19 years respectively, formed a brotherhood whose artistic creed was Sincerity. Because they emulated the spirit of the Italian painters before Raphael, they styled themselves the "Pre-Raphaelite Brotherhood." Each painted a picture to embody his creed — Rossetti's being the *Annunciation*, exhibited 1850. The new style of art was bitterly criticised, but was saved to public consideration by the championship of Ruskin.

Sydney Colvin sums up Rossetti's work thus: (1) 1847–62. Aim, dramatic and narrative art. Subjects and inspirations sometimes Christian, sometimes literary and romantic, very often drawn directly from Dante. Vivid presentment, the idea dominating the matter, the work naïve and often technically defective. (2) 1862–70. Themes sometimes suggested by literature, as "Beata Beatrix" and "The Beloved"; more often single female figures or heads, which are presented as types of rich beauty or are used as symbols for spiritual ideas. This is the period of greatest technical perfection. (3) 1870–82. Marked by decadence of idea and technique.

Parallel with this artistic activity went his poetic work. His volume of poems appeared in 1870. After ten years of poor health and melancholia he died in 1882.

In painting as in verse he was entirely a poet.

Best short life, Radford: Rossetti. London, Geo. Newnes, 1905. Contains 57 plates.

Appreciations, Masters in Art Series: Rossetti. Boston, Bates & Guild, 19–. Contains also biography, bibliography and 10 plates.

RUBENS, Peter Paul.

Flemish school. Born 1577 at Cologne, died 1640 and was buried in Antwerp. Early showed artistic genius and surpassed his masters. At 23 he traveled to Italy for improvement, where he met the Duke of Mantua and entered his service as court painter. His duties took him to Rome and Spain. After eight years he returned to Antwerp, where his services were retained by Archduke Albert, governor of the Spanish Netherlands. His vogue as a painter now became extraordinary. It is said that in two years he refused more than a hundred commissions. During this period he produced (1612) the famous *Descent From the Cross* (Antwerp cathedral) and the huge series of twenty-one paintings illustrating the life of Marie de Medici and Henry IV (1622–5) now in the Louvre.

Through the Duke of Buckingham, who was impressed with his splendid talents in many lines and his persuasive manners, he was chosen to negotiate terms of peace between England and Spain. This was accomplished in 1627–30 with such credit to himself that he was knighted by the King of Spain and by Charles I of England, and loaded with various honors and gifts. During these negotiations he was also busy painting royal portraits. Altogether his output is the most extraordinary in the history of art. Of course he used his pupils freely in all his work; but every picture embodied his conception and received its finishing touches at his hand. The total of such paintings is between two and three thousand, a number several times in excess of the work of the most prolific geniuses. He was enabled to perform this work partly because he possessed abounding physical vigor, and partly by a most severe and simple regimen of life; but the preponderating element was sheer genius.

" The spectacular is his domain. His eye is the most marvellous prism of light and color that has ever been vouchsafed us. Passions, attitudes of the body, expressions of countenance, — all mankind in the multifarious incidents of the great drama of life, — passed through his brain, took from it stronger features, more robust forms, became amplified, but not purified, and transfigured into some unknown heroic mould. He stamps all with the directness of his character, the warmth of his blood and the magnificence of his vision." — *Eugène Fromentin*, as adapted in Masters in Art.

"No other painter has endowed figures with such spirit, with such impulsive gestures, with an impetuosity so abandoned and furious." — *Taine*.

Best short life, H. Knackfuss (trans. by Richter): Rubens. 121 plates.

Best collection of criticisms, Masters in Art: Rubens. 10 plates. Boston, Bates & Guild.

SARTO, Andrea del (Andrea d' Agnolo, called).

Born in Florence about 1486, son of a tailor — whence his name del Sarto, the tailor's son. At seven years he was set to work in a goldsmith's shop, but his ability to draw was noticed by his master and the boy was sent to an artist for instruction. His progress was marvellous. When hardly more than twenty he executed beautiful frescos in the church of the Annunziata. About this time he fell in love with the handsome young wife of Carlo di Recanati, and after the husband's death in 1513 he married her. Lucrezia's beautiful face appears in almost every virgin and saint Andrea ever painted, but she proved to be his evil genius. In 1518 Andrea went to France by invitation of Francis I, but because of his wife's entreaties he secured temporary leave to return. He then betrayed Francis' trust, failed to come back, and squandered upon his wife and her relatives the money entrusted to him for the purchase of works of art. Thus he threw away the prospect of a great and honorable career in France. At home he found plenty of work, but the originality and force of his earlier style slackened. More than once he tried without avail to recover the favor of Francis. He died during the siege of Florence by the Spaniards in 1531, deserted even by his wife, who through fear of the plague left him to die alone.

471

Andrea is classed by critics immediately after Leonardo, Michelangelo and Raphael. He was superb as a technician and a colorist, as his title of "faultless painter" implies; but he lacked the spiritual gifts that admit to the highest rank of artists — inspiration, depth of emotion, energy of thought. Read by all means Browning's wonderful analysis of his character in the poem "Andrea del Sarto."

Best short life, with appreciations and 10 plates, Masters in Art series: Andrea del Sarto. Boston, Bates and Guild, 1901.

More extended account, Crowe and Cavalcaselli: Painters of Florence (ed. Hutton), Vol. 3, pp. 482–514.

SIEMIRADSKI, Hendrik.

Born in 1843 at Charkof, Poland. Studied at Petrograd and Munich, visited France and Germany, and finally settled at Rome in 1872. He executed frescos for the Church of Our Savior, Moscow. His masterpiece, "The Living Torches of Nero," is in the Crakow Museum. He was a member of the Stockholm, Berlin, Rome and Petrograd Academies, and Knight of the Legion of Honor. He died in Rome, in 1902.

SOORD, Alfred U.

Contemporary British school, pupil of Herkomer. Died 1916 (?).

TIEPOLO, Giovanni Battista.

The "last of the old painters and the first of the moderns" was born at Venice in 1696, son of a ship's captain and merchant. His father died when he was a year old, leaving him a fair fortune. Who were his early masters is not known, but his inspiration came from the works of Titian and Paul Veronese. His special excellence is shown in his frescos, of which he executed a prodigious number. In this field he is probably unexcelled, as may be seen in various churches in Venice, Bergamo and Vicenza. In 1750 his fame caused the Prince Bishop of Wurtzburg to engage him to decorate his palace, and in 1762 he began to paint for Charles III in Madrid. Besides his decorative work, Tiepolo produced a number of oil paintings, many of them altar-pieces, of which the picture here studied is perhaps the best. He died suddenly in 1770 at Madrid, and is there buried.

Best short life, with appreciations and 10 plates, Masters in Art series: Tiepolo. Boston. Bates & Guild, 1907.

TISSOT, James.

Born in Nantes, France, 1836; died in 1902. Genre painter. Studied under Flandrin and Lamothe, and exhibited frequently in the Paris Salon from 1859 to 1870. He was of a genial temperament, very popular in the art world of Paris. After the Franco-German war, in which he fought bravely, he went to London and lived as an " artist prince " in a house commonly called a palace of painting, where he entertained with regal lavishness. In the midst of his successes a great change came over him. While painting a series of pictures called " The Parisian Woman," he went to a service in the church of St. Sulpice to get atmosphere for " The Choir Singer." During the mass he had a vision — a disheartened peasant and his wife seating themselves on the ruins of a shattered church, and Christ crowned with thorns taking his place beside them to comfort them: " See! I have been more wretched than you; I am the solution of all your problems; without me civilization is a ruin." The vision pursued him after he left the church and stood between him and his canvas. He fell ill from fever, and on recovery painted his vision. The picture is called " The Ruins," or sometimes " Inward Voices." Henceforth he resolved to dedicate himself to painting the life of Christ. Accordingly in 1886, at the age of fifty, he went to Palestine and in ten years produced 365 water-colors of New Testament incidents. His aim was thoroughly devout: " To be moved directly by the life of the Master, passing through the same places, looking at the same scenes." He desired to get back to Jesus as he was, with Oriental garb and Oriental surroundings, and to present to the world a truer conception of Him than art had yet embodied. When his pictures were first exhibited in Paris in 1895 they called forth a great variety of criticism, some admiring their vivid realism and the erudition they display, others noting their want of spiritual insight and their crudity of coloring. The pictures were first reproduced in two costly volumes by Lemercier (Paris), who paid Tissot one million francs for the right; and afterwards the Tissot Co. of New York made them universally accessible in penny form. The whole series deserves study. After the publication of the book, Tissot withdrew to the Abbey of Bouillon to work on a similar series of Old Testament subjects, but he died without completing the task.

TITIAN, Tiziano Vecelli (called).

Born of good family in 1477 at Pievi in the Venetian Alps. Sent early to Venice to learn art, he studied under Bellini and was influenced by Palma Vecchio and Giorgione. The earliest notice of his work connects him with fresco painting. His first great commission was to paint a battle scene for the ducal palace in Venice, a commission that provoked the jealousy of his master Bellini and that for various reasons not wholly creditable to Titian was not completed till 1538. In 1516 he acquired the patronage of the Duke of Ferrara, and later the Duke of Mantua; from this time on he numbered kings, popes and emperors among his friends. In 1530 he painted at the court of the emperor Charles V. This brought him wealth, a Knighthood and a Count Palatinate. In 1545 he went to Rome to paint for the Papal court, and again in 1548 he spent some time with the Emperor at Augsburg. With indomitable energy he continued to work year after year; his physical power seemed exhaustless. At ninety he was still painting, and when the plague stayed his hand at the age of ninety-nine he was finishing his Pietà, one of his great works. He died in Venice in 1576.

"There is no greater name in Italian art — therefore no greater in art — than that of Titian. If he does not soar so high as Leonardo or Michelangelo, if he has not the divine suavity, the perfect balance that makes Raphael unique, he is wider in scope, more glowing with the life blood of humanity, more the poet-painter of the world and the world's fairest creatures than any of them." — *Claude Phillips.*

"Titian was the foremost artist of Venice, not because he was her greatest master of color, but because no other Venetian painter possessed so many of the essential qualities of great art in so full a measure. Rounded completeness is what stamps Titian as a master." — *Vasari's Editors.*

Best short life, with appreciations and 10 plates, Masters in Art series: Titian. Boston, Bates and Guild, 1900.

UHDE, Fritz von.

Born at Wolkenburg, Saxony, in 1848. He was an army officer until 1877; then his passion for art led him to become a pupil of Munkacsy. He became shortly the chief representative of the new realistic school of painting. His first works were devoted to problems of air and light, and he became one of the most expert in this technique. Then he struck into deeper themes, impressed with the idea of restoring to their rightful place in German thought the ideals of the Christian religion. He did therefore what has been done in every unsophisticated period of art — in the times of Fra Angelico, the Van Eycks, Dürer, Rembrandt — he transferred the events of the New Testament to his own time and gave them a spiritual meaning that reflected the depth of his own sincerity. He is the most successful painter of religious themes of our day. Various honors, prizes and medals have been awarded him. He still lives at Munich, where he is Professor in the Academy of Art.

Reproductions of 285 of his works, with short biography and appreciation (in German), Rosenhagen: Uhde. Stuttgart, 1908.

VAN DER GOES, Hugo.

Born either at Ghent or Bruges or Antwerp about 1435. Nothing whatever is known of him prior to his admission as free master in the painters' Guild of St. Luke in Ghent in 1467. Later he became Dean of the order. He first made his reputation as a designer and decorator, employed by the Flemish princes in connection with their elaborate pageants and festivities. He devised the method of painting on cloth and so supplanting the small triptychs on wood and the brilliant arras, or tapestries, both costly. The canvases were so easily produced and so cheap that he filled the churches and mansions of Bruges and Ghent with them, and made his fortune. In 1476, following his brother's example, he retired to a monastery at Roodenclooster, near Brussels, as a lay brother. There he continued to paint and to receive visits from lordly people, to the envy of his brethren. Latterly he developed melancholia through worry over his inability to complete the pictures ordered — about nine years' work — and over his doubts about the prospect of his salvation! During a journey to Cologne he became violent, and though he recovered temporarily, he died in 1482 and was buried in the cloister.

Although he was a prolific painter and many extant pictures are attributed to him, only two are indisputably his.

Best account given in Crowe and Cavalcaselli: Hist. of Flemish Painting, or (in German) in the Niederlandisches Künstler-Lexikon (*sub* Goes).

VAN DYCK, Anthony.

Born at Antwerp in 1599. Began his art studies at ten, was a pupil of Rubens at fifteen, and a member of the Guild of Antwerp painters at nineteen. *The Betrayal of Christ* was produced in this first period. In 1621 he visited the art centers of Italy, was strongly influenced by the works of Titian and Tintoretto, and himself created great enthusiasm by his genius at portraiture. The most notable families of Italy sat to him. Before he returned home in 1625 he had painted a hundred pictures. Now came his great altar-pieces; and parallel with them, the portraits of all the notables of Europe and the incomparable etchings known as the " Iconography." This Antwerp period marks the culmination of his genius. Visiting England in 1632 he so impressed King Charles I that he was appointed Court Painter, was knighted and pensioned. About thirty-eight portraits of King Charles and thirty-five of Queen Henrietta, besides numerous groups of the children and of English courtiers, are the fruit of this period. Excess of work and possibly excess of pleasure caused his premature death at the age of forty-two, in London, 1641.

"Van Dyck has not, like Rubens, the love of power and of life for life itself; more refined, more chivalric, born with a sensitive and even melancholy nature, elegiac in his sacred subjects, aristocratic in his portraits, he depicts with less glowing and more sympathetic color noble, tender and charming figures, whose generous and delicate souls are filled with sweet and sad emotions unknown to his master." — *Taine*.

Best short life, with appreciations and ten plates, Masters in Art series: Van Dyck. Boston. Bates & Guild, 1900.

VERROCCHIO, Andrea di Michele di Francesco Cioni.

Born in Florence in 1435. We know nothing of his youth except that he was apprenticed to a goldsmith, whose name (Verrocchio) he took. Later he learned sculpture from Donatello, painting from Baldovinetti, and studied architecture, bronzefounding and mechanical engineering, in all of which he excelled.

The Medicis beginning with Cosimo the Elder employed him almost constantly. His large workshop-studio was filled with assistants, many of whom became famous, like Leonardo da Vinci, Lorenzo di Credi and Perugino. His best works are his statue of David, and the magnificent equestrian statue of Bartolommeo Colleoni in Venice. While in Venice he fell ill, probably of fever, and died in 1488. Andrea never married; he was wholly absorbed in his work. "His ideal as an artist was to express with absolute truth the human form in its fullest perfection not only of physical strength but of noble and intellectual beauty. He was a scientific and poetic artist."

Best short account, with appreciations and 10 plates, Masters in Art series: Andrea Verrocchio. Boston. Bates and Guild, 1905.
Fuller account, Maud Cruttwell: Verrocchio, 1905.

VINCI, Leonardo da.

Born in 1452 at Vinci, a town between Florence and Pisa; son of a notary; brought up in Florence. He early became conspicuous for his beauty, bodily strength and passion for learning. At fifteen he entered the studio of Verrocchio where he attracted the attention of Lorenzo de Medici and through his influence soon obtained commissions. From 1481 till 1487 nothing is known of him; then he appears in Milan as a painter and architect of renown in the service of Duke Sforza. The letter in which Leonardo recommended himself to the Duke is extant. In it he claims to be a military engineer, architect, sculptor in marble, bronze or terra-cotta; "and in painting I can do as much as any other, be he who he may." The marvel of it is that this is all true; and Leonardo might have truthfully added that he was anatomist, botanist, physicist, astronomer, mathematician, poet, musician and anything else you please!

For sixteen years Leonardo served the Duke, till Milan was conquered by the French. His works included the model for a gigantic equestrian statue of the Duke's father, model for the cupola of Milan cathedral, plans for a vast irrigation scheme, a treatise on painting, the *Virgin of the Rocks*, and the *Last Supper*. During the next sixteen years he undertook various great tasks for various masters. His great artistic creation was the fresco of the Battle of Anghiari (1440) for the Council Hall of the Palazzo Vecchio, Florence. An unfortunate experiment with plaster caused the loss of the picture in a few years, and the cartoon also has disappeared. Contemporaries judged this to be his masterpiece. To this period belongs also the famous *Mona Lisa*. Troubles now began, caused partly by the painter's loose business methods and a not too delicate sense of honor. He finally made a bid for service with Francis I of France, and succeeded in quite capturing the monarch's heart. He went with him to Paris in 1516. But his health began to fail, and without accomplishing anything of note he died in 1519 and was buried in the royal chapel at Amboise.

"The world, perhaps, contains no example of a genius so universal as Leonardo's, so creative, so incapable of self-contentment, so athirst for the infinite, so naturally refined, so far in advance of his own and of subsequent ages. His countenances express incredible sensibility and mental power; they overflow with unexpressed ideas and emotions. Alongside of them Michelangelo's personages are simply heroic athletes; Raphael's Virgins are only placid children whose souls are still asleep. His beings feel and think through every line and trait of their physiognomy." — *Taine.*

Best short life, with appreciations and 10 plates, Masters in Art Series: Leonardo da Vinci. Boston. Bates & Guild, 1901.

VITI (or Vite), Timoteo.
Born 1469 at Ferrara, died 1523 at Urbino. Brought up a goldsmith, but painted with Francia in Bologna, 1491–5, and settled as a master in Urbino. About 1519 he became Raphael's assistant in Rome till the latter's death the next year. His works are few; the *Magdalen* is perhaps his best.

WATTS, George Frederick.
Born in London in 1817, the son of a piano-tuner. He began to draw almost before he could talk, and at twelve he was an indefatigable illustrator. At fifteen he began to study art, first exhibited when he was twenty, though his first success did not come till 1842 when he won a first prize of $1,500 for a design for decorating the houses of Parliament. With this money he went to Italy. Returning in 1847 he again won first prize of $2,500 in a similar competition, and his fame was assured. In

1856 he joined an archæological expedition to Asia Minor, and traveled by himself in the Levant. In the meantime the idea of the moral significance of art was growing in him, and beginning about 1860 he devoted himself largely to painting pictures that express great truths of life. Many of these pictures are now by his gift permanently housed in the Tate Gallery, London, where they constitute a unique and very impressive collection. Throughout his long life Watts painted portraits, many of the most renowned men of England having sat for him. He was elected a member of the Royal Academy in 1867, received degrees from the English universities and the Order of Merit from King Edward, the cross of the Legion of Honor from France, was made knight of the Order of San Luigi by Italy, and twice declined a Baronetcy. He died in his eighty-eighth year in 1904.

Modest and self-effacing, he yet had an earnest desire to serve the world through his art, because he felt that he had something to say: " My intention has not been so much to paint pictures that will charm the eye as to suggest great thoughts that will appeal to the imagination and the heart, and kindle all that is best and noblest in humanity."

Best short life with appreciations and 10 plates, Masters in Art series: George Frederick Watts. Boston. Bates and Guild, 1905.

ZIMMERMANN, Ernst Karl Georg.

Born in Munich in 1852. Studied with his father and in the Munich Academy, and perfected himself by travel in Belgium and Italy. He then settled in Munich and painted conventional historical scenes, genre pictures and portraits. Became a member of the Munich Academy in 1886. Won several medals for excellence, especially as a colorist. He died in 1899. There is no biography or criticism in English.

INDEX

Italics show the page opposite which the picture will be found; Roman figures refer to the exposition of the picture.

481

a

4

8